VOGUE

Beauty for Life

VOGUE

Beauty for Life

Health, Fitness, Looks, and Style for Women in Their 30s, 40s, 50s . . .

Deborah Hutton

CROWN PUBLISHERS, INC

NEW YORK

Originally published in Great Britain by Ebury Press in 1994.

Published by Crown Publishers, Inc., 201 East 50th Street, New York,
New York 10022. Member of the Crown Publishing Group.

Random House, Inc. New York, Toronto, London, Sydney, Auckland

CROWN is a trademark of Crown Publishers, Inc.

Manufactured in Italy

Jacket design by Linda Kocur

Library of Congress cataloging-in-publication Data is available on request.

ISBN: 0-517-59224-x

First American Edition

CONTENTS

INTRODUCTION

VISIBLES

PHYSICALS

PRACTICALS

HORMONALS

PSYCHOLOGICALS

ALPHABETICALS

For my mother, my sisters, and my daughters.

INTRODUCTION

THERE'S no escaping it. Everything ages and eventually wears out: VCRs, cars, animals, us. Even the universe, 20 billion years old last birthday, has a sell-by date. It's the timing that varies.

Thanks to advances in health care, greater control over our reproductive lives and a personal commitment to fitness and good nutrition, our own time scale has changed beyond recognition. In Japan, life expectancy has risen 20 years in the space of one generation. In the U.S., women are expected to live over four years longer than they were just 20 years ago. As we age, we find ourselves in good company. Western populations the world over are growing older. In the mid-1960s, at the height of the youth cult, half the French population was under 25. By 1995, for the first time in history, there will be more French citizens over 45 than under 30. Such changing demographics allow the new majority to project the reality of their lives upon the media, spearheading a whole new attitude to age.

Already what we think of as middle age has been shunted back several decades. When Grace Kelly, the movie star who became a European princess, reached 40 she lamented that, while it was a marvelous age for a man, it was "torture" for a woman since it was the "beginning of the end." That was in 1968. In the few decades since then, 40 has come to seem like the beginning of the beginning, with middle age, Byron's "brief summer between the end of August and beginning of September," shifted some 10 or 20 years up the line. Writing in American *Vogue* at the age of 45, Erica Jong clearly believed that middle age was still a long way off. "When I was twenty, forty-five seemed an intolerably venerable age, an age to retire to one's countryseat and have a last long love affair with one's garden. Now that I have reached that venerable age, it seems – if not the quintessence of youth – then at least nowhere close to middle age, whatever that may be."

Today's 40- and 50-somethings do not feel middle-aged, dress middle-aged or act middle-aged. In fact, the term middle-aged, with all its fuddy-duddy connotations, has itself had its day and is now hardly used except as a semantic put-down. "The only criticism that really hurt, and one of the few that was really true, was that I'm middle-aged; I could believe when I saw that in print . . ." said 44-year-old Hillary Rodham Clinton during the election campaign of 1992.

As midlife starts later and finishes later, 50 itself has become a midpoint rather than the beginning of the end. A century ago, a 50-year-old woman could expect just 19 more years of life. Worn out by continual childbearing and childrearing, she was sorely in need of rest and repose in the autumn of her life. She looked old, felt old, and was already winding down. If she had more than a handful of teeth in her head, she was something of a medical phenomenon. Today's 50-year-old, by contrast, might be running multinational companies and/or marathons or even, thanks to some stunning new technology, expecting her first baby.

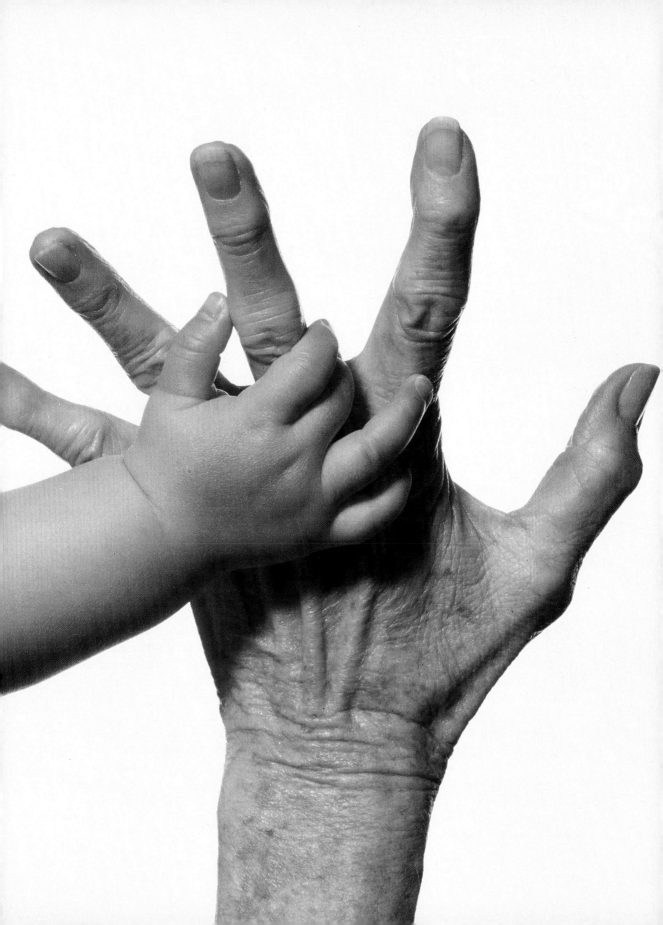

The prospect of 30 mainly active, independent years ahead certainly takes the pressure off the middle decades. For a while, turning 40 has been no big deal; now the milestones of 50 and even 60 are becoming occasions to party. These days, many older women are *celebrating* each new decade instead of succumbing to fits of depression on every successive birthday. A couple of decades ago, it would have been professional death for a Hollywood actress to admit to being 60. Now she invites half the world's press to a party that publicizes the fact. 1992's most sought-after invitation was to Elizabeth Taylor's 60th birthday bash in Disneyland. "I want to have a blast," the celebrated beauty was quoted as saying. "Sixty is a great age to be. You can do things that are completely off the wall."

Once asking any adult their age was considered the consummate rudeness; now the woman who refuses to divulge her age has herself become an anachronism. Gloria Steinem may have been ahead of her time when, on being congratulated on her appearance as she greeted guests arriving at her 40th birthday party, she came out with the memorable line "this is how 40 looks," but since then we have also seen how good 50 looks (Raquel Welch, Lauren Hutton, Julie Christie, Catherine Deneuve), as well as 60 (The Duchess of Kent, Jeanne Moreau, Leslie Caron, Lauren Bacall), and even 80 (Katharine Hepburn). As midlife starts to look good for its own sake, and the culture wakes up to an appreciation of the older face, it is allowing us to turn a more compassionate eye upon our own. The lived-in faces of the women on these pages have a glamour that the unlined faces of youth can never match. Looking fabulous *at* their age and not *for* their age, they show us that continuing good looks and attractiveness do not have to mean preserving the 28-year-old face in aspic, or buying the years from the cosmetic surgeon in an unholy Faustian pact.

If midlife now has a glamorous ring to it, it is still an insult to call anybody Old. Every semantic attempt to reclothe later life in better dress, including the laughable "chronologically gifted" and "silver generation," has met with resounding failure. Where old has come to be shorthand for chronically ill and incapable, the comfort is that it is further off than it ever was – especially for those who have got into the habit of looking after themselves. A longer life is not the only aim, of course. Consider the tale of Tithonus, who married the Dawn Goddess and got her to pray to Zeus to render him immortal – but, in his enthusiasm, neglected to ask to remain young. He became the first recorded supplicant for euthanasia. If we are to enjoy the fruits of longevity, the goal must be, as the advertising copywriters put it, to add life to our years as well as years to our lives. Genetics still count for a lot more than modern egalitarians like to pretend. But within the genetic givens, which remain (at least for the near future) unchangeable, there is much that we can do for ourselves. Studies on identical twins show big differences in life spans, barring accident or inherited disease. "Successful aging" in the sense of remaining active and independent until one is close to death appears a worthwhile and realistic goal, if not a failsafe one.

Encouragingly, there is already some evidence that we are enjoying longer health spans as well as life spans. Two out of three of American 90-year-olds have their wits undimmed, and one in five is still driving. Aldous Huxley's *Brave New World* vision of 70 years of cosmetic youth followed by sudden death, without any decline, may not be too sanguine a vision of the future. In fact, 70 is *unambitious*. There is good evidence from our own new world that individuals who forge healthy habits are not only living well beyond 70, but enjoying extra years of active life and shorter periods of sickness and dependency whenever death takes place – whether at 75 or more than 90. Dr. James Fries, associate professor of medicine at Stanford University in California, has called this phenomenon the "compression of morbidity." Tellingly, there is more evidence of this among Americans, who have taken good health practices into their hearts and lives, than among Europeans, who tend to be more skeptical of the advantages such practices can bring.

Since we can now assume that we will probably live beyond 70 or even 80, we need to plan actively for our later life, wherever we are on the chronological ladder. Fortunately it is never too late to intervene in our own aging process. In fact, as you will read, there is growing evidence that a healthy lifestyle makes even *more* impact at a later age than at an earlier one. Twenty years ago the chances of making it into the ninth decade were so slim as to be positively unlikely, and were not worth counting on let alone planning for. Now it's a probability. It is intriguing to think how much better the lives of some of today's 85-year-olds might be had they been conducted with this longer future in view.

Planning actively for one's later life does not mean pursuing the crazier reaches of life-extension. Deliberately not included in this book, these are untried and untested and in some cases capable of doing great harm. In the last few years, a burgeoning black market for growth hormone has grown up among those desperate to reverse the effects of age, following a breakthrough study in 1991 showing that daily injections of the hormone (which is produced in quantity in young, healthy individuals and falls off by about 30 per cent after the age of 55) reversed middle-age spread, restored waning muscle mass and strength and improved skin quality in a group of infirm elderly men who had been shown to be growth-hormone deficient. Thousands of dollars are now changing hands for this latest elixir of youth, even though it has long been known that over-ambitious doses can dangerously hike up blood pressure, quadrupling the risk of early death from cardiovascular disease, and can increase the chances of cancer.

Fortunately, there are more than enough ways of prolonging our healthy, active lives without also taking the risk of inadvertently shortening them. But in order to do so, we need to be well-informed. Information is power when it comes to planning for our own later lives. It makes us active partners in our own healthcare and fuels the critical feeling of being in control that serves so well even in extreme old age, whatever the genetic luck of the draw. (See page 357 for a survey that proves the point.) As importantly, it also enables us to take advantage of what is now known beyond reasonable doubt – namely that regular physical activity keeps the whole body (and indeed the brain too) vigorous and functional; that certain foods promote health and fight off cancer and heart disease, while others do the body few favors;

that some forms of screening can detect changes early enough to enable us to avert major life-threatening illness. So much is known.

While availing herself of the latest medical research, however, the woman who takes charge of her own aging must also be able to live with uncertainty. At several points in my research for this book, I was amazed to learn that what I had assumed was established fact was actually far from certain ground. In fact, there was a surprising lack of consensus on such crucial areas of women's health as the advisability of hormone replacement at menopause, monitoring and treating women with moderately raised cholesterol levels, and screening 40-year-old women for breast cancer.

Sometimes getting definitive answers from the world's experts proved impossible. Not only did they disagree (at times vehemently) with each other as to how the findings of various surveys and trials should be interpreted, but in many cases the research that would prove or disprove the points at issue had simply not been done. This is partly owing to the age-old cultural bias in medical research, which has consistently left women out of major trials and surveys that hold great relevance for them. The important Baltimore Longitudinal Study on Aging, for example, failed to include women entirely for the first 20 years of its life, even though two-thirds of older Americans are female, while by far the largest study ever to explore the still-vexed relationship between hair dyes and cancer only examined their possible effects in *men*, even though they are by far and away the minority users of these products. As a result of such glaring gender gaps, information regarding women is sometimes so sketchy as to be virtually non-existent. Where I found no ready answers, I have tried to be even-handed, in the belief that, once acquainted with the facts and the arguments on each side, every woman will rise to the challenge of finding her own way forward.

Making up one's own mind on some of the more contentious points at issue is not always easy, however. People like to know who is *right*. It is hard to accept that more than one interpretation is justifiable on the basis of current evidence, which often muddlingly points in several different directions.

"Even now physicians still do not have enough scientific information to respond to a woman's questions about post-menopausal hormone replacement therapy," declared the American cardiologist Bernadine Healy, director of the National Institutes of Health and a great champion of women's health. While some of the most pressing conundrums should be answered by the $500 million Women's Health Initiative she is spearheading, the results will only *start* to come in ten years after the turn of the century, and even then will not tell us everything we need to know.

For the foreseeable future, then, it seems we must continue to live with gaps, inconsistencies, and contradictions. This means keeping our eyes and minds open and coming to our decisions on the basis of the best information available to us. Luckily, the ability to tolerate shades of gray – which is a definite strength and not the miserable capitulation it's so often made out to be – tends to get ever stronger with age and experience.

Their generation: the growing number of 30, 40, and 50-plus models swinging down the world's catwalks are, for the first time in fashion history, of an age with the women who buy and follow the couture. Lauren Hutton, FAR LEFT, and Donna Jordan, LEFT, model Calvin Klein's Fall 1993 ready-to-wear collections; Anna Pawloski, ABOVE, who modeled for Patou in the 1970s, re-emerges for Jean Paul Gaultier in 1993, and Jibby, TOP CENTER, a friend and sometime model for Vivienne Westwood, celebrates the designer's delight in the unexpected.

The uncertainties of the present are, of course, as nothing compared with the speculations of the future. Recipes for longevity have an enduring attraction, and their contemporary appeal remains undiminished by any consideration of logic or common sense. Aspiring immortalists are receiving regular transfusions of their own blood to increase the number of red-blood (oxygen-carrying) cells and give themselves a supposedly life-extending oxygen kick, while others swallow complicated cocktails of vitamins and strange placental extracts. An increasing number, following the lead of the visibly aging but wasted Californian gerontological guru, Roy Walford, are keeping themselves eternally (so they hope) hungry. Their efforts are inspired by reports that rats who have their rations drastically curtailed when still in their growing cycles live 30 per cent longer than their contemporaries, get less cancer and heart disease, and have longer reproductive lives into the bargain. Interviewed in British *Vogue* in the early 1980s, Dr. Walford said he first became interested in the possibility of life extension at high school. "I felt I had so much to do I had to start by living longer." If the idea of staying at two-thirds of your physiological weight does not appeal (bad news for your bones if nothing else), you might profitably go out for a run instead. The National Institute on Aging has shown that when rats are given plenty of daily exercise they display similar gains in longevity – and there's persuasive evidence that humans do too.

What distinguishes Dr. Walford's work from many of the anti-aging hypotheses of the past is that it stems from respectable scientific research. In previous decades, doctors who became interested in life extension and anti-aging research were dismissed as cranks. Now they command a growing degree of respect. Even cosmetic scientists, members of a specialty once considered right outside medicine proper, are being accorded important column inches in the top medical journals as it becomes clear that the broad focus of their research is adding much of value to the quest. As the old barriers come down, and energies and expertise are pooled, questions that we've asked for centuries are coming tantalizingly close to being answered. Molecular biologists claim the research is now where physics was 50 years ago, just before scientists split the atom. By the end of the century, they predict, the progress will be phenomenal. At the annual meeting of the American Association for Advancement of Science in 1992, Professor Michael Rose of the University of California announced that there was nothing deeply problematic about doubling the human lifespan. "Aging used to be mysterious," he declared. "And now it isn't."

It is almost certain that the best way to combat aging will be by postponing its effect at the molecular level. It is now merely a matter of time, scientists say, before we can engineer proteins that will override the messages put out by the master genes that seem to switch on senescence. Already, researchers believe that we can delay our own aging; combating the wear-and-tear factor by stalling the action of free radicals – nasty, disruptive molecules which are a by-product of the body's normal metabolic processes. At the University of California at Irvine, scientists have produced a "Methuselah" fruit fly, which routinely lives to the equivalent of 150 human years, thanks to a specially bred-in genetic trait that produces plentiful amounts of the powerful free-radical-scavenging enzyme superoxide dismutase. At the University of Kentucky, meanwhile, elderly gerbils (who, like elderly humans, tend to grow a little forgetful with age) are finding their way around mazes every bit as expertly as animals several years their junior once they have been dosed with a free-radical scavenger called PBN, a variety of which may soon be tested on humans. The tantalizing question is, what happens when we supply these compounds ourselves via the diet or the skin? While cosmetic chemists the world over are testing these scavengers in exciting new skin creams in the hope of prolonging the dewy blush of youth, some of the world's most respected research establishments are assessing their value in preventing heart disease and cancer when added to the diet in supplement form – swayed by accumulating evidence that such a simple step could keep them young at heart.

As the free-radical research demonstrates, humankind is far from being at a point where its knowledge, enterprise, and energy are exhausted. In fact, we are on the verge of real advances that will be to everyone's benefit – if we only choose to make use of them. Happily, some of them are already reliably open to us. And that's what this book is about.

VISIBLES

THE old decorums are under siege. As women of a certain age throw off the negative assumptions that have prevailed since the dawn of modern time, middle age itself is being redefined. The present generation of late 30-, 40-, and 50-somethings is refusing to retreat into obligatory purdah as "housewives" or "spinsters" as their own mothers did. The once invisible uniform of the middle-aged woman – soft, safe neutrals, sensible heels, and hems in which she tactfully faded from sight and attention – is giving way to a radical midlife chic, as these women are not only looking good but unapologetically looking their age; "happy in their skin" as the Irish say.

Refusing to embrace a second girlhood, modern middle-aged women are inhabiting their own bodies and wearing their own faces with ease and confidence. And, for those who have got into the habit of taking care of them, both are looking good. These women actually have time on their side. Glamour too. As the fashion designer Helen Storey put it to British *Vogue*'s associate editor, Sarah Mower, "There's a difference in how a 40-year-old does it, and how a 20-year-old does it. It's difficult to be glamorous in a convincing way until you're very sure of yourself as a woman. Otherwise it looks a bit as if you're slopping around in your mother's shoes."

Designers in their 40s and 50s (Nicole Farhi, Donna Karan, Betty Jackson, Myrène de Premonville, Catherine Walker) are producing wonderful, wearable clothes for women of any age. Similarly aged models (Isabella Rossellini for Lancôme, Lauren Hutton for Revlon, Catherine Deneuve for Saint Laurent) are hitting the big time, advertising skincare lines for women who, like them, have lived-in faces. Lauren Hutton's career first took off when she was accepted onto Eileen Ford's books at the then late age of 23. Now, at around 50, her career has taken off again. "One of the nicest things about Steven [Meisel – the photographer] is the way he encouraged me to be my age," comments Lauren Hutton of their now-famous partnership, which launched her second trajectory. The same photographer also championed the return of 40-year-old Lisa Taylor, exclusively signed for Calvin Klein after a ten-year retirement at 30, which even then was geriatrically late for a top fashion model. She was said to have landed the job after asking Klein, a friend, "Why are models in the ads not the age of the women who buy the clothes?" and adding, "Twenty-year-olds don't buy your clothes, Calvin."

Like these new role models, many grown-up women are resorting to less artifice in their middle

The first signs of age are often visible on the neck, as gravity and years of sun exposure take their toll. Many women in their 40s and 50s have faces that have not so much as a crease on them, having been lovingly protected from the sun and nourished with the best of creams, but the neck tells a different story. Appropriate skincare, regular yoga-type exercise, and high SPF screens can do much to stay the sag and wrinkle.

years than at any time in their adult lives. While allowing their own faces to shine through more nakedly and visibly than at any time since adolescence, they recognize that just the right amount of make-up rescues them from the drabness that middle-aged skin is often heir to. "I wear much less make-up than I used to," recalled Catherine Deneuve in an interview with American *Vogue* as she took up her new job with Saint Laurent. "But I think it's a mistake to avoid make-up altogether." She should know. Deneuve, who has gone on and on being herself beautifully, exemplifies the French attitude to age to a T. In France, where women are seen to be acquiring rather than giving up their personal magnetism as they get older, the idea of trying to stay a perpetual 25 is incomprehensible. The proper pride that women take in their appearance ensures that 50 or 60 looks very good when they get there. This attitude is light-years away from both the familiar fallback position of holding maintenance in contempt, as though disregard for the outside means there must be riches within, and that of clinging to youth at all costs.

For the woman who cares about how she looks, the abandoning of artifice presents new challenges. The body requires exercise not elasticized underwear to keep it in shape. The complexion deprived of tan foundation must find ways to glow on its own. The hair that forgoes the artificial sheen of the allover permanent tint needs to shine instead with the best possible condition. This health-oriented approach requires a more wholehearted commitment than creating the cosmetic illusion ever did.

Alongside it comes the realization that what really tells on looks and energy is the accelerated wear and tear – the ceaseless battering of sun and wind, the ravages of hard living, the tensions that register on the face and drag the expression down. The best beauty lift of all is not a wrinkle-removing cream or a judicious slice of the scalpel, but laughter and love, time spent with friends and indulged in oneself – an hour of yoga in the early morning, ten minutes flat on the floor putting the realignment principles of posture-control techniques to good effect, an afternoon in the fresh air. "If you do yoga you can postpone facelifts for years," enthused Dr. Karen Burke, attending physician at Manhattan's Cabrini Hospital, putting the centuries-old practice above the very latest in cosmetic high technology. "People who do yoga have those sharp jawlines because they're doing a total stretch."

For all the fighting talk, it would be folly to pretend that even yoga can keep age at bay indefinitely, or that we always like what we see when we stare hard into the mirror or catch sight of our reflection unawares and realize with a nasty jolt that youth is over. For women who are forever gauging the way they look against the way they used to look, the present must always be painful, even unbearable. A new standard is required, since nothing – not the consummate skill of the cosmetic surgeon, nor the glorious alchemy of the hair colorist nor even continuous prescriptions of retinoic acid (Retin-A) – will give a woman back the face she once had, or thought she had. Instead of the quest for a chemically or surgically prolonged youth, it may be that coming to terms with the natural process of aging will transpire as the sanest and safest way of making peace with ourselves and the age we are.

SKIN

BACK in 1924, American *Vogue* saw fit to caution its older readers against idle complacency at their dressing tables. "Effort must be made and pains taken," it declared reprovingly. "No woman of forty-three can safely leave her complexion to look after itself. She must take at least an intelligent interest in its preservation." Happily, late-20th-century skin science has much more to offer such women than it did back then. The good news is that we *can* save our skins. As the processes of aging that were once considered unstoppable come under the microscope, many are found to be avoidable, even when signs of wear and tear are already apparent. Constant care makes the difference. Daylong protection from the unceasing assault of ultraviolet, whatever the weather, will allow the skin to age at its own – gratifyingly slow – rate. While guarding against tomorrow's damage, it may even undo some of yesterday's. If a sun-baked youth is already having dire consequences on the complexion, conscientious use of a sunscreen, together with one of the new cosmeceuticals (cosmetic/drug hybrids), may not only stall the pace of deterioration but also reverse some of these accelerated changes. Just as the lung can partially recover after stopping smoking and the liver after too much alcohol, so the skin can repair some of the damage if only given the chance.

Taking an intelligent interest in the preservation of one's complexion demands a certain realism of outlook. Great-looking skin doesn't mean skin that hasn't a line on it. Even surgery can't erase the years, and total sunblock won't stop the clock. We need to keep a grip on reality. Creams have their virtues, but even the best cannot smooth away wrinkles, take up the slack, or return the dewy look of youth. Lived-in, looked-after faces can look very good in their own right – no longer blandly pretty perhaps, but contoured, expressive, and characterful, especially if the eyes are bright and the complexion clear. As the skin becomes thinner, its texture can often *improve*, taking on an ethereal quality as it becomes more translucent.

KEEPING THE OUTSIDE WORLD OUT . . .

With the exception of the new-generation cosmeceuticals and, possibly, some anti-oxidant product lines, all skincare products work on the uppermost layers of the epidermis, and have a negligible impact deeper down. This is as Nature herself would have it, since the most important role of the epidermis is to keep the outside world out and the inside world in.

In one sense, the epidermis never ages, as it is constantly renewing itself. In the basal layer, several cell layers below the surface, freshly minted skin cells divide and move upward to the surface of the skin – a journey that takes 14–21 days in a young person, up to twice as long in an older one. As they ascend, these cells are transformed from succulently rounded living entities to flat, desiccated shadows of their former selves. By the time they reach daylight, they are dead and compact and they gum together to form the stratum corneum (horny layer), where they gradually flake away.

Exfoliation enthusiasts declare war on this "dead" layer, vigorously scrubbing till all the old, jaded cells have been dislodged and new, pink, tingly skin emerges from underneath. In reality, caution is required. The stratum corneum is now known to be metabolically active and not dead at all. In addition, it forms an essential protective barrier against the more hostile forces of the environment – pollutants in the air, as well as ultraviolet and infrared radiation (the possibly equally damaging heat element of sunlight) – defusing the dangerous free radicals that are produced on the surface and preventing them from doing harm deeper down. (See page 239 for a fuller description of these unfriendly molecules.) In fierce sunlight, the stratum corneum doubles its thickness within days to create a radiation-absorbent safety blanket. As over-enthusiastic removal techniques take away this first line of defense, they could have an effect opposite to the one intended: a sunsensitive skin deprived of its protective dead layers will actually age *faster* in sunlight. Over-zealous exfoliation can also lead to tiny broken veins, redness, pinkness, dryness, and irritation.

The consensus now among many cosmetic dermatologists is that you *can* have clearer, better-looking, smoother skin by encouraging the top cells to slough off. But most feel that this is best achieved by using one of the deeper-acting acid-containing creams (alpha hydroxy, salicylic, or retinoic, for example), which don't so much exfoliate from the surface as appear to change the maturation schedule of skin cells. Increasing cell turnover from the bottom up, the dermatologists say, is preferable to a surface assault.

As you get older, use any exfoliant with great care. The ideal is a gentle product, used gently. Don't be swayed by the language. Exfoliating "scrubs" suggest a vigorous action more suited to laundry than to skin and encourage a dangerous tendency to overdo it. A gentle swipe with a washcloth or cheesecloth, a weekly face mask, or the very restrained use of a Buf-Puf-like sponge (never with soap) will brighten the complexion by removing loose cells, allowing the light to scatter. Some of the new alpha hydroxy ("fruit") acid formulations have much the same effect, when applied twice-daily in cream form. Remember that any exfoliant makes the skin more receptive to products applied subsequently (not necessarily a good thing if the products are potential irritants). On the positive side, this allows moisturizers to do their job more efficiently and enables a makeup base to glide more smoothly onto the skin.

. . . AND THE INSIDE WORLD IN

In addition to keeping the outside world out, the upper layers of the epidermis are also beautifully designed to keep the inside world in. A fine oil (sebum) in water (sweat) emulsion on the surface of the skin acts as an occlusive film, preventing the cells' increasingly precious water supply from escaping into the atmosphere. Since sweat is a natural moisturizer – many components of which have recently been hijacked by the skincare companies and incorporated into their creams – a certain amount of sweaty exercise actually encourages the skin to moisturize itself.

A few cell layers further down in the epidermis, intra-cellular lipids form a second critical barrier. Sometimes called the permeability barrier, this prevents absorption of chemicals into the body and regulates the passage of water through the skin and into the atmosphere. The same lipids also form the important outer membrane of the cells themselves. Unfortunately, since these lipids oxidize as a result of free-radical activity, they are one of the first casualties of ultraviolet radiation, which explains why sun-damaged skin gets so much drier and why regular use of a sunscreen does more to keep the skin's own moisturizing capabilities intact than any expensive wonder cream. Harsh chemicals, particularly those used in strong-acting cleansers and toners, are another threat to the permeability barrier, since they can whisk away more than the oils left behind by make-up or cleanser, so rendering the skin more permeable *and* more likely to react to whatever is subsequently put upon it.

PRESERVING THE SUPPORT STRUCTURE

Beneath the epidermis lies the elusive target of every cosmetic company's most strenuous efforts: the dermis, where wrinkles originate. Here, just beneath the basal layer, an intricate support system of blood vessels, nerve endings, hair follicles, and oil and sweat glands is buoyed up by a supportive network of connective tissue, called collagen and elastin, of which collagen forms by far the larger part. Collagen is sometimes referred to as the skin's "scaffolding" because it supports the other tissues and blood vessels and holds it all together in a close organic embrace. Collagen is not just found in surface skin. It is found around nearly every organ and joint, where it acts as Nature's shock absorber; by relaxing and then returning to its original state of tension it absorbs the force of impact that would otherwise jar the joints. In the skin, collagen supplies stretchability, allowing the skin to expand as in pregnancy and then return to shape.

In fairly young skin that has not been exposed to the sun, collagen fibers criss-cross in an orderly wavy configuration like latticework. But as the skin suffers sun damage, these neat orderly bundles become disrupted and the individual fibers weaken, break, or contort as their inherent strength is lost. An enzyme called collagenase, which is normally brought into play to break down "old collagen," wreaks havoc, cross-linking collagen molecules to create an inelastic tissue. This process, which is called solar elastosis, is the main reason sun-ravaged skin looks so dreadful. Natural wear and tear cannot even begin to compete with sunlight in this respect. (Interestingly, although a cosmetic catastrophe, this process is a health saver, as it acts as a defense mechanism against damage to the organs deeper down.) As the collagen collapses, the skin sags like a mattress giving way.

Yo-yo fluctuations in weight actually accelerate the process by raiding subcutaneous fat stores. This has a devastating effect on skin that no longer has the happy elasticity of youth, leaving a legacy of stretch and sag that no amount of exercise can tighten.

In addition to the long-avowed aim of preserving what collagen we have intact, cosmetic dermatology now increasingly aims to stimulate the collagen-making cells, or fibroblasts, to produce more of their own. The French swear by a technique called electroridophorèse, in which a mild current is conducted through minuscule needles that have been inserted into facial lines in the hope of electrifying the fibroblasts into action. Cosmetic companies are also hard at work, devising ever more ingenious carriers for vitamin C, which is also thought to be important to fibroblastic productivity.

PERPETUAL PULLING
The face muscles, unique of all the muscles in the body, are directly attached to the underside of the skin rather than lying independently beneath it. Indeed it is precisely the pulling of these tiny muscles on the skin that makes the face so uniquely expressive, since the skin moves with every muscular contraction. The downside is that the repetitive pull of the muscles on the skin eventually stretches it beyond the point of no return, creating lines that are evident even in repose: frown lines that don't unknit once the crisis has passed, laugh lines that outlast the joke. Dermatologists are skeptical of most "face-lifting" exercises, though British *Vogue* found effective results from a course of isometric-type exercises tested for, and written up in, the magazine in November 1993. The official line, however, is that the facial muscles move more than enough in the normal course of events, eventually stretching the overlying skin with them, and need no help in this direction. (Some experts are also critical of the time-honored practice of facial massage, pointing out that since facial skin is attached to the muscle, heavy-handed rubbing can stretch out the connective tissue and should be avoided.)

INCREASING DRYNESS
Accompanying these all-too-visible changes, increasing sensations of dryness and tautness are common, especially after the menopause, when sebum secretions level down to about half those of a man of the same age. Sun damage aggravates the tendency, due to the oxidizing, and destruction, of the skin's own oils – so explaining why a sunscreen not only helps the skin moisturize itself more effectively but may also allow women to use lighter, less occlusive creams as they get older.

Many dermatologists rate humidifiers above day and night creams in helping to keep the skin moisturized. Humidifiers hold upwards of 40 per cent of water in the atmosphere, a boon in heated/air-conditioned houses and work environments where humidity is often kept artificially low for the sake of the office equipment.

Unfortunately, while computers prefer humidity at 30 per cent or less, human skin will dry out to the point of itchiness in the same atmospheric conditions.

Sensitivity and cosmetic overkill

As women get older, they tend to use more products and increasingly heavy formulations: super-rich night creams, heavy-duty exfoliants, strong-acting cleansers to remove an increasingly occlusive layer of make-up, along with a whole range of differently formulated products for specific areas of the body. Surveys show that, by midlife, the average American woman is using 15 to 20 products on her skin a *day*, containing over 200 chemical ingredients in all. Dermatologists hold this hodgepodge responsible for the rising number of adverse reactions being brought to their attention: blocked pores and follicles, breakouts of small white spots beneath the skin, a compromised barrier function, and, often, an insatiable thirst that no amount of moisturizer can slake.

***

Use oil or cream to remove dirt and makeup. Give it a few seconds to dissolve, wipe off with a dry tissue, and, if you like, rub gently with a wet washcloth. If you prefer soap and water, use cleansing bars or superfatted soaps. Skip astringent toners. Add a moisturizer only if the skin requires it. Be guided by your skin's own needs. Consistent use of a fairly high SPF sunscreen, applied in the morning, and at regular intervals throughout the day if outdoors for extended periods, should optimize the skin's own moisturizing capabilities, and may even enable you to graduate to lighter lotions rather than the heavier formulations generally assumed appropriate for the aging face.

If skin feels dry or acts irritated, the first response tends to be to load on yet more creams to put the problem "right." Since this is more likely to intensify the problem, the opposite strategy is called for. If you are having trouble with irritation, or your skin is dry and itchy, give it a break. In later life, the biggest "treat" skin can often have is to be left to itself.

***

As we get older, the skin's ability to keep the outside world out and the inside world in is nearly always compromised. As moisture evaporation increases, tiny cracks and fissures may appear on the surface which then invite incoming irritants. This scenario is worsened if the barrier function is impaired by heavy-handed exfoliation or harsh-acting toners, since substances, getting in as well as out more easily, will cause the skin to react to a wider range of substances. Cosmetic chemists call this dermatological bad temper "chronic irritation syndrome." Although the

IS YEAR OLD SKIN

Stratum Corneum (dead layer) is smooth and sloughs off regularly.

Melanocytes (pigment bearing cells), are evenly distributed and act as natural sun protection factors.

Blood vessels suffuse cells with oxygen and nutrients.

Sebaceous glands keep surface oiled, preventing water loss via evaporation.

Basal layer; epidermal cells reproduce perfectly each time.

Sweat glands release sweat which contains natural moisturizing factors.

Dermis is beautifully plump and spingy.

Collagen and elastin fibers are neatly ordered, supplying tone and stretchability.

Subcutaneous fat cushions the skin giving youthful bloom.

45 YEAR OLD SKIN

Melanocytes (pigment cells) get sparser, so skin color fades, and may clump together leading to brown spots.

Stratum corneum thickens and becomes uneven as surface cells clump together. Cell turnover slows.

Sebaceous glands shrink and output drops by half. As more water is lost to the atmosphere, cells dry out.

Basal Layer; cell reproduction becomes flawed as DNA is damaged.

Sweat glands become less active, reducing surface protection.

Collagen becomes fibrous and elasticity is lost.

Dermis gets thinner, eventually becoming transparently thin. Subcutaneous fat shrinks, leading to sagging and wrinkling.

As blood vessel walls weaken, they may stay permanently dilated, ("red veins").

Cross-sections through teenage and older skin, showing how its structure and function tend to change over time. Though common, much skin aging is not inevitable. In fact, top dermatologists now agree that over three-quarters of these so-called "age-related" effects are accelerated if not entirely caused by the ravages of ultraviolet light. Despite huge advances in cosmetic formulations, staying in the shade is still your best way of cheating on chronology.

skin may itch maddeningly, it is not equivalent to a true allergic reaction. These actually get less common with increasing age, as there is a natural decline in histamine output which produces the classic inflammatory response.

RESTORING THE BARRIER FUNCTION

Appropriate skincare can help to restore the skin's barrier function. "Appropriate" in this context means both gentle and restrained. As the barrier function falters, and the skin reacts to a wider and wider range of substances, products need to be more carefully chosen. Many women soon discover they cannot forever proceed on the assumption that their skin is normal. All skin changes over time.

Moisturizers can be made more effective by first spraying a fine mist of water on the face and then applying the cream while the skin is still damp (such a spray can be a real ally since it doubles up to keep hair under control between shampoos – see page 51); as the uppermost cell layers take in water, they plump up and feel softer to the touch, making lines and wrinkles less obvious. There is nothing magical about this process. Anything that allows water into the skin, including sitting in a bath, will have the same effect. The difference is that, three minutes out of the bath, the water evaporates, leaving the skin as dry or even drier than before. The present generation of moisturizers, by contrast, can lock in moisture for 12 hours or more, or even attract it into the skin from the atmosphere if the humidity is sufficiently high.

Moisturizers tend to be one of two types. Humectants (phospholipids, urea, sodium pyrrolydocarboxylic acid [NA-PCA], lactic acid, hyaluronic acid, propylene glycol, glycerine) draw water up from the depths of the dermis or suck it into the skin from the atmosphere; occlusives (petrolatum, lanolin, Vaseline, mineral oil, collagen) create an oily film over the surface which seals water into the skin by preventing undue evaporation into the atmosphere. Most of the so-called wonder ingredients listed in the glossary opposite are no more than moisturizers, in that they keep the skin feeling smooth and comfortable and looking well-conditioned, though some do the job remarkably well and for prolonged periods of time. While you cannot overload the skin with moisturizer or interfere with the output of the sebaceous glands (the skin, being an eliminative organ second to none, will simply expel the excess), not all skins appreciate heavy, expensive creams, so keep it simple. Use what feels good – everywhere. The biggest benefit of "zoning" (using different products for different areas of the face and neck) is enjoyed not by the customer but by the manufacturer, who has the chance to sell three products in place of one.

ANTI-AGING GLOSSARY

Alpha hydroxy ("fruit") acids, or AHAs, are naturally occurring compounds which, being more forgiving than retinoic acid, can be sold without prescription. Of more than a dozen different types, the four under closest scientific scrutiny are malic acid (derived from apples), glycolic acid (sugarcane), pyruvic acid (papaya), and lactic acid (fermented milk). These "fruit acids" are available in a wide range of strengths, also expressed as percentages. Used regularly, they will break up the intercellular glue that causes redundant skin cells to stick together. With the cells sloughed off, the pores unclog. The overall texture is generally finer and brighter too, since the new, smoothed-down skin reflects the light more evenly. AHAs may also boost production of hyaluronic acid, an important naturally occurring humectant (see below), and may in addition promote collagen synthesis. For more details see pages 34-5. Users of these creams should make sure they don't undo potential benefits by washing with alkaline soaps, however, and should always apply the cream to bare skin, giving it at least ten minutes to penetrate before adding further products. Creams featuring AHAs include NeoStrata, M.D. Formulations (doctors and beauticians only), Avon's Anew Perfecting Complex, Chanel's Day Lift, Estée Lauder's Fruition, La Prairie's Age Management Serum, Prescriptives' All You Need.

Anti-oxidants (vitamins A, C, E and the minerals selenium and zinc) are said to soak up the dangerously reactive energy of the free oxygen radical in the manner of blotting paper, transforming it into a new compound which is harmless and can be easily eliminated by the body. Applied externally, they may protect against environmental pollution, smoke, and, especially, UV-mediated aging. As skin does not synthesize its own vitamins, some companies, including Estée Lauder, Dior (Capture Lift), Shiseido, and Avon, are supplying them.

Beta glucan (trade name Nyad) is derived from the cell walls of yeast. Known in traditional medicine for its powerful healing capabilities, it is said to repair sun-damaged skin by stimulating the immune system via the skin's Langerhans cells, which are positioned, like sentries, in the upper layers of the epidermis. Beta glucan is also claimed to regenerate collagen and elastin, reduce fine lines, and promote a healthier glow. Though many dermatologists consider such claims unfounded, even bogus, several cosmetic companies now have it under close scrutiny in their laboratories.

Ceramides and cerebrosides are natural components of sebum, with good moisturizing qualities. Found in Elizabeth Arden's Ceramide Time Complex Capsules, among others.

Collagen has wonderful occlusive properties and cuts right down on water evaporation when applied to the surface of the skin. Any inference that it travels down to the dermis to replenish the body's own dwindling supplies, however, is biologically implausible, since the collagen molecule is too large to get into the dermis (except by injection – see page 37).

Hyaluronic acid (sodium hyaluronate) is a naturally occurring substance in the deep dermis, where it forms part of the nourishing matrix that wraps around the collagen and elastin fibers. When applied to the surface, it acts as a pleasantly greaseless moisturizer with a near legendary ability to attract and retain moisture (it is said to be able to hold up to 200 times its weight in water). Products containing it include Lauder's Advanced Night Repair and Shiseido's B.H-24 Day/Night Essence.

Liposomes are little round taxis carrying anything from toxic anti-cancer drugs to rejuvenating lipids and antioxidants. Their compatibility with our own skin membranes enables them to penetrate more deeply into the epidermis and to deliver the vital component. Critics charge that the principle is like dumping a load of bricks on a building site and expecting them to self-assemble into a building. Nevertheless, their effectiveness as a delivery system has recently been proven in trials and they are also being used in one of the world's first gene therapy trials to combat cystic fibrosis. Cosmetically, there is some evidence that the slow-release system allows for more prolonged hydration. Products containing them include Dior's Capture, Lancôme's Niosôme Plus, L'Oréal's Plénitude Eye Contour Cream Gel, Lancaster Skin Therapy.

Phospholipids are components of the cell membrane which help keep it strong and watertight. Aging epidermal cells, having fewer phospholipids, lose water and so become dehydrated. Phospholipids in creams are said to be able to restore the integrity of the cell membrane. The chemistry is contentious, but they make excellent moisturizers for older skin.

PLAYING WITH FIRE

While women can happily go without certain products, there is one they should never be without. A modern woman would have to be living in outer space not to know that sunlight can be lethal to her health and looks – and even there she'd probably still need a sunblock. Wreaking unspeakable damage that starts in the cradle and continues to the grave, the sun causes 80 per cent of the changes we associate with aging. Deep wrinkling, sagging and bagging, leatheriness, visible blood vessels, sallow yellow coloring, and brown spots are due to excessive sun exposure, according to the American Academy of Dermatology, and not to age at all.

As the sun's rays hit the skin, free radicals are produced. These then go on the rampage, oxidizing lipids both on the cell membrane and between the cells, triggering damaging chain reactions that result in an outpouring of malevolent molecules, such as arachidonic acid and the anti-inflammatory agent interleukin-II. Research at the Lauder Laboratories in New York suggests that these chemicals act as distress signals that have a knock-on effect in cells deeper down: rising levels of interleukin-II in the epidermis, for example, parallel those of the marauding molecule collagenase (see page 21) in the dermis.

Antioxidant vitamins have long been used by cosmetic scientists to stop creams from going rancid. Now it's hoped they may be capable of rendering free radicals impotent on arrival. Experiments at Duke University in North Carolina have shown that when vitamin C is suspended in an aqueous solution and rubbed lightly into the skin, it seems to stall the free-radical damage that can lead to cancer and probably prevents collagen disruption too. In animal studies, antioxidant-containing creams have been found to prevent skin cancer.

A second source of harm is the direct damage from the ultraviolet radiation itself. Packaged in little packets of energy called photons, like bullets, it is sometimes deflected by the dead cells on the skin's surface and bounces off (hence the importance of allowing the stratum corneum to stay put), and sometimes absorbed and disarmed by the pigment-producing cells known as melanocytes in the upper dermis. At other times, however, it evades both defenses and penetrates deep into the dermis. Here it hits the heart of the skin cell, the nucleus, which contains the DNA that carries the genetic blueprint for all subsequent cell reproductions. When this happens, a photochemical reaction changes the chemical structure of the DNA so that, the next time the cells divide, they are not perfect: there is a flaw.

DAMAGE LIMITATION

Luckily, the skin has a remarkable surveillance and repair system capable of mending the damage. Unluckily, it too depends on the structural integrity of the DNA. As the DNA gets damaged, so the ability of the skin to repair itself progressively diminishes. Over time, the number of damaged cells that are overlooked starts to rise, and with it the risk of skin cancer and visible "photo" aging (sun damage). Excitingly, it now seems that simply giving the skin time and space to repair itself may be enough to mend some of the damage. New research suggests that if we can only give our natural repair processes a break by putting a stop to the relentless onslaught of ultraviolet light, they will be able to undo some of the so-called "extrinsic" damage that ages us. This is a surprise. Until very recently, it was thought that harm caused by sunlight was irreversible; that any woman fool enough to sit in the sun in youth could only wait with trepidation for the day of reckoning, decades later, when all the lines and wrinkles would start to show. Now some preliminary new research at the University of Pennsylvania suggests that conscientious daylong use of sunscreens with UVA and UVB protection, especially in sunny weather, may undo some of the damage deep below the dermis. Kept out of the sunlight, even visibly abnormal tissue can improve and collagen reform. These findings tally with research showing that when individuals with a particular form of sun-related pre-cancer, called an actinic keratosis, can be persuaded to change their lifestyles and either stay out of the sun entirely or use high-protection sunscreens, the skin's repair mechanisms spring into action; over a year the lesions do regress, and may even disappear entirely.

SUN PROTECTION

The message is clear. Skin protection *is* sun protection, from childhood onward. However encouraging recent research findings on the cosmetic front, good behavior in later life is no weapon against permanent damage of a more serious nature than wrinkles. As sunscreens are now routinely to be found combined with other products, such as foundations and moisturizers, you can give your skin the protection that it needs without so much as adding an extra step to your skincare routine. And this must be more than a seasonal preoccupation, reserved for the sunniest summer's day. Fair, sun-sensitive skins are particularly in need of protection from the "casual sun" they are exposed to on city sidewalks, in backyards, even via the sunroofs of cars. They tend to age far faster than tougher, darker-pigmented skins, as they have less of the protective melanin pigment capable of absorbing ultraviolet's destructive energy.

The choice of sunscreen is critical. While the shorter-range component of the ultraviolet spectrum, UVB, was being vilified for its role in causing skin cancer, the longer-range UVA was being singled out by sunscreen makers and sunbed manufacturers for its supposedly "gentle" tanning action. No such simple distinctions exist any more. There is now conclusive evidence that much of the visible damage wreaked by ultraviolet light comes from precisely this part of the spectrum. This explains why airline pilots, who spend their working lives behind glass in full sun at high altitudes, do not get more skin cancer but do have deeply furrowed faces: UVA penetrates window glass, whereas most of the UVB is deflected. It is its depth of penetration that is to blame: while 95 per cent of the short-wave carcinogenic UVB is absorbed by the uppermost layers of the skin, up to 80 per cent of the longer-wavelength UVA passes through unimpeded and reaches right down into the dermis. Here it transforms the youthful, orderly bands of connective tissue into the all-too-familiar sag and wrinkle.

As the weight of evidence against UVA accumulates, manufacturers are changing their products. For the moment, a broad-spectrum (UVA plus UVB) sunscreen is, without any doubt, the most important anti-aging skincare measure open to us – even better than the much-vaunted retinoic acid (see page 32), since that new wonder cosmeceutical only undoes some of the damage a sunscreen can actually *prevent*. Many very good moisturizers are already incorporating UVA and UVB screens, some, with numbers climbing as high as 15 or more (Neutrogena, Clinique, Elizabeth Arden Immunage), fully justifying their claims to be anti-wrinkle creams.

Do scrutinize labels and ingredient listings, however, to make sure that UVA protection is included with the UVB. While UVB screens tend to be made from chemicals, such as para-aminobenzoic acid (PABA) and its derivatives, benzophenones, cinnamates, camphor derivatives, and benzimidazole salicylates, UVA protection usually takes the form of light-reflective opaque physical barriers (zirconium, titanium dioxide, ferric oxide, zinc oxide); the only really effective chemical to screen out UVA is Parsol 1789, or butyl methoxy-dibenzoylmethane. Physical barriers may also absorb infrared and many reflect UVB into the bargain.

While physical screens used to be thick, white and embarrassingly obvious, technological advances now allow the protective particles to be pulverized to sheer nothingness in a process known as micronization. As well as being more cosmetically acceptable, sunscreens based on micronized particles are much less likely to cause reactions than the chemical screens. (Find them in many Piz Buin and Uvistat creams and in the entire Estée Lauder Advanced Suncare range.)

A broad-spectrum sunscreen applied every day, irrespective of the weather or the season, is the best thing you can do for your skin apart from staying indoors permanently. So don't leave home without one. (Year-round protection is necessary since the UVA part of the spectrum is present throughout the year at pretty much constant concentrations.) A sunscreen contained in moisturizer or foundation is fine, so long as the SPF is 4 or more. An SPF of 15 is a bare minimum on very sunny days; for extended exposure, use higher SPFs – approximately 20 to 25. Be sure to apply the cream at least 30 minutes before going outside. And stay off sunbeds.

For those who cannot bear to forgo a tan, the new generation of self-tans is putting more acceptable stain on the skin. These use a chemical, dihydroxyacetone, which reacts with proteins on the skin's surface, darkening it within hours. At first, each daily application deepens the colour but after five days the maximum depth is achieved. (Try Estée Lauder's Self-Action Tanning Creme, Lancôme's Self-Tanning Milk, Sisley's Botanical Self-Tanning Lotion, Clinique's Self-Tanning Formula). Be aware that these bottle tans carry no protection against real sunlight (unless sunscreens are also incorporated). In fact, it could be argued that they offer *less* protection than normal, since, in order to obtain an even cover, they require the skin to be lightly exfoliated, so removing some of the skin's natural protection, as explained earlier in the chapter.

Sun protection is important for everyone, even the black and the olive-skinned, but it is particularly critical for those sunsensitive individuals known as Types 1 and 2. (Type 1 always burns and never tans; Type 2 tans with difficulty and burns frequently.) These fairer-skinned types not only have skin that ages faster in sunlight, but they also have a five-times greater risk of developing skin cancer than the more seasoned Types 3 (who tan easily and burn rarely) and 4 (who never burn and always tan). And they have a three-times greater risk of getting a malignant melanoma – the most deadly of all skin cancers and the fastest-rising cancer in Britain and the United States – than either of the hardier types. The lifetime risk of melanoma in the U.S. was one in several thousand in 1930. It had risen to one in 105 by 1991 and, some predict, will soar to one in 75 by the year 2000. This risk is increased further if an individual has light-colored hair, skin, and eyes, and/or large numbers of moles. It also rises hugely if severe sunburn was suffered as a child or if long stretches of time were spent in hot sun before the age of ten. Even recent sunburn can be sinister. In 1981, researchers compared 120 melanoma patients with 120 people who did not have skin cancer and found "clear evidence" of severe sunburn in the last five years in the melanoma group. A later study established a connection between these cancers and the regular use of sunbeds.

Skin cancer is on the increase. Check your body regularly for changes to existing moles or pigmentation spots (70 per cent of melanomas arise in pre-existing growths), and for the arrival of new growths, and get them checked out. In particular, be aware of any of the following changes, and, should two or more apply, report them to a doctor or dermatologist: a mole that is ragged at the edges; that is varied in color; that has changed in shape or grown in size and is now over ⅜ inch (1 centimeter) in diameter; that is inflamed (surrounded by redness and slight swelling), bleeds, or crusts; that itches or has an otherwise altered sensation; a sore that doesn't heal.

RETINOIC ACID

A decade and a half ago, anyone who claimed that skin rejuvenation was possible was lying. Not any more. While nothing (yet) can undo the carcinogenic consequences of sunlight – a compelling reason for being vigilant for signs of change on the skin – the visible consequences can, to a limited degree, be undone by a simple application of cream. The breakthrough came in the late 1970s, when acne sufferers who had been prescribed an experimental new cream noticed that, as their spots disappeared, so the general appearance of their skin was also improving. They returned begging for more. Their observations – namely, that they had fewer fine lines, less deeply etched wrinkles, lighter freckles and brown blotches, and a general "brightening" in tone and texture – held up when put to the test in the laboratory. Computerized measurements and microscopic analysis of skin samples confirmed that the skin's structure really *had* altered in a more youthful direction. Marked changes in cell metabolism were apparent. Skin cells were multiplying at a more rapid rate, leading to faster turnover on the skin's surface, declogging dead cells from the pores and keeping the surface clear. Even more remarkable, collagen and elastin, source of the skin's strength and resilience, appeared to be being reformed. The result was a dermis that was springier, and an epidermis that was thicker and plumper, than previously – more like the dewy skin of a baby than the thin, near-transparent covering of the elderly person. There were other surprise effects too: the blood vessels, which had become feeble and fewer with age, appeared to have multiplied in number, so improving the circulation and better oxygenating and nourishing the skin cells. "We saw increased anchoring fiberls in the top part of the inner layer of the skin of the dermis," reported a Michigan research team in one of America's top scientific journals, every bit as breathlessly as if it were announcing the first sightings of life on Mars.

In the real world, some of this excitement has now worn off, as it has become apparent that these dramatic effects can be duplicated only with the very high-concentration cream, generally 0.1 per cent, which also provokes a high degree of irritation – swelling, soreness, peeling, redness (its champions call it a "rosy pink glow"), and such a pronounced degree of sun sensitivity that a sunblock must be worn at all times. In a major research program at the University of Michigan, more than nine out of ten volunteers developed a serious-enough skin irritation at the higher concentration to warrant withholding the cream for a few days.[1] Further studies at the Boston University School of Medicine, using more cosmetically acceptable concentrations of the active ingredient at between a half and a hundredth of this amount, suggest that the more dramatic changes in the dermis, such as the reforming of collagen and elastin, are observable only when the highest concentration is used; at the lower concentrations, the cream could not be shown to offer anything a normal moisturizer could not.[2]

For the moment, this means that women wanting to reverse sun damage on their skins will have to make a choice between subtle (often imperceptible) improvements on the low-dose, less irritating creams; or opt for noticeable improvements on concentrations that will make the skin suffer for the privilege. In the Boston study, 47 per cent of the higher-concentration group were still reporting adverse reactions in the 24th, and last, week of the trial, so gainsaying the view that virgin skin hardens off as it gets used to the assault of the active ingredient.

R etinoic acid is available (by prescription) in a number of different strengths and as either a gel, lotion, or cream. Although more dramatic results are achieved when the strongest concentration of retinoic acid is used (0.1 per cent), the skin is also more likely to react. At this higher concentration, women commonly find their skin becoming so dry it actually flakes off. Those who don't want red, shiny, itchy, and exquisitely sun-sensitive skin should start with a lower concentration (0.025, 0.05 per cent), using a tiny, pea-sized amount over the whole face, diluting it with a simple cold cream to begin with, and gradually working up, according to a schedule agreed with a dermatologist. Avoid applying the cream to the delicate eyelid area, since it can cause such tightening of the skin that it pulls the eyelids back, exposing the inner surface, a complication known as ectropion. While responses to retinoic acid are very individual, women with Type 1 and Type 2 sun-sensitive skins (see page 31) are more likely to react adversely, as are women whose skin is generally sensitive.

After a year or so of regular use, both the dose and frequency of application can be tailed off and a maintenance schedule embarked upon, say once or twice a week, which must then be maintained for ever more to keep up the improvements. On stopping use of retinoic acid, many of the benefits slide off, though some changes have been shown to persist for years.

Professor Albert Kligman, who has had more experience with retinoic acid than anyone, likes to start women on a low concentration, using the tiniest amount every second or third night, and moving up by degrees to 0.1 per cent as soon "as the skin can tolerate it." Interviewed in American *Vogue*, he pointed the finger at indiscriminate prescribing, and usage, as the main reason for the disillusionment and side-effects that put so many off. "You don't just hand somebody a tube," he criticized. "The average person will press out the same amount they use for brushing their teeth, which is about eight times too much."

Intense research is already underway to find new, less corrosive, but equally effective retinoids. Some companies, cashing in on the hype, are making much of skin creams containing ingredients such as retinyl acetate and retinyl palmitate, which, although loosely related to vitamin A, have been incorporated in cosmetics in tiny amounts for years and, in the words of one dermatologist, "bear as much relation to the original as coal to diamonds."

For the best results, retinoid treatment needs to be continued indefinitely once embarked upon, since the most marked effects fall away soon after stopping. Sunbathing must also be renounced, both because the skin becomes so sun-sensitive and because it will cancel any therapeutic benefit. Although the irritation does usually lessen over time, treated skin will always remain more susceptible and demand greater care than the old leather it replaced, even after years of use. Patchy use merely heightens problems of irritation, since the skin reacts badly on being re-introduced to the cream. An appropriate skincare regime is also essential. As the vulnerable new skin stimulated by the drug is more permeable to substances coming in from the outside, products tolerated perfectly well in the past may irritate. The catch-22 is that, although the skin is more likely to react to what is put on it, the use of products is more necessary than ever: Moisturizers and oil-based foundations are required to counteract the dryness, sunscreens to protect against sun damage, and thicker, denser make-up to cover that "rosy pink glow."

More seriously, there has been some concern about the possibility of birth defects among babies born to women who use the cream in early pregnancy, since the drug is known to be capable of causing malformations in the babies of women who take it in tablet form when pregnant. However, a reassuring study was published in 1993 showing no increase in congenital disorders in the offspring of 215 women who had used the cream in early pregnancy.[3]

"FRUIT ACIDS"

Another family of acids, the alpha hydroxy ("fruit") acids, or AHAs, are also being described as cosmeceuticals. While these naturally occurring compounds seem capable of delivering more than the average skin cream, more dramatic claims have yet to be quantified, since the many respectable research studies that retinoic acid has to its credit are still noticeably absent here. Nevertheless, a paper published in the *Journal of American Academic Dermatology* showed that alpha hydroxy acids plump up the epidermis rather in the way of retinoic acid, normalize skin color by fading age-related pigment changes, and increase the skin's own stores of hyaluronic acid. At the moment, glycolic acid, going through intensive trials at the University of California at Los Angeles, appears the most promising, having even been shown, albeit only in a test-tube, to stimulate fibroblasts to produce more collagen.

Promisingly, these substances also appear capable of rendering other cosmetic ingredients more effective. For example, when applied in combination with corticosteroid creams in the treatment of eczema, they give better results than when the creams are used alone. They also have good effects on liver spots (lentigines) when used with the usual preparation, hydroquinone. Dr. Eugene Van Scott, who developed these acids, predicts their real value will turn out to be as combination preparations that "potentiate" other ingredients, both making those ingredients more effective *and* minimizing side-effects. They have been shown, for example, to spare the skin from the worst effects of potent cortisone drugs. Certainly, most of the top skincare companies are now including these new buzz substances in their formulations (see page 27).

CHEMICAL PEELING

Those who find the results of using these acid creams disappointingly subtle can get a more dramatic effect by having stronger-acting acids applied to the skin's surface. The application of these acids, in a process known as chemical peeling, will literally eliminate surface skin – obliterating shallow lines, smoothing out deeper wrinkles, and fading uneven color spots to boot. It sounds drastic and it is: the cosmetic equivalent of voluntarily immersing your face in an acid bath, these chemicals corrode the skin's topmost dead layer before burning on down to the live skin below. As the uppermost half millimeter of skin is eliminated, so are the finer lines and wrinkles. The astonishing healing capabilities of the skin are then brought into play, and it constructs itself afresh. The result is skin that both looks and acts younger (after all, it actually *is* younger), and feels softer and smoother to the touch. These terrific results are, not surprisingly, achieved at some cost. Chemical-peel procedures are not only agonizingly painful, they *must* be carried out by an experienced practitioner, who will be able to achieve precisely the degree of control required. The results can be excellent . . . or catastrophic if the procedure goes wrong, leaving bad scarring where the chemical has penetrated too deeply and uneven patches of skin color.

Of the two types of acid used, the most dramatically effective results are achieved with phenol, a frighteningly corrosive substance that reaches right down to the deep dermis. It literally wipes the slate clean – entirely erasing every line and wrinkle in its path and restoring a somewhat shiny, baby-smooth surface to previously corrugated areas, such as above the upper lip. Since phenol shrinks the skin, it has the additional effect of pulling the skin tight. Unfortunately, the price to be paid for such effectiveness is that, on its way down, phenol also wipes out the pigment-bearing melanocytes in the upper dermis, so leaching color from the complexion. (One advantageous side-effect is that undereye darkness vanishes.) For this reason, better results tend to be achieved on pale-skinned individuals. However pale the skin, a phenol peel will always leave a demarcation line between the old, naturally pigmented skin and the new, bleached-out skin next door – unless the whole face is peeled, an ambitious maneuver that can result in an all-over ghostly pallor. If, as is more common, just a few areas are being treated (such as around the mouth and eyes), the chemical should be applied so as to make any color contrast as inconspicuous as possible. Even then, makeup is a must if the contrasts in color are not to be apparent. A phenol peel demands commitment: not only does it hurt horribly, but it can take fully three weeks before the redness, swelling, and discomfort recede to a point where a woman feels happy to resume normal life, let alone be seen in public. And it can be months before the full effect is apparent.

In the early 1990s, the number of chemical peels undertaken in the United States increased by nearly half, making it the fastest-growing cosmetic procedure, thanks to the introduction of a milder form of acid, trichloroacetic acid, or TCA. This has less of a depigmenting effect and cuts down dramatically on recovery time, requiring several *days* rather than weeks. Like retinoic acid, trichloroacetic acid is available in varying concentrations – but should always be applied by a skilled dermatologist/ plastic surgeon. The mildest can be used as a cosmetic treatment; penetrating no more than two or three cell layers, it acts as an ultra-effective face-mask or exfoliant, which noticeably improves the texture and look of the skin for three to four months at a time. The stronger concentrations penetrate as far as mid-dermis, obliterating fine lines, refining texture, and fading pigmentation differences. It has been described as "wonderful for that 40-something look." But even at the highest concentrations, TCA won't penetrate quite as far as phenol, inevitably leaving some of the lines that phenol would have erased, though on a second application almost as good results can often be obtained. Some surgeons prefer to carry out a series of small TCA peels at, say, weekly intervals rather than one major one. Adding methyl salicylate or solid carbon dioxide can increase penetration and gives a more even peel (known colloquially as a "hot rod"). TCA is certainly preferable to phenol for women over 60 and those with certain health problems, because the latter has been known to disrupt kidney, heart, and liver function.

The risks and degree of discomfort involved have to be taken into account. Nevertheless, to date, chemical peels are unarguably the best way of getting rid of fine lines, especially in the center of the face, such as above the upper lip, where a face-lift has least impact. Even better results can be obtained by priming the skin with Retin-A for at least six weeks before treatment to make it more receptive, and by following a strict post-treatment skincare schedule with (in particular) conscientious use of sunscreens for ever afterwards.

DERMABRASION

An alternative to using a chemical is a surgical technique, called dermabrasion, which uses a rotating sander to plane off skin cells to the mid-dermis. Some surgeons claim that they can control the depth of peel more easily, and vary it according to the part of the face being treated. Dermabrasion can also have a permanent depigmenting effect, though it is less likely than with phenol. Scarring is a risk, too.

LINE FILLERS

Increasingly, non-surgical solutions are being brought to the rescue of the aging face. In the 1970s, the idea of bypassing the operating theatre with simple, single injections promised to be the perfect answer for scalpel-shy women. When first introduced in 1976, bovine collagen (which closely resembles the collagen in human skin) was said to be serious competition to surgery. Injected directly under the creases, it seemed a wonderful way of filling out lines and furrows and restoring fullness to those areas of the face where the underlying collagen was disintegrating.

Fifteen years and over half a million patients later, public enthusiasm for the procedure continues unabated (in the United States, collagen implants have now shoved breast augmentation out of place to become the second most popular cosmetic procedure, after eyelid surgery), while professional enthusiasm (like the results of the implants themselves) has worn thin. When Eugene Courtiss, past president of the American Society of Aesthetic Plastic Surgery, addressed the American College of Surgeons in Atlanta in the mid-1980s, he passed around before-and-after pictures of patients he had treated with this new wonder line-filling material. Invited to determine which were the befores and which the afters, his fellow surgeons were unable to tell.

While it does stay in place for a while, it is highly unlikely that bovine collagen permanently integrates with, or "replenishes," one's own collagen. Even the heavy-duty version is quickly reabsorbed by the body – disappearing in as little as a couple of months if injected into the more mobile areas of the face, such as between the eyes or around the mouth, which, of course, is precisely where the deep expression lines form. Allergic reactions are occasionally a problem too. To get around this, some surgeons are now separating out the skin's own collagen after liposuction and injecting that. The consensus among U.S. dermatologists now is that collagen must be looked on as a temporary fix requiring a regular maintenance schedule, in the same way as tinting one's hair or waxing one's legs, rather than a permanent solution. There seem to be many women who, quite resigned to its short life span, are happy to submit to these regular repeats, however. Hopes that Fibrel, a gelatin powder derived from porcine (pig) collagen, would outlast the bovine variety, are foundering. While it can help push up indented scars and prominent, deeply etched lines, Fibrel does not appear any more longlasting, in spite of claims to the contrary.

Everyone agrees that liposuction – taking fat out of the body (see page 89) – works; but there's intense disagreement about the effectiveness of putting it back in. The appealing idea of having one's own unwanted fat "harvested" from the abdomen, buttocks, or thighs and then reinjected to fill out the lines of the face, hands, and even calves where one's own fat and muscle have wasted with age, is, of course, the stuff of fantasy. Thus far, however, the results have been somewhat short of fantastic, as the fat seems to be just as speedily reabsorbed as collagen. Often it doesn't even survive the transfer, especially in older patients – a fact that has not stopped the fast-buck clinics from advertising it as safe and effective, despite well-documented hazards in the fat-removing process (see page 89).

Although silicone has a history of disastrous use, in careful, experienced hands it is the most satisfactory of all the line-fillers and the only one that stays permanently where put. When pure, medical-grade silicone is injected in small microdroplets right underneath the dermis, it stimulates the formation of collagen around it, rather as sand in an oyster leads to the formation of the pearl, and pushes the skin up like a pillow. Unlike collagen, Fibrel, and fat, silicone really can produce permanent results. This is its great disadvantage too, of course, since in the wrong hands it can lead to lifelong disfigurement. Disaster stories of silicone migrating away from the site of injection into the lungs, with occasionally fatal consequences, or causing ugly raised lumps at the site of the injection can be ascribed to inexperience, the use of impure silicone which has been contaminated by additives, or the introduction of over-ambitious quantities – sometimes all three at once. If silicone is pure, "medical-grade" quality, and built up over a period of months, with at least two weeks allowed between treatments, the results can be truly impressive, especially on very pronounced lines. If these cautions are not observed and the surgeon goes all-out for an instantly gratifying result, ridges are likely to appear as the new collagen forms around the silicone. Since fine judgment and considerable experience are required to deposit just enough but not too much, and since the effect will last forever, an experienced practitioner is infinitely more important here than for any other line-filling technique. Because of the many problems associated with silicone, not least the still-unresolved questions about its capacity to provoke serious immune disorders, the American Food and Drug Administration outlawed its use as a line-filling substance in 1992 to a chorus of protest from U.S. dermatologists and surgeons who complained that the best was now banned. In Europe, where it continues to be used, albeit by a minority, it is still seen as the most effective option of the lot.

Unsatisfactory as the first generation of line-fillers may be, they are an improvement over the disastrous wax injections women flocked to have in the early years of this century. The technique's most famous failure was Gladys Deacon, "the most beautiful woman in the world" and ninth Duchess of Marlborough, who, hoping to improve on an already exquisite profile, had wax injected into the bridge of her nose. Over the years it gradually melted and slipped down, giving her a second jawline. Her biographer, Hugo Vickers, tells of a visitor who, sitting with her by the fireside, noted that she refused to look him full in the face "and appeared to be gently massaging the wax, melted by the heat, back up into the bridge of her nose."[4]

Today's improving options aside, as little as ten years may bring a safe, effective, permanent solution to the lines we'd rather live without. Already, research on wound healing is turning up intriguing prospects for future injectable substances, such as natural enzymes and hormones called epidermal growth factors, that will spur the body's own ability to regenerate tissue, so pushing its own lines out again.

COSMETIC SURGERY

For all the wonder creams and cosmeceuticals, the line fillers and myriad other anti-aging weapons that are continually being added to the older woman's armamentarium, surgery remains the only effective solution to the eternal age-related problem of overlarge, sagging skin. Nothing can make the skin shrink a size, except cutting out the slack.

Many women find the very idea of having a scalpel cut into their flesh physically and philosophically repugnant. Acceptance of the aging process is the hallmark of adult maturity, they say. One feminist has gone as far as to draw a parallel with the genital mutilation carried out in some African societies – charging that both practices, although ostensibly carried out for aesthetic reasons, demonstrate "the pressure on women to comply with male standards of desirability and eligibility and are thus a mirror of male domination."[5] Another compares it to tribal scarification, with each woman under a growing pressure to have the requisite younger look carved into her flesh. Squarely occupying the moral high ground, this growing and increasingly vocal group condemns women who voluntarily submit to the knife as unduly vain and narcissistic, overpreoccupied with the externals, guilty of the cardinal crime of caring too much.

Other women see nothing particularly wonderful about wrinkles, especially their own, and cannot wait to get rid of them. Taking the same coolly professional attitude to this form of self-improvement as to any other, they feel entitled to take advantage of what modern medical expertise can offer them, maintaining that having the slack skin on their face excised or the fat sucked from their thighs is simply part of a general thrust toward self-improvement – the logical end-point of visiting a gym or watching their weight. This is also a growing group: in the United States during the 1980s eyelid surgery increased by over a third and face-lifts by a quarter.

Unlike other operations, the presence of the patient on this particular operating table is entirely a matter of choice. If she goes into the technicalities, even the most confident applicant will find herself blanching at the prospect of having a scalpel slice into a face that looked (more or less) all right to begin with. She will also find herself confronting the uncomfortable risk of visible scarring and, more remote but still real, that of paralysis of part of the face due to nerve damage. Neither eventuality can be quantified because no firm statistics exist and because the outcome depends to such a degree on how well the patient heals and the competence of the doctor, both of which are highly variable. Less traumatic but more common, a woman's choice of hairstyle or the way she puts on her make-up may be forever restricted as a result of the operation.

If her researches are thorough, the face-lift candidate will be aware that, even in the best of hands, she has to be prepared for a line or scar that may be more or less successfully hidden but will never entirely fade. In the more immediate aftermath of the operation, she can expect several days of acute discomfort, and at least two weeks of looking swollen, bruised, battered, and considerably worse than she ever did in her life before. Pounding headaches may accompany the slightest exertion for

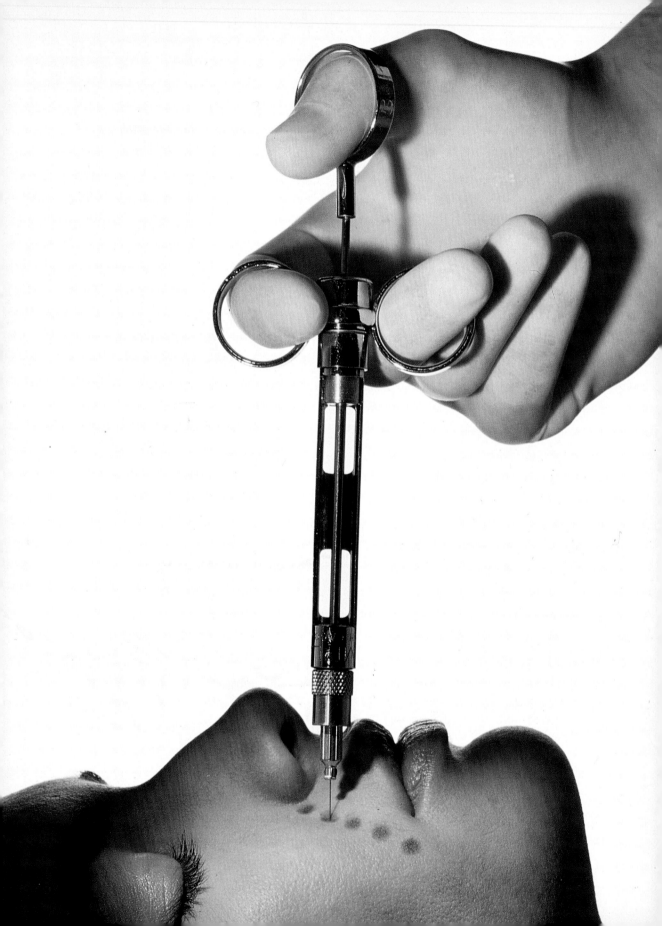

several months. A numbness around her ears and cheeks will give a curiously detached sensation on making up and may never entirely disappear. Someone else's smile may even temporarily flash back from the mirror. Here is Saville Jackson, writing up the experience for British *Vogue* a month after the operation.

> Unless I lie down frequently my head still feels as though it were in a vice. I shop in sunglasses, making sure I am there earlier than my neighbours. I really didn't know what I was taking on. I knew that it would be very painful for a while, but fondly imagined that by now I would be back to my routine. I can swim very gently but cannot play golf, as any effort makes my face tighten. This includes carrying anything heavy. The itching still drives me mad – caused, I suppose, by the nerve ends wriggling like decapitated worms.[6]

Even after the operation, a woman may be disappointed to find that the scalpel has not entirely erased every line and wrinkle. Those around the eyes and midface remain where they are. Every single line, every millimeter of loose skin that so gratifyingly disappears when the skin is pulled tight at the temples by the index finger, cannot be tightened to the same extent by surgery, since the scar cannot take this degree of tension. Saville Jackson, who was thrilled with the result of her lift (lucky, after all that pain), declined to sit for the before-and-after portraits *Vogue* hoped to publish alongside her piece, pointing out that we would have to wait for the eye-lift scheduled in six months' time. "When I smile," she protested, "all the lines crinkle around my eyes and it looks a bit odd."

For women who are fundamentally dissatisfied with the way they look, a face-lift will always disappoint, since the old face never pleased them anyway. For women who just want to look a little fresher and tighter, however, and for whom the re-emergence of the familiar face beneath the bandages comes as a big relief, a face-lift can make a positive difference. One study, comparing psychological before-and-after profiles of 75 cosmetic surgery patients against patients presenting for general surgery, found them much less anxious, less distressed, and more extrovert a year after the operation than they had been before and concluded "cosmetic surgery really can cheer you up." In the end, it all comes down to one's expectations. And, these days, women whose expectations are realistic and researches are thorough are likely to find them met to the full.

In the best hands, cosmetic surgery has reached extraordinary heights of technical excellence. The slack skin can be cut away with no sacrifice of expressiveness, and the scars are so consummately hidden as to be all but invisible. The effect is simply, well, fresher, though all but the most eagle-eyed would be hard-pressed to say why. Needless to say, these results are achieved by only some of the thousands of surgeons now setting their scalpels to the face of contemporary womanhood.

The basic face-lift operation was developed in France at the turn of the century and is still

In the 1970s, the idea of bypassing the operating theater with simple single injections promised to be the perfect answer for scalpel shy woman. Two decades on, however, most line fillers have been shown to offer a fleeting improvement that must be looked on as a temporary fix, in much the same way as having highlights put in the hair or one's legs waxed.

widely practiced. It entails detaching the skin and fat from the muscle underneath, pulling them up, cutting off the excess, and stitching them back down (so a mark on the cheek, for example, ends up nearer the temple). There was a brief fashion in the 1970s for the "mini-lift," which involved making the smallest possible incision and removing as little tissue as necessary in order to "rejuvenate" the face at a fraction of the cost and effort. But the effects hardly lasted beyond the removal of the stitches. These days, nobody talks "nips" and "tucks" any more. Instead, from the early 1980s on, cosmetic surgery has itself had a kind of face-lift with the introduction of deeper and more dramatic techniques.

The relatively new SMAS lift (it stands for superficial musculo-aponeurotic system) takes up not only the skin but the muscles underneath. Since a more substantial section of flesh is cut away, it can be anchored more firmly, giving longer-lasting results than the conventional lift. If, as is often the case, the underlying muscles have become slack, skin lifted in the conventional way will soon start to sag again. The SMAS lift looks more natural too: as the skin is not as stretched, the artificial, pulled look is avoided. The deep nose-to-mouth lines, which the standard lift has little impact on, are softened. The SMAS lift is now the most commonly practiced face-lift in the U.S. But many European surgeons have hesitated to take on this new technique, fearful of side-effects as the more radical slicing takes them ever nearer the critical facial nerve, which controls the muscles of facial expression. American surgeons counter with the claim that some complications are actually *lessened* by cutting deeper. There is less risk of bruising and post-operative bleeding and hemorrhage, they say, since few blood vessels lie between the layers where the SMAS is separated.

A newer, even more audacious technique, just beginning to gain popularity on the world's operating tables, goes deeper still. In the subperiostial or "Mask" face-lift the surgeon burrows in through the brow and the roof of the mouth and delves right down to the bone itself, hauling virtually everything up into place, and even chiseling away at the bone if needs be – recontouring the eye sockets, fining down the nose, and supplying cheekbones by grafting implants onto the originals. One enthusiast described it in British *Vogue* as "like getting the foundations in before you hang the wallpaper." Once the framework is satisfactorily remodeled, the soft tissues and muscles, which are now free from the bone, are lifted upward and secured in the position they occupied before gravity took over. The eyes can be attended to at the same time, so often avoiding the need for a further "eye-lifting" operation. Enthusiasts rave that this type of face-lift really allows them to change the "underlying architecture" of the face. But the procedure is still experimental, prolongs recovery time, and causes considerable swelling and bleeding. Furthermore, it is not suitable past the age of 50, when there's too much slack skin on the surface to make it feasible.

All cosmetic surgeons like to operate earlier rather than later, making the "maintenance lift" a growing trend in cosmetic surgery. Some leading U.S. surgeons report that nearly half their customers are in their 40s. The idea is that, rather than recreating youth, the surgeon maintains it – not so much erasing the signs of time as forestalling them.

Whatever the age of the patient, the scalpel is increasingly being deployed on several different fronts, with surgeons carrying out multiple operations that aim to correct every aspect of the aging face at one time – eyes, brows, chin, cheeks, even nose. "Extras" include procedures to shorten the earlobes; to flick up the ends of the lips, counteracting gravity's depressing downturn; to restore fullness to the mouth by slipping in grafts of one's own skin; to lift the tip of the nose a fraction and so counteract the natural drooping that occurs with age. The new attitude is that it's often the small adjustments rather than the major changes that have the truly rejuvenating effect. The corrections may be imperceptible to the untrained eye but they can make a real difference to the overall look. If nature omitted to supply you with them, for example, cheekbones (malar implants) can be provided that will instantly remove the gauntness that can come with age by returning the fuller face of youth. These hard, transparent shells can be positioned above, on, or under the bones, where they fill out the face, expanding the skin surface and stretching out some of the lines. A particularly popular midlife option, they prolong the life of a lift to boot. The lucky few to be born with naturally good bone structure have faces that age less fast because the cheekbones act like a frame to support the skin, helping to maintain the tension – hence the tendency now to supply them for those not so naturally blessed.

The use of liposuction on the neck, with ultra-fine tubes, is enabling surgeons to restore a clean right angle at the neck, eliminating jowliness and the soft fleshiness under the chin (especially when the broad sheath of platysma muscle is also cut and tightened). In a minority of women – usually those under 45 – suction alone can sometimes produce the required result with no need for surgery. As women pass 40,

Would you make a suitable candidate for cosmetic surgery? Study your face in a mirror while sitting, then lie down, still holding the mirror. If you feel your face looks better and tauter on the horizontal, it is because the slack skin has shifted. According to one surgeon, this gives a good idea of what surgery can do, since "there has to be something to take out." Pulling the skin smooth with the fingers is not a good guide since surgery never stretches the skin to this extent.

Identifying a good surgeon must be a priority. Find someone who has had something done and is pleased with the result. Ask several doctors whom they (or their colleagues) would recommend, and pick the name that comes up most often. Look at examples of their work and ask to talk to someone who has had the operation. Be clear that you are both in agreement about the effect you are hoping to achieve. All surgeons have their own ideas about what a beautiful female face/body looks like, so make sure your aesthetic preconceptions are compatible.

Beforecare is important: lose weight first (if necessary) to maximize the potential of a lift, prime the skin with retinoic acid, and stop smoking to aid healing.

Aftercare is crucial too, since skin following a face-lift is more vulnerable than it was before. Keeping the skin well moisturized is important, as is keeping out of sunlight for the first month and strictly limiting exposure thereafter. Keep weight as stable as possible and avoid crash dieting since a drastic weight loss will soon undo the results.

however, surgery is generally necessary if the newly swanlike neck is not to look odd with the face above. While occasionally used to reduce pouchy cheeks, suction is not common on the face itself, since few older women actually have *enough* fat there.

With modern surgical techniques, the scars following a face-lift should be imperceptible. When the neck and lower part of the face are lifted, the incision is made behind the ears, preferably buried well back in the hairline if the scar is not to show when the hair is put up or pulled back. When the classic face-lift (which attends to the midface) is also performed, the incision line runs up behind and in front of the ear, where the scar is buried in the natural crease. You'd never notice it unless you knew exactly where to look. In many practices now, the use of staples, rather than stitches, is preferred when the incision is made in the scalp area, since it is less likely to disturb the line of the hair. These are removed within a few days of surgery.

Increasingly, women are also electing to have their brows lifted. This procedure involves a radical cut across the top of the brow. The incision is buried about an inch (a few centimeters) back in the hairline and the skin peeled forward as though pulling a swimming cap over the front of the face. If well done, it can do more to lift the expression of the face than any other single procedure, restoring the original upward arch of the eyebrows and removing the glowering, beetle-browed look that so often accompanies their descent. Surgeons love the brow lift because once the forehead skin is lifted up, the eyebrows also return to their original position and any pouching and bagging on the lids instantly improves.

Many women, reluctant to have what they perceive (rightly) as a radical operation, opt for less extensive eye surgery, known as blepharoplasty. The change is not very drastic – one just looks wider-awake and refreshed. Generally, surgery is carried out from the *inside* of the eyelid, so avoiding visible scarring. While surgery here can be entirely indiscernible, in less practiced hands over-ambitious removal of eyelid skin may prevent the eyes from closing completely and create a lopsided look infinitely worse than the bagging that preceded it.

Such disaster stories point up the importance of gaining as much information as you can if you are contemplating cosmetic surgery of any kind. Explore your options with a number of surgeons not just one. Disappointment is not always due to unrealistic expectations or less than expert surgical skills; the importance of selecting the appropriate procedure is also critical. As often as not, a poor result comes down to a woman not having fully acquainted herself with the various options open to her and so having missed out on the one that would have suited her best.

A far cry from advertising instant coffee and washing detergent . . . forward-looking skincare companies are increasingly using models with lived-in faces that their customers can both identify with and realistically aspire toward. Actress Isabella Rossellini, ABOVE, now in her early 40s, has been Lancôme's "face" for over ten years. Also acting as inspiration to their generation are Patti Hansen, now in her late 30s, house model for Alexandra de Markfoff, a skincare, treatment, and color cosmetics range aimed at women of 35-plus, Catherine Deneuve (Yves St Laurent) and Lauren Hutton (Revlon Results), both in their 50s.

SKINSAVING STRATEGIES

WHAT WORRIES	WHAT MAY WORK	WHAT PROBABLY WON'T
forehead furrows	The *surgical brow lift* can smooth (though not erase) them. *Cutting the frontalis muscle* prevents lines returning, but may render the face strangely expressionless. *Injecting a toxin* (botox) paralyzes the muscle for months at a time and after a year or so (theoretically) breaks the furrowing habit. *Silicone injections* (Europe only) can also be effective, but proceed with extreme caution. While short-lived, *collagen* has better results on horizontal than vertical lines.	*Line-filling options* are disappointingly temporary, since the repetitive pull of the muscles on the skin caused by the habitual expression quickly disperses the material.
frown lines	The *surgical brow lift* will minimize these lines but the repetitive pull of the muscles will soon etch deep grooves back between the eyes. Permanent improvements can now be gained by *cutting the corrugator muscle*, with scalpel or lazer, so removing the ability to frown. The *muscle toxin* (botox) is effective. In experienced hands, *silicone injections* (Europe only) can fill the grooves, especially once the muscle has been put out of commission.	Although temporarily impressive on very early lines, *collagen* has only the most transient effect on the established scowl, since the marks soon return as the familiar expression is pulled. It may have longer-lasting results when used following treatment with muscle toxin.
crow's feet	*Retinoic acid* has impressive results (which is why the eye area always features in "before-and-after" pictures). Spot *chemical peels* can also be very effective, with phenol's depigmenting effect supplying a surprise bonus by lightening dark circles beneath the eye. *Tightening the orbicularis muscle* can eliminate crow's feet, but many surgeons prefer to leave most of these lines in place for an authentic result: perfectly smooth skin around the eyes is unusual even in a 20-year-old, and can give an unreal, blanked-out look.	The *classic face-lift* has no impact on these lines, though a separate eye lift (blepharoplasty) will soften them (especially if the orbicularis muscle is also tightened). Even in Europe, *silicone* is not advised since the skin is so thin there is a strong risk of visible lumps post-treatment. *Dermabrasion* is also unsuitable due to the thinness of the skin.

WHAT WORRIES	WHAT MAY WORK	WHAT PROBABLY WON'T
nose-to-mouth lines	*Collagen injections* can be effective early on, though once the line becomes a fold, they are ineffective. Some surgeons are now threading strips of *Gore-tex* through the inner edge of the nostril to push out entrenched lines to good effect. *Liposuction* may help minimize pouches but best results usually require a *full SMAS face-lift*.	As the flesh starts to pouch and the line becomes more of a fold, *line-filling techniques* are of no use, nor are *chemical peels*. *Liposuction* is usually only partially helpful at best, as is the *traditional (skin-lift-only) face-lift*.
lipstick (pucker) lines	*Dermabrasion/chemical peel* can often be dramatically effective. Although phenol gives the best results (literally erasing the lines), it also leaves the skin much paler, making full-time make-up a must. Trichloroacetic acid (TCA), while marginally less effective, leaves color intact. Of the line-fillers, *silicone injections* (Europe only) are the only permanent answer. Where lipstick bleeding upward is the problem, *collagen* can be injected along the upper lipline, creating a (sometimes visible) ridge.	*Surgery* has no impact on lines around the lips since it intentionally avoids pulling on the mouth.
marionette lines	Small "commas" at the corners of the mouth can be temporarily softened by *collagen*, though *silicone* (Europe only) provides a longer-lasting alternative.	*Surgery* usually has no impact on these lines.
mouth-to-chin lines	Once the lines become prominent, a *face-lift* will minimize them by removing the excess flesh that casts the shadow.	*Peels* tend to be disappointing since these are gravitational lines caused by sagging flesh, which no amount of acid can remove.
horizontal neck lines	Nothing very well . . . Neck lines do not come with age but are there from birth, an ingrained pattern like "ringlet" lines on the wrist. A *neck lift* will make them less obvious but never obliterate them. A *chemical peel* performed on its own, or three months after surgery, can also help soften these lines.	*Surgery* will help smooth the neck, but lines close to the throat often remain disappointingly evident.

HAIR

CATCHING sight of that thread of pure white amid the dark or light is often the first shock of the old. It can make a woman feel she has aged ten years in an instant. The happy conviction of unassailable youth takes a hammering. Middle age has arrived.

Corkscrewing madly up from the scalp as though it had a life of its own, the offending strand may also provoke the more mundane realization that the graying head is going to need "managing" in a whole new way. The woman whose hair has always been pleasingly biddable, needing little more than a blob of mousse to persuade it into place, may now start finding it a "problem." Either it is a furious frizz defying all attempts at control, or it is so limp that the style it once held happily for days falls apart after just a few hours. She "cannot do a thing with it." Permanent waves flop out after a couple of weeks, the ends snap, and there's so much static after washing it's like there's an electrical storm raging over her head. To make matters worse, her crowning glory is not quite as glorious as it used to be – not as thick, nor as lustrous, nor as healthy-looking. The products used for decades are no longer working. To regain control, she exchanges her six-weekly wash 'n' cut for a weekly "do." Placing her head in the hands of her hairdresser, she finds herself caught in a dependency trap that works as long as her beauty caretaker is available, but leaves her feeling helpless, and looking terrible, when he or she isn't.

Alternatively, if haircare has always come low down on her list of priorities, she may let out an exasperated sigh and give up on it for good, leaving it to its own unpredictable devices, unaware of how much can now be done to improve it.

PROFESSIONAL HELP

If she hasn't already, the woman whose hair looks, feels, and acts quite differently to the way it did at 20 should adapt her haircare. If she is serious, she will enlist the aid of a professional. In New York, women commonly consult trichologists (scalp and hair specialists) about all the minutiae of haircare, especially if they cannot get satisfactory help from their hairdressers, recognizing in their pragmatic way that "problem hair" is only a problem because they haven't yet found a solution – and there are solutions to be had in plenty. Elsewhere, however, many women are reticent about consulting a trichologist for something that the prevailing culture holds to be as trivial as the way they look. Trichology is still associated with dreaded scalp diseases when, in fact, these specialists (whose training overlaps both the medical and the cosmetic) are experts at improving the condition and look of "normal" hair. They are also perfectly positioned to advise on the risks and benefits of chemical processing, since there is no capital to be made from persuading you into (or out of) any particular course of action.

The next ally on any woman's agenda is a stylist who can cut her hair and keep it looking current. Half a century ago, once women arrived in their 20s, they did away with childish things and put on the face, fixed the hair, and stepped into the clothes that would last them a lifetime. As far as the hair was concerned, the color and style remained constant through several decades. "My own grandmother wore Revlon's Windsor on her nails every day of her life," marvelled Julia Reed writing in American *Vogue*. "And the same man gave her the same hairdo for 35 years. (He even gave it to her after she was dead.) She never once looked anything else than perfect." In those days, the man who wrought such perfection was not so much a master of art as artifice – the color making little reference to the shades beneath, and the shape defying gravity and movement, with each strand stiffly sprayed into place; a mummified tribute to how the hair had been in its heyday. (And a time-consuming one, demanding weekly visits to the hairdresser to maintain it.)

These days women, continually reconsidering the way they look, recognize that a change of cut is the fastest passage out of the dumpy, frumpy, and lumpy middle-age syndrome. The challenge is finding a professional to whom they feel happy entrusting their heads. At best a collaboration, at worst a passive submitting to the scissors, the rapport between a woman and her hairdresser has a big impact on the result. Skimping and saving is usually a false economy. What money buys, and the top stylists can provide, is a look that the hair can't achieve on its own. What makes a cut *right* goes beyond matters of technique. Ultimately it's a question of instinct. A runaway stylist is every woman's nightmare, but equally disastrous is the maintenance man (or woman) who simply performs "the usual?" without so much as a second thought, when a change can be long overdue. Hairdressers are notorious for making assumptions about what their older clients want, and performing it, without so much as taking in the shape or character of the face beneath.

THE KINDEST CUT

While there are no rules, after 30 hair generally looks better shorter, and either drawn well off or away from the face. London hair stylist Andrew Jose, who has cut hundreds of older heads into shape, almost invariably finds that the best look is "very short or all one length, often touching at the jaw, showing off the shape of the head." Jose delights in showing his clients how the proportion of the hair – determined by the features of the face – should be designed to draw attention to, say, the slant of the cheekbone or the width of the mouth. When the focal point is emphasized in this way, a haircut can really transform a face in the short space of an hour. According to many top stylists, once hair reaches older shoulders, it looks best swept right off the face – with combs, in a braid, or in a timeless French pleat. Even here the soigné chignon that French women wear to such effect can soon end up as a schoolmarmy bun in less practiced hands. And loose is no better. We all know women who keep their hair long for too long, unaware that a tousled mane and alluring curtain of hair work only if you're under 17, and not always then. Once a totem of youth and freedom, flowing locks can actually be *aging*. Short is a sign of having grown up, not given up. It looks sharp. It means business. Hillary Clinton's move from housewifely hairband and bangs as supportive campaigner for her husband to uncompromising power cut once in the White House with a job of her own in the administration is a perfect example of just how much such a makeover can signify. It also had the effect of bringing her right up to date – instantly. Fashions may change, but short stays contemporary, and has done since the bob first took New York in 1917.

Make an ally of your hairdresser. A professional acquainted with your hair's condition and history can give valuable advice on color or condition. Because you will be returning for repeat appointments, he or she is likely to take a long-term view rather than going for the instant result – which might be achieved at the expense of your hair. Unless you have had a specific recommendation, ask for the most experienced stylist/colorist on your first appointment at a new salon.

Have your hair cut regularly, at least once every two months. The basis of any style is the cut underneath and, since the hair grows at different rates on different parts of the head, a cut can grow out of shape quite quickly. Although hair tends to grow more slowly as a woman ages, regular visits are still essential to keep split ends cut back and the whole well conditioned. If hair is fine or thinning, a blunt one-length style, such as a bob, is an excellent option, since it will give an impression of volume. Graduated, feathered, or layered effects generally make hair look thinner. Ask your hairdresser to show you different ways to wear a look – smooth or messy, up or down – and also how to use gel and other products that might benefit your hair.

Cutting the hair is an act of both self-assertion and self-approval. Plucking up the courage to make themselves over, many women have found that junking the old and putting on the new can literally be a heady experience – allowing them to cut free from the too long lived-in image of their youth and to move on beyond the luscious long-haired stereotype of (early) womanhood. Short is also the perfect answer for women in a hurry. New techniques in cutting and razoring give shape and style while still allowing a woman to shampoo her hair, run a dab of gel through with her fingers, and leave it to the air to dry – a liberation from the bother of blow dryers. As long as there's some degree of layering, the haircut will usually fall easily into place, aided by the new generation of gels, mousses, and sprays.

THE NEW-GENERATION OF STYLING AIDS

New styling aids have helped render the old "shampoo and set" obsolete. They are deservedly popular. Hairdressers love them for the easy control that they give. Applied sparingly after washing onto nearly dry hair, light sculpting lotions leave a thin film which can transform the frizziest mess into a sleek, controllable delight. Silicone serums also lend wonderful frizz-control. In addition to making combing wet hair blissfully easy, these clear, odorless fluids coat the hair shaft with a glistening protective film that stops hair both from absorbing moisture and from losing it. They are thus great for coarse hair that frizzes in humidity (as they seal *out* unwanted moisture) and for hair that suffers from dehydration (as they seal *in* essential water). As the silicone actually coats the cuticle and fills in any holes, each strand is made more uniform, with the result that the hairs can lie obediently side by side, creating a more light-reflective surface and giving a wonderful shine. For fine hair, however, which can be weighed down to a point of lankness by these serums, it's essential to choose the lightest formulations (Shiseido's Hair Cuticle Treatment is one). Styling products containing polymers that expand and set in the heat give an even stronger fix. Mousses are particularly versatile, since they can be applied to hair that is either wet or dry. The effect is natural and casual, with lots of movement and just the right element of control – enabling women to do what they want with their hair while avoiding the rigid haystacks created by the old-style setting lotions.

Gels, mousses, and sprays offer an ideal solution for the woman whose hair is frizzy, fine, or difficult to style and who desires a free, unstructured look. As formulations vary widely, experimentation is often in order. Hair texture is more important than oiliness or dryness when choosing the right product, and a number of ranges now address these differences.

Quiz your hairdresser about the best way of using these new styling products. Be mindful, too, that the effects of mousses and gels tend to change in different weather conditions; you will need less (or none at all) when humidity is high, more when humidity is low.

In general less is more: over-application of mousse and gel will flatten the hair, giving the exact opposite impression to the one intended. Use the smallest amount – a coin-sized quantity – and run your hands through your hair, concentrating particularly on the ends. If it hasn't had any effect, wet your hair again and apply a little more, styling to the shape you want. When gels and mousses are applied wet, the hair must be styled and then dried or left to dry undisturbed or the holding effect will be lost. The more you fiddle, the more you cancel out the end result. The style created by the gel can often be revived by spraying the hair damp and combing or finger pulling through as before.

PEAK CONDITION

Short does not mean unchanging. Several top stylists suggest changing the style "at least a little" every year, in order not to get stuck in a time warp and to enjoy the new look and sense of proportion that can come from that subtle snip of the scissors. Condition often benefits with cutting too. Short hair almost invariably looks shinier and glossier, if only because its condition actually *is* better. While shoulder-length hair has been washed hundreds of times and bleached out by two or three summer holidays, close-cropped hair has freshly emerged from the scalp and is just a few weeks old. New to sunlight and shampoo and all the other paraphernalia of hair "care," it is hardly surprising that it looks so much better by comparison.

While peak condition is essential to the new short cut, especially when scissored into a one-length bob, bigger boosts in sheen will come from overhauling the way we live than from anything we can put onto the hair. This is because the hair cell is one of the most prolific in the body, second only to bone marrow in its speed of replication and growth, and it demands a continual supply of nutrients. Unlike bone marrow, which is indispensable, hair comes low down on the body's priority list. This means that it is the first to miss out when supplies are scarce and the last to benefit in times of plenty. Because of its second-class status, the look of the hair (and also the nails, which are made of exactly the same protein, keratin) is an excellent indication of your general health. It's no coincidence that the hair of malnourished or anorexic individuals grows dull and lank and eventually falls out, or that the color actually

Vogue once noted that the very sight of Dawn Mello, the vice-president of Gucci known for her timeless style and innate fashion sense, "makes people straighten their backs." Nearly always to be seen in impeccably tailored pant suits, she has her hair expertly cut and keeps it in best-possible condition, knowing that it sets off her appearance perfectly. While fashions may change, shorter nearly always looks more modern after 30, with the hair drawn well off or away from the face. It is also the ideal low-maintenance option: a little gel at the roots and a few blasts with the blow-dryer will ensure that such a style lasts all day.

changes in the presence of severe nutritional deficiency. Less drastically, crash diets, protein-deficient diets, and even skipping meals all tell on the hair's condition, thickness, and growing characteristics since they literally deprive the follicles of their lifeblood.

We reap what we sow. And many of us reap a thin, poor crop, the roots starved of nourishment, the ends similarly famished. If we want our hair to look its best and behave brilliantly, we have to feed our 100,000-odd follicles with everything that they require. Putting the nutritional guidelines on pages 228–238 into practice should allow it to regain best-possible condition, though the benefits may not become apparent for some months since the hair receiving this new bounty is still underneath the scalp and, hence, invisible to the eye.

Externally, condition requires a paradoxical-sounding combination of attention and restraint. In young hair – and well-treated older hair – the outer layer, or cuticle, forms a very effective barrier. Just six to ten cells thick, its overlapping scales are smoothed flat like the scales on a lizard's skin by sebum secretions which slide along the length of each strand and reflect the light, giving a lovely luster and sheen. As we get older the activity of the sebaceous glands slows down and the supply of sebum, a natural oil made up of waxes and fats, falls off. As the cuticle loses its natural protection, moisture evaporates. The result is dry, thirsty, even frizzy hair that requires more care if it is going to look as good as it did 10 or 20 years earlier.

Various chemical and environmental assaults (shampooing, heat-abuse with electrical styling appliances, permanent waving, some forms of coloring, ultraviolet radiation) aggravate the situation by temporarily or permanently lifting the cuticle. This not only *looks* worse – ruffled cuticle scales scatter the light to dull effect – but also *is* worse, since the hair becomes porous and less watertight as a result. As other substances seep in, including some of those that we put onto our hair in the hopes of improving it, condition inevitably suffers.

KILLING WITH KINDNESS

Once their hair is in this compromised state, women who lavish love and attention on their lank-looking tresses may actually be systematically spoiling them with overcare. Once the cuticle has lifted, it soaks up whatever comes its way, and all the conditioner in the world will not improve the way it looks; indeed it will only worsen it. Overconditioning is now considered one of the main (and least recognized) reasons for dull, lank, lifeless hair, and for the shorter than expected lifespans of permanents, since if the hair shaft is weighed down some of the curl is invariably lost before time. The new polymer products that pump up the volume of fine hair are extraordinarily tenacious in this respect, and must always be scrupulously rinsed out. Often, the problem is self-perpetuating: the more out-of-condition the hair, the more products get lavished on it, and so the build-up builds up. The *Journal of the Society of Cosmetic Chemists* showed that penetration of these products into the cortex can reduce the strength of the hair by a sixth and makes split ends, stress fractures, and longitudinal splits more likely.

The answer is to use a very gentle shampoo that doesn't contain conditioners, to rinse really thoroughly afterward and to skip conditioner in favor of an acid rinse (add the juice of a lemon to a pitcher of water), which will persuade the cuticle to lie flat again and help restore the hair's acid mantle. If you've ever wondered why the professionals carry on rinsing until your shoulders ache and your neck cries out for mercy, this is it. It's the most important part.

When washing hair, comb it first from the scalp down to untangle it and loosen dirt, skin cells, etc. Then, holding your head close to the shower head, soak your hair and scalp with warm (not hot) water until thoroughly damp. Apply a little shampoo and massage well into the scalp, treating the ends with extra care. (If hair is excessively greasy, or you've been using styling wax, good results can be obtained from shampooing "dry" first and rinsing, before putting on the second, "wet" application; if the scalp is greasy but the ends are dry, use different formulations for each.)

As hair gets drier, just one application of shampoo is usually enough, especially if washing every day or two. A switch to a milder formulation, and less of it, may also be in order, though baby shampoos will not shift the dirt effectively. If you cannot find a shampoo that suits your hair, ask your hairdresser, since the salon sells retail versions of the professional line used on your visits. If you have colored your hair, harsh-acting anti-dandruff shampoos can cause the color to fade sooner. pH-balanced shampoos can be helpful on very damaged/chemically processed hair.

If the hair requires it, apply conditioner lightly through towel-dried hair after a shampoo, holding the ends firmly and combing toward the roots; leave on for the required time and rinse off thoroughly. Conditioners are not always necessary and can turn fine hair lanky by slipping through the cuticle and weighing it down. If this describes your hair, use a shampoo (such as Neutrogena) that doesn't contain conditioners or try a weekly protein treatment instead. And avoid all but the lightest formulation silicone serums.

The tendency to blame the product rather than the process is endemic to hairdressing. The haircare market is notorious for consumer change and near-zero "brand loyalty." Always on the lookout for a better, more effective product and inspired by extravagant advertising claims, we really do believe that there is something magical out there that can, in a single wash, transform the way we look – when the truth is that most of us do more damage to our hair through what we do to it than through using the "wrong" products. As the old normal/dry/greasy demarcations are replaced by more specific ones that pay attention to texture – fine, coarse, frizzy – it's going to get harder and harder to misuse the products on sale. The degree of "care" we give (or deny) our hair can affect its growing characteristics as well as its condition: unthinking stresses applied to wet hair in the form of blow dryers and styling aids are the main culprits.

Although the length of one's hair is genetically determined, and growth slows with age, hair can fall out before time if subjected to unfriendly forces. Under normal circumstances, up to 150 strands are shed each and every day in an unnoticeable ongoing process of loss and replenishment. In early adulthood, every hair on the head has a "growing phase," which lasts about three and a half years, a "resting phase" of about three months, and a "falling-out" phase where the follicle surrenders the hair. After three decades of constant replacement, each strand spends more time idle – six months, nine months, even a year – and less time growing. Cell division slows up too, closing down some follicles entirely.

THINNING HAIR

Although baldness may be a male trauma, many women do find their hair getting noticeably thinner once they are into their sixth decade. At 50, few women have anything like the volume they had at 20, by 65 the thinning is often marked, and in extreme age very sparse, wispy hair (like the babyfine hair of a one-year-old) is common. This is partly owing to a fall-off in the number of follicles on the scalp – at the age of 50 the number is down by nearly half from that at the first year of life – and partly to a change of texture.

Although the menopause is often blamed for thinning hair, the process actually starts earlier. It may only become apparent at the age of about 50, since at least 15 per cent of the total must be lost before it feels or looks any sparser. It's at that point that women notice that their parting seems to be widening or their hairline is receding or that their hair does not create as thick a bunch when pulled back into a chignon or braid.

Take especial care when your hair is wet, as it loses nearly a quarter of its elasticity. Once stretched by the weight of the water, any further pulling, in the form of brushing, combing, excessive toweling, or even a heavy hairdryer leaning on it, could push it past "breakpoint" so that it snaps as it dries. When blow-drying, the golden rules are to squeeze water out first, towel dry, and only start to blow when the hair is already half-dry, using the warm (not hot) setting. Blow-dry downward to keep the cuticle flat, and keep the dryer constantly on the move to avoid overdrying an area of hair. Switch to a cool setting toward the end of the drying time and stop before it's totally dry.

As hair gets finer over the years, clever blow-drying can add more volume. Center- or side-part the hair and clip back the sides and top. Starting with the underneath sections, take small, manageable amounts and furl around a brush to get a firm pull on the hair. Direct the air flow from root to end, persuading the cuticle to lie uniformly flat and the individual hairs to lie happily in formation, before rewinding and eventually removing the brush. Take down the side sections and finally the front, raising the hair off the head at a 90-degree angle and drying *beneath* the strands.

Finger drying can loosen overtight curls produced by a permanent and can also create more volume, rather as beating egg white introduces more air. Although invaluable for adding volume to limp, fine hair, no blow-dried shape will hold its style for long if it's very fine. Ultimately a light permanent might be a better option.

Fortunately, modern technology has come to the rescue with some great salon products, most notably sprays and gels containing polymers, also known as volumizers. When applied to wet hair before blow-drying, the heat from the dryer swells the polymers, which cling to the hair shaft and make it thicker. Non-sticky, leaving the hair natural to the touch, these products also guard condition with their glistening protective film. There are some very effective chemical solutions too. Tinting, particularly the new tone-on-tone colors (see chart on pages 64–7), can pump up the individual strands, creating an impression of volume.

In early adulthood each hair spends 3½ years growing, and 3 months resting. With age, these phases alter.

Outer cuticle is smooth and flat, sealing in moisture.

20

Rate of growth starts to slow. Number of hair follicles in production drops as each strand spends longer in its resting phase, and less time growing.

40

This series of hair strands at the ages of 20, 40 and 60 shows typical structural and textural changes over time. Generally hair becomes drier, as sebaceous gland activity slows, and finer in texture, as its diameter shrinks. By the age of 50, the central core of the hair shaft, the medulla, has usually disappeared completely. Hair may also get noticeably sparser as the number of follicles in production drops off. Thinning is generally most apparent around the crown of the head and hairline, and is accentuated by hormone changes at menopause. Condition can suffer too as the outer cuticle, which is flat and smooth in youth thanks to plentiful sebum secretions sliding up the hair shaft, gets ragged – a consequence of sebaceous activity falling off and chemical processing, which becomes more common. The good news is that the right sort of care can help stall and even reverse some of these changes.

60+

Outer cuticle can become ragged and porous, hair dries out.

Sebaceous gland activity slows. Sebum supply dwindles. Hair becomes drier.

Hair becomes thinner and finer in texture losing a third of original diameter.

tyling tools can be a great answer to midlife loss of volume, but use them with caution. Be especially careful with heated rollers, winding them on carefully and checking that the spikes used to secure them are put gently into place. Heated curlers are a great way to boost a style, and lift hair at the roots, so giving more volume, but the curls are weaker and shorter-lived, and the method is potentially much more damaging. If you have to use heated rollers or tongs, try to restrict their use to twice a week. Opt for steam models with a mist spray to counteract the otherwise unavoidable dehydrating effect, and make sure hair is cool before taking them out. If styling cold, avoid metal rollers or those with plastic spikes or hard brushes inside, which may tear the hair when you remove them. Look for kinder alternatives, such as the fun bendy foam-rubber pieces now available from many salons. If you are styling your hair yourself, a lightweight setting lotion will help you coax it into the style you want while avoiding the old heavily sprayed look.

PERMANENT SOLUTIONS

Assuming the hair's condition is good enough, a permanent can be the perfect solution to the limp, fine hair that is so often a problem in midlife, as long as the hair is not too fine to hold it. While the early permanents were stiff and unnatural-looking, modern ones – when skillfully executed on hair that's in good condition – can look sensational, adding volume and looking so real that no one would ever suspect they weren't. The subtlest give a slight lift at the root that restores an impression of fullness. While these modern "body" or "acid" waves do not last quite as long as the old version, needing to be renewed after about three or four months, they are softer and more natural, lending movement without corrugated curls.

Such is the pace of change that an experienced stylist who is thoroughly conversant with new techniques is essential. Timing is especially critical, since a permanent left on the hair to "develop" for too long degenerates into a frizz, while one not allowed to develop for sufficient time will fall out almost immediately.

For the permanent chemical reaction to take place, the chemicals must not only penetrate the cuticle but also break through to the cortex inside. To speed penetration, the permanent is applied to wet hair, as washing swells the hair slightly and causes the cuticle scales to rise, allowing the chemicals easier access. Their job is to soften the sulfur bonds in the cortex, which are organized like steps on a ladder. When these bonds are softened and the hair is put into its new shape, usually by means of rollers, the sulfur bonds change their configuration. The addition of a neutralizer then seals them into this new, chemically altered line. This is quite a brutal job, even with the new, kinder chemicals, and it may be more than very fragile hair can take. Acid waves use heat lamps instead of ammonium compounds to open up the hair shaft and let the active ingredients in and are therefore regarded as less damaging since they spare many more of the sulfur bonds. The effect is certainly less pronounced, leading to delight for some, disappointment for others. When it comes to the hair texture that will benefit most from a permanent, there is a fine line between the improvement that can be expected and the risk of taking already fragile hair beyond breaking point, leaving a woman with even frailer hair than she started out with. And less of it.

If you are considering having a permanent, a skilled operator is crucial; do not take shortcuts, save money, or attempt to give yourself a permanent. Always listen if a hairdresser advises that your hair is not in sufficiently good condition to withstand it, and nurse heat-damaged or chemically abused hair back into condition first. If your hair is really very fine and wispy, you may be advised that a permanent will not take at all, since there simply isn't sufficient volume left at the roots to hold the wave up. Unfortunately the chemicals used in the new-style permanents tend to provoke more allergic reactions, so a patch test is essential first.

Look after hair that has had a permanent by treating the curls very gently, not pulling or stretching with a brush or rollers after shampooing but gently finger drying them back into shape, and use conditioner conscientiously. The better you care for it, the longer it will last. Do not tint at the same time, since the permanent wave lotion continues to be active for some days afterward and lifts the color from the tint, altering the shade. Do the permanent waving first and leave at least a week before tinting.

TO GRAY OR NOT TO GRAY?

Chemical assistance of all kinds is increasingly sought as women grow older, with surveys showing that a third of women over 35 and nearly half of women over 45 use a permanent and/or a color on their hair. Although so-called premature graying, in which the whole head is white by the teens, is a real phenomenon, most of us look on our gray as premature – whenever it starts to come through. For Caucasian women, this is at the age of about 34, with half the population having at least half a head of gray hair by 50. Black women begin to go gray much later, not even starting to detect the first strand until nearly 44. Japanese and Asian women, coming somewhere in between, generally start to gray in their late 30s.

If men are acutely conscious of their balding heads (a displaced sign of castration anxiety, according to classic psychoanalytic theory) many women are as painfully conscious of their gray. "Only God, my dear," quipped the poet W. B. Yeats, "could love you for yourself alone, and not your yellow hair." Having most likely displayed no real attachment to their yellow or brown or red in the past, lots of women get racked by nostalgia for the "old" color once they start to lose it. Forgetting how dull and uninteresting they found it, they determine to retrieve it. This is the first mistake. The old color is literally the old color. Age leaches color out of the skin as well as the hair, leading to increasing pallor from the late 20s on and that lovely see-through translucence that gives so many older complexions their quality. The woman who was once dark or auburn and continues to cling to her (or even more dangerously her husband's or lover's) fond remembrance of the "old" color, picking the identical shade from the shelves each time she tints her hair, is heading for an unflattering, over-strong contrast between the old hair color and the new skin tone, with hair that no longer quite fits the face, neck, or even hands for that matter.

Through history, women have always declared war on their gray. In the 1940s and 1950s, new permanent tints promised a measure of control. These dyes wrought permanent changes by bleaching out the color and depositing heavy, dense pigments in its place. Although the new chemistry of color technically allowed a woman to cover up all signs of advancing age and return to a more "youthful" color, in reality this amounted to a somewhat restricted choice of inky black, dark brown, brown, Titian, or a Jean Harlow platinum blonde that took on a most unfortunate hue of beige when applied to gray/white hair. But the dyes certainly worked. And they were permanent: it took at least three days to get the color off the forehead.

In the event, the sense of control turned out to be illusory. Once women set out on the irrevocable path of covering their gray, they found they had embarked on a rite of passage that committed them for ever more to three- or four-weekly touch-ups as the telltale strip of white started reappearing at the roots. It soon became crystal-clear that every self-respecting woman had to take a policy decision in her 40s – to gray or not to gray? – and then rigidly adhere to it. There was no turning back. There was also a price to be paid for prolonging youth. The corrosive chemicals that were used crucified the hair by stripping out all condition until it resembled nothing so much as straw – an effect that was then perfected by setting and spraying the unfortunate crown into place. It is questionable too whether these dyes really enhanced a woman's appearance, since they worked by coating the hair with a single color (which no head of hair ever is). This killed what highlights were already there, along with the offensive gray, and lent a flat, unnatural look that became ever flatter and more unnatural as color drained away from the skin, leaving the hair in over-strong contrast. Although flat, one-color tints are still used to great effect today, having an unreal, larger-than-life look, in their case artificiality is the point.

These days everything has changed, from the chemistry of color itself to the way we perceive our gray. Now that older women have acquired more power, control, and influence over their own lives and those of others, gray itself is coming to look less of a threat and more of a promise – reflecting the authority, strength, and steeliness of purpose that sums up what many older women are about. The Indira Gandhi white streak is a perfect example. As more and more women are glad to be gray, they need to pay close attention to condition, using a brightening shampoo every third or fourth wash to prevent discoloration and keep their gray shiny; deep-conditioning salon treatments can also ensure it stays soft and manageable.

COVERING THE GRAY

If a woman decides to cover her gray, she will find that the present generation of tints has revolutionized the hair-coloring process, combining the removing of the old and depositing of the new in one quick, gentle step – gentle because the pigments are combined with emollients that condition as they color. With a tint, it is possible to transform nondescript light brown into burnished auburn or to exchange a dull gray for a rich nutty brown in just half-an-hour, without damaging the hair. Advances in the chemistry of color are now so impressive that almost anything is possible in the coloring line, both more quickly and with less damage to hair than ever before. Yet color specialists report that women are often more afraid of tinting than of having a permanent.

The options are wider than ever before as well. Women do not have the stark choice that confronted their mothers and grandmothers. If gray is less a color than a

Glad to be gray: as older women acquire more power, control, and influence, gray is coming to look less of a threat and more of a promise, reflecting the authority, strength, and steeliness of purpose that sums up what many older women are about.

Among the new grays: FROM LEFT, Evangeline Blahnik, confidante, muse and manager of brother Manolo's international shoe empire; Liz Tilberis, editor in chief of *Harpers Bazaar*; Polly Allen Mellen, creative director of the beauty magazine, *Allure*; Christian Lacroix's muse and sometime model, Marie Seznec. Margot Smiley, ABOVE CENTRE, British *Vogue*'s "Mrs Exeter" from 1949 to 1963 (see pages 109–10), made a point of letting the white creep in – an act of great professional daring at the time.

state of mind, then the woman who is not of a mind to go as gray as Nature intends quite as soon, will find degrees of natural: ways of allowing the gray to creep in without taking over or giving that stark pepper-and-salt contrast that she finds so hard to live with; ways of improving on the gray she does go, using one of the soft, semi-permanent colors to transform her gray to silvery white or deep slate and give it a dazzlingly healthy shine into the bargain.

THE NEWEST SALON TECHNIQUES

For the woman who is just starting to lose her color, the chart on pages 64–7 gives an idea of the options ahead. With the help of a good colorist, the results can look sensational – much better than before the gray started to creep in. Whereas the old coloring strategies relied on reducing hair to a single monotone (the "old" color), many of the newer strategies rely on adding *more* color to the hair, in highlights, lowlights, bolts, and slices, to mimic its natural pied effect. Even the dullest-looking head of hair has several color tones and, as the hair starts to gray, the best effects are achieved by adding to rather than subtracting from these. Taking their cue from colors already in the hair, skilled colorists weave in new tones that lie between the gray (or white) and the dark (or blonde or red or auburn). These "lowlights" get rid of the pepper-and-salt effect, which is what many women object to, while leaving many, even most, of the gray hairs in place but a lot less noticeable. The overall effect is a little lighter, which is probably appropriate, since white is Nature's way of diluting the normal hair color, thereby keeping pace with the loss of color in the complexion. Much the same technique can be applied to a single white streak or a few patches of gray, but this time by weaving in strands of the original color; the gray hairs that are not tinted soften the whole effect so that it looks completely natural. Whichever the chosen tone, colorists work, as with highlights, in zig-zag horizontal lines to ensure that the hair will never fall into vertical stripes.

If you are planning to color your hair yourself, start your search with well-known brand names (L'Oréal, Wella), since the large companies spend a lot on research and development and make very good products.

Chemically treated hair demands extra care and maintenance. Choose shampoos and conditioners with neutral to acid pHs (such as those labeled "pH-balanced" or containing citrus fruit, milk, or beer). Alkaline products can disturb the cuticle, reducing shine and causing color to fade; slightly acidic shampoos, by contrast, make the cells of the cuticle lie flat, helping to keep moisture in the hair, increasing shine and prolonging color. To help color last between applications, try a color-enhancing shampoo and/or conditioner, which works by depositing a small amount of pigment onto the hair (Redken's Interval Color Enhancing Shampoo, ARTec's Color Enhancing Shampoos, and J F Lazartigue's Color Reflecting Conditioner are some). Or use a leave-in conditioner and so eliminate excessive rinsing.

Ultraviolet can dramatically shorten color-expectancy, as the color lightens quickly and dark hair may end up distinctly reddish. In addition the UVB rays destroy the sulfur bonds that maintain the hair's strength – bad news for permanents. When in the sun for any length of time, wear a hat, coat the hair with a leave-in conditioner, or comb a specially formulated alcohol-free, water-soluble hair sunscreen through the hair. Rinse hair thoroughly after swimming.

While temporary, semi-permanent, and vegetable colors can also be applied effectively at home, a pair of professional hands is still the best option when contemplating highlights, lowlights or a permanent tint. The schedule for the latter is both expensive and time-consuming, with out-and-out tints requiring renewing as often as every three weeks, but the results will look better and, while demanding more cost from you, may be achieved at less cost to the hair.

Women who a generation ago took the tinted route and have come to regret it – the effect often rendered increasingly improbable by the traces of gray now appearing in their daughters' hair – commonly carry on dyeing regardless out of fear of the stripe that must be endured as the white grows in. Such a fear is years out of date; a transition from unnatural color to a more aesthetic gray can now be managed seamlessly, the margins effectively broken up with highlights and lowlights, and the hair looking so natural no one would ever suspect you of trying to get rid of anything.

If you have never had your hair tinted before, an allergy (patch) test is essential. One in ten people suffers an allergic response to the chemicals used, which can be problematic since it often triggers wider allergies to a whole family of chemicals, including some local anesthetics.

THE CANCER CONTROVERSY

There is also the long shadow of cancer. A worrying increase in certain cancers of the lymphatic system (non-Hodgkins lymphoma and Hodgkins disease) and bone marrow (multiple myeloma) among regular users of *any* permanent or semi-permanent hair coloring product was reported in the *American Journal of Public Health* in 1992, backing up previous reports.[1] While some of the recognized carcinogens (cancer-causing substances) have been removed over the last 20 years, suspect aromatic, nitroso, and amino compounds remain in both types of product. These are present in greater concentrations in permanent products and in darker dyes (blacks, browns, and reds) than in the lighter and semi-permanent tones, and researchers tellingly found that users of these products were between a third and half again as likely to develop these cancers as non-users. The risk also increased "significantly" with duration of use and young age at first starting. Although the evidence is still not considered sufficiently strong to warrant withdrawal of these products, the safety-first principle should hold in pregnancy and total tints be avoided at this time. The experts agree it's not the penetration of the hair shaft, but of the dye through the scalp, that may be hazardous to health. This occurs when a full head of hair is dyed or the roots are retouched. Within two hours of application, traces of dye can be found in the urine.

In June 1993, British *Vogue* investigated the renewed controversy that has sprung up over the use of hair colorants.[2] Its author, Judy Sadgrove, interviewed Dr. Stan Venitt, a biochemist at the Institute of Cancer Research, who has been monitoring the research on hair dye for nearly 20 years. He stated that none of the 40-odd studies conducted so far had been able to demonstrate "satisfactorily" that hair dyes cause cancer – though he acknowledged that it was hard for scientists to separate a single factor from all the other lifestyle variables, such as smoking, diet, and exercise, and prove that it must be to blame. Asked how real the risk might be for the one woman in four who dyes her hair, Dr. Venitt said:

> When you consider how many women dye their hair and how long they've been doing it, a strong connection would have surfaced by now. These chemicals can be absorbed through the scalp and passed around the body into the bloodstream. Some probably do induce lymphomas – and bone marrow is particularly sensitive to these benzene-based chemicals – but the association, if it exists, is nowhere as strong as that between smoking and cancer. These cancers are so rare that any elevated risk – although a problem – is still only a small risk.

Women worried by the possibility of any risk, however small, and at the same time reluctant to forgo coloring their hair entirely, should consider methods of application which protect the scalp from contact with the dye, such as highlighting or lowlighting, since these certainly minimize and probably abolish any health risk. Natural "vegetable" colors are another safer option, as are lighter-colored dyes, which have lower concentrations of chemicals.

FUTURE OPTIONS

Graying remains a mystery. Nobody knows why the melanin supply seizes up in some cells but continues in others. Laboratory studies suggest that the melanocytes (pigment-supplying cells) do not die but continue to be present in the scalp, although no longer functional. When such mysteries are unraveled, the chemistry of hair color will enter a brave new phase, as biochemists manipulate the triggers that stimulate the melanin receptors, and so preserve the color of the graying head.

GOING, GOING, GONE

DEGREE OF GRAY	BEST OPTIONS
a few stray gray hairs	Highlights, lowlights, vegetable conditioning colors
10% gray	Highlights, lowlights, vegetable conditioning colors, semi-permanent colors
pepper and salt	Highlights, lowlights, semi-permanent colors, tone-on-tone colors
50% gray	Highlights, slices, tone-on-tone colors, permanent tints
almost entirely gray/white	Temporary color rinses, tone-on-tone colors, permanent tints

COLORING BY DEGREES

THE OPTIONS	THE EFFECT
temporary color rinses	Add a hint of warmth and vivacity to light colored hair while successfully concealing the gray.
vegetable/conditioning colors	Kindness itself to the hair, since they only coat the surface. The colors are derived from natural sources such as walnut extract, and last for six shampoos; a very temporary option, therefore, which may not even last a week if you wash your hair every day.
semi-permanent colors	Add richness and depth as they deposit their color, giving a wonderful sheen.
highlights	Up to three different tones two or more shades lighter than one's own color.
lowlights	Any color up to one shade lighter or darker than one's own hair color.

WHAT'S INVOLVED

When applied to pre-washed hair, a low positive/negative charge allows the color to cling to the cuticle, which then washes out with the next shampoo. The effects last longer on already permed or sun-damaged hair: being more porous, it absorbs the color more readily.

Home colors are washed in along with the shampoo, and rinsed off as normal. Salon colors are applied to pre-washed hair.

Most products shampoo into already dampened hair and wash out after around six shampoos. The so-called "oxidizing" semi-permanents (or "color baths") penetrate the hair slightly and have more holding power, washing out after up to 12 shampoos (still a very temporary option for women who wash their hair every day). Color mistakes can be canceled by frequent washes with a clarifying shampoo (the sort that rids the hair of chlorine).

Wrapping strands of hair in foil packets, allowing color to develop and then washing out. The color is permanent and grows out with the hair. As there is no hard margin at the roots, highlights only need repeating every three to four months. Skillful application is essential.

See highlights. A good colorist is essential: in inexpert hands, lowlights can look stripey, and less natural with each reapplication as there must always be some overlap. Professionals often like to attend to the roots alone between whole-head applications. For those worried about a possible cancer risk (see pages 62–3), these techniques may represent a safer option than permanent or semi-permanent colors, as the chemicals in the dyes do not come into contact with the scalp.

WHAT IT LOOKS BEST ON

White or gray hair that just needs a lift to look wonderful. A silvery mauve rinse can remove the yellowing effects of cigarette smoke and pollution, slate gray adds depth, and, yes, a "blue rinse," left on for just a moment, can make white hair sparkle.

Darkish hair that looks dull; hair that is just starting to gray – although it won't conceal it. By increasing the intensity of the original color and giving a glorious shine, the whole head will appear healthier.

Any head, providing there is sufficient color (not more than 20 per cent gray); they add intensity and richness to the original color – chestnut tones to dark hair, for example. While not returning the gray to the same color as the rest of the head, they will look (fleetingly) less obvious; great for women who are nervous about coloring their hair and want to see what richer tones can do for them without altering or compromising their base color.

Dark blonde or fair hair that is losing its color. By supplying several shades between the base color and the white, thereby softening the contrast, it is a great way of going gray or white, or any color in between, gracefully.

Darkish hair that's losing its color, deeper blondes, and reds. It is generally a more subtle option than highlights since it entails adding tones that are very close to the base one; weaving in new tones avoids a pepper and salt contrast, while leaving much of the gray as it is. The colors can also be taken down progressively as the natural color lightens and the volume of gray increases. An especially good option for dark hair that has just a scattering of gray; once hair is more than 50 per cent gray other options may be worth considering.

C O L O R I N G   B Y   D E G R E E S   *(C O N T I N U E D)*

THE OPTIONS	THE EFFECT
bolts	Similar to high/lowlights but rather more emphatic – i.e., more strands are contained in each foil packet and they are placed farther apart, giving a more defined look.
slices	A strong defined look, which enhances the movement of a cut, following high/lowlight principles but worked through the hair in definite sections.
tone-on-tone colors	Full-head cover, halfway between a conditioning color and a permanent tint. It offers only the option of darker and richer but the range is much wider than with a semi-permanent color – you can go as dark as you like, even black.
permanent tints	Can look wonderful or dreadful, depending on the choice of color; will mask any gray/white entirely.

WHAT'S INVOLVED

The chemistry and method of application are as for high/lowlights, with renewals required every three or four months.

WHAT IT LOOKS BEST ON

Curly, coarse hair which high/lowlights often reduce to a misty frizz of color. As hair falls into waves or curls, the movement is accentuated by the bolts of color. On straight hair, however, bolts just look stripey.

Instead of weaving out individual strands as for high/lowlights, thin sections of the hair are colored in bands; these are applied as highlights, with recoloring necessary after three to four months.

Hair that is now over 50 per cent gray – it's a great alternative to the whole head tint; best on layered choppy hair of short to medium length – the effect is too geometric for one-length hair.

A whole new chemistry of color that does not require ammonia and contains a fraction of the oxidizing agents used in permanent tints, thanks to the development of color molecules just small enough to slip inside the cuticle. The process does not take the color out of your hair, just adds to it. While not permanent except on more porous hair, the color only fades slightly over time, so regrowth is less apparent and touch-ups needed less often.

Almost any degree of gray, where it can be made as subtle or as dramatic as you like, albeit always in a darker direction. It can turn white hair silver, and dull gray a strong slate; it can turn mouse a rich dark nutty brown or even a dark blonde. A wonderful option for women with fine, frail hair as the microcoating of color clinging to the cuticle actually thickens the hair.

Modern tints contain just enough peroxide both to lighten the original color, where necessary, and to act as a catalyst or "color developer," and just enough ammonia to open the cuticle and allow the new color in, making it permanent. The tint is applied to dry hair, left on to "develop," and then thoroughly rinsed off. Roots need recoloring every four to six weeks. As the color starts to fade, the gray will come through first, even with a so-called permanent color; a semi-permanent rinse, applied about three weeks after tinting, should keep the base color as is while encouraging the gray to disappear.

Any color and texture: when there is a lot of gray, the best results are obtained when a tone rather lighter than the remaining color is chosen. A good option for hair that is 50–70 per cent gray. As white hairs resist the tint more than the colored ones, they remain less intense than the rest, giving a less "solid," more natural effect.

NAILS

WELL cared-for hands speak volumes about the woman who has them. While nails that are neat, clean, and natural reflect competence and proper pride in one's appearance, the reverse speedily sabotages any attempt at professionalism. "It's horrible to be caught out, mid-gesticulation," groaned Sarah Mower in British *Vogue*, "by the realization that your nails are a mess – and it's not grown up to resort to hiding your hands under the table like some overgrown schoolgirl . . ."

While the number of American women getting regular manicures quadrupled over the 1980s, many women still perceive a manicure as the ultimate in unforgivable idleness and self-indulgence. Although essential nail maintenance takes only a couple of minutes a day, ten minutes at most at weekends, many are loath to lavish even this much time on their hands.

VISIBLE NEGLECT

Neglected, battered by the elements, and regularly exposed to substances that no self-respecting woman would ever contemplate putting on her face, hands soon suffer the ravages of time. Many women in their 40s and 50s have faces with not so much as a crease on them, having been lovingly protected from the sun and nourished with the best of creams, while their hands are lined and leathery and spattered with brown pigmentation spots. It's hardly surprising, therefore, that hands are invariably the great give-away of a face-lift.

Always on show, hands eternally reproach us for our lack of care. Nails, particularly, are caught in the spotlight of neglect. By midlife, they are usually thicker, drier, less transparent, and more likely to break and splinter – a consequence, it's thought, of several decades spent intermittently immersed in water. A study at the University of Arkansas suggests that the passage from wet to dry takes more toll on nail condition than any of the more common suspects, including paint stripper. When researchers collected nail clippings from doctors and students and subjected them to various chemicals, such as acetone (a common ingredient in nail polish remover), they found that, while it took three weeks of exposure to acetone before the nails started to peel, repeated wet-and-dry treatment produced visible peeling in less than 48 hours. Their conclusion: the more often you expose your hands to water, the more likely your nails are to suffer. It's thought the "drying-out" period (which cannot be sidestepped by towel or hot-air drying) dissolves the gluelike structures that hold the nail layers together, so making them more likely to split. The only solution is to get your hands wet as little as possible.

Diet has always been considered critical to the strength, length, look, and luster of the nails. One French woman built an entire, very successful beauty practice in London on her legendary ability to transform the nails of her clients by giving drops of iodine in water – the number mystically varying from client to client. She also gave a mean manicure. In truth, anything that benefits the hair (protein, vitamins A, B, C, and E, zinc, calcium, iodine, sulfur, and iron) will also benefit the nails – though there is no evidence that specific substances such as gelatin, long promoted as a nail conditioner, have any specifically good effect. White spots and ridges are less likely to be caused by vitamin deficiencies than by damage to the nail matrix or wear and tear (being rarely seen on the toenails, which are better protected). Illness can temporarily put a stop to nail growth, causing a line or furrow to form at the base which then grows out with the new nail. The pace of growth of nails also gets more sedate with age.

Faces have their own natural oil, hands have less, and feet have none at all. Keep both looking good by moisturizing several times a day, using a handcream that also has a sunfilter. Alternatively, rub a sunscreen into your hands whenever applying it to your face.

Use lined rubber gloves *whenever* immersing your hands in hot water, which is desperately drying; or, if you are not using them, keep the temperature tepid. Station a large tub of hand cream by basins and sinks and slather it on every time your hands get wet.

A useful nutrient for feeble nails may be biotin, a component of egg white, sometimes referred to as Vitamin H. An intriguing research study was published in the *Journal of American Dermatology* in December 1989, following some Swiss research where scientists, having noted that vets commonly give racehorses biotin supplements to heal cracks in their hoofs, tried it out on humans. After three to four months, the nails of eight out of ten volunteers showed a "very significant" improvement.

Until relatively recently, long nails were a status symbol. In ancient China, where they were irrefutable proof of wealth and leisure, spans of up to 12 inches (30 centimeters) were recorded. In our own time, the supremacy of the work ethic has revolutionized nail aesthetics. Today, short is modern, practical, ready for business. The fashionable length is a full ⅜ inch (1 centimeter) shorter than it was in the 1950s when impractically long nails announced that a woman had a husband successful enough to enable her not to work in or out of the house. The ideal shape has also changed: the perfect oval (the curve at the tip reflecting that at the base, which was so fashionable in the 1970s) has given way to a more workwomanlike shape – squarer across the top, with the sides left straight for support.

A PERFECT TEN

Keeping the nails short and clean is as much as any modern woman needs to do. There's no need to fiddle with bowls, Q-tips, orange sticks, and cuticle removers; in fact, it's actually better not to. The cuticle should be left to itself. Liquid cuticle removers can also cause inflammation with subsequent infection, while the use of metal instruments may injure the nail matrix – the damage later showing up as white spots or dents in the usually smooth surface of the nail. If the cuticle does overhang the nail, entrust it to a skilled manicurist, who should be able to persuade it back without redness, soreness, or subsequent infection, or try the gentle alternative detailed below.

> For maximum strength, keep nails fairly short and square, especially if prone to splitting; too sharp an arc will weaken them. Scissors are not ideal as their shearing force can split the nails – a wooden (not metal) emery board, held at 45 degrees and used in one direction only, preferably from sides to center, is better. Nails will need weekly attention if you don't use scissors, however.
>
> If cuticles do hang over onto the nail, soak them in warm water for 15 minutes (easiest when having a bath; alternatively, hold a dampened face cloth over them) and then gently work them back, using an orange stick cushioned with cotton, persuading rather than forcing them off the nail.
>
> Rubbing almond oil into nails each night will help nail layers adhere together and prevent peeling. Alpha hydroxy acid creams (see page 27) are also said to have a fabulously strengthening effect.

Happily, nails can be rendered better-looking in minutes. Buffing every two to three weeks with a special buffer that has differently graded abrasive surfaces, or with the traditional chamois buffer and abrasive cream/powder, will give a real gleam as the dull top cell layers are sanded away and the circulation beneath boosted, so pinkening the nail.

On unpolished nails, all that is then needed is to run a white pencil under the tip. The result is instantly, believably, pretty. The so-called "French" manicure uses clear pink polish and an opaque white polish at the tip. American manicurists, finding the contast too stark, often opt for softer whites or simply use the white pencil as described above.

Women who have only ever used polish to stop a run in their stockings will be pleasantly surprised to find that it can become a well-groomed hand like little else, provided there's not a chip to be seen, of course. Professionals get their perfect results by applying four coats of polish to the newly manicured nail: a colorless base coat, two coats of color, and a transparent gloss on top to help prevent the color from chipping. The secret of their success is using top-quality products and not hurrying. Some allow 15 minutes for the base coat alone to dry. The process can be speeded by placing the fingers under a gentle trickle of cold water or using a quick-dry spray. When applied as thinly as possible, the base coat adheres to the nail and provides a smooth surface for the color. Since the nails are porous, it also prevents the yellow staining caused by applying red polishes direct to the nail.

U se polish to protect weak and brittle nails. A hardener that includes strengthening agents in the form of nylon fibers and resins can helpfully reinforce the strength of the nail. Many contain formaldehyde; despite its unappealing association with embalming fluid, it is only a problem if you are allergic to it.

Nail polish needs replacing regularly. Keep it in the fridge to extend its lifespan, and throw it away as soon as it stops gliding easily onto the nail. Leave off polish for a few days a month to allow air to get to the nails.

Although you can disguise out-of-condition nails with a coating of color, all nails appreciate time to themselves, devoid of polish. Leaving the nails to daylight is essential if you are wearing custom-made sculptured (artificial) nails, which are sanded onto the originals. Because they form an impervious surface that interferes with normal vapor exchange, nail sculptures should not be worn for more than three months continuously, even when polish is left off. (Sculptures are so natural-looking now that they even look good without a disguising layer of polish over the top of them.)

There are myriad different techniques and systems for enhancing the length and strength of the nails – ranging from emergency repair services for recreating the tip of a single broken nail to a full set of "nail extensions" which are painted on layer by layer over a metal bed, set, and stuck onto the nail. Nail extensions can look very impressive, but they all ultimately weaken and damage the originals. A choice must therefore be made.

BETTER FEET FORWARD

A pretty foot, wrote Goethe, is the one element of beauty that defies age. In fact, distinctly unpretty dry, cracked skin and brittle nails are the lot of most aging feet. As the feet, in common with the rest of the body, lose their subcutaneous fat padding, they become less resilient and more infection-prone and in need of extra special care.

If the hands miss out on most of the attention that's lavished on the face, the feet are hopelessly neglected. In one survey conducted by Scholl on over 1000 adults, six out of ten admitted that they had not even *looked* at their feet in the previous week.

And this was in spite of the fact that four out of ten women acknowledged their feet had a big bearing on the way they felt generally. Interestingly, just as dress size often changes with age, so the foot also grows. Most women imagine that they have a set shoe size for life, but as the foot ages, the arch tends to drop a fraction and the foot spreads and becomes larger, increasing by as much as three width fittings between the ages of 12 and 55. It's therefore always a good idea to try one size up from time to time when shopping, and see if the shoes fit your feet better. In one survey carried out by the American Orthopedic Foot and Ankle Society on 356 women between the ages of 20 and 60, 313 of those questioned were found to be wearing shoes that were too small; four out of five not surprisingly also complained of foot pain and problems like hammer toes, bunions, or corns.

> **F**eet should be washed and scrupulously dried at least once a day and hard skin removed with a file, pumice, or even (many a grown woman's guilty secret) sandpaper. Podiatrists commonly take a scalpel to the heel. Frequent application of moisturizer – either body/hand lotion or a foot-only product – is essential to guard against cracking, infection, and snagged stockings. Toenails should be clipped straight across. As toenails thicken up with age, they may need regular attention from a podiatrist. Monthly pedicures are also a good idea.

A regular podiatry session is a near guarantee against developing most of these problems, and since it can also transform the way that the foot, and the whole body, feel afterward it should certainly be part of every woman's health care schedule past the age of 50. Reflexology – an extraordinary technique that claims to give the body organs a kind of long-distance massage via the exquisitely sensitive sole of the foot – makes feet feel wonderful even in the absence of any more esoteric benefit.

TEETH

THERE's reason to smile. The last decade of dentistry has made the prospect of keeping one's teeth for life a reality. Thanks to new techniques in cleaning, veneering, and orthodontia, methods of treating gum disease and, where all else fails, a revolutionary new implantation procedure, there is no reason why anyone should have unattractive or missing teeth.

More people than ever are keeping their teeth well into extreme old age, and so they should. Dentists tell us that a healthy tooth will outlast its owner by several *hundred* years. Yet most modern teeth don't display anything like this degree of longevity. The most recent survey by the National Institute of Dental Research in the United States revealed that while toothlessness "has been almost eliminated in middle-aged adults" (a significant improvement when compared with the early 1970s), 42 per cent of adults over 65 were missing all their teeth, and only two per cent still had all 28 "permanent" teeth.

In the relatively recent past, individuals were condemned to toothlessness because rampant decay rotted the teeth in the jaw until abscesses and intolerable pain took them to the dentist, who mercifully yanked the offending teeth out. But before Sir Walter Raleigh's historic cane of sugar became the ubiquitous sugar cube, decay was rare: pathologists examining the skeletons of the crew of the Tudor battleship, the *Mary Rose*, hauled from the deep off the English coastline in 1981, found evidence of tooth decay in only seven per cent of the crew. Decay is now less of a threat thanks to greater awareness of sugar's destructive corrosiveness and of the importance of oral hygiene. The use of fluoride in water supplies, in tablets as the teeth are forming and in sealants that can be painted onto young teeth, not to mention virtually every brand of toothpaste now on the market, has also helped.

Although unusual after the age of 25, decay can become a problem in later life if sugar-based medicines and antacid preparations are taken on a regular basis. If age or gum disease causes the gums to recede to a point where the roots of the teeth are exposed, they become very vulnerable to decay – a problem suffered by nearly a quarter of adults and a majority of over-65s, according to a U.S. National Institute of Dental Research survey. Later-life decay tends to creep in at a different point – lower down toward the roots – and can be counteracted by renewed oral hygiene, diet control, treatment of gum disease (where appropriate), and rinsing with fluoride mouthwashes.

These days, teeth are more likely to be jeopardized by gum disease, whereby bacteria can become ensconced beneath the gumline and ultimately erode the bone that holds the teeth fast in the jaw. This preventable catastrophe is a good example of where state-of-the-art technology comes a poor second to daily tooth care, since, with motivation, regular checks, and a good technique, virtually everyone can prevent and even brush and floss their way out of teeth-threatening problems, so ensuring that they keep their own teeth for life.

DAILY TOOTH CARE

The point of brushing and, as essential, flossing is to remove the sticky, colorless film of plaque – an unsalubrious mix of food debris, sloughed-off skin cells, and bacteria – that continually collects on and between the teeth. If every last bit is not brushed and flossed off at least once every 24 hours, the minerals in saliva will start to calcify and, within a short time, set rock hard – after which this tartar, as it is called, will have to be painstakingly scraped off by the dental hygienist.

Unfortunately, the up-and-down or back-and-forth brushing style most of us employ removes rather less than half of the plaque in the mouth and particularly fails to get into those critical crevices between the gum and tooth where the bacteria lurk. While glossing over the hard-to-clean corners at the back, this heavy-handed approach also tends to wear down the enamel on the front surfaces. All the effort is

Regular visits to the dentist are essential for everyone, the intervals depending on the condition of your mouth. Everyone should see their dentist at least twice a year for a check-up, cleaning, and a check for oral cancer. Anyone with diagnosed gum disease or other dental problems may require more frequent visits. Let your dentist help you determine how often you should be seen.

• Ask your dental hygienist to give you feedback about where you are failing to brush – build-up of tartar is a good guide – and, if necessary, to teach you a new, more thorough brushing habit. The most widely approved method involves angling the brush at 45 degrees to the gum/tooth margin and wiggling it against the teeth so the bristles poke in between: you count to five and then move on. Areas requiring special attention are the back teeth, the spaces between the teeth, and the gum/tooth margin. It is a job that cannot be rushed, nor replaced by an anti-plaque mouthwash, though it can be helped by one of the new electric toothbrushes with rotating bristles. Oral irrigators may also help.

• Your toothbrush should have a small, neat head that fits the curve of the jaw – about the size of the head on the average child's toothbrush. Most brushes on sale are much too big to fit sufficiently snugly against the teeth. The bristles should be medium or medium-soft, and the brush should be changed as soon as it starts to splay out.

• A fluoride-containing toothpaste is a necessity throughout life, not just in childhood. A therapeutic, breath-freshening, "plaque-removing" mouthwash is unnecessary if you clean your teeth well, and ineffective if you don't. Avoid mouthwashes with alcohol: a U.S. National Cancer Institute study has suggested that a mouthwash with over 25 per cent alcohol may raise the risk of oral cancer.

• Brushing *must* be followed up by the use of dental floss, at least once every day, since even conscientious brushing removes only about 50 per cent of plaque. Rather than forcing the floss between the teeth with a sawing motion, curve it into a "C" around the tooth and sweep it up and down. This is easiest with the extra-wide waxed variety, and impossible with toothpicks or a prethreaded flosser. Interproximal brushes can be useful between the teeth.

thus concentrated where it is least necessary. (Sensitivity problems, caused by exposure of the sensitive inner dentin layer, are usually a sure sign of this sort of overbrushing.)

Do not rely on "pre-brushing" rinses to do the job for you. Although they promise to polish off plaque, they fall into the dubious category between cosmetics and drugs, and are thus more likely to get away with exaggerated claims. While test users of one of the original products did show three times less plaque than a non-rinsing control group after three months, the scientist conducting the experiment suggested that the mere act of rinsing could have loosened the plaque and that simply slooshing the mouth with water prior to brushing "may point to a new important strategy in the control of plaque [that] would be considerably more cost-effective than using the test rinse . . ." Try it.

THE PERILS OF PLAQUE

As long as the right tooth-brushing technique is employed and plaque removed once a day, the bacteria are quite harmless, even beneficial. Allowed to remain on the teeth, however, Jekyll-like, they change their nature. Long-stay bacteria form into colonies which delve into the gum, provoking redness, inflammation, and bleeding on brushing (the first signs that all is not well). Once the bacteria move beneath the gum, they create pockets that cannot be reached, or even detected, except during a thorough professional examination. Usually unsuspected and always inaccessible to the toothbrush, the bacteria are then free to attack the surrounding tissues and, eventually, to destroy the bond that supports the teeth. By the time the teeth actually wobble and become loose in the jaw, the disease has reached its near-terminal stage.

This silent and sinister process is the cause of most tooth loss in Western countries yet few people feel it enough of a threat to change their brushing habits. It is astonishingly common. The American Dental Association estimates that, by the age of 35, three-quarters of all Americans have signs of the disease – namely, bleeding, inflamed, and receded gums – though most are unaware of it. This is because even very advanced gum disease creates little discomfort. Often, it is only when the dentist probes the teeth and finds deep pockets, or the teeth become loose and start to wobble, or an abscess appears, that the extent of the disease becomes apparent. X-rays can be uncomfortably revealing, since they show just how much bone has already been lost to gum disease and how little remains before the bone relaxes its grip on the tooth and it becomes loose in the mouth. This new technology is revealing frightening losses of bone in patients as young as 35, confirming that gum disease is a condition that tends to gallop in midlife – although the teeth may not actually fall out till much later.

In the early stages, regular scaling of the hardened tartar and root planing, which scrapes away bacterial deposits below the gumline, can keep the disease in check, but once it reaches a certain stage, the best dental hygiene measures in the world will no longer be sufficient to reverse it and surgery may be necessary to eliminate the

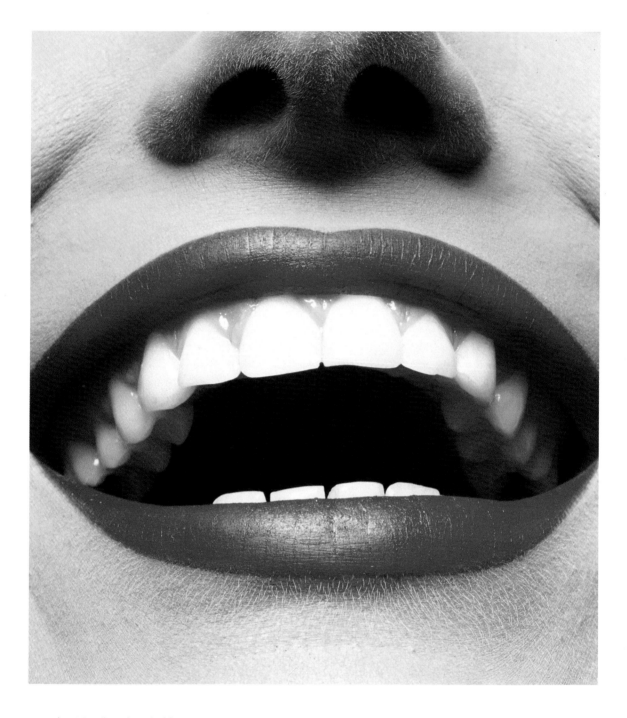

A certain smile can be anybody's
these days with the help of some
stunning new advances in cosmetic
dentistry.

pockets and make the mouth cleanable again. Even when a tooth starts to wobble, it may not be too late to save it. New treatments range from slow-release high-dose antibiotics to kill the bacteria to the new "Gore-tex" procedure, whereby a semi-permeable plastic material, originally patented for use by raincoat manufacturers, is placed over the bone and beneath the gum in the hope that it will stimulate the bone to renew itself.

> **O**nce teeth start to wobble, drop-out point is imminent and you should *run* to the periodontist (gum expert). As long as the tooth is still in the jaw, the situation may well be salvageable. Question any routine decision to extract by your regular dentist, insisting on a second opinion.

COSMETIC DENTISTRY

It is not just the gums that change with age. Decades of wear and tear tell on the teeth, yellowing them and rendering them more brittle and so more likely to chip and fracture. They also become blunter, where the cusps have worn flat with use. Increasingly, cosmetic dentistry is turning its attention to supplying clients with younger-looking teeth. At the less subtle end of the market this generally means making the mouth conform as closely as possible to the cultural *idée fixe* that the best teeth are perfectly white, evenly spaced, and regular as piano keys – properties usually seen only in the cheapest type of dentures. Such questionable aesthetics aside, in skillful hands cosmetic dentistry becomes an art form that really can transform the look of the mouth, often returning a sense of harmony and proportion to the face too. As the chart on page 79 demonstrates, there is very little now that dentistry cannot deliver when it comes to improving appearance – whether it is brightening teeth that have yellowed with age, covering chips, eliminating gaps, improving the alignment of twisted or crooked teeth, or supplying tooth-colored fillings and inlays to replace the tell-tale flashes of unflattering metal.

The arrival of veneers, thanks to bonding techniques perfected in the development of the space shuttle program, has added hugely to the possibilities open to the cosmetic dentist. These fine, custom-made shells, usually of porcelain, slip over the front face of the tooth. Not only do they hide a multitude of irregularities, they also last remarkably well and look indistinguishable from the teeth next door, restoring harmony to the mouth in only two, albeit prolonged, visits. In a few selected cases, they also offer a short cut to more involved adult orthodontic work, sometimes enabling orthodontists to straighten crooked front teeth. Porcelain is longlasting and, unlike the resin composites sometimes bonded onto the teeth to correct minor imperfections, it resists chipping, cracking, and staining.

STRAIGHTENING ADULT TEETH

For all the impressive advances, there are still limits, however, to what can be achieved without permanently rearranging the teeth. Although orthodontia is generally perceived as a child-oriented specialty, increasing numbers of adults are now seeking appointments for themselves, ready to embark on the long treatment schedule necessary to shift their teeth into a more acceptable position. Every year Americans spend nearly twenty billion dollars straightening their smiles, assisted in their decisions by video technology that allows the orthodontist to redesign the length, shape, and spacing between the teeth on screen and so show their patients what can – and, as importantly, cannot – be achieved.

Informative as they are, these instantly gratifying after-images belie the tremendous amount of time and motivation required. The truth is that while adult orthodontia can transform a face, a great deal of motivation and a realistic outlook are essential. Once a person is out of the teens, orthodontia will rarely give as good a result as if the program had been started at around the age of 12, when the adult teeth are fully through but the bone still has more growing ahead and can therefore adapt to the new configuration. As the face "grows" into itself, the result looks more natural. Once growth has finished, however, everything is programmed to remain where it is or to return there.

Many individuals are misled by their regular dentists into thinking that orthodontic work will be simple, requiring no great sacrifice on their part, especially if only a minor adjustment is required. Unfortunately, what looks minor to a patient is rarely minor to the specialist. The two twisted front teeth, which appear only to need to be persuaded away from each other, usually cannot be treated in isolation because their position has an impact on what happens all the way around the jaw. Since the lower jaw closely meshes with the upper one to form the bite, corrective maneuvers may stretch to the top as well as the bottom jaw, or vice versa. One orthodontist puts it simply: "You can't clap with one hand."

Aside from the expense, which is nearly always considerable, one of the great turn-offs of most orthodontic work is that visible fixed braces must usually be worn for up to three years. Orthodontists commonly take short cuts to spare their clients' vanity and cut wearing time to a minimum. Yet few of the less visible options are as good as metal. So-called "artificial sapphire" braces, for example, may be transparent and so less obtrusive, but they break and discolor very easily, and stick so fast to the fronts of the teeth they can be very difficult indeed to remove.

Even after the braces come off and the teeth have been shifted to their new position, most adult orthodontic work demands some form of braces be worn full-time – usually in the form of a millimeter-thin steel bracket glued onto the *backs* of the teeth. If for some reason this restraining influence breaks or is removed, the teeth can return to their old tricks in as little as a week, even after being held in position for 20 years. As an alternative to a permanent restraint, some orthodontists suggest a "retaining plate" only be worn at night. This is not generally thought advisable, however, since the infinitesimal movement of the tooth as it is persuaded into the

TEETHSAVING STRATEGIES

WHAT'S WRONG	WHAT'S INVOLVED	WHAT TO WATCH OUT FOR
gaps between teeth	Having fine porcelain *veneers* attached to the front surfaces. The teeth are etched with a mild acid before the veneers are cemented onto them, eliminating the gaps and lasting for at least ten years. *Bonding* (see below) can also work.	Well-done, veneers take considerable time to fit and finish, as the joins must be smooth if they are not to stain. If not adequately polished, they can be thicker at the tips, making crunching into a crisp apple (for example) impossible.
chipped teeth	*Bonding*, whereby a composite resin is built up on the tooth and set with ultraviolet light, can render chipped teeth whole again. Some dentists prefer to fit *veneers* (see above).	Bonding has a short life expectancy; it chips and stains, particularly around the margins if not perfectly finished. When expertly applied and scrupulously looked after (avoiding smoking, black coffee, and red wine), bonding may last as long as 15 years, but two to three is more usual.
missing tooth/ teeth	A single missing tooth is best disguised by a *bridge* which attaches a dummy tooth to the existing teeth next door by means of a crown. When more than one tooth is missing, *implants* are an option.	Implants demand considerable motivation. Though impressive, they are only as good as the dentist who fits them. Even at best, up to ten per cent never integrate, and there is a risk of continued pain, swelling and infection. An oral surgeon, periodontist, or prosthodontist is essential.
yellow/stained teeth	Now the number one dental cosmetic procedure in the U.S., though temporarily suspended in the UK. owing to fears about gum damage, *bleaching* can be used at high concentrations for immediate effect in the surgery, while a milder, carbamide peroxide solution can be used at home with a custom-made mouth guard. It is usually worn for 30-minute or hourly periods for two to four weeks, depending on the degree of whitening required. Additional treatments are necessary every six to 12 months. Over-the-counter kits are not advised: some dissolve the surface of the enamel while others are too mild.	Have teeth professionally cleaned first, since plaque prevents the whitener from getting to the enamel. Bleaching works best on porous enamel – which is some sort of natural justice since this is the sort that stains most readily in the first place. As bleach will not lighten plastic-composite fillings, porcelain inlays, veneers, and crowns, be prepared for a mismatch. Smokers should avoid bleaching because studies on animals have linked the interaction of tobacco and hydrogen peroxide to oral cancer. (Note: Teeth stained from early antibiotic use or otherwise discolored will not usually respond to bleaching; veneers are a better option.)
visible fillings	*Tooth-colored composites* are fitted in the chair and set with a strong blue light. These are best for small holes at the front of the mouth, while specially made composite or *porcelain inlays* are best for medium-sized fillings at the back of the mouth. Very heavily filled molars are best with *crowns*.	All filling materials have their disadvantages since nothing is perfect (except the original tooth). Gold is strongest (but generally unacceptable for reasons of aesthetics), porcelain and resin composite inlays come next, in that order, followed by amalgam and, lastly, tooth-colored fillings.
crooked teeth	Crooked teeth can often appear straighter after *veneers* are fitted but are more likely to require *orthodontia*.	See gaps between teeth, and page 78 for comment on orthodontia.

desired position at night and drifts away during the day, can, when multiplied by, say, ten years (that's over seven *thousand* tiny movements), loosen the tooth or create problems in the mouth or with the bite.

TITANIUM IMPLANTS

The ultimate failure of preventive dentistry is, of course, that point at which the teeth fall out. Dentists have always dreamed of developing alternatives to false teeth. As long as 200 years ago, they were embedding cylinders of gold, porcelain, or lead into the jaw, and crowning them. (The results, though initially pleasing, were eventually horrific due to infection, rejection, and even poisoning from the implants.) Now, at last, there is a means of anchoring false teeth directly into the jawbone that offers a permanent, safe, effective alternative to false teeth. Developed in Sweden, and known as the Branemark system after the man who invented it, it can be used to replace a single missing tooth (or several) or to recreate all the teeth in a jaw. As other good systems have come on the market, the popularity of the procedure has grown; the number of implants performed in the United States, for example, has tripled in the last four years.

The technique bypasses the age-old problem of bonding inert metal to living bone by using titanium implants, which the bone attaches to via an oxide layer produced by the metal. Rather than rejecting the material, as always happened in the past, the body actually adopts titanium as its own, creating a permanent fixture stronger than a natural root. The procedure is carried out in three stages. First the bone is drilled and titanium "pegs" are screwed tightly into the jaw. Three to six months later the gum is reopened and blunt posts screwed onto them. These stick out of the gum and can be covered or disguised by a temporary plate or bridge for a further week or two, after which permanent prosthetic "teeth" are attached. As will be appreciated, this is a time-consuming, painful, and expensive procedure, demanding such high levels of motivation and commitment on the part of the patient that orthodontic work fades into insignificance by comparison. But for those people who cannot endure the indignities of life with ill-fitting false teeth, it is a godsend.

S H A P E

THE fitness movement has revolutionized our concept of what a middle-aged body looks like, can wear and is capable of. As fitness wear has traveled beyond the gym, loosing Lycra and bodyhugging lines on the world outside, bodies have come into sharper focus – at every decade of life.

In many cases, the focus has become relentlessly sharp. The desire to be thinner now starts earlier and continues later than ever before. In a recent U.S. study, two-thirds of a sample of 850 girls aged 12 to 13 were unhappy with their weights, while a British survey carried out in 1992 found nearly half of a sample of 400 nine-year-olds expressing the desire to be thinner and cited an ideal weight "at odds with their impending physical development."

If girls are feeling fat at ever younger ages, grown women are yearning to be unrealistically slim at ever older ones, certainly well into their seventh decade. As the years pass, the desire to conform to what the American writer Naomi Wolf has called "the official body" – flat-as-a-washboard belly, firm high breasts, and improbably pert bottom – continues to exert enormous power, even though it bears not the slightest relation to a body that has given birth to one or more children and seen 50 summers come and go.

While the nubile ideal is visible everywhere, the reality of the grown-up female form is virtually nowhere to be seen. Confronted with this single invidious standard for comparison, it's hardly surprising that the older woman gazes with dismay at her sagging breasts and stretch marks. No wonder, too, that, complying with the prevailing cultural pressure, she quickly covers up. It doesn't take her long to realize that the permissiveness that allows the nymphet to strip to promote cars or power tools will soon turn into tight-lipped censoriousness if she has the unpardonable bad taste to sport a low neckline or, worse, step onto the beach in a bikini.

Significantly, the only women applauded for showing off their older bodies have retained perpetual cheerleaders' figures – trimmed by relentless dieting, endless leglifts, and possibly the sharp edge of the scalpel, to conform to the younger version. The negative feelings women have about their changing shapes can only be intensified by the fact that they see so few older bodies unclothed till possessed of one themselves. When the only naked 50-year-old form a woman has glimpsed belongs to her mother, she may have the strange sensation of stepping into her mother's skin as her own flesh starts to give and sag. "Lately, I look in the mirror and I'm so afraid I'm going to look like my mother," shuddered one young slave to Betty Friedan's *The Feminine Mystique* more than 30 years ago. It's significant that, in traditional cultures, where nakedness is seen in all its variety right across the age spectrum, older flesh is readily accepted and continuing sexuality is seen as normal (see page 277).

Bucking the trend, some women like their older bodies better than they ever did when they were youthfully taut. Indeed, they may come to treasure them in quite a new way – not so much for the way they *look* as for what they can *do*, are capable of, and have been through. The amazing physical feat of giving birth can instill new respect, while an injury or illness can lead to the realization that one has only one body and it needs care if it is to last a lifetime. The late actress Lillian Gish summed it up in American *Vogue* at the grand old age of 85. "Now I realize that this thing I live in, I can't get a second one. I can get another apartment, another sofa, but I can't get another pair of eyes or another body. So I have to take care of them."

It's not so surprising then that, rather than starving their bodies into submission or flogging them to a state of aerobic exhaustion as they may have done in earlier days, many grown-up women prefer to challenge their bodies in kinder, more compassionate ways. As they take up hiking, dancing, rock climbing, martial arts, or yoga, unexpected strengths and abilities often come to light that deepen these feelings of appreciation. Putting the postural principles on pages 195–200 to good effect has the double advantage of preserving structural health and transforming shape. Instantly.

MUSCLE GIVES WAY TO FAT

Whether we will it or not, bodies change shape over the life cycle. The 50-year-old woman who weighs exactly the same as she did at 20 cuts a different figure – fuller in some places, more angular in others. Her tummy will be more convex, her waist a bit wider, her hip-bones less defined, her collar-bones more pronounced, her breasts less full and high, the flesh over her thighs and upper arms apt to give a bit with every passing year. The effect is generally softer and squashier as muscle gives way to fat. This tendency is independent of, though obviously exaggerated by, the reduced activity levels of later life. From the early 20s on, unless a woman increases her activity level considerably, working out several times a week every week, she will sacrifice about half a pound (200 grams) of muscle for the same amount of fat *every year*. The visible consequence is spreading middle, bottom, and thighs, and clothes that feel as though they must have shrunk in the dry cleaning. Since fat is a lot lighter than muscle, the woman who steps on the scales and discovers to her delight that she hasn't put on an ounce may also be mystified to discover she has gone up a whole dress size, or even two.

By the age of 60, women cross-culturally are as much as 40 or 45 per cent fat, and have as little as two-thirds of the muscle mass they had at 20. Thanks to this changing muscle/fat ratio, it gets harder and harder just to stay the same size. While muscle requires plenty of nourishment to do its work, keeping the metabolic rate high, fat just sits there as a storage tissue, lowering it. As muscle disappears, the metabolic rate slows by around two per cent every few years from the mid-20s on. If activity levels drop sharply, as they are wont to do, it will dive faster and even more flesh will accumulate – in the form of fat, of course, so throwing the fat/muscle ratio even further out of kilter. Because this extra fat gets harder and harder to shift, a strict healthy eating/exercising strategy pays enormous dividends by preventing fat from accumulating in the first place.

For women who are only marginally larger than they'd like, a tape measure, a favorite pair of jeans, or a three-monthly check on body-fat percentage will give a better guide to progress than a weekly appointment with the scale – especially as trading fat for muscle will add pounds anyway. Assessments of body fat can now be made at most gyms and health clubs. The optimal range for women at any age is between 18 and 24 per cent fat. The old pinch test with a pair of callipers is not the most reliable test, but it can give a guide if always performed by the same person. Newer, computer-generated methods rely on shining infra-red rays or running a weak electrical current through the body and then measuring the differing degrees of resistance offered by fat and lean tissue.

Past the age of 35, take weight loss at a snail's pace for reasons of aesthetics and health. A weight loss of between one or two pounds (half and one kilogram) a week is quite enough. The emphasis should always be on changing your eating habits permanently. No special diet is required, just a life-long commitment to the low-fat high-fresh-food alternatives outlined on pages 228–238. Stepped-up exercise regimes should accompany any diet.

HEALTH ASPECTS

A sense of proportion is important too. Although the waist may thicken and the hips may broaden, your size may stay well within the bounds of the healthily acceptable. Looking at the Body Mass Index (BMI) chart opposite should make it immediately apparent that the upper range of "normal" (i.e. at which there is no ill-effect to health) allows considerably more latitude than any self-respecting Western woman would permit herself. These tables derive from the pooled experience of life insurance companies, who have worked out exactly what every extra pound is likely to cost them in early deaths, ill health, and lost premiums. So you can rest assured that there is a big distinction, easily blurred in the weight-conscious West, between wanting to lose a little weight for appearance's sake and being so big that it is a risk to your health. Although you may prefer for reasons of aesthetics to keep your BMI down to a low 20 or 21, you will be no better off from a health point of view than if you were a much better-covered 24 or 25. In the United States, several official bodies have now relaxed their guidelines, allowing a certain increase in heaviness with age. The life-shortening risks of obesity are highest under the age of 50. As long as you are not overweight already, studies suggest you can afford to gain a bit as you get older.

While there are certain health risks associated with increasing size, and we would be foolish to disregard them, the specters of heart disease, breast cancer, and diabetes do not become significant until a woman is substantially overweight and sailing toward obesity (Body Mass Index of more than 30). At this point, the extra weight certainly requires shifting in the interests of health. This is best achieved by following a specific diet, both devised and supervised by a dietician.

Lesser degrees of overweight, however, are not necessarily health-threatening. One of the most respected surveys in the world, the still ongoing, half-century-old investigation into the lives and health habits of the citizens of Framingham, Massachusetts, has found that, far from prejudicing their health, mildly overweight women enjoy the best survival record of the entire population – much better than the thinnest group, who were actually found to be more seriously at risk than the fattest.

For most of us, the disadvantages of being a size or two larger than we'd like are aesthetic. We have a shape that we dress around. Once that shape changes, we feel stuck for choice or make the mistake of continuing to dress the same way or, worse, squeezing determinedly into the same size, regardless of straining seams. Size itself often becomes a talisman of youth, a sort of numerical monument to the way we were, when a more generous cut would not only fit better and feel better but look better too. Some women, shuddering at the thought of the visible bulge, take refuge in ever more disguising layers, bereft of hope or style.

Work out your Body Mass Index (BMI) by drawing a line between your weight, on the left of the chart, and height, on the right, and seeing where they intersect at the center. Anything between 19 and 25 is acceptable for health. If in the low 20s, losing pounds will not give a leaner line and better body shape; what's needed is to swap fat for muscle and tone up what you already have by taking action – literally. If less than 19, your body's fat/muscle stores are too low and you are likely to be lacking nutritionally. A BMI between 25 and 30 signifies a degree of overweight that is possibly damaging to health, if only because it disinclines to activity and stresses the body's joints, while one of 30 or more takes you into the obese range and is definitely hazardous.

WEIGHT
(KG)(LB)

BODY MASS INDEX
(W/H²)

HEIGHT
(CM)(IN)

90
85
80
75
70
65
60
55
50

•180
•170
•160
•150
•140
•130
•120

40

OBESE

30

OVERWEIGHT

25

ACCEPTABLE   20

UNDERWEIGHT   15

140
145
150
155
160
165
168

56
58
60
62
64
66
67

When our size deters us from exercising, or embarking on new relationships, or taking pleasure in clothes and the way we look – when it makes us feel uncomfortable, unhappy, and insecure – then it's time for action; but judicious action. Dieting down below the lower level of normal in the misplaced belief that thinner is always better may well be hazardous to health. Building more activity into our lives is the better option; though, be warned, this can be taken to excess as well.

YOU *CAN* BE TOO THIN

Nearly every woman in the Western world wants to be thinner, and, according to a panel convened by the American National Institutes of Health, this includes many normal and even underweight women. If they succeed in their goal of losing weight, it could well be at some cost to their health. You most certainly *can* be too thin, especially as you age. As the years pass, being underweight (doctors call it "unphysiologically thin") becomes a substantial health hazard in its own right.

Thin is particularly bad news for the skeleton. A certain amount of heaviness helps fend off that peculiarly female scourge, osteoporosis because following menopause most estrogen is formed not in the ovaries but in the fat. In addition, the load of flesh rebounding on the bones and the pull of the muscles on the ligaments provides a positive stress that stimulates bone formation and promotes the uptake of calcium. Very skinny women might be a designer's dream but they are an orthopedic physician's nightmare, since their much-envied small size puts them at greater risk of painful fractures, deformed spines, and warped widows' humps.

When Susie Orbach's groundbreaking book *Fat is a Feminist Issue* was published in the late 1970s, one doctor remarked that the emphasis was wrong; the book should have been called "Fat is a Feminine *Tissue*." This pun becomes a tough biological truth past menopause, when a woman's fat cells become the main factories of her dwindling female hormone. While a dribble of estrogen is still secreted from the ovaries and adrenal glands, most comes from the fat cells that process the "male" hormone, androstenedione. There is some evidence that, thanks to their extra estrogen, well-covered women have less miserable menopauses, stronger, fracture-resistant bones and perhaps even healthier hearts.

> **W**omen who become thin and bony as they age should attempt to push their BMI above the lower limit, not by stuffing themselves with high-calorie foods and fat, but by ensuring their diet is nutritious and by building muscle, which adds both weight and stability, through supervised strengthening exercises.

Just as women must be wary of messages implying they should be superslim for the sake of their health, so they should also recognize that the relentless effort to keep their weight down by dieting can ravage their looks – leaving them wasted, prematurely wrinkled shadows of their former selves. Sixteen may look good skinny as a rail; 60 just looks skeletal. Crash diets are especially ruinous, since they draw both on precious, fast-diminishing muscle reserves – which may never be replenished even if the weight is regained – and on equally precious stores of succulent subcutaneous fat just beneath the skin. As older skin loses its ability to contract back to the old snug fit, crash diets write new lines onto the older face faster

WHAT WORRIES	WHAT MAY WORK
saggy skin – arms, thighs, abdomen	*Surgery* is still the only way of removing excess flesh – and there are specific operations for every conceivable body part, from the ankles upward.
jodhpur thighs, bulging hips or buttocks	*Exercise* using weight machines and the services of a one-to-one personal trainer can sometimes achieve results, especially when paired with a strict *low-fat, low-alcohol diet* for at least a year. Faster effects can be had with *liposuction* provided general shape is good, skin tone is reasonable, and only a modest amount of fat is removed. The new, "circumferential" approach allows the whole upper leg to be treated not just one area as previously. While liposuction can give a better shape beneath clothes, the flesh may be left slack, rippled, and dimpled, especially after age 50 and so can actually look *worse* naked.
"cellulite"	A new *liposuction variant* actually breaks down the fibrous bands of tissue that tether the muscle to the skin via the fat (defying the usual laws of sag and give, these actually contract over time, causing fat cells to bunch up). It is said by some to be effective, by others to be unimpressive and short-lived. *Cellulolipolysis*, a French technique using long acupuncture-type needles, claims to electrify fat cells into non-existence over six (expensive and often uncomfortable) sessions. It is said by some to reduce volume and minimize dimpling.
drooping, "deflated" breasts	*Surgery* firms the breasts by cutting away slack skin and usually raising the nipple. Lost volume can be compensated for by inserting an implant at the same time (saline for preference, pending the outcome of trials on silicone). The most aesthetic results are achieved by using implants with a roughened, textured surface and siting them behind the pectoral muscle. Although some women dislike the less breastlike texture of saline, and complain they can hear or feel the water sloshing around, it appears less prone to subsequent hardening (a common complication with silicone).
spider veins	*Sclerotherapy, lazer therapy* (sometimes)
stretch marks	*Retinoic acid*, sometimes, in the early (red) stages; once white, the only solution is *surgically* removing the skin.
post-baby bulge	*Abdominoplasty* (see saggy skin), or a new less invasive experimental procedure (see right).

WHAT'S INVOLVED	WHAT DOESN'T WORK
An incision is made (inside the bikini line in the case of the tummy, or in the groin fold for the thigh). The skin and fat are detached from the muscles beneath, pulled up and trimmed away, leaving the area as smooth and flat as possible. In *abdominoplasty*, the navel is repositioned (unfortunately not always correctly – further surgery is sometimes required) and the abdominal muscles may also be tightened if they have been stretched. These operations require major surgery and often leave extensive and prominent scars. Some are more discreet than others, such as those on the thigh, whereas those on the upper arm stretch from the elbow to the armpit and that on the tummy from hip to hip. Mostly it's a question of trading improvements in shape for scars which are always visible to some degree.	*"Firming lotions,"* such as those containing ivy and horsetail which are said to "tighten" the skin (a physiological impossibility, since once the skin has stretched, only a scalpel and needle and thread can tighten it), *exercise*.
Liposuction entails a general anesthetic, several "stab" incisions, and a good deal of discomfort after the operation, including pronounced bruising and swelling and the wearing of an elasticized corset for several weeks. Skin can take months to regain its original tone and texture. In addition, lumps and bumps forming around the remaining fat cells will require strong pummeling massages to disperse them.	*"Reducing"* creams, most forms of *firming exercise*.
For *liposuction*, see above. *Cellulolipolysis* entails having pairs of needles inserted around the problem area and a pulsating electrical current passed between them so theoretically exciting the fat cells into relinquishing their stored energy and reducing volume.	*Creams with extract of ivy, caffeine, theophylleant* will not improve a "cottage cheese" texture; *skin brushing* and any other form of exfoliation; massages designed to promote *lymphatic drainage*.
Mastopexy involves cutting away excess skin and pulling up the rest; usually relocating the nipple centrally, often with subsequent loss of sensation. In less extreme cases, just the skin around the nipple is cut away and the rest pulled up and stitched into place; the incision and stitches can be restricted to the areola (pigmented circle around the nipple). Lifting very large, droopy breasts may leave extensive scarring in an inverted T-shape from nipple to breast crease. Since pregnancy should be avoided to prevent the scars from stretching, this is an option for the finished family.	*"Firming"* creams; exercises (as the breast is not a muscle, the gradual stretching of the supporting ligaments produces the droop, not a slackening in muscle tone). The best anti-gravity device is a good-fitting bra.
Sclerotherapy, the more usual option, injects an irritant solution which causes the vessels to swell shut and cut off the blood flow. After a few weeks the escaped traces of blood fade into the obscurity from whence they came.	Though successful on the face, lazers are generally proving disappointing on the body.
See saggy skin.	*Creams; vitamins;* wonder *body treatments* such as seaweed wraps.
A new technique gains access to the muscle via two tiny incisions, one in the navel and the other in the pubic hair. A vertical pleat is made from the breastbone to the pubis, and the fold of slack muscle is then stapled together (the staples remain in place and are not removed).	*Dieting; liposuction* (the problem is slack muscle, not too much fat); if bulge is pronounced, *exercises* will have only a small impact because of underlying damage to abdominal muscle.

than whole seasons on a sunbed, leaving the face cavernous, the cheeks gaunt, and inches of unflattering slack across neck, arms, abdomen, bottom, and thighs. For sure, weightwatching is important if the BMI is creeping past the mid-20 mark, but the skin must be given time to adjust to a gradual loss of flesh. Once the skin has stretched, there are no exercises known to woman capable of shrinking it. People talk of "tummy tucks" as though they were as inconsequential as going to the hair salon to have one's ends trimmed, when in fact abdominoplasty is a major, sometimes even life-endangering operation, involving big scars and a lengthy convalescence. Avoid the need for such drastic action by keeping weight within bounds, so you never need to shed more than four to five pounds (a couple of kilograms) at a time.

LIPOSUCTION

As just about every Western woman knows, bulges unresponsive to diet or exercise *can* be resculpted by suctioning out fat from beneath the skin. It sounds simplicity itself. A small – ¼ inch (5 mm) – incision is made, where possible in a fold of skin, the fat is separated from the skin, and a maximum of about 9–11 pounds (4.5 kilograms) removed, though more often just half this amount. The fat is suctioned from any area of the body through a fine tube or cannula or, increasingly, an even finer syringe. Since the fat cells themselves are removed, they will never reform.

While the procedure is often described as slight or minimal, the aftermath can be quite traumatic, involving days of intense discomfort, weeks of spectacular bruising, and months of swelling so pronounced that it can take fully a year to judge the finished result. Complications include infection, blood loss, and even deaths due to fat embolisms (clots) forming and lodging in the lungs. The final results depend enormously on the experience and skill of the operator, so it's essential to find a superb surgeon, especially as the techniques used, and results now achieved, by the leading surgeons bear no relation to those of even ten years ago.

Though some women are thrilled after liposuction, the aesthetics are not all they have been made out to be. Even good results can be spoiled by overeating, as the remaining fat cells expand to fill the void. The cruel reality, too, is that liposuction is most effective on the women who least need it – namely those who are fairly young and slim and have taut skin that will spring back to shape post-treatment. But even in young people with very good skin tone (the single most important determinant of success), the skin on some parts of the body seems especially resistant to contracting back to shape – the flesh on the upper arm is one such. Liposuction may offer improvements in shape that would previously have been impossible without drastic surgery, but it does nothing to tighten slack skin: the bane of so many otherwise shapely women over 50. Neither can it tighten dimples and corrugations. As skin loses its spring with age, it is almost certain to sag as a result of liposuction, and the final appearance

In great shape, personally and professionally: one of a new generation of actresses in their mid-40s who are as far removed from the "lumpy, dumpy, and frumpy" middle-aged stereotype as it's possible to imagine, Charlotte Rampling has confessed herself pleasantly surprised by the number of attractive roles still open to her in her 40s. Interviewed by British *Vogue*, she said, "There used to be an attitude that after the age of 40, women shouldn't be seductive or want a man to want them. Now a woman of 40 can be very desirable. We've been given another ten years."

will therefore be marred by "waves" or ripples of fat. For women over 50, then, it is usually a case of knowingly trading the unwanted fat for a better overall shape, albeit with some loosening of skin and lumpiness of texture. What can be expected is a slimmer line that can increase the number of wardrobe options open to you. While looking better in clothes, however, your body may actually look *worse* without. It all depends what you object to most – the fat or the slack. The best results are achieved when the amount of fat removed is kept strictly within the limits of what not-so-elastic, aging skin can take, or if skin is removed simultaneously, for example, via a "tuck" in the groin.

THE DOWNSIDE OF YO-YO DIETING

Whether taking the surgical route or not, the key to preserving one's health as well as one's shape lies in constancy – which is obviously a blow for the nine in ten dieters who are slaves to seasonal slimness. Unless you're truly enormous, surveys confirm that keeping the size you are is actually better for your health than changing size; and if you do change size, the result should be a lasting one. Covering up with outsize sweaters and leggings in winter and then taking fright and scaling down for slim, figure-clinging shapes and swimsuits in summer – a national pastime now – is bad news for bodies, however big.

American research studies not only confirm that there is no health advantage in losing weight if it is promptly regained, but have also shown that chronic yo-yo dieters may have worse health and shorter lives. Furthermore, lighter women may be putting their health in greater jeopardy by this practice than heavier women. "Weight cycling," as it is called, appears to increase the risk of several conditions, heart disease in particular.

APPLES AND PEARS

The truth is that, much as we all dislike it and eternally try to pare it down, the familiar female pear shape (heavy around the hips, bottom, and thighs and much despised by virtually every woman in existence) is actually good news in health terms. It is the pot-bellied apple shape, on the other hand, with its barrel-like accumulation of fat around the middle and lack of a clearly defined waist, that has been strongly associated with an increased risk of diabetes and heart disease. Preliminary evidence suggests that it might also be linked to breast and endometrial cancer and even infertility.

Under biochemical scrutiny, fat cells from the center of the body can be seen to be behaving differently – being more resistant to insulin and having both unusually high levels of more potent "free" estrogens and lower levels of a key protein known as sex hormone binding globulin. These hormonal differences may explain why apple-shaped women also have a three-fold higher risk of developing a tumor in their breasts, and also why they are as much as 15 times as likely to get cancer of the endometrium (lining of the womb) if the waist swells to a point where it measures *more* than the hips. Although men are generally more apple-shaped than women –

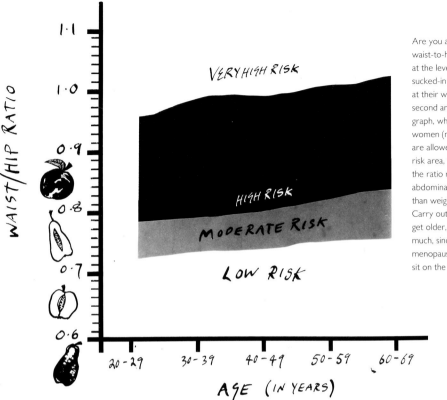

Are you an apple or a pear? Assess your waist-to-hip ratio by measuring your waist at the level of your navel – in a relaxed, not sucked-in state – and your buttocks and hips at their widest point; divide the first by the second and check the result against this graph, which gives the acceptable limits for women (men, being naturally apple-shaped, are allowed more latitude). If you are in the risk area, work at reducing the excess until the ratio rights itself – the good news is that abdominal "apple-type" fat is easier to shift than weight that settles around the hips. Carry out regular waist-to-hip checks as you get older, even if your weight does not vary much, since hormonal changes over the menopause mean that fat is more likely to sit on the middle than on the hips.

which is why it is often referred to as "male-pattern obesity" – when a woman's shape deviates from the norm for her sex, and becomes plumper around and just above the waist, it puts her into the higher risk category sooner than a man.

WHY DIETING MAKES YOU FAT

Just as changes of shape must be permanent, so the diet that leads to it should be permanent also. For sure, short-term strategies such as liquid meal replacement, drastic calorie-cutting, or excising the last meal of the day work some temporary magic. The pounds drop off and the belly flattens out. But it's a fleeting phenomenon, caused by loss of the body's glycogen, a form of carbohydrate. Just as dietary carbohydrate – rice, potatoes, pasta – bulks out when cooked, so physiological carbohydrate also absorbs water and, when lost, takes three times its weight in water with it. The problem is that the body replenishes its stores the minute eating patterns return anywhere near normal, so water is retained again and with it the problematic weight and bulk.

Another reason that on–off starvation strategies are ineffective is that the body, which evolved over millions of years to store food as fat as efficiently as possible, interprets any shortage in supply as encroaching famine, shuts down inessential bodily processes, and so lowers its metabolic rate – like a frantic shopper stockpiling cans in the supermarket to guard against future shortage. In fact, decades of chronic dieting teaches the system to become so defensive it actually gets accustomed to subsisting on starvation rations, so that every new diet requires more and more self-denial for less and less result. In this worst of all worlds, women are neither getting the nutrition they need nor losing the weight they'd like to shed. And there are many such. In 1988, a survey of post-menopausal women in Sydney, Australia, was published in the *European Journal of Clinical Nutrition*. This revealed that over a third of the sample were eating less than 1200 calories a day, on which, claimed the researchers, "it is difficult to provide an adequate intake of essential nutrients." They recommended that women "be encouraged to increase their physical activity rather than reduce their energy intake to control weight."

INCREASING ACTIVITY

Since dieting can shrink the body's muscle stores and drive the metabolic rate down, it is a poor second to increasing levels of activity, which keeps muscle mass and metabolic rate *up*, the weight stable, and the body lean and well-defined in later life. Research at the University of Pittsburgh has shown that, although weight gain is common in midlife, with an average 5½ pounds (2.5 kilograms) accumulated over three years at around the age of menopause, the tendency is more strongly linked to reduced physical activity than to the menopause itself[1] even though this is a time traditionally associated with weight gain. Throughout life, regular exercisers put on substantially less weight than their underactive contemporaries.

Stepping up activity instead of subjecting your body to yet more punitive diet regimes will encourage the spreading middle to retract and the fat/muscle ratio to regain a healthier balance. The washboard tummy may not reappear. The belly may still be rounded and the hips well covered. Weight may not change much. But the general impression will be much improved. You will be able to reclaim much of your outgrown wardrobe, and your metabolic rate will be raised. Permanently.

As you become more active, you will find that weightwatching becomes less of a necessity. Dr. William Haskell and his colleagues at Stanford University have demonstrated that when the body is treated to some exercise every day, it will find

---

The fitness regime most conducive to noticeable changes in shape, and to loss of excess body fat, includes fairly low-intensity aerobic exercise carried out for 30 minutes or more on a near-daily basis and a supervised weight-training program.

To help you get results fast, consider engaging a personal trainer. Most gyms in the United States now have a number of trainers on their books; some offer a few free sessions as part of the membership. Always ask for a trial session first since it is essential to work with a trainer you feel comfortable with.

its optimal healthiest (albeit not its lowest) weight and stay there obligingly as the years pass by. The activity taken can be quite light. You don't have to pulverize your body into the dust to see the benefits, indeed you *shouldn't*. Lower-intensity exercise not only reduces the likelihood of burn-out and impact-related injury, but also leads to better body shape – since it targets hard-to-shift fat stores and, research suggests, preferentially reduces higher-risk abdominal fat.

While short bursts of hard exercise, such as sprinting or fast running, draw on a ready source of energy (glycogen), which is stored in the muscles and quickly used up, a less vigorous but more prolonged activity like jogging or fitness walking will burn up body fat. The energy that drives the muscles in both cases is adenosine triphosphate, or ATP, but it can be produced either from glucose and glycogen already in the muscles and lean tissue – a near instantaneous process – or from triglycerides lodged in the body's fat stores. The triglycerides must be broken down within the cells to free fatty acids before they can enter the bloodstream and travel to the muscle. There, in the presence of plenty of oxygen, they are further broken down to help form the ATP that the muscles can use. Since this process takes at least 20 minutes, an activity only qualifies as a "fat burner" when it is both prolonged (to enable the free fatty acids to be mobilized so that fat-to-fuel conversion can take place) and aerobic (as fat can only be broken down in the presence of plenty of oxygen).

Although many women are resistant to the idea of using weights, increasing numbers of women are finding that as little as 15 minutes' weight-training three times a week tightens the sag and increases strength, bringing benefits beyond the purely aesthetic. Visible results can be seen after just six weeks. As the weight-training systems available in most gyms isolate specific muscles more effectively than free exercises, they have impressive flab-fighting effects, especially on the upper body and the thighs. They are also safer than free (hand-held or anklestrap) weights, which risk stressing joints while strengthening muscles, particularly when used as part of an aerobics workout. Weight-training systems, such as Nautilus, Cybex, and Camstar, support the back and encourage slow, fully controlled movements in both directions, without permitting momentum to take over. But supervision is still essential to begin with, since the machines only put you in approximately the right position. In addition to straining muscles and joints, the wrong technique could provoke dangerous rises in blood pressure if the contraction is held for too long.

Recognizing that there is all the difference in the world between unstructured activity – great for general health – and these fitness specifics that can transform the look and line of the body, increasing numbers of American women are now availing themselves of the services of a personal trainer – and getting results they are convinced they could never have achieved on their own. A personal trainer is more than just another modern status symbol like a Mercedes convertible or a Chanel suit. By helping you set suitable goals and prescribing the appropriate weights, graduating them as necessary, you see results much sooner than when working out on your own.

MAKEUP

MAKEUP is a grown woman's great ally. An instant lifter of the spirits, brightening the face and the day ahead, it is a great way of keeping up the standards and bringing a touch of glamour into an imperfect world.

While these advantages can be – should be – lifelong, makeup always needs reconsidering when the first flush of youth is over. This alone can turn a certain age into an uncertain one. It's all part of the midlife style crisis that hits with such force in fashion. Just as sticking to the same clothes can fix one in a time warp that is actually aging, so too can the look that once worked so well now appear heavy, tired, and, yes, distinctly dated. The no-makeup brigade may also be at sea as they gaze upon their freshly scrubbed faces and find them fresh-looking no more, wondering whether it isn't time to trade the natural look for something a little more polished.

Makeup can be used to better and better effect as the years pass by. As the face softens and loses its early sharpness – taut skin over prominent bones, sharp creases above the eyes, strong color in the brows and lashes – cosmetics can lend the definition that the middle-aged face cries out for. The more defined, more polished look that works to such effect on the older face does not mean denying the changes that age brings – but rather acknowledging and taking account of them. Often it also means having the confidence and courage to let go of an earlier look, which can operate as a sort of cosmetic security blanket. New York makeup artist Kevyn Aucoin, who has attended to virtually every older American female celebrity face around, notes that even they – especially they – get locked into certain looks. Just as they are often determined to stick with the look they had in their heyday, so we too can get stuck in the rut of the old, too nervous or unaware to put on the new.

Most makeup professionals deplore strict rules. It's by breaking the accepted conventions, they say, that the most striking results are achieved and new fashions born: a montage of quarreling colors on the eyelids; a set of long, false, *clumpy* lashes; red eyeshadow; a scarlet nail with white polish at the tip and base. Such inspirations aside, the few time-honored principles that distinguish the makeup that works from the makeup that doesn't, become more important as the face ages.

THE LIVED-IN FACE
No longer the blank canvas that allowed any sort of look to be superimposed onto it, the lived-in face defies wipeout. It has a landscape of lines, crevices, depths, and hollows, and a much greater play of light and dark, which must be taken account of, like it or not. Nothing can be achieved by trying to obliterate the years except inadvertently adding them on. The hard reality is that, while care, skill, and well-chosen products can knock ten years off the apparent age of a face, five minutes of the wrong type of product or a heavy-handed technique can soon add 15, rendering the eyes reptilian and the complexion a grizzled disaster zone.

When it comes to the base (foundation, concealer, and powder), the first principle is less is more. Always. Wonderfully enlivening effects can be achieved with very little – the less the better, in fact. As the women who were the most heavily made-up teenagers in history approach middle age, this is a principle not always put into effect. Makeup supremo Barbara Daly, who has a terrific-looking skin and, unless dressed to the nines, appears to be wearing no makeup at all, says, "You can do amazing things with very little product." In Daly's wide experience, a 17-year-old girl and a 57-year-old woman require identical makeups: a spare, simple look applied with the lightest of hands. The first has skin good enough to take this bare minimum, so that any more would look heavy and artificial, while the second has skin not sufficiently smooth to take more. Other makeup artists advise making a choice between the eyes and the mouth, emphasizing one and leaving the other. While a few go for the eyes (Liza Minnelli is one), more go for the lips, using commanding colors, penciling in the brows for balance, and leaving the eyes (almost) bare. Think of Paloma Picasso in her signature red, Mon Rouge, or Jean Muir's mauve.

The techniques are simplicity itself. It is *savoir faire* that makes the difference – knowing both what to do and what to do it *with*. As formulations get better, the difference between one lipstick and another, one foundation and the next, is widening. The addition of new ingredients such as silicone to products as various as foundations and lip crayons is allowing smoother application than ever. But you need to know what to buy. While this may mean investing in better-quality makeup, confident purchasing can whittle down the actual number of products required.

THE LIGHT TOUCH

While not – quite – needing a Ph.D. in chemistry to get to grips with the new makeup formulations, some knowledge stands you in good stead. As a general rule, the heavier, stickier, and more occlusive a product is, the more you should pass it up, unless you *want* to look 100 years old. This is because, as the face becomes animated, moving this way and that, the makeup moves too – right into the lines and creases where it stays, loudly calling attention to them. The aging effect is intensified if the external or emotional temperature rises, since the resultant warmth melts the makeup, which then slides over the face and sinks into the cavities just as water does when draining on an uneven floor. This phenomenon, which makeup artists call "migration," applies just as much to eye-shadow (which settles into the creases) or lipstick (which bleeds into the pucker lines above the lip) as it does to foundation or powder. In order to minimize this creeping effect, both the product and the hand that applies the makeup must be as light and sparing as possible. You should also have the courage and commonsense to withhold makeup altogether if your face, or eyes, or lips, look better that way.

Hiding lines is not what makeup is about. For all the tricks that are sometimes advocated, like laboriously infilling each and every line on the face with white pencil to throw the light up and so minimize the crevice (believe it or not, some women *do* do this), even the cleverest makeup can't disguise these signs of age on your face. Be comforted that those lines that look horrifyingly stark in the cold light of day will be thrown into relief as the face moves and changes in different plays of light, appearing much less apparent than they do when glowering at yourself in the mirror.

Ask yourself whether complete makeup cover is still appropriate. You do not have to wear the works: foundation, powder, *and* blusher may be too much. If your skintone is relatively consistent with a few uneven patches, artfully applied concealer and a little powder may be all that's required. If skin color looks generally good but a bit washed out, a hint of a blush or sweep of pink powder whisked over cheeks, forehead, and browbone can cheer up the face (and you too when you see how easily it's achieved) in minutes. If red veins are creeping over cheeks and nose, or if brown spots are emerging, a whisk of foundation and concealer patted on over the top will bring the color into line with the rest of the face. Moles, deep pigmentation spots, shadows thrown by lines, and the occasional spot will also fade from view.

R ather than trying to correct your basic skin color with foundation, go with it. Since the fluorescent lighting in most stores throws the color, making it seem lighter than it really is, take new colors to a window or door and assess them in daylight, having brought a small mirror in your purse for the purpose. Always test new shades on the jawline, not the back of the hand. The one that disappears into your own skin wins.

BACK TO BASE

How appropriate are your current products? Put on your usual foundation; if you notice tidemarks around the jawline, the makeup is too dark – a common mistake as the advancing years drain color from the complexion. According to Barbara Daly, accustomed tones of foundation commonly become inappropriate in the 40s. Matching makeup to skintone becomes an increasing challenge, she says, as skintone itself becomes uneven. Makeup artist Kevyn Aucoin warns against the wishful thinking that sabotages makeup choices. Women buy foundation for the skin they *want* to have, he says, rather than respecting the skin's own color and buying a product that suits the skin they've got. Resist the temptation to buy a brownish-toned foundation to transform your new, not-uninteresting pallor into a "healthy" look, and do not be persuaded into buying pink- or peachy-toned products to "warm up your complexion" – they may give you candy-colored cheeks or cast a disastrous orange hue over skin that now bears no relation to that on the neck and rest of body.

Makeup can be used to better and better effect as the years pass by. Paloma Picasso's iconic good looks exemplify the polished finish that works so well in midlife. Not for her the depressing, self-effacing neutrals that women of a certain age are traditionally expected to wear. Like many confident, assertive women of her generation she uses intense lip color – always in the same deep red – to call attention to what she has to say as well as how she looks.

There is one exception to this rule: the addition of yellow casts a softer light on all skin tones (particularly pale, older Anglo-Saxon complexions). Think of the outrageous flattery of candlelight, and you will realize why yellow pigments are now being included in many of the newest makeup formulations and powders (such as Yves Saint Laurent Banane Soie de Poudre, Chanel Poudre Lumière, Lauder Lucidity Translucent Loose Powder, Ultima II The Nakeds Pressed Powder).

If an appropriate tone of makeup still eludes you, you could try a personalized foundation (such as Prescriptives Custom Blended Foundation, or Cosmetics à la Carte). These are made up individually at the counter by the consultant to match the idiosyncrasies of your own complexion. You'll need to subject them to the same rigorous daylight scrutiny as pre-packaged foundations, however, since they are mixed and matched in artificial light and the color may not be true when seen in the cold but real light of day.

It may not only be a change of color that's required; texture often needs to become lighter too. The new superlight formulations (such as Lancôme Maqui Éclat) have a near magical effect as they slide over the skin, smoothing out color differences and eliminating large pores, red veins, and pigmentation spots. They look as though you are wearing nothing at all, only better. An oil-based foundation is generally most appropriate for skin that has become drier and may even cancel the need for a separate moisturizer underneath. The type of foundation is also important. On the principle that only the lightest wash of color is desired, with concealer for heavy-duty cover, liquid formulations give the lightest coverage. Cream and mousse foundations tend to have superior moisturizing capabilities but denser coverage, which will accentuate underlying wrinkles and crinkles.

When putting on foundation, apply a perfectly light wash of color with a damp sponge wedge, having first allowed your moisturizer at least ten minutes to settle. Put the sponge under a stream of tapwater and wring it out well, then place it on top of a tissue on the palm of your hand and squeeze hard so there's not a drop of water left. Put a blob of foundation about the size of a small coin on the back of your hand, add a spritz of water to thin it, and press the sponge well down until the makeup is absorbed. Starting from the middle of your face, sweep the sponge outward – taking the color just under the jawline so that it fades into the neck, up to and onto the lipline but not over the entire mouth, over the cheeks, forehead, and eyelids and up to the hairline but not into it. Do not rush this stage, and use just the lightest wash you can. If you overdo it, rinse the sponge, wring it out, and buff foundation off until the effect is just as you want. If you underdo it, a second application can intensify the cover. Finally, blot with a tissue.

The finish has an impact too. Ultra-matte formulations look dull on any skin, especially one that has lost its early bloom. The indelible older woman's rule never to wear pearlized or frosted anything – foundation, eyeshadow, blusher, or lipstick – stands corrected. While bright white, frosted highlighters and shimmering shadows might look terrible on crepey eyelid skin, a healthy complexion has a luminous sheen which needs replacing if it has disappeared. Light bounces off plump, young skin multidirectionally, so that the skin shines as the light scatters, while older skin, being flatter, reflects the light much less abundantly. Smart women have always known this – wearing jewelry, and particularly gemstones, on the ears and around the neck to catch the light and flatter the complexion. Belatedly taking their cue from such *savoir faire*, cosmetic chemists have recently come up with some wonderful light-reflecting foundations (such as Lauder Just Perfect Light-Diffusing Creme Makeup and Dior's Reflet du Teint). Very different from the sparkly glitter variety of the late '60s, these contain finely milled silica-coated particles that act like microscopic mirrors, bouncing the light off in myriad angles and lending such radiance they are many an older woman's most prized (cosmetic) possession.

CORRECTIVE STRATEGIES

Once you have a well-matched foundation, the best way to add or correct color is through the (very) restrained use of a blusher, through an undercover cream (such as Estée Lauder Color Primers) or through the subtly enhancing effects of shaded loose powder. Some undercover creams and shaded powders carry a pinkish hue to cheer up a dull complexion and add a rosy glow; others a light purple to take away sallowness or a pale bluish-green tone which, in combination with foundation, can calm down the redness caused by dilated veins, hot flashes, or rosacea. If the skin is very discolored and mottled, however, a white pearlized undercover product (such as Chanel Base Lumière or Clinique Allover Face Lustre) that contains titanium dioxide but no color pigment, can whiten the discolored skin. Although very strange-looking before makeup, a moderate-cover foundation on top can render the skin porcelain-perfect, softening fine lines out of existence, thanks to the minimizing effect of the finely ground titanium dioxide or mica.

Unless you are very skilled, avoid the "corrective" makeup strategies touted to reduce jowliness, eliminate a double chin, introduce cheekbones where none were before, or generally refine the shape of the face. Their purpose – reducing the face to a perfect oval with regular-as-clockwork features – becomes increasingly unattainable as the lived-in face departs from the restrictive Western ideal and develops its own interesting dips and concavities. Anyway, in reality, nothing save the scalpel will really change the structure of the face. True, you can fine down a bulbous nose with a judicious shading of mole-colored eyeshadow but even this simple trick requires a practiced hand. Too often, the tendency is to overdo it, producing glaringly amateur stripes that wouldn't fool anyone into thinking there is now a nice clean jaw where once a double chin had been.

"Concealers," by contrast, truly are the older woman's ally – helping to alleviate world-weariness by lightening the dark curves under the eye, minimizing deep shadows, and masking the dark pigmentation spots, or lentigines, that come with age due to clumping of melanin-producing cells, not to mention covering the occasional spot. These maximum-coverage products contain high amounts of titanium dioxide, which acts as an ultra-efficient UVA cream, an unexpected bonus protection when applied to the sunsensitive eye area. They should always be worn oncealer sticks tend to suit women better than fluids or mousse-tipped wands, which have the double disadvantage of giving imprecise cover and drying into giveaway patches. Sticks work even better when applied with a lipbrush rather than direct. As with foundation, match the shade as closely as possible to skin tone (though this can be difficult, as there is much less choice) and use a light touch. Apply *over* the foundation, adding more as (and if) necessary and, most important, *not* blending into the skin, but patting firmly into place with the fingertip so it stays where you want; then set with powder.

over the foundation base, as the subsequent application of makeup would either cause the concealer to move or obliterate the lightening effect. Applying concealer after foundation also makes you less likely to be heavy-handed with it.

Women are traditionally advised to avoid powder in later life, since the mythology holds that it clumps into lines. Visions of ancient-looking floury faces notwithstanding, the newer, microfine formulations return luminosity to timeworn skin, smoothing over differences of tone and giving a unifying coherence to a face that is only partially made-up. Many makeup artists prefer to use pressed powder rather than loose powder on older faces since it allows for more control, and they often choose to apply it with a sponge rather than a brush. Powder (and before that, foundation) should always be applied to eyelids prior to brushing on powder eyeshadow, to keep the color of the shadow true and make it last longer. In Kevyn Aucoin's view, this simple step makes all the difference between a professional look and an amateur one.

Blushers should be applied lightly. Women who have been unthinkingly swiping on the tawny stuff since their 20s should ask themselves whether it is giving them the high Slavic cheekbones that Nature carelessly omitted to supply them with or a rigid swath of color that looks like, well, a rigid swath of color. For many women, it's not so much the rosy cheeks of youth that need imitating, as the unwanted redness produced by broken veins or hot flashes that requires toning down.

EYEBROWS AND EYES

Eyebrows, which may have anyway been plucked into near non-existence or become sparser with age, can be made bolder or brushed up with an old toothbrush, instantly creating a more alert look. If the color is lighter than that of your hair, they can be dyed at the salon along with the hair on the head (*never* attempt this yourself). As thin, sculpted arches come back into fashion, many women can console themselves that their thinning brows are now the height of chic. If too sparse, however, they can be filled out with an eyebrow pencil of an exactly matched color

Liza Minnelli's evergreen urchin haircut and sock-it-to-you signature eyelashes and eyebrows draw the eye where *she* wants it – a perfect illustration of the clever cosmetic confidence trick that separates the women from the girls.

or one shade lighter. Strong brows look great on older faces but short, feathery strokes applied with a paintbrush are more natural than a single hard line. If eyebrows are untidy or erratic, pluck from the underside (stray hairs only) and from the middle of the forehead if they are contributing to a crosspatch glower. A slick of gel can keep brows orderly. Some women are darkening and thickening their brows with injections of tiny pellets of color.

Since eye colors quickly creep into the myriad small lines on and around the eyelids, making the lines more obvious and the eyes appear smaller, many women sensibly forgo eye makeup completely once into their 50s or 60s and opt for sock-it-to-you lipsticks instead. Others also get it right by continuing to emphasize the crease and to line the upper lid, compensating for gravity's unkindness by drawing the eye upward, and by wearing very little on the lower lid.

There is still no perfect formulation for eye makeup. Waterproof products, containing pigments in petrolatum, cocoa butter, or lanolin, migrate swiftly into eyelid folds, as do the creamier formulations which many women mistakenly choose, thinking they will provide moisturizing benefits along with color. Pressed powder shadows and eyeshadow crayons tend to be more obliging about staying where they are put. Setting creams (such as Elizabeth Arden Eye Fix) contain wax, which seals the skin, and talc and cyclomethicone which provide an adherent base to which the pressed powder shadows can then cling. Some eyeshadows actually incorporate a setting cream in their formulation (Clinique Touch Base) or include a separate fixer in the product (Max Factor Dawn to Dusk).

Bright strong eye colors are harder (but not impossible) to carry off successfully on lived-in faces. Slabs of straight blue or green look odd on everybody. The glorious earth tones which can now be found in all major cosmetic ranges are more natural. The best combine warm browns and tans with another tone – wonderful lavendery taupes, for example, muddy olives, and chestnutty reds – and these can be most effective when chosen to echo colors in the eye or clothes. Flashes of more emphatic jewel colors, such as emerald, can look sensational when applied sparingly to lower or upper lids at night, but for day the one-color eye is very effective – simply providing that extra definition that brings the eyes forward. It takes about ten seconds. Minimalists might try using the same color on eyes, cheeks, *and* lips; the effect is extraordinary, as though one's own coloring has somehow, inexplicably, improved.

Although shadows should not be so highly pearlized as to make the skin look more crinkly, they should have a certain luster and sheen. The flat colors developed in the 1980s at the height of designer-matte mania can look dull and lifeless.

An eyeshadow just one stop darker than your foundation can give additional depth and definition to the eyes for daytime, while retaining a no-makeup makeup effect. A hint of pink on the brow bone and cheekbone can also look naturally pretty. Keep techniques simple. Eyes do not have to be an elaborate mosaic of differing colors – just two can be used to great effect, and the one-color eye can also look great. Complicated plays of shadow are more likely to give the impression of closing the eye than opening it up. As the skin around the eye folds and creases, keep shadow on the upper rather than lower lid.

Liners should be used with great restraint. Misapplied, as they often are, dark lines can obliterate the lid (which gets smaller with age as the flesh descends) and call attention to dark circles around the eye. A precise line also gets harder to draw as the skin itself becomes lined. Eye-pencils are more versatile than the liquid types, and easier to apply; whereas the former demand a defined line that requires a steady hand, the latter give a smudgy line that can look very good.

As with the hair on the head, eyelashes lose color and become sparser. Mascaras are described by professional makeup artists as *extremely* important at this time of life, together with an eyelash curler. A more lustrous illusion can be created by dotting eyeliner onto the upper and lower eyelid and by using one of the many proprietary lash thickeners and lengtheners, which contain talc/kaolin and nylon/rayon fibers respectively. (They must, however, be allowed to dry completely between applications to avoid caking.) Some products contain polymers which give a more even coating (Lauder More than Mascara). All mascaras can be irritating, but if applied in several coats only to the tips, the lashes can be emphasized while contact with eye and skin is kept to a minimum. Black looks hard and aging on most eyes; dark browns, grays, and charcoals are a better option. Many women forgo mascara entirely and have their eyelashes dyed; again browns, grays, and blues are usually better options than black.

> **W**hen applying mascara, roll the wand around the underside of the lashes as you go, rather than simply sweeping upward, and you will get better, more even coverage and the desired curl. Coverage is so good that it's not necessary to apply it to the topside of the lashes too. Use an eyelash comb to thin out clumps, and always replace the product once it loses its liquidity.

LIP COLOR

Lips look great in the bold colors that women of a certain age are generally advised to eschew in favor of safe soft peaches and apricots. Why succumb to the conspiracy to be so subtle one is near invisible? Why *not* wear bright and bold? Red is there to be noticed – and so are you. It will call attention not only to how you look but what you say. While red is the swiftest way of escaping middle age's beige syndrome, take care! The effect can look ghastly when overdone; the scarlet gash that bleeds messily upward into the lines above the lip takes on positively frightening proportions. Luckily there are some clever tricks (see page 104) that will not only staunch the wound, but prevent the hemorrhage in the first place. Remember, too, that as the lips lose fullness with age, very dark tones can give a mean, hard set to the mouth.

Lip color demands more careful application with every passing year. Some surgeons tattoo liplines by inserting a red pigment along the vermilion border, but it can look disastrously false. A simple lip pencil will do the job as effectively. Because it contains less oil and stiffer waxes, such as carnauba wax, which have a higher melting-point, it acts as a barrier to the softer, more slippery waxes used in lipsticks proper and prevents them from wandering upward. But it must be allowed to function as a barrier by containing the chosen color: too many women undo the effect by rolling their lipsticks over the line they have just drawn.

The formulation of the lipstick is critical for both staying power and staying-where-you-put-it power. As a rule, the more easily a product glides on, and the better the sheen, the more oil it contains and the shorter the wear time. More oil also makes a lipstick much more likely to slip into the lines, where infuriatingly it then displays very much longer staying power. The formulations are changing, however. A new generation of lipsticks has been cleverly developed to remoisturize and recolor every time the lips come together. Color and conditioners are encapsulated in a web which breaks when pressure is applied; once lipsmacking stops, the web reforms (examples include Lancôme Rouge Absolu, Avon Color Release Long-Wearing Lipstick, Lauder Perfect Lipstick).

To encourage lipcolor to stay where you want, make sure your lips are in the best possible condition. Use a specially formulated cream (such as Orlane B21 Lip Line Reducing Cream) twice a day. You may find that the application of a lip sealant (such as Coty Stop It! or Elizabeth Arden Lip Fix) prevents the color from bleeding and encourages the lipstick to stay in place; allow the sealant to dry before adding the color. To keep the lipstick on the mouth and off the teeth and to set the finished look, take a tip from the experts: place a one-ply tissue over the mouth, make a V with your fingers at the sides to hold it in place, and brush a sweep of powder over the top.

Lip color can also be prolonged by rubbing the first coat well onto the lip skin with the finger and creating a stain. Kevyn Aucoin suggests two further alternatives. The first: buy a much darker, bolder lipstick than you would normally do (but the same tone as your favorite); put lots and lots on, give it ten minutes to settle, and then, taking a tissue, blot and blot and keep on blotting until nothing is left but the stain. Putting a transparent slick on top to give shine (confine this to the middle of the mouth only, keeping well away from the treacherous margin) will ensure color and shine and no bleeding. Another way of getting both shine *and* wear is to line the lips and also fill in with the crayon (nothing, but nothing, will shift this), then cover with a creamier lipstick in a toning color, keeping well inside the lipline. Use a lipbrush rather than applying color straight from the applicator. The shape of the lipstick soon smudges with wear, giving an imprecise line.

STYLE

"FASHION is general; style is individual. Some people have it, some haven't," declaimed Edna Woolman Chase, the redoubtable editor-in-chief of American *Vogue* from 1914 to 1952. Some would add that if you haven't got it at 40 you never will; that you are born with a good eye or not at all, rather as you are born with or without a musical ear. But just as the ear can be made more musical, so the eye can also be trained. We all know women who take fully two decades to arrive at their own sense of style, and look a million times better at 40 or 50 than they ever did at 20. At its best, grown-up is glamorous in a way that youth cannot match. Think of Jackie Onassis, still fabulous in the look she made her own 30 years ago; the modernist architects' pin-up and French interior designer, Andrée Putman, breaking every rule in her mid-60s in clingtight Alaïa and sky-high heels; Paloma Picasso in uncompromising black and *that* red; Yoko Ono in her unstructured layers. Impossible to imagine them any other way. Take away royalty and you realize that the best-dressed list features almost exclusively women over the age of 35.

The woman who has learned how to make fashion work for her has a confidence that can make these mid-decades, quite literally, a "certain age." While younger women flirt with every change of fashion coming off the catwalks of New York, Milan, Paris, or London, the grown woman is no chameleon. Having developed her eye for style and quality, cut and color, she knows what looks good on her and has the confidence to carry it off. As the years pass, many women come into a new enjoyment of what fashion has to offer *them*. They revel in wearing fabulous lingerie next to the skin, know the pleasure of slipping into the beautifully cut dress that does their figure such favors, enjoy the fall and the feel of silk or linen or cashmere, appreciate the superior look of velvet, leather, suede, and beautifully woven tweeds. Anna Wintour, editor-in-chief of American *Vogue*, sums it up for women of her generation: "I think the point is that after a woman has worn good clothes for a period of time, she can develop a great style that has got to be fun for her and a treat to the eye of all who come to know her."

THE POWER IN DRESSING

While much of the pleasure in dressing may be private ("The aging woman who wears a diamond necklace on a picnic," states Germaine Greer, "is pleasing only herself") there is a wider audience out there. Like it or not, clothes do more than cover one's nakedness. The woman who makes her appearance a priority (not *the* priority) and feels good about the result, advertises her self-esteem, and encourages others to hold her in equally high regard. She doesn't have to power-dress in slay-'em-dead shoulder pads to make her impact, but she must recognize the power *in* dressing. The importance of the first impression, fairly or unfairly forged in the first few *seconds* of any encounter, may dawn only after three or four decades.

Just as the girl dresses to draw attention to her curves, so the grown woman finds that the crisp Chanel jacket or the understated Jean Muir dress that cost half a king's ransom justifies the expense many times over when worn to equally deliberate effect. "When I wear that jacket I can feel the bullets flying off me . . ." said one woman who has come gloriously and colorfully into her own style at 40 after spending her early adult years as a shrinking beige.

For every woman who discovers the power in dressing, several never quite manage to negotiate the yawning gap between girl and grown-up. Some stay girlishly "young" well beyond their season while others become needlessly frumpy, taking refuge in the dowdy uniform of middle age: the dirndl, the tweeds, the track suit, the shapeless pair of jeans, the ubiquitous A-line skirt and sweater in insipid pastels and safe neutrals. This monotony of habit, in both senses of the word, must be distinguished from the stylish singularity of such women as Diana Vreeland. Editor-in-chief of American *Vogue* from 1963 to 1971, she had an entire wardrobe of identical black turtlenecks which she wore nearly without a break for 20 years, and had the same pair of shoes custom-copied by the same shoemaker because she simply couldn't find better. The addition of original jewelry and distinctive makeup made the whole inimitable.

> **I**f you feel stuck in a fashion rut, reappraise your shape and style. Borrow another eye: that of a ruthlessly honest friend, whose way of dressing you admire, or a genuinely helpful saleswoman. (Some top department stores have an executive shopping service for the purpose of guiding prospective customers.) When trying on clothes, keep both an open mind *and* the casting vote: do not be lulled into a willing suspension of disbelief if the outfit looks terrible and the salesperson is working hard (for her commission) to persuade you otherwise.

For those without such style, the passing years demand a rethink. The old has been outgrown and the new appears elusively out of reach. Often it's not as simple as trying on something else when shopping. It's a question of graduating to new stores, different fabrics, a new sense of proportion. It means developing an eye for quality, reconsidering colors as the pigment fades from skin and hair, and adding as much as another zero to the price of an outfit. Naturally, this can seem threateningly expensive and very perplexing.

"As in all rites of passage, mistakes are inevitable as we grope towards a changed image," wrote Lesley Cunliffe in a piece for British *Vogue* in which she compared the midlife style crisis to the great identity upheaval of adolescence. "We

Anna Harvey, deputy editor of British *Vogue*, in characteristically pared-down style. In common with other formidably well dressed women, she edits her wardrobe ruthlessly twice a year and evicts anything, with the exception of evening wear, that has not had an outing in the last two years.

For most of this century, age had its own wardrobe. In the '50s, British *Vogue* even supplied its own model to show it off: "Mrs Exeter" (in reality, the model Margot Smiley) became synonymous with older style. Here, photographed at the cocktail hr)r in October 1957, she wears a decorous version of the little black dress (arms covered, neckline stopping well short of décolletage, buttons strategically placed to slim the torso). She sets it off with "the topical, exciting fashion-boost of a hat made in deep fuchsia satin and feathers (realizing that fuchsia is a wonderful no-age-tag colour) plus a pearl rope, and a black suede bag . . ."

aren't quite who we have been used to being. We look different – we hardly recognize ourselves as the person with whom we have lived on such intimate terms for so long. We are living in a different body. How to clothe it? How to inhabit it?" Taking her cue from Alison Lurie's classic work, *The Language of Clothes*, Cunliffe described the crisis in terms of a transition to a new fashion vocabulary. "The wardrobe of a woman *d'une certaine age* will inevitably contain words and phrases which are no longer appropriate, just as she may be captivated by certain trendy expressions (which she has finally latched on to just as they have become outdated). She should discard the first and not be tempted by the latter."

The woman in her mid-decades unquestionably wants to dress eloquently, but often she can't seem to summon the right words let alone find her own voice. She can dress down brilliantly (casual clothes are easy to get right – the rules have relaxed and there are any number of eminently wearable, easy, unstructured options), but dressing up, as she is increasingly expected to do, is a different matter.

"We grew up in jeans and sneakers, comfort clothes," observed the designer Donna Karan speaking for her generation in American *Vogue*. "That other look is not for us. I'm a naturalist at heart, but I'm at the age when I need a little help." Like Karan, the woman in a midlife clothes crisis is not comfortable with the overdone trussed-up chicken look. But at the same time, the old warning about mutton dressing as lamb rings in her head. Not for the first time she wonders how mutton is *meant* to dress. What does mutton wear? How short are its skirts, how bright its colors, how body-skimming its cut? She finds few ready answers. Even in the top echelons of fashion, where you would expect a sense of style and proportion to arrive intravenously as part of the job, women of 40-something have been heard agonizing about whether it's okay to wear flares, how high they can hike up their hemlines, and how see-through their blouses can be. These days, the increasingly fine line between the appropriate and the inappropriate is one that all women are expected to arrive at by osmosis.

Some fashion commentators airily assure us (wrongly) that there are no rules, that "anything goes," just as egalitarian spirits insist we not only are all born equal but stay equal. Like race and gender, they affirm, age is no bar. Anyone can learn anything, do anything, wear anything. Well, of course, they *can*. But any woman possessed of a shred of judgment knows that now that all the rules have been blown away there is more room than there ever was for the visual *faux pas*.

It was all easier, if half as much fun, when one only had to follow the rules. For most of this century, age had its own wardrobe. Throughout the 1950s, British *Vogue* actually made over part of the magazine to late middle age. Every second month, Mrs. Exeter, "our heroine of 50-odd" (in real life, the model Margot Smiley, who was only in her late 30s) paraded the clothes befitting her generation. Stylish, classic, and impeccably cut, they took her to luncheon parties and weddings, private views and exhibitions, hunt balls, and the opera. Mrs. Exeter held tremendous sway. Younger women took comfort that there was a stylish future ahead of them. Older women, identifying with her, assembled themselves in accordance with what they saw on the pages. After all, Mrs. Exeter shared their limited budget and 33-inch waist. Sensible of her influence, she picked out high-waisted girdles that flattened the abdomen and smoothed the hips, and modeled the more sedate styles thought fitting to her generation: long tunics and skirts tactfully pleated at the front to hide the tummy that could no longer be held in on its own.

STUCK IN A TIME WARP

As Mrs. Exeter knew full well, the illusion that dressing "young" keeps one young is a snare and a delusion. Her own scrupulous attention to detail was light-years away from those who strive so hard and so unsuccessfully for youthful looks and end up stuck in a time warp. Simone de Beauvoir, writing at around the time when Mrs. Exeter made her first appearance on the pages of *Vogue*, painted a frightening picture of 50-somethings who, panicked by the passage of time, launch themselves into a second girlhood that is in every sense vain.

> One and all, they declare they never felt so young. They want to persuade others that the passage of time has never really touched them; they begin to "dress young"; they assume childish airs. The aging woman . . . tries to disown her independence; she exaggerates her femininity, she adorns herself, she uses perfume, she makes herself all charm, all grace, pure immanence. She babbles to men in a childish voice and with naive glances of admiration, and she chatters on about when she was a little girl; she chirps instead of talking.[1]

We can all think of several contemporary women who cross that fine line between looking modishly smart and being a figure of fun – sporting a look that's too trendy or clinging to a "youthful" style of dressing that, often itself out of date, is curiously time-warping. According to Anna Wintour, "Nothing is sadder or more frightening than seeing a woman of the more interesting age in clothes too girlish or revealing. It makes her appear as if she is out of touch with herself. And she is." Lesley Cunliffe, writing for British *Vogue*, put it more brutally:

> To cling pathetically to the style of one's youth is a sign of dementia. I recently saw a woman in perfect '60s Little Girl dress – complete with long, thick blonde plaits ending in bows – little strapped shoes, tiny handbag, pink gingham mini. According to the current mode, she was right on target. The only problem was that she had obviously had the entire get-up since 1964, when it must, indeed, have looked charming. Wearing it nearly 30 years later, she looked like someone on day release.

Keeping current, paying some attention to fashion while not being enslaved by it, is what keeps a woman looking contemporary and modern *at any age*. For sure, it means having the discrimination to pass up some looks, but, as the wilder reaches of fashion are relinquished – the clanking costume jewelry, heavy platform soles, flirty skirts, dangling shirt tails, and lingerie as outerwear – new possibilities open up. As one gets more practiced at reading fashion, so one develops a better eye. Absorbing what is happening on the catwalks of the world's fashion capitals by reading magazines and newspapers and studying the advertisements of the designers, one can incorporate the essence of the new into one's own scheme of things. Fashion-literate women of 30-plus have the judgment and experience to make the critical distinction between the *directional* – the wildly creative looks seen on the catwalks of Paris or Milan that make the papers next morning – and the *wearable* that emerges out of it.

Just as "young" is not the plus adjective that it's so often made out to be, so "feminine" is equally suspect. Women who stick with broderie anglaise, puff sleeves, pussy cat bows, ruffles, and ribbons under the misconception that frills and frippery are necessary compensation for the precipitous drop in female hormone as they near menopause would do well to remember that the Peter Pan collar takes its name from a boy who refused to grow up. (It is the same subconscious motive that induces women to keep their hair long when shorter and sharper would look infinitely better.) At this age, classic is a better guide than "young," soft and fluid better watchwords than "feminine," simple and easy better than complicated and fussy. Dresses that drape deliciously about the person, sweaters that are loose and flowing, comfortable pants in marvelous natural fabrics look stylish and modern at any age.

Work out where you spend most time, and buy for the life you lead. Many women find it hard to break the habit of buying clothes for the lifestyle they used to have. The result: wardrobes stuffed with smart-occasion clothes and no place to go, or vice versa.

Remember, too, that what isn't in fashion doesn't go out. The classic jacket, the jeans, the jodhpurs, the big white shirt, the cashmere woolens, the wonderful leather belts, the wrap wool coat, the trench . . . These hardly change from season to season, and are worth buying in the best quality you can afford. More ephemeral, throwaway, fashion-tied looks (examples in the last few years might be sarongs, cut-away tops, animal-print leggings, flared pants) can be cheaper.

BODY CONSCIOUSNESS

As the fabric alters, so should the proportion. All women have a shape that they dress around – whether it's wide shoulders, long legs, or a handspan waist and curvy hips and bosom. As shape changes, so too should the cut. Mrs. Exeter knew that. "No, this is *not* for me," she says, shaking her head a touch sadly as she holds up a tightly belted little Balenciaga number. "It's for my granddaughter, and the size of her waist does come as a rather sobering reminder of the – well, *mature* size of my own. But I made peace with my figure some years ago, so it doesn't disturb my plans at all." Unity Barnes, the fashion editor responsible for the Mrs. Exeter pages in *Vogue* throughout her reign, remembers tracking down every outfit they planned to feature in order to ensure it was available in larger sizes. "Everything I chose went up to reasonably large sizes. It had to . . . to appear on the pages."

These days women who have honed their bodies into marvelous shape with the twin disciplines of diet and exercising have no need of corsetry, and are damned if they are going to take a larger size. Ever. They want to show off their well-worked-out bodies. Their motto is, "If you've got it, flaunt it." The prevailing doctrine that anyone can wear anything, provided that they've got the shape for it, is certainly aspirational, since shape can always be changed, or so we are led to believe, whereas age cannot. But while a few looks *are* determined solely by shape – jeans and pencil-slim pants are good examples – others are the exclusive province of the young, however much one's figure may be equal to them. Microskirts slashed to mid-thigh, bathing suits cut as high as the navel at the hips, and bicycling shorts that draw the eye magnetically to the crotch are three.

Of course not all women of 40, or even 20 for that matter, are in wonderful shape. Many women whose bodies have seen slimmer days have wardrobes crammed full of outfits of every size and shape. Like an archeological excavation, the layers, vertical rather than horizontal, bear witness to fashions that went in and out and a body that went in and out with them. Loath to throw the smaller sizes away, the numbers become totems of the way they were (and, often, what they hope to return to). For such women, moving up a size or three and reconciling themselves to the fact that they will never again slide into the size eight jeans can seem like the final submission in the desperate race against time, when in fact it is the start of sanity, and a wardrobe that works. Women who stick grimly through thick and not-so-thin with the size they used to be are condemning themselves to a wardrobe that not only leaves red welts around the waist at the end of the day, but that looks terrible too. Tight seams, straining cloth, and gaping buttonholes always *emphasize* the extra, looking for all the world, as P. G. Wodehouse described one of his heroines, "as if she had been poured into her clothes and had forgotten to say 'when'."

As women who frequent certain fashion designers know full well, clever dressing can do much to give one's body more pleasing proportions, eliminating unwanted contours and adding curves – playing up the good and down the bad. Yet one consultant makes the point that many women dress in a way that emphasizes their *worst* points: the too small shirt straining over the big bosom, the brief hemline cutting across the wobbly thigh, the frills and flounces "disguising" a short neck.

Donna Karan, female designer with an instinctive understanding of the way that women need to feel, above all, slim, uses new fabric technology, such as woolen Lycra, to accentuate the natural curves of the female body while smoothing out the bulges that women feel happier without. "I watched my mother wriggle into her corset," she told Suzy Menkes of the *International Herald Tribune*, "and I do the same with Lycra. All women feel insecure about clothes. All women have hips." Rumored to design naked in front of a mirror, she has turned her own imperfections and insecurities to every woman's advantage. "I'm in front of that mirror all the time, looking at my body and the clothes on me," she explained to Sally Brampton in

Vogue. "That way I find what works and what doesn't. I don't have a perfect body. Who does?" As with many of the designers listed on page 115, trying on Karan's clothes can be a closet encounter of the most agreeable kind. Since mass-market clothes tend to be skimpily cut, while designer clothes are more generously proportioned, women who make the jump from Benetton and Gap to designer ready-to-wear labels may enjoy the illusion of remaining a size ten while being able to breathe out in comfort.

Cleverly chosen clothes can elongate and slenderize the body, drawing attention away from the not-so-good to the better. Let fashion flatter your body.

• Experiment with different proportions – lengths of jacket in relation to a skirt, for example, or dimensions of a coat. If you take a bigger size than average, tailored well-cut clothes look a lot better than loose layers.

• Wearing shoes and stockings (best in sheer or opaque shades) and even skirts, too, of similar color can add inches to the apparent length of your legs, especially if the chosen color is dark. Drama and interest can then be added above the hips or waist. A higher heel can add an illusion of length.

• Lengths vary from season to season, but as a general rule skirts, pants, shorts, and leggings should end at a narrow point on the leg – just below the calf, for example, rather than bang on it – so drawing the eye to a thinner rather than a thicker area.

• Keep shapes simple and uncomplicated; ditto colors and patterns. Remember that dark colors draw the eye away and light colors highlight, as do matte and shiny fabrics.

• If you are going to be baring your body, go for the neck and chest or *embonpoint* (a Donna Karan tip, this), an area which nearly always looks better on well-covered women than skinny ones.

THE WELL-ORDERED WARDROBE

Women who don't (yet) have much style can gain a lot from watching those women who have it in abundance. They will note that, virtually without exception, well-dressed women have well-ordered wardrobes. Their clothes sit comfortably on good hangers, not the metal type that could double as car radio aerials. They are unstained, their buttons, hooks, and zippers are all in place and they are subjected to regular ruthless scrutiny. The unworn are discarded on the grounds that they don't fit, they look shabby, or they have simply outstayed their welcome in the wardrobe. "Once I'm over something I want it *right out* of my wardrobe," says Anna Wintour firmly. "I give it away immediately."

In wardrobes of the well-dressed woman, everything hangs for a purpose; nothing hangs around. Not for her a rail of clothes unworn for half a decade. The season, the size, the style are all current. No woman is immune from making mistakes, but her mistakes do not sit there reproaching her.

Clothes need to come out of the closet. The discipline of taking everything out and sorting through at least once a season is where the editing starts. If you follow the advice of one leading fashion consultant you will also notice how your clothes look when heaped up on a bed or the floor (or even when tumbled together in the laundry basket) since the random coupling may spark new connections that had never occurred to you before. As well as engendering new ideas, a biannual shake-out can actually *eliminate* a lot of unnecessary buying, as old, forgotten, near invisible outfits reclaim your attention – do you really *need* a fifteenth big white shirt? Another navy jacket? As old items come to the forefront of your consciousness, so the wearable options expand. Careful analysis of what you have, and what you haven't, can also point up the gaps.

At least once a season, pare down your wardrobe. Take everything out, and consider selling or giving away anything you haven't worn for two years. Check everything is clean and mended and then rehang your clothes on good hangers, making sure everything is on view; it will all instantly look more appetizing. Separate the halves of suits so that jackets, skirts, pants present themselves – visibly – as separate options.

SPENDING MORE ON LESS

Disciplined shopping is a quality possessed by many (but not all) better-dressed women. We are all swept away by impulse from time to time, and the results can sometimes be the best buys of all time, but limiting yourself to a few good items each season – a great jacket or a pair of beautifully cut pants, for example – is the surer way to a better wardrobe, especially if your own looks unredeemably tatty. One fashion editor advises counting how many things you will be able to match a prospective purchase to and, if it's less than three, leaving it in the fitting room – unless it's truly wonderful and justifies buying more to go with it.

The idea of the capsule wardrobe – namely, a small, considered collection of clothes centering on a jacket and including a skirt, pants, sweater, white shirt, coat, raincoat, and accessories such as shoes and belts, all of which can be worn *inter alia*, need minimal updating, and can be worn until they fall apart – is extremely helpful. Donna Karan sums them up as her five or seven "easy pieces" and includes them in every "Essentials" collection she produces.

As the old makes way for the new, the principle is to spend more (often a good deal more) on less. Often women do have more to spend as they get older, and have acquired the time and taste to buy things that are beautiful: a silk T-shirt instead of a cotton one, cashmere in place of lambswool, a one-off hand knit, an immaculately cut jacket, authentic amulets instead of endless kitsch. The cotton T-shirts can still come from Gap and the white tennis shoes from sports stores. But it gets harder to get away with nothing but cheap clothes as one gets older. Some part of each outfit, with the exception of the most casual, should either be immaculately cut or be made in a delectable fabric. "In youth almost any sort of frock can slip over a pretty young head and look appropriate. The older woman must not hope to be clothed in bargains," declared American *Vogue* in April 1924 in a piece entitled "Odds Against Chic in Middle Age." Spending large sums of money on a few classic outfits does not come easily to many women, however, who, while quite happy to invest huge sums in their children and their house, come to regard spending any amount of money on themselves as immoral.

Surrendering her eye for quality, if indeed she ever had it, such a woman espouses the virtues of make-do and mend, has her dressmaker run things up for a fraction of the cost – and looks like it. As she accumulates more and more, worse and worse, keeping it long past its wear-by-date, she looks at her cramful wardrobe and wails, "But I don't have a thing to wear!" Be warned. She may have given up, she may have sold out. But she doesn't have to be you.

Department stores bring together collections of many different designers' clothes under one roof. Designer discount stores stock end-of-line and last-season items often at hefty discounts. Labels that are particularly worth exploring include:

AFFORDABLE: Alexon, Aquascutum, Liz Claiborne (easy, casual, lots of choice), Norma Kamali, Jaeger, The Gap

MIDDLE MARKET: Nicole Farhi (loose, comfortable, unstructured), MaxMara (wonderful coats and jackets), Calvin Klein (elegant, classic daywear), Kenzo, Myrène de Premonville (smart, fitted day and evening wear); all the so-called "diffusion" (i.e. more moderately priced) lines of the top international designers – Ralph Lauren Roughwear (good-quality denims, cottons, linen), Donna Karan DKNY, Issey Miyake's Plantation, Kors by Michael Kors, Emporio Armani and Mani, KL by Karl Lagerfeld, State of Claude Montana

EXPENSIVE: Giorgio Armani (classic, easy, fluid clothes), Bill Blass (smart urban and evening wear, luxurious fabrics), Jean Muir (wonderful wool dresses), Sonia Rykiel (woolens and crepe suits), Jil Sander (structured daywear, suits), Catherine Walker at The Chelsea Design Company (tailored, beautifully cut day and evening wear), Jasper Conran (smart, wearable clothes), Geoffrey Beene (chic urban daywear), Betty Jackson (workable, wearable shapes and patterns), Isaac Mizrahi (understated, relaxed styles, beautiful fabrics, fine detailing), Donna Karan, Ralph Lauren; Manolo Blahnik and Stephane Kélian (shoes); Renaud Pellegrino (handbags)

ASTRONOMICAL: Chanel, Dior, Christian Lacroix

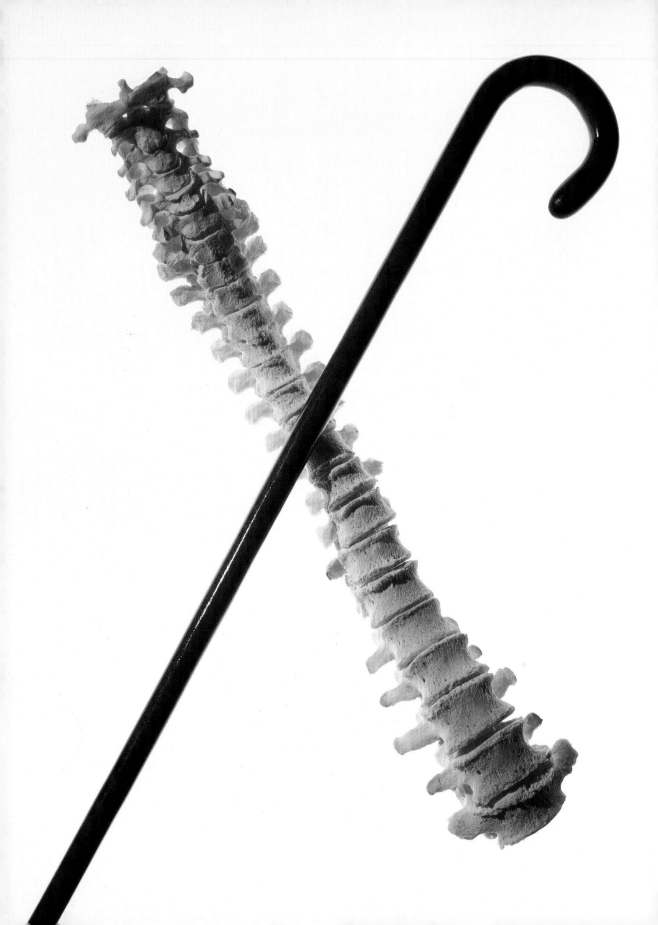

PHYSICALS

TIME takes its toll on every body – albeit invisibly at first. Some say that we start to age from the moment we are born, when we are most lavishly endowed with everything from brain cells to hair follicles, and it is numerically downhill from then on. Happily, however, we can afford to lose more than half of many of the body's cells with no impact on efficiency.

The real aging process becomes measurable from the fourth decade. From the mid-30s, our bones take longer to knit and our wounds to heal, and our organs lose a little of their efficiency with every further decade. Our ability to bounce back from injury, infection, and physical stress takes a knock, as the armies of white cells responsible for fighting invaders disband. As censorship of mismade cells becomes less sharp, the likelihood of developing a malignancy creeps up. Crossculturally, graphs for nearly all cancers show a steadily rising curve from the 40s on.

The scenario sounds depressing but it needn't be. In many cases, the slowdown can be forestalled by a lifestyle that spares the system so that it isn't loaded with more than it can take. Screening, and self-awareness, can bring still-treatable problems to light that might become health- or life-threatening later. Action points, which can be found in the boxes throughout this section, point the way to proper prevention, maintenance, and care.

To a great extent, we are the lucky generation. Many conditions, from high blood pressure to osteoporosis (thinning of the bones), that used to be attributed to aging and were neglected because they were considered inevitable, are now recognized to be largely preventable. Osteoporosis, for example, can be delayed by a decade or more. But preventive action should begin well before the first fracture. Building up strong, dense bones in our 30s and 40s through a well-balanced diet and a certain amount of athletic activity gives us a head start, which we can then build on by making wise choices about hormone replacement at menopause.

The message is that we can forget about being graceful about it. Aging does not have to be a one-way process of decreasing vitality, diminishing health, and fading looks. Where previous generations might have resigned themselves to a gradual loss of mobility and vitality, stoically bearing the "inevitable" aches, pains, and inconveniences of midlife and later, we can if we wish have it otherwise. The traditional *laissez-faire* attitude is way out of date. In the 1990s, women want to remain well-informed and in control. That's how they have become accustomed to feeling about every area of their lives – from managing their

With up-to-the-minute information, and the readiness to make the most of it, modern women are perfectly positioned to benefit from the new, rapidly changing technology of screening. If state-of-the-art scans reveal bones that are more fragile than expected, for example, taking appropriate action at the menopause will reinforce the strength of the spine, so rendering the walking stick redundant and keeping a woman walking (and running and jumping) unaided well into later life.

own finances to confronting tough contraceptive conundrums or the multitude of different childbirth options. Aging, as they see it, is no different.

Information, as ever, is power; it enables us to know what must be accepted, and allowed for, and what should not be written off as one of later life's inevitables and can be helped. Information also gives us the confidence to seek and get a second opinion and to insist on referral to a specialist when appropriate. And there is no doubt that, when illness does strike, the more a woman knows about the health-care options open to her, the more likely she is to get the best treatment available.

Some changes in physical health are inevitable as the years pass. Yet the popular assumption that after 50 or 60 good years, all that remains is a one-way journey to decrepitude is mistaken. When put to the test, even octogenarians emerge as much more spry than they're generally given credit for. When researchers recently asked a group of healthy women in their early 80s to rise from a chair with their arms folded, and then timed them, how long do you think it took them? A minute? 30 seconds? Nine out of ten achieved it in *less than two seconds*.

Aches, pains, malfunctions, and memory lapses are not the "inevitable" corollaries of older age. Often, they are either treatable or caused by medication given for some other problem and are entirely reversible. While medicines can help preserve the quality of later life, they can provoke complications often written off as the effects of age itself. Anti-hypertensive drugs can lead to dizziness, faintness, and falls; sleeping pills and tranquilizers can muddy mental clarity and lead to frightening memory lapses; high doses of aspirin can interfere with hearing.

In later life, the drugs of habituation are less likely to be of the illegal cocaine and cannabis variety and more likely to be prescription drugs. Women are the more medicated sex through life, but the number of medicines taken increases exponentially after age 65. A survey recently revealed that most Americans over the age of 65 use more than five medications, and ten per cent use more than 12. As the efficiency of the kidneys and liver, which are responsible for removing drugs from the system, falls off, side-effects become more likely. The best way of reducing the rising number of adverse drug reactions would come from doctors questioning the need for drugs and stopping all unnecessary medication. But you can – and should – question the medications you are given too. Make sure you are not merely kept on maintenance drugs, with repeat prescriptions replacing face-to-face consultations, and ask that any medication taken for a long-term problem be regularly reviewed. Get written details of any new drug regime you are prescribed, and inquire about side-effects. Notify a new doctor of any drugs you are taking, including those bought over the counter yourself.

B R A I N

THE idea that anyone past the age of 40 is also past their best mentally is one of the enduring myths of the 20th century. And it has a lot to answer for, from agist employment practices that refuse to recruit anyone beyond the first flush of youth to the reluctance of older people to take up any form of further education.

One of the most damning pieces of "evidence" for an age-related decline in intellect came in the early 1900s, when the newly introduced intelligence tests found an ever-steepening downward curve after the tender age of 20. This depressing discovery has had a lasting grip on the popular consciousness and lingers on in the closing years of this century, even though the tests themselves, which were originally designed to predict academic achievement in children, have long since been declared inappropriate. When adults are tested at different points along the lifeline, using tests appropriate to their style of mental function, a surprising stability emerges.

What has become clear is that younger and older adults' mental attributes are different. While young adults have a gift for rapid flights of thought, older ones, processing chunks of information both differently and more efficiently, seem better able to synthesize and integrate what they learn. In his paper "Death and the Mid-Life Crisis" the psychoanalyst Elliott Jaques gives many examples of artists whose work entirely changed its nature in the mid-30s, moving from what he calls hot-out-of-the-fire spontaneous inspiration to a more "sculptured" and considered creativity. Certainly, major scientific and artistic achievements tend to have their own chronology; great mathematicians jump out of the bath in early adulthood, while philosophers, integrating the thoughts of a lifetime, make their most significant contributions in their 60s and 70s.

NEURONES AND NUMBERS

To suppose that an individual peaks intellectually at 20, and declines from then on, is to suppose that intelligence owes everything to physiology, and nothing to the accumulated effects of experience, knowledge, judgment, and practice. The number of cells, or neurones, in the brain does indeed fall off as we get older, and the brain shrinks, so that by the age of 90 it is about four-fifths of its original volume and has plenty of space around it, like a walnut in its shell. Luckily for us, however, it has a "built-in redundancy," and some neurologists even maintain that periodic clear-outs of some of the 1000 billion or so brain cells we are born with may actually be beneficial, since we are losing cells we are probably better off without.

Different bits of the brain age at different rates. Reaction time slows and blood flow to the brain drops slightly as the blood vessels become a little less elastic. The number of synapses – the points of contact between the nerve fibers – also falls by about 15 per cent, slowing the split-second transmission of information a fraction.

But since essential skills remain not only intact, but also well-ingrained with use over the years, our additional experience in organizing material generally makes up for any shortfall in speed.

MID LIFE MEMORY LAPSES

As if one needed reminding of the fact, memory, short-term memory especially, does get blunter with age. At 35, a woman will not be able to recall as much as she could at 25, and at 45 even less. But the sort of memory loss many women find themselves contending with in midlife often has more to do with straight overload than with chronology. The complex lives many women lead in their 30s and 40s, with at least four high-priority must-dos on their mental agendas, can interfere with the laying down of new memories, especially if the next thing is mentally embarked upon before the one before was ticked off. The result is that recall of the simple details of day-to-day life eludes them in a way it never did before, leaving them increasingly dependent on lists and gimmicks to jog the memory. Midlife memory loss, as it is sometimes colloquially called, is especially common among women who have young children. Such women joke among themselves about having left their gray matter behind in the delivery room, but the ensuing cerebral fog is infinitely more likely to be the result of tiredness and distraction than any deficiency in cognitive processing.

Sleep deprivation may also have something to answer for. Researchers have found that the shallower, dozing stages of sleep do not seem to be as restorative as the deeper stages. If individuals are prevented from descending into deep sleep, as can happen as a consequence of having one's nights constantly disrupted by, say, a wakeful baby, they may underperform the next day. Women who suffer miserable menopauses and are assailed by hot flashes and sweats at night, often complain of memory loss and poor mental function. Some even fear they are losing their minds. Though these women are used to having their complaints airily waved aside, there is growing evidence that tiredness can take a toll on memory. Many specialists believe that there is a shift when asleep from short-term memory to long-term memory almost as though the information taken in when awake is processed and sorted in sleep. Lack of the right kind of sleep can cut through mental capabilities the following day.

Be warned that recourse to sleeping pills is not the answer. Ever. Far from inducing sleep – which is an active, positive phase of mental activity – sleeping pills merely induce a state of semi-coma which is almost useless in providing the real rest and unconscious problem-solving that goes on during a good (unmedicated) night's sleep. Even young people demonstrate measurable memory failings in objective tests after a medicated night's sleep. As one gets older and one's body is less able to rid itself of chemicals, sleeping pills are even more likely to compromise waking life.

MEMORY LOSS IN LATER LIFE

The sort of memory loss that is associated with age, and is independent of tiredness and lifestyle overload, becomes apparent much later in life, and even then the fear is overdone. The expectation of mental decline leads a lot of elderly people to take needless fright at memory lapses they would have blithely shrugged off 20 years earlier. Although short-term memory is the commonest cerebral casualty of later life, it doesn't necessarily signal anything sinister. Some researchers have found that the ability of older people to remember the names of those they are introduced to or the items on a shopping list may be as little as half that of a younger person – but this is not necessarily a problem unless you can't remember where you put the list! Although no indication of an ominous slide into senility, such forgetfulness can be frustrating, as Elizabeth Taylor made clear in her valedictory novel, *Mrs. Palfrey at the Claremont*, when the elderly heroine finds yet another name escaping her.

> It was hard work being old. It was like being a baby, in reverse. Every day for an infant means some new little things learned; every day for the old means some little thing lost. Names slip away, dates mean nothing, sequences become muddled, and faces blurred. Both infancy and age are tiring times.[1]

In the United States, Mrs. Palfrey would be said to be suffering Age Associated Memory Impairment (A.A.M.I.), along with well over half her contemporaries. According to American diagnostic criteria, individuals can be said to have this worrying-sounding condition if they are over the age of 50, they have no signs of medical/psychiatric problem, and their subjective complaint of memory loss is backed up by tests showing performance measurably lower than that of the average young adult. British psychiatrists, who have their own less precise label, Benign Senescent Forgetfulness, consider the use of young adults as the "norm" inappropriate since it is well known that memory declines with age, just as vocabulary and wisdom seem to be enhanced. Making a normal event into a disease suffered by a huge proportion of normal elderly people is not only questionable, they say, it ignores the fact that general intellect tends to be preserved with increasing age by alteration of the balance of its components.

A QUESTION OF PERFORMANCE

Increasing numbers of Americans of all ages are now attending "smart bars," where they gulp down cocktails of ginseng, vitamins, and certain amino acids that the brain is known to use, such as carnitine and tyramine, despite no evidence of efficacy. Others, more riskily, are taking experimental drugs in the hopes of boosting their brain power. New compounds still under trial, such as phosphatidylserine and ondansetron – the so-called "smart drugs" – claim to enhance the performance of both brain cells and neurotransmitters (the chemical substances that transfer impulses between brain cells), but a big question mark still hangs over their safety and possible side-effects. Since most are not yet out of research and many have been adequately tested only on *mice*, the U.S. Food and Drug Administration has resolutely refused to countenance their use.

While short-term memory sometimes fails with age, longer-term memories remain unaffected, partly because these are etched more deeply into the brain and partly because the long-term memory stores are differently located. But even short-term amnesia is not inevitable. Some specialists believe that failing memory has as much to do with circumstances as with fading mental faculties, pointing to evidence that independent elderly people recall recent events better than those of a similar age who are institutionalized. When present-day existence becomes drab and unmemorable, who wouldn't take mental refuge in the past?

WARDING OFF DECLINE

Variation, stimulation, and the challenge of learning new things are the best ways of warding off the mental cobwebs. The "use it or lose it" label applies as much to the brain as to any other part of the body. Research confirms that practicing mental and verbal skills keeps them well honed and nearly as good as new: when psychologists took a group of expert crossword-puzzle solvers aged between 45 and 80 and set them a series of puzzles, they found they all performed as well as each other, regardless of age, and did much better than novices of all ages. Animals thrive on stimulation too: in experiments at the University of California, at Berkeley, adult rats that were treated to an enriched, stimulating environment showed a thickening of the cerebral cortex (the part of the brain involved in intellectual processes) at all ages.

While it's often assumed that the mind seizes up after 60, mental deterioration is not an inevitable part of aging in the way that graying hair and loss of near vision are. In fact, most people remain in full possession of their faculties throughout their lives. Surveys show that the old can be good, even quick, learners. When teaching methods are appropriate to their style of learning, which does change with age, septuagenarians pick up languages as quickly as school children, with only pre-school children outperforming both. In one well-known Australian experiment, a class aged from 60 to 90 years learned German from scratch, using the same books and teaching methods as 15-year-olds. After four months, half of them passed an examination normally taken after four years of study.

OTHER FACTORS AFFECTING MENTAL CLARITY

While frightening memory lapses leave many people dreading imminent dementia, too fearful to go to their doctors, such lapses are as likely to be associated with reversible, treatable conditions as with any of the devastating degenerative brain diseases. Severe depression, for example, which is by far the commonest psychiatric problem in older age – way ahead of the degenerative brain diseases that get so much publicity – can closely mimic Alzheimer's disease, even in those as young as 40, causing apathy, inertia, alarming self-neglect, and loss of memory and responsiveness. Depression consistently emerges as the major cause behind people's attendance at memory clinics, especially when still in midlife. It is essential that the depression is recognized, since it is often entirely reversible on properly managed anti-depressant therapy. Certain types of illness, such as thyroid conditions and severe anaemia, can also muddy mental clarity.

The side-effects of drugs are responsible for a lot of confusion and amnesia,

Keep a tally on the drugs you are taking, asking about side-effects when any new drug is prescribed. If you do find memory lapses becoming much more common, consult your doctor. Nobody should take benzodiazepine-type tranquilizers and sleeping pills for more than a few weeks; they accumulate in the body and are prime causes of memory loss and confusion.

especially when several drugs are given at once. All drugs have unwanted side-effects, which tend to become commoner with age, and an enormous number can interfere with memory. Recent studies have shown that drugs that inhibit the action of acetylcholine, a neurotransmitter in the brain, can produce significant memory loss; common offenders include over-the-counter remedies for diarrhoea, nausea, and coughs and several prescription drugs, principal among which are the benzodiazepine family of tranquilizers and sleeping pills.

Of course, brain function can be knocked sideways by degenerative diseases, but these are generally hazards of much later life. Alzheimer's disease and multi-infarct dementia account for about 90 per cent. Both are rare under 65 and affect only about two per cent under 70. They do, however, become more prevalent with age. By 85 one in five is affected and by the early 90s the figure is closer to one in three – which still makes dementia in advanced old age the exception rather than the rule.

VASCULAR DEMENTIA AND STROKE

Vascular, or multi-infarct, dementia is a form of stroke disease, in which the small arteries deep within the brain get blocked by blood clots, usually the result of high blood pressure or diabetes. The result is a series of "micro-strokes" which cause a progressive step-like deterioration of mental function. This may go unnoticed, unlike a major stroke, which, being caused by one big blockage or bleed, has a dramatic effect on mobility, function, and speech.

Although three times as many women suffer a stroke as develop breast cancer, few realize that stroke, unlike breast cancer, is often preventable. Half of all cerebrovascular deaths (those relating to the brain and its blood vessels) under age 70 are said to be avoidable "solely by application of existing knowledge." Keeping very high blood pressure under control (most strokes can be linked to systolic pressures above 160), and learning to live with the side-effects of medication is perhaps most important. Unfortunately, although a rise in blood pressure is common with age, the tendency to assume that it is "normal" and that quite steep rises require less attention in the elderly contributes to the casualty toll. Other preventive measures consist of catching diabetes before it gets a runaway hold on the circulation, stopping smoking, and keeping drinking in check – though a small amount of alcohol appears protective.

Have your blood pressure checked at least every two years, if well within the normal range, and your urine preferably examined at the same time for signs of creeping glucose intolerance. If your blood pressure is known to be borderline-high, or if you have a family history of high blood pressure or diabetes, have it checked more frequently. If, having made the lifestyle attempts to lower pressure detailed on page 369, you are prescribed an anti-hypertensive drug, take it, and if this doesn't control it ask to be referred to a specialist physician.

Diet may be important. There are suggestions that a high daily consumption of fruit and vegetables may protect against stroke and that keeping up one's intake of potassium, found in abundance in many fruits, such as oranges and bananas, may have a protective effect above and beyond its lowering tendency on blood pressure. Although these findings are preliminary, they constitute yet another good reason for overhauling your diet in a healthier direction (see Eating chapter). A glass (or two at most) of wine at night has also been linked with a lower risk of stroke.

ALZHEIMER'S DISEASE

The short-term memory loss that accompanies Alzheimer's disease is dramatic and progressive. Unpreventable, untreatable, and unstoppable, the disease initially causes losses of recent memory. Gradually the loss of memory worsens as it attacks the cells in the cerebral cortex, the province of thought, language, and learned movement. The result is increasingly bizarre behavior, more radical memory loss and, tragically, the loss of those qualities that make others want to care: humour, kindness, special interests, skills, or talents. Eventually loss of control of the muscles follows, along with incontinence, paralysis, inability to speak or, in the final stages, even to swallow. The disease was described by one awestruck neurologist as "a dismantling of the human being, starting at the most organized and complex point and proceeding with the failure of the central nervous system components." Its course is relentlessly downhill, and the earlier it sets in, the steeper the slope.

For the moment nothing can be done to prevent this catastrophe, since its causes are still unknown. Suspects include slow-viruses (which, one psychiatrist admitted, "terrifies pathologists who have cut up more brains than is good for them"), environmental contaminants, rogue genes, even a propensity for picking one's nose! The presence of aluminum at the center of the abnormal plaques and tangles is also causing great interest, but the link to environmental contamination is unclear.

In 1990, a rogue gene on chromosome 21 was identified as being responsible for the very aggressive early onset of the disease – which accounts for about ten per cent of cases. In late 1993, a further genetic link was found by researchers at Duke University, North Carolina, this time to the more common, late-onset type of the disease. While every relative of an Alzheimer's sufferer lives in dread of being similarly struck, the risk is most likely to be raised in families where several members have had the disease, especially if onset was early. Although reliable genetic tests are available for such individuals, they are not widely advertised since nothing can be done even if the gene is identified. The rationale of screening will become compelling, however, once effective treatments have been developed that can be given before the brain is half-destroyed.

Positron Emission Tomography (PET) scans provide a window through which the brain can be watched in action. Minute doses of a radioactive chemical are injected into the bloodstream, where they bind to glucose molecules. Since brain cells increase their uptake of glucose as they become more active, particular areas can be seen to light up during different kinds of mental activity. In this series, RIGHT, red and yellow correspond to high metabolic activity and blue to least activity. Counter to the common misconception that advancing age lowers intelligence, PET scans show no perceptible fall-off in brainpower over time in healthy individuals.

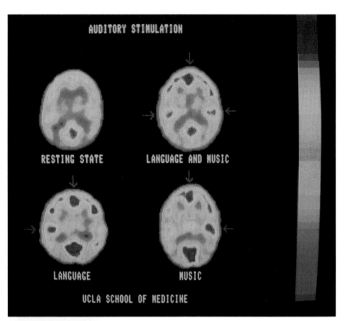

AUDITORY STIMULATION

RESTING STATE   LANGUAGE AND MUSIC

LANGUAGE   MUSIC

UCLA SCHOOL OF MEDICINE

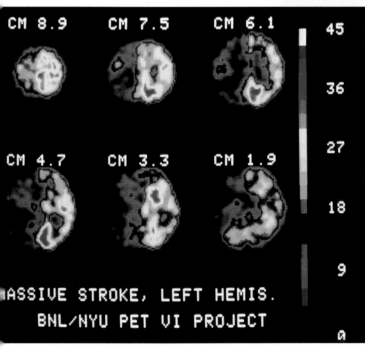

CM 8.9   CM 7.5   CM 6.1   45

36

27

CM 4.7   CM 3.3   CM 1.9

18

9

ASSIVE STROKE, LEFT HEMIS.
BNL/NYU PET VI PROJECT

A

Scans, LEFT, taken following a stroke, show near-complete cerebral wipe-out in the left hemisphere. Like the arteries surrounding the heart, the blood vessels supplying the brain can become dangerously narrowed and so more prone to clots or hemorrhages. This often preventable catastrophe might be averted by following a healthy low-salt diet and keeping a careful watch on blood pressure.

PET image of the brain of an Alzheimer's disease sufferer, RIGHT, showing the typical irreversible slide-off of function. As cells responsible for memory, thought, emotion, and movement become choked by hard proteins, mental activity gets confined to ever fewer areas of the brain.

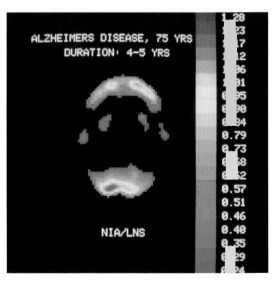

ALZHEIMERS DISEASE, 75 YRS
DURATION: 4-5 YRS

1.28
1.23
1.17
1.12
1.06
1.01
0.95
0.90
0.84
0.79
0.73
0.68
0.62
0.57
0.51
0.46
0.40
0.35
0.29
0.24

NIA/LNS

SENSES

TAKEN for granted until they threaten to desert us, all five senses dim slightly as we get older. During the middle decades of life any fall-off in sensation is so small as to be generally imperceptible, however, with the marked exception of eyesight, which changes for almost everyone in the fifth decade. Hearing, one of the best developed senses at birth, starts to deteriorate from about the age of 30 (earlier if it has been continually exposed to "sonic drugs," such as loud rock music and personal stereos, whose low-pitch stimuli can literally prove deafening), but it may be another three decades before any dulling becomes noticeable.

SMELL, TASTE, AND TOUCH

Other changes are equally subtle. The sense of smell, for example, quietly and progressively becomes less well able to distinguish the subtler nuances. This may explain why some women find their perfume preferences undergoing a sea change in midlife and particularly post-menopause, with previous favorite scents seeming watery and no longer possessed of the richness that originally attracted.

A search for new, more pleasurable essences can often be a joy as one gets older and should take in such heady, longlasting scents as Guerlain's Mitsouko, any of the Lauder scents, Chypre de Coty, Fracas, Chloé, Joy, L'Air du Temps, Madame Rochas, Femme, Ysatis, Bijan, Coriandre, Montana, Yves St Laurent's Paris, or Opium.

As the sense of smell becomes less sharp, so the appreciation of flavor (80 per cent of which is determined by smell) also dulls, with the over-65s rating their sense of taste as about half as sharp as it used to be.

Touch, however, stays central to psychological and physiological well-being throughout life. Of all the senses, it is said to be the first to arrive and the last to leave us. Massage is a particular pleasure at every stage of life. In the United States now, there are literally dozens of different types of massage, ranging from aromatherapy, which uses strong-smelling essential oils said to penetrate the bloodstream with specific therapeutic effect, to shiatsu, which uses fingertips, fists, elbows, knees, and sometimes feet (usually on the back) over traditional acupuncture points, or reflexology, which involves massaging the sole of the foot. Rolfing and other types of connective tissue massage claim to remold the underlying connective tissue and so realign a body that has become out of kilter, by delving about as deep as it's possible to go without a general anesthetic.

In the hands of a sensitive masseur, any massage will help undo knots of tension and give a deep feeling of relaxation. Some are pleasurably energetic and leave one feeling tingly as well as loosened up. More esoteric benefits are contentious. Some promise to stimulate lymphatic drainage – the system which relieves body organs of excess fluid, then dumps the clutter of dead cells and waste in the lymph nodes where it is passed into the bloodstream. Supposedly freeing the body of toxins and shifting fat ("cellulite") into the bargain, such treatments are bound to disappoint. But those promising to re-energize or to boost feelings of well-being are likely to be close to the mark. In one study, chronically anxious individuals who had failed to respond to several different types of medication showed measurable decreases in muscle tension, skin resistance, and heart rate after a course of ten 35-minute deep massage sessions. Subjectively, they reported feeling better too.[1] In a review of seven different forms of massage in British *Vogue*, Catherine Bennett concluded:

> It is for *relaxation*, not the dubious privilege of being reshaped or diagnosed by a medical amateur that one should visit a masseur. It seems only fair that the body should occasionally receive some undivided attention, and anyone who can ease the protective hunch of the shoulders, or assuage one's worries, has a skill worthy of respect.[2]

While the skin never loses its responsiveness to touch, it does lose its exquisite sensitivity to changes in temperature. Old, immobile people are more susceptible to cold because they do not realize that they are becoming dangerously chilled. Where young adults can register changes of about one degree Fahrenheit (half a degree Celsius), older ones may be unable to detect fluctuations many times bigger.

HEARING AND SIGHT
Unfortunately, the two senses we most depend on deteriorate most markedly with age: hearing falls off quite dramatically in later life, particularly in the high frequency range, and some changes in sight are so common as to be virtually universal. Appropriate screening at regular intervals is essential to pick up early losses. Often treatment can be given to avert the catastrophe of losing one's vision. And, while little can be done to undo the high-frequency hearing loss that comes with age, early detection may prevent the isolation that can so quickly encompass those who are no longer able to catch what is being said. As in any other area of health, it pays to be vigilant. Loss of ability to hear or see may be so gradual as to be imperceptible until both are compromised. In addition, because some blunting of the senses is generally believed to be inevitable, people often feel fatalistic about their failing faculties and do not realize they can be helped.

CHANGES IN VISION
As we get older, some changes in vision are almost inevitable. A young lens easily adapts focus between near and far objects, but its elasticity starts to diminish from the tender age of ten. From around the age of 40, most people have the sensation that their arms have become too short: newsprint starts to swim, maps require reading at

From the age of 40, near sight usually becomes noticeably less sharp, but more dramatic losses of vision are generally confined to later life. This series shows how normal sight, LEFT, suffers in the advanced stages of glaucoma, LOWER LEFT, a preventable, often inherited, condition caused by rising pressure inside the eye. The tiny specks of opacity on the lens known as cataract are more common than not after the age of 60. As the lens continues to cloud, sensitivity to light and glare increases and sight becomes blurred, LOWER RIGHT. There are suggestions that high intakes of fruit and vegetables rich in vitamin C may check the course of this condition. The dark patches, BOTTOM LEFT, are typical of damage to the blood supply arising from uncontrolled diabetes. Though it is very common in midlife and later, half of all diabetics are not aware of their condition, to the detriment of their health as well as their sight. Everyone should be conscious of the warning signs (see page 366) and, if any apply, get their blood sugar levels checked out. Loss of central vision is typical of macular degeneration, BOTTOM RIGHT, an age-associated condition caused by breakdown of the circulation supplying the central part of the retina. It can sometimes be arrested in the early stages and, like cataract, may even be preventable if the diet is high in foods containing anti-oxidant vitamins and minerals.

arm's length and the eyes of needles appear teasingly less wide than formerly. By the age of 65, near sight often stabilizes as a result of the formation of cataract, since this tends to nudge sight in the opposite direction.

It is rare to escape wearing glasses altogether. Those amazingly spry octogenarians who have never needed a pair of glasses in their lives generally have one eye that is long-sighted and one eye that is short-sighted and use the first for perceiving distant objects and the second for reading. While this may seem the ultimate chronological gift, it is a mixed genetic blessing as depth perception may suffer, so affecting the ability to judge distance when, say, reversing cars, catching balls or returning a serve at tennis.

As the lens thickens and hardens, light scatters on the retina at the back of the eye, making glare more of a problem and the fluorescent lights in supermarkets and department stores a source of annoyance rather than additional illumination. As the pupil shrinks and allows less light to reach the retina, the eye becomes less well able to see in low light too. It has been estimated that a 60-year-old's eyes need three times as much light to see an object as clearly as a 20-year-old's. Dark backgrounds therefore pose a problem, making the figures on the mandatory matte black hi-fi equipment, and television channel-changers, difficult to decipher.

Never ignore changes in your sight. If you are aware of pain in the eye or blurred or distorted vision, see your doctor, optician, or ophthalmologist. Many degenerative eye diseases have early warning signs and are most treatable at this stage. The big exception is glaucoma, which is never painful or even usually noticeable in the early stages. A simple pressure test, however, can detect it before harm is done. Two-yearly checks for glaucoma are essential for anyone who has a family history of the disease (which multiplies the risk tenfold), and these checks should become at least yearly on reaching the age when the parent or sibling got it. Glaucoma checks should be part of everyone's self-care schedule from the age of 40, and repeated at least every two years. These can be carried out by opticians and can be twinned, where appropriate, with sight tests to check that the glasses prescription is still correct. Checks for early signs of cataract, for macular changes on the retina, and even for diabetes can be carried out at the same time as the tests for glaucoma. People with known diabetes should have annual eye checks.

Nine out of ten people over the age of 65 have some signs of cataract, tiny specks of opacity on the lens, though most are unaware of any problem beyond a small loss of clarity. But as the lens continues to cloud, sight becomes increasingly blurred. By the age of 75, half of the population notices that their vision is markedly less sharp than it used to be – either cataract or macular degeneration is usually to blame (see Alphabeticals). While little can be done for the latter, which causes loss of central vision, treatment for the former is nearly always dramatically successful; it was a cataract operation at 82 that enabled Monet to finish his water-lilies.

Fortunately, most changes in eye health are only too apparent; you only need to act on them. Chronic glaucoma is the exception. Caused by rising pressure inside the eye due to obstruction of normal fluid drainage, it accounts for about ten per cent of blindness in the United States. The pity is, it is preventable.

HEARING LOSS

Changes in hearing are common with age. While just five per cent of people have hearing difficulties at age 50, over the age of 65 more than a quarter have some hearing loss and around one in ten complains, as Beethoven did, of tinnitus, or distracting noises in the head. (This condition can also come on – reversibly – as a result of very heavy aspirin use and may be triggered by syringing the ears.) By 70, the proportion of the population with hearing loss severe enough to benefit from a hearing aid has risen to a third and by 80 it is thought to be half.

The most common form of hearing loss, presbyacusis, follows a predictable pattern, with a gradual, initially imperceptible, fall-off in the ability to hear very high-pitched (high-frequency) notes. This occurs as the hair cells within the snail-shaped cochlea, which help convert sound into nerve impulses, are progressively lost. Since the high-frequency bands cover the upper part of the human voice in most languages, giving it its timbre and tone, it gradually becomes difficult to distinguish pitch, and eventually speech itself, from background noise, such as television and music in restaurants and supermarkets. As hearing worsens, people may notice that they no longer enjoy music in the way they once did, since they can now only pick out the lower-pitched instruments in the orchestra. It also becomes increasingly difficult to pick out the one voice addressing them among the babble of a large group.

The best screening test for presbyacusis is pure-tone audiometry. Any loss can then be compensated for by use of a hearing aid, which selectively amplifies high tones. A hearing aid takes some getting used to: unlike the human ear, which has evolved a blissful selectivity, it amplifies everything within range. Prompted by the prospect of an up-and-coming style-conscious generation, manufacturers are at last investigating cosmetically acceptable devices. Under development: a hearing aid that can be fitted inside a single tooth, tuned to pick up acoustic vibrations and conduct these to the inner ear via orthodontic braces that act like a miniature receiver; and a device said to be hearing's equivalent of the contact lens, which is cleverly smuggled into earrings and necklaces of the individual's choice.

If picking up sounds is becoming difficult, have an audiogram to assess the sharpness of your hearing; the quicker a hearing aid is fitted, and the more residual hearing remains, the less the danger of becoming isolated and cut-off. Signs that indicate a need for assessment are:

- having to ask people to speak up
- other people commenting that the television or radio is turned up too loud
- failing to hear the telephone or doorbell ring
- finding oneself saying "what?" more frequently
- leaning forward and tilting the head to hear better.

B R E A S T S

As we get older, our breasts change both outwardly and inwardly. Their appearance alters partly as a result of birth and breastfeeding, partly thanks to the pull of gravity on the key supporting ligaments, and partly as a result of an inward shift in composition: as hormone levels change in the lead-up to the menopause, a process already underway by the mid-30s, the glandular tissue inside the breast shrinks and is gradually replaced by fat. The visible consequence is a gradual slackening and loss of volume, particularly at the top, as the breast and nipple slide southward.

There are compensations. Women who have been troubled by cyclical changes throughout their fertile years can look forward to blessed respite from soreness, lumpiness, and fluid retention as the post-menopausal breast settles down. The exception is women who take hormone replacement therapy, which may switch the breast cells back on and cause problems to recur with a vengeance. The good news is that, as the breasts become quieter, cysts are much less likely to form, as are benign growths such as fibroadenomas. The bad news, of course, is that where there are changes in the breast, they are more likely to be cancerous.

THE SHADOW OF CANCER

Breast cancer has a unique power to terrify. All women live in dread of finding a lump in their breast. While a woman's lifetime chance of developing a tumor is only about a fifth that of developing heart disease, breast cancer is a growing threat to her health. All the industrialized nations of the world (the United States, Canada, Western Europe, Australia, New Zealand) report increasing numbers of cases. In the United States – where one woman in nine develops breast cancer, the highest incidence in the world – detection rates have been rising at a rate of about three per cent every year since 1976, with a recent dramatic upturn in the last five. And in Britain, which has the highest death rate from the disease in the world, the chance of a woman getting a tumor in her breast has risen from one in 17 to one in 12 in the last ten years, to become the likeliest cause of death in women in their middle years.

THE WOMAN AT RISK

Breast cancer may be common, but its causes still mystify and its patterns elude prediction. Until it is known what changes healthy, law-abiding breast cells into anarchic miscreants, the opportunities for taking preventive action are limited. The traditional picture of the woman at risk (having a close relative with breast cancer, a late menopause, children at a late age, etc.) confuses more than it clarifies, since these classic risk factors fit only one in four women who develop the disease. Between 65 and 75 per cent of women who develop breast cancer have no risk factors other than their sex and their age. Age is important. Women over the age of 65 represent just 14 per cent of the American female population, yet they account for more than half of the breast cancers. The number of new cases diagnosed each year per 100,000 women rises from about 27 at age 30 to 212 at age 50 to 404 at age 70. Although family history plays a part, women with an afflicted relative often overestimate the threat to themselves. According to an analysis in the *Journal of the American Medical Association* in 1993, a woman whose mother or sister developed breast cancer before the age of 45 is around two-and-a-half times more likely to develop it herself than a woman with no such family history. If her mother or sister developed cancer at the age of 55, her risk drops to just over one and a half. If the cancer appeared in a so-called "second-degree" relative such as an aunt, grandmother, or cousin, her risk is thought to be only minimally raised – if at all.

Although over three-quarters of the benign changes found in the breasts (cysts, fibroadenomas, general lumpiness) are innocent, in a small minority of cases a sample of cells taken by biopsy and examined under the microscope can reveal cell changes on the far end of the benign spectrum. This condition, called atypical hyperplasia (also known as epitheliosis or papillomatosis), may increase a woman's risk of eventually getting breast cancer.[1] A history of persistent breast cysts may also slightly raise the risk.

THE ESTROGEN FACTOR

In a sea of uncertainty, the estrogen connection is key. An early start of periods (before age 12) and/or late menopause (after age 55), which expose a woman to greater amounts of the female hormone, are associated with a higher risk, whereas women who have an early menopause or have their ovaries removed in their 30s have a dramatically reduced one (not a recommended course of action since their risk of heart and bone disease also soars).

Although estrogen is not itself a carcinogen (cancer-producing substance), it is a growth-promoting hormone that stimulates cell division. With each division the chance of a mistake resulting in a cancerous change rises and, once tumor cells are present, they may depend on estrogen in order to grow. The additional breast cancer risk on long-term hormone replacement therapy (lasting more than five years), which exposes a woman to more estrogen over her lifetime than she would otherwise get, is thought to be due to the extra hormone encouraging a pre-existing cancer to grow, and points up the importance of having an all-clear mammogram before embarking on therapy (see pages 332–3 for a fuller discussion).

In addition to these risks, having no children or having children "late" in life (after the age of 35) more than doubles the risk of getting breast cancer, when compared with childbearing at the tender age of 19 or 20. Breastfeeding over several pregnancies for several months at a time appears protective in some studies. Some doctors believe that the protection afforded by childbirth at younger ages has been overplayed, however. The oncologist Susan Love, now assistant professor of surgery at UCLA School of Medicine, has criticized the message for being "delivered in a tone that smacks of the attitude that if women stayed home and had babies like they're supposed to, they wouldn't get breast cancer."[2]

Estrogen levels are also raised by certain fat cells in the body. As discussed more fully on pages 90–1, "apple-shaped" fat women (who store their fat around their middles) may have a greater risk than "pear-shaped" fat women (who store their fat on their hips and thighs) although the studies are still somewhat conflicting. This is thought to be due to higher levels of "free" estrogens, typically seen in women with this fat distribution pattern.

Keep your weight within limits; this is particularly important post-menopause. Watch your waist-to-hip ratio (see page 91) and if fat starts gravitating to the center of the body, make concerted efforts to take it off, without crash dieting.

Research at the University of Pittsburgh suggests that post-menopausal women who drink modestly may raise their estrogen levels, perhaps because alcohol helps convert the male hormone, androgen, which is naturally present in women as well as men, into estradiol, a form of estrogen. In other words, women who enjoy a couple of glasses of wine a night may be paying for a reduced risk of heart attack and stroke with an increased risk of developing breast tumors. Find out more about this controversial connection on pages 249–50.

THE FAT FACTOR
Researchers have known for half a century that high-fat diets promote mammary tumors in laboratory animals and that a country's rate of breast cancer correlates closely with the amount of fat in the diet. Japanese women, for example, suffer a quarter of the breast cancers that afflict American and British women and eat a quarter of the dietary fat (11 per cent). As Japanese eating patterns change, however, and hamburgers and Western fast food take off, the breast cancer rate is starting to rise – as are heart attacks and cancer of the colon.

A high-fat diet is thought to provide the conditions in which abnormal cells flourish. The fat-in the-diet connection fell down somewhat, however, in the biggest survey to date, the U.S. Nurses' Health Study, which failed to find any clear link between fat intake and breast cancer, possibly because virtually all 90,000 women in the trial had relatively high-fat diets, at 32 per cent and upward of total intake;[3] three other, smaller studies, however, did find a link between breast cancer and dietary fat. Some epidemiologists argue that, to lower their risk, women should restrict animal fats to between 20 and 25 per cent of total caloric intake – a goal that demands a high degree of discipline on a Western-style diet. Although the evidence at the moment is not strong enough to recommend that all women rigorously overhaul their lifestyles purely on the grounds of protecting themselves from breast cancer, reducing dietary fat would also keep weight steady and the risk of diabetes and high blood pressure down, while probably helping to protect against heart disease and cancer of the colon.

It may be just as helpful, however, to eat more fruit and vegetables, together with natural sources of vitamin E (such as blackberries, asparagus, tuna in oil, avocado, and nuts). When one study measured women's vitamin E levels and divided them into five groups, women in the lowest group were found to have five times the number of breast cancers of those in the highest. In Singapore, meanwhile, breast cancer has been found to be less common in women eating beta-carotene-rich foods (orange/yellow fruits and vegetables, and dark green leafy vegetables, such as apricots, broccoli, carrots, cantaloupe melon, pumpkin, spinach, sweet potatoes, watercress) and soya, which appears to have the capacity to alter the "estrogenic pattern." Cruciferous vegetables (bok choy, broccoli, Brussels sprouts, cabbage, cauliflower, kohlrabi, turnips, rutabagas) have nitrogen-containing compounds called indoles, which also seem capable of converting active estrogen into an inactive type.

Faced with the threat of breast cancer, most thinking women want to know what they can do to protect themselves against it. The answer to date is a limited amount. The case against fat and alcohol remains inconclusive and, if there is an association, it may be that it will only be a very low-fat diet and teetotal life that afford any protection.

It may also be that good behavior in middle age comes too late to make much difference, and that the key period is in adolescence, when the breast tissue is developing and is most hormonally sensitive. Certainly this is when exposure to the contraceptive pill seems significant, and the same may be true of alcohol and high-fat, high-calorie diets. European women who went through adolescence in the 1940s and had low calorie and fat intakes, due to rigorous wartime rationing, are now getting many fewer breast cancers than expected.

A VIRTUE IN VIGILANCE?

So how can we help ourselves? The consensus now among specialists the world over is that breast self-examination, long-touted as a woman's own personal best protection against the horrors of advanced breast cancer, is not the answer. It is a ritual that cannot be counted upon to bring cancers to light at a point sufficiently early to make a life-or-death difference, they say, and has a negligible benefit in comparison to mammographic screening.

In the United States, experts are coming to the conclusion that the benefits of breast self-examination have been oversold. In 1991, an expert panel convened by the American Cancer Society concluded that the scientific evidence for breast self examination was "not compelling," though it was a simple, low cost, non-invasive procedure that might at least encourage older women to see their doctors before the horrendous late-stage. (Such cancers are still seen on both sides of the Atlantic, as a result, it's thought, of women's disregarding obvious signs of something amiss, out of a combination of fear and ignorance.) Similarly, Britain's Cancer Research

Campaign recently concluded: "There is currently no evidence to support the view that BSE [breast self-examination] should be regarded as a primary screening technique nor that it should be conducted on a routine basis following a set technique which requires formal instruction." Instead it urges women to replace formal breast self-examination with "breast awareness," regularly to ask their doctors to examine their breasts for suspicious signs, and to present themselves for regular mammograms.

Those who argue that breast self-examination cannot hurt are right provided that it does not lull a woman into a false sense of security that means she then bypasses her mammogram. The small tumors that carry such an excellent prognosis on X-ray are well below the threshold of touch.

Make sure you have regular yearly clinical examinations. Surveys show that many tumors found on mammogram could have been felt by a doctor, and also reveal, contrary to popular belief, that doctors are more likely to detect abnormalities than women carrying out breast self-examination.

Be breast "aware." You do not need a certified technique. In place of the old formal session, simply become familiar with both the appearance and the feel of your breasts so that you know what is normal and what is not. It is change that is important.

Standing before a mirror, check for obvious changes. Place hands on hips and press inwards to tense chest muscles, then look for any puckering, dimpling, or discoloration in the skin; a change in the shape or direction of the nipple; discharge or bleeding from the nipple. Raise your arms and turn slowly from side to side. When in the bath or shower, use a soapy hand. Take the flat of your middle three fingers in sweeping movements from the armpit in toward the center to feel for unusual lumps or changes in size and shape. If you do this as a matter of course, you will soon be familiar with the texture of your breasts.

In a feature on the subject in American *Vogue*, Patti Wilcox, director of the Breast Evaluation Center at Johns Hopkins Oncology Center in Baltimore, stated: "Women think their breasts should feel like Jell-O, but they normally feel more like lumpy oatmeal . . . I tell women: you're looking for something that feels different – like a piece of gravel, or a peanut, or a grape – from the other lumps in the oatmeal." If your instinct tells you something is different, see your doctor.

When it comes to breast self-examination, then, women must make up their own minds, though they may be persuaded by a study, published in spring 1993, suggesting that the practice does lead to earlier diagnosis and, perhaps, a small survival advantage.[4] Pointers to help you become more breast-aware are given above. If you want to learn a formal technique, ask your physician to show you. If you hate having to treat your breasts like segmented grapefruits or spokes on a wheel every month, and are among the two-thirds of American women who never do it with any regularity anyway, be sure to ask your physician to give you yearly clinical examinations.

MAMMOGRAPHY

As far as early detection of breast cancer goes, mammography is quite simply the best method available, though research is underway on new techniques, such as magnetic resonance imaging, infrared light screening, and analysis of biomarkers in

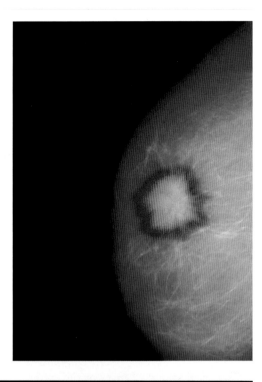

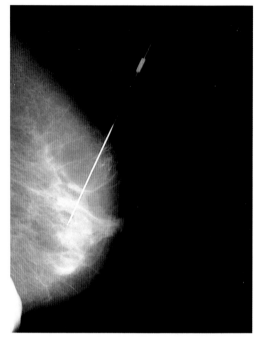

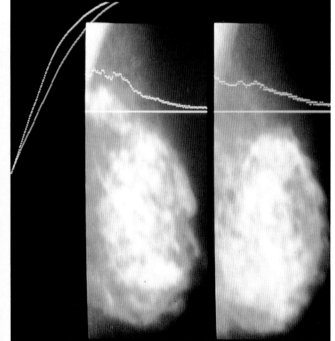

As a screening method for breast cancer, mammography (soft tissue X-ray) has everything else beaten . . . for the moment. In the mammogram, TOP LEFT, a cancerous tumor shows up as an orange mass with an uneven border. As many as five out of six suspicious mammograms turn out to be normal after a biopsy, ABOVE, which entails inserting a fine needle and taking a sample of cells – in this case from a non-invasive growth. A new computerized imaging technique, digital mammography, promises to improve detection rates by clarifying hard-to-see areas of the breast. Pilot studies have shown that when a computer is instructed to flag suspicious specks of calcium with a brightly colored ring, detection rates improve significantly. In this example, LEFT, the asymmetry between the densities at the top of the breasts (as indicated by the diverging blue and yellow lines) prompted the radiologist to take a closer look. In the event, there was a cancer in the inside upper margin of the breast on the far left.

the blood with the hope of identifying the presence of a cancer at an earlier developmental stage.

While X-rays may not be the ideal diagnostic tool, there is a difference between the nature of tumors picked up on a mammogram, especially a regular one, and those that come to light in the bath or by clinical examination in a doctor's surgery. By the time a breast cancer is big enough to be felt by a woman or her doctor, it is generally over ⅜ inch (one centimeter) in diameter and contains 100 billion cancer cells, some of which may well have broken loose and begun to infiltrate brain, bones, liver, or lungs. The lymph nodes will be involved in almost half the patients. It has been estimated that, by the time you can feel it, a tumor is between eight and ten years old, though what scientists call the "doubling time" (the time it takes for one cell to become two cells or two million to become four million) can be as little as three days for exceptionally aggressive cancers or as much as a year for indolent ones.

Mammography can bring tumors to light a couple of years before they are able to be felt. A skilled radiologist can find a tumor of less than ¹⁄₁₂ inch (2 millimeters) in diameter. The big advantage of finding a tumor at this early stage is that it can generally be removed with conservative surgery – and just the lump and a margin of surrounding tissue taken away. While this is still no guarantee of cure, since some cancers spread early in their biological life, it is more likely *not* to have broken off and migrated by way of the lymph and bloodstream to other distant parts of the body.

The stage at which cancers are found is important: 91 per cent of women are still alive ten years later if they have stage 1 disease (a small, movable tumor confined to the breast) whereas only 30 per cent are still alive if their disease has spread to the lymph nodes. It is a subject of fierce medical debate whether the small tumor coming to light on a mammogram is an early tumor caught in the nick of time and so prevented from growing into a large invasive cancer later on, or whether it has been there for some time and was never destined to spread beyond the breast. At the moment one of the fiercest disagreements centers on a form of cancer known as ductal carcinoma in situ (DCIS), which is thought to have about a one in three chance of turning into an invasive cancer. In the past, less than one in 20 cancers were of this type, but the widespread use of mammography, which is particularly good at picking up DCIS, has upped the ratio to one in six and it is even higher in women under 50. In a review of 117 women under the age of 50 whose breast cancers were found by mammography at Massachusetts General Hospital, 40 per cent had DCIS.[5] In the future, it is likely that better ways of distinguishing different sorts of DCIS will be developed, allowing more conservative ways of treating some of these slow-growing "precancers." Already, analysis of suspicious cells using a technique called fine needle aspiration can give important clues as to the relative aggressiveness or indolence of a tumor.

The benefits of mammography are unarguable over the age of 50. The most reliable findings are widely acknowledged to come out of Sweden, where regular two-yearly mammograms have been shown to increase a woman's chances of surviving her cancer by about 30 per cent. In 1960, before their breast screening program got underway, 62 per cent of Swedish women with breast cancer died of their disease; now it's 36 per cent. This big improvement, however, only applies to women over the age of 50, the age group in which over two-thirds of all cancer cases are concentrated. The greater success of screening older women is probably due both to better detection – the structure of the post-menopause breast, being mostly fat and connective tissue, allows suspicious lumps to stand out very clearly – and to the fact that post-menopausal tumors may be slower-growing, so presenting a "window of opportunity" that is less apparent for younger women.

The evidence for the usefulness of screening varies enormously with age. For women aged over 50, the evidence is now so compelling that there is universal agreement throughout the Western world that this group should have regular mammograms – ideally at least once a year. Annual screening should continue at least through the 69th year, and some claim even longer. "Mammography is significantly less utilized in women 65 years and older compared with young women," criticized the American Cancer Society's expert forum in 1991. "This is striking since breast cancer incidence rises sharply with age . . . and so the majority of women affected with breast cancer will be 65 years or older."

Women of all ages find excuses not to go for their mammograms. It comes too low on their list of health priorities or it is too expensive or they are fearful of what it might reveal or they are anxious about the procedure itself. Despite repeated promotional campaigns, only five per cent of American women over the age of 50 have regular mammograms. Interestingly, in one U.S. survey, half the women questioned said they found mammography less painful if they were able to control the degree of compression themselves.

The hottest controversy in breast cancer screening concerns women under the age of 50. To date, the findings are conflicting. Most of the world's largest, longest-running studies have been unable to show that mammography makes a life-or-death difference for women under 50. This includes a huge Canadian trial of 50,000 women, published in late 1992, in which breast cancer deaths in the screened group actually outnumbered those in the unscreened group.[6] Although the trial has been criticized for the low quality of much of the mammography, the findings highlight the controversy over exposing women under 50 to additional radiation unnecessarily. With modern equipment, a mammogram is said to amount to less exposure than the dose received on an average transatlantic plane trip (a maximum of 0.4 rads per exposure), but the younger breast sometimes requires higher doses to obtain a readable picture.

A Swedish overview, published in 1993, however, reassuringly found "no evidence of any detrimental effect of screening in terms of breast cancer mortality in any age group."[7] Of nearly 300,000 women followed for 13 years, significant reductions in death rates of nearly 30 per cent were noted in women between 50 and 69, as was expected. Less predictable was the finding that, after eight years, a "small and delayed" benefit began to become apparent in the 40 to 50 age group. This finding backs up those few smaller-scale studies on women in their 40s that suggest a survival advantage of around five per cent from screening. While this is small, women will understandably consider it is a benefit worth having. They might, after all, be the one in 20 where screening makes the vital difference.

There is rarely justification for low-risk women in their 30s to have mammograms. In one survey, published in the medical journal *Cancer*, one in six women in their 30s had had a mammogram within the previous year, and 19 per cent of physicians said that they ordered regular screening mammograms for between 80 and 100 per cent of their 30 to 39-year-old female patients. In one's 30s, the dense glandular tissue of the breast can make a mammogram virtually unreadable, with tumors more likely to be missed and any reassurance that is given at best unreliable. Even in one's 40s, the detection rate, which is over 90 per cent post-menopause, falls to less than 70 per cent and the number of "false positives" requiring further investigation also rises enormously. In the Canadian trial, nearly 20 per cent of the under-50s in the mammography group were subjected to further tests. This is because the milk-producing glands in the breasts show up uniformly white on the X-ray film and cancers also appear as small white specks: telling white from white is hard even for a very practiced eye.

BREAST SURGERY

While our current state of knowledge is limited, modern treatment for breast cancer has advanced considerably. Surgery, where it can, now spares the breast, with no

Have mammograms a year apart from at least the age of 50, or yearly from the age of 40 according to your personal inclination and your physician's recommendation. If you are in your 30s, have no family history of the disease and your doctor recommends a mammogram, ask him or her to tell you why it is necessary. U.S. cancer experts have recently recommended there should be no upper age limit for mammography, although some feel that annual screening beyond age 69 may be of little benefit. The importance of good quality mammography cannot be overstated, as there is a great diversity in screening standards. Be sure to go to a center accredited by the American College of Radiology; many aren't. And always ask beforehand about the arrangements that will be made for you to be checked should any abnormality be found.

● If a first-degree relative (mother, sister) had pre-menopausal breast cancer, be guided by your physician as to screening intervals and age of starting.

● If a biopsy for benign disease revealed a rare condition called atypical hyperplasia, or epitheliosis, earlier and more frequent screenings are advisable; be guided by your doctor.
● If you are pre-menopausal and your physician advises a mammogram, schedule your appointment for the second half of your cycle. Although it will be more uncomfortable, some specialists believe that it could have a bearing on your prognosis should a cancer be found.
● Remember that a negative screen does not eliminate the possibility of cancer. Stay vigilant to any changes in the breast and bring them to your doctor's attention, even if you have had a recent negative mammogram. According to American researchers, there is some evidence that women in screening programs are "aware of breast changes but await their next screen rather than seek immediate evaluation."
● Ensure you have a mammogram before starting hormone replacement therapy, to rule out an existing tumor that might then flourish on the extra estrogen.

compromise on survival. Provided the tumor is small, confined to a single area, and readily accessible to the scalpel, just the cancer is removed along with a margin of normal-looking surrounding tissue and, where appropriate, the underarm lymph nodes. The breast bears a slight scar at the site of the incision but the tissue soon adjusts to fill the gap and the breast regains its former shape. When radiation is given to the remaining breast tissue, the approach has been shown time and again to save as many lives as more extensive surgery. The aptness of lumpectomy, as the conservative approach is called, formed the core recommendation for treatment of early breast cancer in a consensus statement prepared by U.S. breast experts in 1985. Yet it remains a minority procedure in the United States. While some women prefer to have their early breast cancers treated radically "just to be sure" (Nancy Reagan, to a chorus of criticism, was one), many candidates for lumpectomy are simply unaware of their options and are never offered a choice. According to experts, it is unusual that a woman wouldn't be a candidate for lumpectomy if her cancer was detected during a regular mammogram screening, so a second specialist opinion is always worth seeking if a full mastectomy is the only strategy discussed.

Even the minority of women still needing a radical mastectomy may be able to awake from the operation and be reassured that nothing appears to be missing. The Food and Drug Administration is allowing the use of slicone implants for breast reconstruction (many women prefer their more natural feel and texture to the saline alternative) providing they agree to take part in a controlled trial, so that the safety, or lack of it, of these implants can be established beyond reasonable doubt. The results of the trial will not be available for at least ten years. Increasingly, the tendency is to build up the breast at the time of operation, the breast surgeon working in concert with the cosmetic surgeon. Every survey carried out to date shows strong psychological advantages in doing so for women for whom the loss of a breast would be devastating.

FUTURE PREVENTION OF BREAST CANCER

One of the most useful weapons in the anti-breast cancer armamentarium is tamoxifen, a hormone-like substance which works by blocking the estrogen receptors in the breast, and significantly reduces the recurrence of the disease in older women. Excitingly, the drug may also be capable of disrupting the development of breast cancer, or even entirely preventing it in high-risk women. This is now being put to the test in a joint five-year trial in the United States and Britain, and already reports are drifting through that many less tumors have been found than expected. Tamoxifen is controversial. In pre-menopausal women, it temporarily removes fertility and may induce menopause-like side-effects like hot flashes and nausea. On the positive side, it appears to have a beneficial impact on blood fats, to lower cholesterol, to protect the bones, and possibly lower the chance of getting ovarian cancer. But the discovery that it causes liver tumors in rats, and may also provoke endometrial cancer (a greater-than-expected number of tumors are being reported in treated women), has dented much of the early optimism and has led to much stricter criteria on its use on healthy women. By the time the results of the tamoxifen trial come through, a second generation of safer, tamoxifen-like drugs is likely to be available. Already trials of a more potent, tamoxifen-like compound, idoxifene, are being carried out, and tests on a second hormone, GnRH (gonadatrophin releasing hormone), which inhibits ovarian function and causes estrogen levels to decline, are underway in southern California.

In the future, high-risk groups of women might be pinpointed by means of a blood test, which would sound an early warning by showing up "markers" of very early malignancy, as is being developed for ovarian cancer (see pages 187–8). In some cases, blood tests can already be used to identify a genetic predisposition (thought to apply to between five and ten per cent of breast cancer cases), which would indicate the need for closer surveillance. In one tantalizing new lead, over a quarter of breast cancer sufferers have been found to have abnormal proportions of a growth-promoting gene on chromosome 17. Women with high levels, which can be as much as 20 times that of the norm, appear not only more likely to get cancer but also to have three times the risk of recurrence once it is diagnosed. In the future, tests may be able to identify such women, and gene treatment, using antibodies to lock onto the gene and incapacitate it, could keep them free of cancer.

HEART

MANY of the body's organs deteriorate with age, but the heart remains wonderfully well preserved. This tireless muscle carries on beating 100,000 times a day, every day, without respite, for a lifetime, and it would often go on considerably longer if the profuse system of arteries that supplies it with its lifeblood were kept in better shape.

You're as old as your arteries, the saying goes. But how old are they? Silted-up blood vessels are so common in Western societies now as to be virtually the norm. As the Coronary Prevention Group has put it, "The relevant question is not so much 'Do I have heart disease or not?' as 'How *much* heart disease do I have?'" It is estimated that one in nine American women between the ages of 45 and 64 has some form of the disease and this climbs to one in three over the age of 65.

THE MALE-ONLY MYTH

Because much heart disease is preventable, avoiding it means being aware both of the risks (and eliminating or minimizing them where feasible) and of the danger signs. Most women do neither. They do not see damaging habits, such as smoking, as a threat to the health of their hearts. Nor do they take chest pain seriously. Although heart disease is the leading killer for both sexes in the United States, women continue to live under the illusion that they are somehow gloriously immune to it. In fact, *more* American women than men die from heart disease and associated conditions, such as stroke. The difference is that a woman's "dangerous decade" comes in her 70s rather than at the prime of life, in her 50s.

The result is that the normally well-informed, health-conscious woman worries far more about developing breast or cervical cancer than clogging up her coronary arteries – even though she is four times as likely to develop fatal heart disease, which quietly kills off one in every two American women over the age of 50. Culturally conditioned to see herself as being at no great risk, the modern woman ignores the health messages and worries by proxy – steering her mate onto a low-fat diet, outlawing butter, and keeping a strict tally of the number of eggs he eats.

If millions of Western women are sublimely unaware of their own sick circulations, doctors are not much better. The American cardiologist Bernadine Healy, the first-ever woman appointed to the prestigious post of Director of the National Institutes of Health, has charged that the "male-only myth of heart disease" permeates medical practice and health education. Such attitudes help to explain why heart disease is more likely to go undiagnosed in women and to go untreated even when found. In 1991, *The New England Journal of Medicine* published two surveys showing that American female heart patients are less likely to receive critical life-saving procedures, such as bypass surgery and angioplasty, which widens clogged arteries and reduces the chances of a heart attack. Even when treated, women do not do as well, probably because the intervention comes later in the disease process and because their arteries, being narrower to start with, are both harder to fix and more susceptible to damage during surgery itself.

In our agist culture, medical research is invariably geared to saving the lives of middle-aged men. This is not totally unreasonable seeing that men are three to four times more vulnerable in midlife, whereas women are seemingly protected before the menopause, but it is remarkably neglectful given the overall mortality figures. One international review of cholesterol-lowering studies, published in the journal *Circulation* in 1992, included no one over the age of 69 and, hence, only a small number of women. In addition, four out of every five projects on coronary health specifically *exclude* women as subjects. This sexist, agist bias spills into all cardiovascular research and has led to a glaring lack of information about the health of women's hearts – what is normal and abnormal, what may prevent and what will make worse, what helps and what doesn't.

CONTRIBUTORY FACTORS

While so little continues to be known about the nature of heart disease in women, and more particularly the risks that predispose to it, doctors can only guess how best to prevent and treat it. One of the most far-reaching surveys ever conducted on health and the myriad variables of lifestyle is the still-ongoing inquiry into the health and habits of the inhabitants of the town of Framingham, Massachusetts, which has followed about 5000 men and women for over 40 years. The survey found that the so-called classic risks of raised blood pressure, smoking, and high total blood cholesterol were no help in predicting which women would get heart disease – but that having children and a badly paid, routine, repetitive job doubled the risk.[1]

The perceived notion that high-stress, high-flying jobs increase a woman's risk of heart disease, that "as women start living like men they will start dying like men" as some alarmists have predicted, has no basis in fact. In fact, women with well-paid, satisfying jobs seem if anything to be protected from heart attacks. The U.S. National Longitudinal Mortality Study has clearly shown heart disease risk to be highest among women whose socio-economic circumstances are lowest, being particularly marked in women whose incomes are less than $20,000 a year and who have not gone on to any form of higher education.

So what are women who want to rustproof their hearts to do? Should they follow the advice given to men or simply ignore everything as irrelevant to them, cross their fingers, and hope for the best? The picture is confused and confusing. While it should, at last, be clarified when the results of the keenly awaited $500 million U.S. Women's Health Initiative come to light, these are not expected until 2008 *at the earliest*. In the meantime, a few things are certain. One is that having a parent or sibling who has had a heart attack or stroke before the age of 60 is bad news whatever your gender.

Just as bad, but mercifully preventable, smoking accounts for more than half of all pre-menopausal heart attacks in women and triples the risk of stroke under the age of 50. This may be due partly to its lowering effect on HDL ("good") cholesterol,

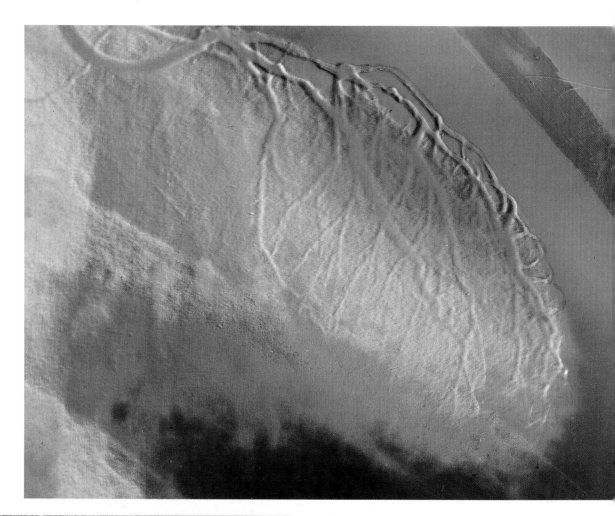

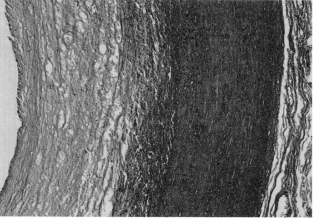

Silted-up arteries are so common in Western societies as to be virtually universal. The angiogram, ABOVE, shows multiple obstructions in the artery immediately above the heart on the image, while healthy blood vessels appear as continuous pink ribbons. The cross-section through an obstructed artery, LEFT, shows signs of atherosclerosis (the holes in the pale pink represent glistening streaks of cholesterol and other metabolic detritus on the once smooth arterial muscle as shown by the denser pink area on the right of the image). Because the heart's arteries are no wider than a drinking straw – and a woman's are even thinner than a man's – the chances of a clot blocking the blood supply to the heart increase as the arteries narrow. Encouragingly, recent U.S. research suggests that if women switch to a diet of 20 per cent fat or less, some of these changes can be reversed.

partly to its tendency to exhaust supplies of free-radical-scavenging vitamin C, and partly to its stimulating effect on catecholamines, which cause the arteries to constrict, the heart to beat faster, and the blood pressure to rise into the bargain.

Many studies show that the additional risk of heart attack falls rapidly on stopping smoking – a powerful argument for stopping well before menopause, when heart disease risk really takes off. Smokers who use oral contraceptives face double jeopardy – being 20 times more likely to have a heart attack and up to 22 times more likely to suffer a stroke than women who neither smoke nor use birth control pills (which is why gynecologists are always so anxious to steer smokers onto safe methods of birth control).

I f you smoke, give it up. Smoking is the major cause of heart disease in pre-menopausal women, so you could remove the main risk factor more or less instantly. New research shows that the dangerous higher risk of blood clotting in smokers returns to normal levels within a matter of *days*, rather than the decade that was previously thought.

THE ROLE OF CHOLESTEROL

The picture regarding cholesterol, one of the most intensely researched areas in coronary heart disease, is much less clear. Cholesterol is a soft waxy substance, essential for the formation of cell membranes and the action of certain hormones. Being insoluble in water, it must join with proteins to form particles called lipoproteins before circulating in the bloodstream. There are high-density and low-density variants of cholesterol. The low-density lipoproteins (LDL) are bad news. Under certain circumstances, they collect in the arteries in a waxy plaque that narrows the vessels with all the dire consequences already described. High-density lipoproteins (HDL) are good news. They remove cholesterol from the arteries and return it to the liver for reprocessing, and may even scoop up cholesterol from atherosclerotic plaques, so-called "reverse cholesterol transport."

Interestingly, the importance of high levels of LDL (the "bad" lipoproteins), thought to be so ominous for men, have been called into question by some researchers.[2] This stems from the fact that women tend to have higher levels of HDL cholesterol, which are protective and counterbalance the effects of high LDLs. But if levels of HDL (the "good" lipoproteins) are *low*, a woman's risk of heart attack rises significantly, especially once she is past menopause.

Activities that raise HDL levels may have especial value in warding off heart disease in women. Examples are 30 minutes of brisk walking or any other form of fairly vigorous activity at least three times a week; keeping weight within reasonable limits; strongly considering taking estrogen at the menopause; and, happily, enjoying a glass of wine two or three times a week. All these measures can potentially raise HDL levels some 10 to 20 per cent and in some studies have proved themselves more effective in lowering a woman's risk of fatal heart attack than many cholesterol-lowering drugs, which lower HDL levels along with the LDL.

Have a cholesterol check at least once every five years from the age of 20. If your results are unhealthily high or you have a family history of raised cholesterol, or if your physician advises it, have your cholesterol checked again after making dietary changes: if the levels are still high, investigation of other blood fats, such as triglycerides and fibrinogen, may be thought advisable.

Differences in opinion as to the wisdom of watching out for and treating high cholesterol levels rage in the top echelons of cardiology. Some experts (though now a decreasing number) still recommend frequent cholesterol checks across the nation combined with aggressive treatment measures to bring above-normal levels down to the upper level of 200 mg/dl recommended by the National Cholesterol Education program (NCEP). Others take a more cautious line, pointing to the lack of definitive evidence that cholesterol-lowering drugs work in men, let alone women, especially low-risk women, and prefer to reserve treatment for only very high levels. They also point to several studies showing that too little cholesterol can also be bad for you. Healthy pre-menopausal women needn't worry about their cholesterol levels, they say, and should certainly avoid aggressive, drug-oriented attempts to lower them. The consensus for now: women should have both their total cholesterol and HDL cholesterol measured every five years from the age of 20 onward. More frequent checks may be advised if the original reading was high or if you are hypertensive or diabetic, you smoke or you have a family history of early heart disease – along with investigation of other blood fats, such as triglycerides, and fibrinogen.

REDUCING DIETARY FAT
While arguments over the risks of raised cholesterol and the wisdom of medication designed to lower it look set to go on for years, restricting the amount of fat in the diet is good health practice whatever your cholesterol count. Women who already suffer from occlusive arterial disease – angina or atherosclerosis – particularly stand to gain, since research now shows that narrowed arteries can actually unclog to some extent when a prudent diet is followed. There are sex differences here too: whereas male heart disease patients have to cut back drastically to less than ten per cent total fat before such changes are reversed, there are signs that women may be able to start clearing their gummed-up arteries on a more palatable 20–25 per cent.

HIGH BLOOD PRESSURE

While most studies suggest that high blood pressure raises the risk of heart disease in women as in men, an impassioned debate is raging on the value of universally treating all women with raised blood pressure. While black women, who suffer hypertension more severely throughout life and get it at an earlier age, tend to respond positively to drug therapy, two large studies suggest little benefit from treating all white women with elevated blood pressure.[3] If blood pressure is very high, medication has undoubted value in reducing the risk of stroke it's at lesser levels that its use is controversial.

Since pressure-lowering drugs have unpleasant side-effects, those with borderline high blood pressure should push hard to lower it by making the lifestyle changes listed below before embarking on therapy.

Have your blood pressure checked at least every two years if it is well within the normal range. If pressure is known to be borderline-high, or if you have a family history of high blood pressure, diabetes, or heart disease (one parent dying at or before the age of 60), you'll need to have it checked more frequently (talk to your doctor about an optimal screening interval). In addition, keep the risk of a rise at bay by not adding salt to food, avoiding processed foods, taking more exercise if you lead a sedentary lifestyle, having no more than two alcoholic drinks a night, and keeping your weight within limits.

OTHER RISK FACTORS

Other distinctions are emerging between male and female risk factors. Late-onset diabetes, for example, which becomes common in the years after the menopause, appears *more* ominous for women than for men. The U.S. Nurses' Health Study, which followed up over 100,000 women, revealed that diabetic women had six times the risk of heart attack and four times the risk of stroke as non-diabetics did. This is thought to be because the metabolic changes that accompany diabetes damage the small blood vessels supplying the heart and brain. The study also showed that the risk of circulatory disease rose even more if the women also smoked, had high blood pressure or high cholesterol levels, or were obese – a discovery that fits the current understanding of heart disease risk multiplying as these separate risk factors accumulate.

Although being overweight is firmly fixed in the popular mind as a sure way to heart failure, in the absence of diabetes and high blood pressure, shape may be truer indicator of risk than weight alone. The apple shape, with fat accumulated around

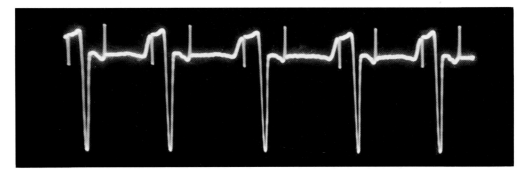

There is no straightforward screen for the heart; the best-known test is still the resting electrocardiogram (ECG), ABOVE. Taken when the individual is lying down, it supplies a tracing of the electrical activity of the heart. Its drawback is that it can give an all-clear in the presence of quite severe coronary disease. In one study, more than half the people dying of heart disease had had normal ECG readings less than 12 months previously. The test becomes more reliable when taken during exercise, with anomalies more likely to show as the heart comes under strain. False alarms are common, however, especially in younger women.

the midsection, is associated with more heart disease and diabetes than the good old pear-shape, with a waist-to-hip ratio of more than 0.8 clearly shown to raise the risk, according to the American Heart Association (instructions for checking your own are on page 91).

I f you have a family history of diabetes, had sugar in your urine or developed gestational diabetes when pregnant, or gave birth to a very heavy baby – over 10 pounds (4.5 kilograms) – be especially vigilant, since these increase your chances of developing diabetes in later life. Follow a heart-healthy diet, take regular exercise and do not allow your weight to rise more than a few pounds (a couple of kilograms) over the recommended level (see page 84). These are all ways of keeping your risk as low as possible and the system optimally insulin-sensitive. In addition, whether the above risk factors apply or not, be aware of the signs of glucose intolerance (see Alphabeticals: diabetes), asking your doctor to check them out if you suspect you may have one or more of them.

The picture for women may be muddy but that for men is not as clear as doctors often pretend. There are many anomalies. The Inuit, for example, have stratospheric cholesterol levels but virtually no heart disease. The French eat more saturated fat than Americans do, yet they have healthier arteries. The Greeks smoke heavily and have both the highest red meat consumption and one of the lowest rates of heart disease in Europe. Japanese men smoke more cigarettes and have higher blood pressures than American men, and yet are rewarded with the highest male life expectancy in the entire world, suffering just a fraction of the number of heart attacks that Western men do.

THE PREVENTIVE APPROACH

The truth is that the classic foursome – high blood cholesterol, high blood pressure, smoking, and family history – explains somewhat less than half of all heart disease in men (and a quarter in women). The rest is unknown, though there are some tantalizing leads. Some think it likely that a low consumption of fruit and vegetables may be as risky as any of the above by depriving the body of vital anti-oxidizing vitamins C and E. These are now known to prevent the free-radical damage that renders low-density cholesterol dangerous by enabling it to penetrate and stick to the artery walls (see pages 240–2). One big European study found low vitamin E levels the biggest single predictive factor of whether an individual would later go on to develop heart disease, with high levels appearing protective even if the individual also had high levels of cholesterol and/or high blood pressure.[4] A U.S. study published in 1993 on more than 80,000 women found that those who took vitamin E supplements of at least 100 IUs a day for two years or more cut their risk of heart disease by a third.[5]

Make a few heart-healthy changes to your diet – cutting down on total fat and, especially, saturated fat; upping intakes of fresh fruit and vegetables for free-radical scavenging vitamin C; considering a vitamin E supplement of up to 200 IU daily (to get an equivalent amount from food you would have to eat a lot of oil); eating oily fish (mackerel, herring, tuna, salmon, trout, red mullet, sardines) twice a week; enjoying a glass of wine at night.

Certainly, lifestyle plays a big part in heart disease. Over the last 25 years the death rate from heart disease in the United States has plunged by a quarter as Americans have quit smoking, put on their jogging shoes, and taken prevention into their hearts and lives. By contrast, in Britain, where people remain stolidly resistant to the idea that action can have any impact on health, and where fat consumption – which is responsible for virtually half of all the energy supplied by the British diet – has remained static for 15 years, the mortality rates have merely dipped a fraction.

THE VALUE OF ESTROGEN REPLACEMENT

Non-smoking women are very unlikely to suffer heart disease pre-menopause because they are protected by the hormone estrogen. Produced in abundance by the developing follicles in the ovary each month, it has the effect of keeping LDL levels low and HDL levels high. Some research indicates that it protects the blood-vessel walls from the changes that cause fatty plaques to accumulate and probably keeps the blood vessels stretchy too.

Some years before menopause, the picture changes, however, and women start to lose these advantages. From the mid-40s, HDL cholesterol falls by about 15 per cent and LDL rises by the same amount, while weight starts accumulating around the middle. Women losing their natural protection before time, through either premature or surgical menopause, may be as much as four times more likely to get heart disease than if they had gone through their menopause at the usual time. Such women are well advised to take estrogen replacement therapy – at least until they are 50, the average age of menopause – if only to bring their risk down.

It makes perfect biological sense that replacing this heart-friendly hormone to pre-menopausal levels should also protect the arteries of women going through the menopause at the usual time. Indeed, the current headlong enthusiasm for hormone replacement therapy is partly based on its much-stated ability to cut heart disease deaths in half, as was recently shown in a ten-year follow-up study of nearly 50,000 female nurses by researchers at Harvard Medical School. Tablets appeared more effective in this respect than those creams or skin patches. And especially big reductions were noted in women with existing heart disease.[6]

With news like this, it's no wonder that 50-somethings everywhere have started clamoring for hormones – unaware that this magical protective effect does not occur for every treated woman. In fact, the estrogen-only regimen that produced these results is now only followed by the minority of HRT-users who have had a hysterectomy. Those with an intact womb generally take their estrogen combined with progestin to stimulate a monthly bleed and so protect them from the known estrogen-related risk of cancer of the lining of the womb. Unfortunately, the progestins incorporated into the current HRT formulations push a woman's blood-fat profile in an unfavorable direction (see page 331 for a fuller discussion), in particular lowering HDL levels and raising LDL levels, and so they probably undo some, if not all, of the benefit provided by the formulation's heart-friendly other half.

The results of the important PEPI (Postmenopausal Estrogen/Progestin Interventions) study in the United States, which is looking at the effects of estrogen alone and estrogen-plus-progestin on heart-disease risk factors in nearly 1000 women, should clarify the picture but results are not due in before the mid-1990s. Hopefully, by the end of the decade, hormone replacement formulations will anyway have changed so they protect the lining of the womb, while having minimal metabolic effects on the rest of the system. This would make the therapy virtually unmitigated good news for millions of menopausal women. But in the meantime, calls for mass prophylaxis are definitely premature.

NON-HORMONAL MEASURES: ACTIVITY AND ASPIRIN

Estrogen therapy is not the only answer. Other ways of forestalling or reversing some of the more negative health effects of the menopause can be as simple and non-invasive as taking a brisk walk on a daily basis. Researchers at the University of Pittsburgh have found that active women have lower blood pressure, lower total cholesterol, and higher HDL cholesterol than their sedentary peers and suggest that physical activity may protect against the increasing heart disease risk associated with the menopause. Other studies have found that regular exercise can inhibit some of the clotting factors in the blood, so reducing the chances of a clot forming and blocking the coronary arteries. Tellingly, one of the most definitive studies to date, which came out of the Institute of Aerobics Research in Dallas, found an eight-fold difference in risk of death from heart disease when the least-fit women were compared with the fittest.[7]

Aspirin also has positive protective effects against heart disease for both men and women. This humble 100-year-old headache remedy has been proven to protect people who have already suffered a heart attack or stroke from a recurrence – reducing their risk by about 30 per cent. It can help prevent heart attacks in patients with diagnosed heart disease and angina, and newer research suggests that it may also keep the hearts and brains of still-healthy individuals in good shape.

The effect is said to be due to the drug's effect on the platelets, the smallest of all the particles in the blood, which normally clump together to staunch a bleeding wound. Aspirin keeps the platelets from excessive clumping – a process which constitutes a vital step in the formation of a blood clot. Though it will not prevent the

---

Keep active. Like any other muscle in the body, the heart responds positively to exercise. Recent studies show that the negative changes in blood fat chemistry that pave the way toward later heart disease, and are often well established by the middle years, can actually be reversed by a regular program of moderately vigorous exercise. It can also lower both blood pressure fractions by as much as 10mm permanently. Even walking is associated with big improvements in heart health, and it's working out at relatively low levels for longer that's beneficial.

---

accumulation of fatty deposits in the artery, it may make the blood fluid enough to keep it flowing through.

The exciting news is that doctors are not talking about huge amounts. Since the 1940s, when U.S. research first showed that a daily aspirin reduced the likelihood of stroke and heart disease in monkeys, the protective dose has come down by three-quarters; it now amounts to just half a standard tablet every other day, or one aspirin twice a week. A retrospective survey of the self-medication histories of 87,000 American nurses between the ages of 34 and 65 who had no known heart disease revealed that those women taking one to six aspirin a week had an astonishing 32 per cent fewer first heart attacks.[8] Women over 50 and those who already had established risk factors, such as diabetes, smoking, or high blood pressure, gained the greatest apparent benefit, so it looks as though the drug was protecting those who needed it most. There was no evidence that regular aspirin use was helpful in preventing heart attacks before the menopause – an important distinction since the risk of side-effects, such as gastric bleeding, and the more remote chance of serious harm would outweigh any benefit. Along with fewer heart attacks, as was expected, one trial noted a worrying 20 per cent rise in brain hemorrhages due to uncontrolled bleeding thought to be provoked by the drug.

L ow-dose aspirin is not appropriate for everyone, but worth serious consideration if you are already at risk of heart disease by being over 50 and either smoking or having diabetes, high blood pressure, or abnormally high cholesterol or fibrinogen levels. But it must be a decision made in consultation with your physician, since the drug does have serious side-effects in a small proportion of people. Side-effects like stomach upset and small gastric bleeds can be reduced by taking the tablet with a meal or plenty of water.

SCREENING FOR HEART DISEASE

The current belief that one should get every important piece of one's anatomy checked out for signs of incipient malfunction is not straightforward when it comes to the heart. The resting ECG (electrocardiograph), which supplies a tracing of the heart's rhythm and is a mainstay of many so-called preventive health checks-ups, is notorious for its false negatives. As many as nine out of ten people with heart disease but no symptoms and no previous heart attacks will have normal ECGs, with the underlying abnormality only apparent if the heart is put under strain. Although the exercise electrocardiograph, which supplies a tracing of the heart's rhythm under stress – when bicycling or running on a treadmill – is more reliable, it has a tendency to throw up "false positives," especially in younger women. This can obviously prove a problem if such tests are insisted upon before a woman over 35 joins a gym. Although a majority of women testing positive will have perfectly healthy hearts, the suggestion that something is wrong can only be discounted by a radioactive scan. This involves injecting a short-acting radioactive chemical, known as thallium, into the bloodstream and tracking its passage with the aid of a special camera. The camera picks up the radioactivity, and the resulting image reflects how well blood is flowing to the heart muscle; areas of severely reduced flow indicate dangerous narrowings in the arteries supplying the corresponding part of the heart. However, even a thallium scan is not absolutely conclusive.

The only conclusive test is still the invasive angiogram, which requires a small

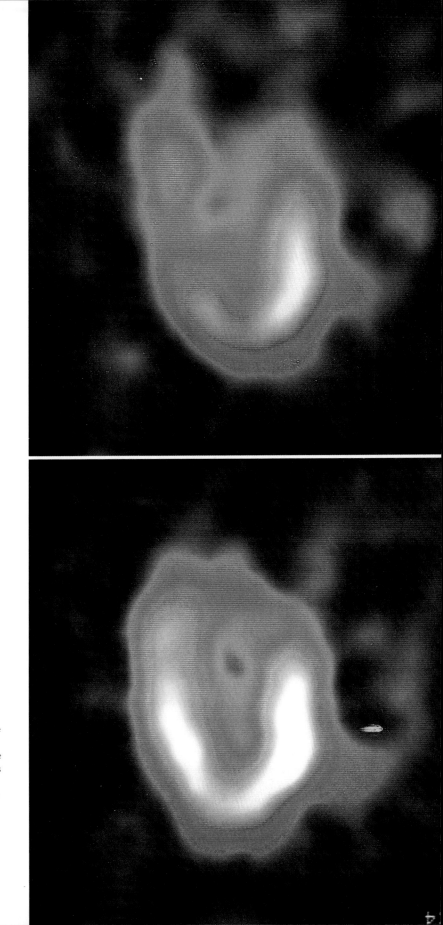

The thallium scan, one of a new generation of screens for the heart, involves injecting a radioactive chemical into the bloodstream and tracking its passage through the system so the specialist can see how well blood is flowing to the heart muscle. The diminished flow, TOP RIGHT, points up severe heart disease, which only came to light during exercise even though the heart appeared normal, BOTTOM, when the individual was at rest.

tube to be inserted into the heart to take pictures of the coronary arteries – a procedure which has risks of its own and certainly cannot be used as a routine screen. In the future, color Doppler ultrasound, which tracks the velocity of the blood flowing through the arteries and can show up areas of obstruction or restricted flow, could prove a valuable screening tool (as might magnetic resonance imaging, another non-invasive screening technique); but for the moment most of the coronary arteries remain frustratingly out of reach.

MUSCLES AND JOINTS

For all the lip-service paid to the well-toned body, modern women are conditioned not to care too much for muscle, looking on it as yet more unfavorable flesh. Even now, the cultural belief is that muscles are for men and that "the weaker sex" should have soft contours. Yet strength training is arguably even more important for women than for men, since women start off with less muscle, are consistently weaker than men of the same age at every stage of life, and have bones that are especially susceptible to fractures if they fall. In fact, maintaining strength gets ever *more* important with age. Though often neglected, it is a key determinant of independence in later life. Sufficient muscle can literally keep a woman on her feet – mobile, steady, and physically self-assured.

Even today women are likely to resist recommendations that they increase their strength. Back in 1972, Susan Sontag made the point that, whereas boys are encouraged to develop their bodies, "to regard the body as an instrument to be improved and to invent their masculine selves largely through exercise and sport, which harden the body. . . . girls are not particularly encouraged to develop their bodies through any activity, strenuous or not; and physical strength and endurance are hardly valued at all. . . ."[1]

Twenty years on, despite contemporary rhetoric about the well-worked-out female physique, an attractive woman's body, so far as most women are concerned, remains a light one, bereft of both fat and muscle. The mid-1990s generation of featherweight models wafting down the world's catwalks sums up the ideal exactly.

Since women almost universally want to be lighter as much as they want to be slimmer, and since muscle is heavier than fat, there are strict limits to how much muscle is regarded as "permissable." Even though more women now work out with weights than ever before, the motivation is mainly cosmetic. As any gym manager or personal trainer knows, women worry enormously about over-developing their muscles, particularly those in the calves and at the front of the thigh which are so important for stability and balance.

LOSS OF STRENGTH

Neglecting their strength, many women become enfeebled unnecessarily early in life. The American Academy of Physical Education found that 40 per cent of women aged between 60 and 64 were unable to carry, and in some cases even lift, a load of 28 pounds (13 kilograms) – the equivalent of a couple of bags of groceries or a one-year-old child – and a quarter could not manage to walk a quarter of a mile (400 meters).[2] Two separate Scandinavian studies have shown that, at 70, well over half of women are unable to negotiate a 20-inch (50-centimeter) step without a handrail, and that ten years later virtually none, though apparently healthy, could muster sufficient walking speed to keep up with the timings set for pedestrian crossings. All these basic day-to-day activities are determined by muscle strength; without it, a woman can soon find herself incapable of many of them.

As with so much else, loss of strength is not one of later life's inevitables. At the same age as women are having trouble going up and down steps or getting to the store or lifting their grandchildren, others are running marathons or practicing demanding yoga postures or lifting weights. We do have a choice about how weak we get how soon. Our strength does not suddenly desert us; it ebbs away from lack of practice and is a direct consequence of an ever more sedentary way of living in which every last ounce of effort is taken from us by some labor-saving device. Once the critical point is reached where the maximum strength that can be summoned for a particular activity is equivalent to the minimum necessary to do it, any further loss of strength takes a woman from the point where she is just able to do that activity to the point where she is just unable to. The result is an ever more restricted and immobile life.

PREVENTING FALLS AND FRACTURES

In trials, women suffering osteoporotic fractures have consistently been found to have weaker and more wasted muscles. An American survey that compared women who had been admitted to hospital suffering fractures after falling, with female patients of similar age and circumstances who had not fallen, found the calf circumference of the former "significantly" smaller.[3] Sophisticated new bone scanners are also revealing a close relationship between muscle strength and bone density; the stronger the muscles, the denser the bones. Recognizing that well-developed muscles also increase strength and balance and help prevent falls, preventively minded physicians are beginning to prescribe specific exercises for their post-menopausal female patients.

While aerobic exercise, such as brisk walking, particularly on uneven terrain, will help maintain muscle mass, adding a resistance training component to the workout will actually increase it. Machines (under supervision) are the safest option. Strength training should be done every second day at the most, as muscles need a recovery period between sessions.

Seize the opportunity to use the weight machines at your gym, but make sure you do so under strict supervision for the first few sessions. For the best results, the resistance needs to be carefully gauged so the muscle group is worked to the utmost after eight or ten repetitions; if you can easily manage a dozen or more, the resistance is too low. The American College of Sports Medicine recommends that the exercise be rhythmical, performed at a slow or moderate speed (no "explosive" or jerky movements), continued through the full range of motion, and done so as not to interfere with normal breathing. It also cautions that lifting heavy weights can dangerously raise blood pressure. If you have high blood pressure, or think you might, check with your physician before embarking on strength-building exercises.

Any activity that uses the body's large muscle groups, from carrying the groceries to running up the stairs, will help keep muscles strong and functioning well.

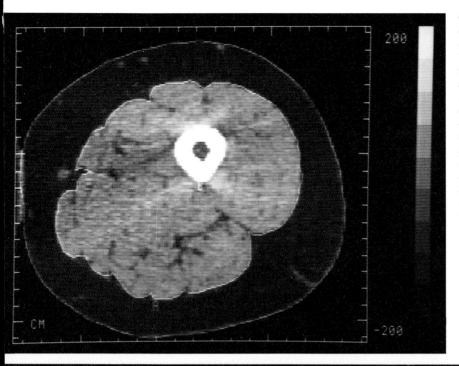

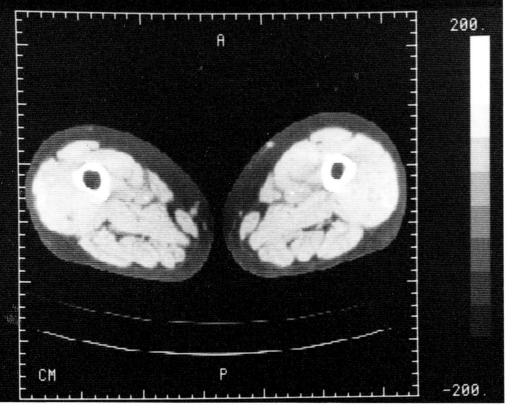

Once into their 30s, and particularly past menopause, most women lose strength at a rate of one to two per cent each year. These soft-tissue X-ray cross-sections through the thighs of, LEFT, a fit 35-year-old and, BELOW, those of an averagely inactive 57-year-old woman, show how lean muscle mass (light area) gradually breaks up and disintegrates. By the age of 60, most women have just two-thirds of the muscle they had at 20. The consequence is a dramatic loss of muscle tone and, more seriously, increasing enfeeblement. It used to be thought that only young adults could build strength, but research shows that muscles respond beautifully to training at any age, with impressive gains in strength of up to a quarter in as little as six weeks.

A POWER OF GOOD

Women who exercise in such a way as to maintain and build up their muscle can do their bones a power of good without recourse to hormones (although research now suggests that some post-menopausal muscle loss can be forestalled by HRT) or expensive rounds of calcium tablets. Upright yoga postures, brisk walking, and cycling (stationary or otherwise) will develop the muscles at the front of thighs and the calf muscles; doing the right type of sit-ups will strengthen the tummy.

The pay-offs of increasing strength persist throughout life. "I'm enjoying the feeling of being thin-and-strong as opposed to being only thin," confided Gloria Steinem, having newly taken up yoga and weight-training in her 50s. "Recently a woman I didn't know came over to compliment me on my muscle definition. *Muscle definition!* It was a compliment that made me more body-proud than all media references to the 'the pretty one' combined."[4]

Encouragingly, not a great deal of exercise appears necessary to give muscle definition and improve strength, and you are never too old to benefit. Counter to common preconceptions, an impressive degree of strength and muscle can be restored even in advanced old age. At the Human Nutrition Research Center at Tufts University, Boston, Dr. William Evans, who is chief of human physiology, has shown that 60-year-olds can gain strength and develop their muscle mass just as easily as 20-year-olds. In fact, he states that he has seen "increases in muscle size and strength in people up to age 90 and even 100." His ongoing research study into the effects of twice-weekly resistance training in post-menopausal women in their 50s and 60s confirms positive effects on bone metabolism, with gains in density of one and two per cent recorded, as Dr. Evans himself says, "at a time of life when losses would be expected." In addition, the women's muscular strength has almost doubled, and their muscle mass increased by 15–20 per cent, with consequent elevations of their metabolic rate.

LOSS OF MOBILITY

As we get older, the easy freedoms we enjoy can gradually slip away – so gradually, in fact, that they proceed unnoticed until ease of movement is quite severely restricted. A national fitness survey carried out in Canada in the early 1980s revealed marked losses of flexibility in the over-50s when compared with younger adults, with increased stiffness a commonplace in later life. Although loss of agility is not one of aging's inevitables, most of us take our mobility for granted until it threatens to desert us; at which point – as the novelist Elizabeth Taylor so well described – it can have a devastating effect on physical self-confidence.

> Mrs. Palfrey was trying to walk off a stiffness in her hip, but it would not be walked off. It seemed, instead, to be settling in, locking her joint, so that every step was consciously achieved. She realized that she never walked now without knowing what she was doing and concentrating upon it; walking had been like breathing, something unheeded. The disaster of being old was in not feeling safe to venture anywhere, of seeing freedom put out of reach. Her fall had deepened her uncertainty.[5]

As twinges in the hinges become part of everyday experience, and joints start to feel stiff and uncomfortable, it is essential that you do not let them circumscribe your life and that you put your body (gently) back into use. Mobility is your next most important asset after your wits, and the best way of preserving it is by continually calling upon it, putting each of the body's main weightbearing joints through their full range of movement every day.

When you use a joint, it squeezes the bones on either side and pumps blood around the network of capillaries under the bone surface, allowing a crucial exchange of nutrients from the blood to the synovial fluid that encapsulates the cartilage around the joint. The cartilage must be kept thoroughly awash in the synovial fluid if it is not to chafe, split, or otherwise dry out. Although all the body's major joints get drier as we get older, they can dry out unseasonably soon. Immobility, in particular, restricts the free circulation of fluid around the joint. Deprived of essential nutrients and oxygen and lumbered with its own cellular waste, which is no longer being washed away, the cartilage becomes worn and tatty. The blood capillaries also atrophy. Samples of tissue show a direct relationship between the number of vessels under the cartilage and the degree to which the cartilage above is worn. Once the blood supply is compromised, the bone thickens and the joint becomes stiff and sore.

Interpret pain and stiffness that doesn't resolve in a couple of days as a cue to see your doctor. If your joints often hurt or are causing you to cut out activities you previously enjoyed, don't adjust your lifestyle around the condition – get it checked out before it renders you even less mobile.

Sitting around all day is an occupational hazard. Both it and the shuffle that so often passes for walking take the hips through only a quarter of their full arc of movement and, if that is all the hips are asked to do, will eventually limit their freedom. In developing countries where the natives squat into advanced old age, osteoarthritis in the hip used to be virtually unknown – although it is now beginning to creep in among the more affluent due to the sedentariness their "privileged" lifestyle affords. The problem is extraordinarily common in Western societies: surveys show half of all the over 60's have some evidence of osteoarthritis on X-ray.

THE BENEFITS OF MOVEMENT

Mobility is determined by the ability of the joint to move freely about in its axis, whether nearly 360 degrees in the case of the shoulder or about 200 degrees in the case of the hip. The principle of "use it or lose it" really does apply. Light calisthenic exercises and, particularly, yoga twists and stretches will take each of the major joints through its full range of movement – the joints of the spine included. Far from being the immovable fused column it's often thought, the spine is actually a supple, jointed structure that needs to be moved every day for health. Long, slow stretches, held for several seconds at a time, are what's required; short, bouncing stretches can make joint problems worse.

Yoga is particularly beneficial, having evolved to bring the more uncommon "accessory" actions of the joints into play. One of the best insurances against later life seize-up is to find a yoga teacher, and to carry on practicing the postures you learn at home. Yoga can be started at any age and at any level of physical fitness. As well as keeping the joints fluid, daily practice soon uncovers unsuspected strengths and abilities, bringing physical self-confidence of the sort that usually diminishes with age. To begin with, the discipline of daily practice may come as a chore. But as joints that were seizing up start to loosen and muscles that had come to ache on the slightest exertion become strong and robust again, the surge of well-being acts as both reward and reinforcement, making it easier and easier to find time to practice.

Try a yoga class. If it doesn't appeal, try another; teachers and techniques vary enormously. Walking, swimming, and many of the martial arts can also keep joints free and mobile from midlife on. Regular exercise is especially important if joints are already stiff. Although the instinct is often to spare them by removing what little use they are put to, the opposite strategy is called for: light exercise that gently persuades the joint to move and loosen up is your best guard against any further loss of use. Always warm up muscles well *before* working the joints (see pages 216–19).

BONES

BACK in the not so dim and distant past, the skeleton was looked upon as little more than the frame on which the rest of the body was built – solid and unalterable as a table leg. If older people broke their bones more often, it was because they fell down more often. Now that the devastating bone-wasting condition, osteoporosis, has blasted to the forefront of the collective consciousness, we know that bones can become so frail that you don't even have to fall down to fracture them. Sneezing can crush a vertabra, stepping off a sidewalk fracture a hip.

A woman would have had to have been on a distant planet for the last ten years not to have heard of osteoporosis or to know that it is a rising scourge for her sex. Campaigning organizations say this is a condition one in three of us will not escape. While critics charge that talk of an epidemic is overdone – benefiting only the purveyors of vitamin pills, calcium tablets, skim milk, and hormone replacement therapy, all of whom play on our fear of fracture to promote their products – brittle bones are both common and becoming commoner at all sites of fracture. Campaigning organizations have drawn our attention to the fact that this is a condition one in three of us will not escape. In the United States, the National Osteoporosis Foundation estimates that one in two women over 50 now has an osteoporosis-related fracture.

Our sedentary lifestyle is the major cause for this steep upturn, and smoking doesn't help. In the years to come, some predict yet further rises as weight-obsessed women who spent their teenage and early adult years starving themselves come of age and suffer the consequences of decades of calcium-deficient diets and anovulatory (estrogen-deficient) menstrual cycles. Frighteningly, X-rays of the spines of some anorexics in their 20s are now revealing the sort of spinal crush fractures that normally afflict elderly women in their 60s and 70s.

DEGREES OF DENSITY

The 206 bones in the skeleton are composed, in differing degrees, of a mixture of "compact" and "trabecular" bone. Compact bone is dense, intensely strong and makes up bone's hard outer surface, or cortex. Trabecular bone acts as a filler and is much lighter than its compact counterpart. It is this latter, loofah-like bone that crumbles in osteoporosis; while the length and width remain unchanged, the internal composition becomes gappier and gappier until its ability to resist the forces of everyday activity suffers. The different bones of the body tend to have a different fracture timetable. First the wrist may fracture, then the spinal vertebrae crumble, then finally, and often devastatingly, the hip cracks. More than three-quarters of hip fractures afflict the over-75s.

Far from being solid and unchanging, we now know that the skeleton is one of the most dynamic parts of the body – constantly being broken down and built up again.

The secret life of the skeleton was beautifully summed up by the anatomist Dr. A. M. Cooke more than 40 years ago when he wrote:

> The skeleton, out of sight and often out of mind, is a formidable mass of tissue occupying about nine per cent of the body by bulk and no less than 17 per cent by weight. The stability and immutability of dry bones and their persistence for centuries, and even millions of years, after the soft tissue has turned to dust, gives us a false idea of bone during life. Its fixity after death is in sharp contrast to its ceaseless activity in life.

So ceaseless is this activity, in fact, that a young woman turns over around ten per cent of her total quota of bone a *year* – a process which verges on the credit side in adolescence, when there is a steep rise in bone mass, and then settles into equilibrium in the 20s, when it reaches its peak. The amount of bone we have at this point is largely genetically determined. If, as orthopedic surgeons only half-jokingly suggest, we could choose our parents none of us would ever need to suffer an osteoporosis-type fracture.

Race, another genetic unalterable, is important too. Black women have so much bone that osteoporosis is virtually unheard of, while white fair-skinned women have considerably lighter skeletons, and Asian women even lighter bones again. Women of Hispanic and Mediterranean origin appear to fall halfway between. But even within racial groups, the range remains wide and is, some maintain, determined more by income and degree of Westernization (i.e. inactivity) than by any genetic advantage or disadvantage.

From the mid-30s on, more bone is destroyed than replaced whatever our frame, race, or gender. While men also get osteoporosis, they have a much smaller (five per cent) risk, against our 25–30 per cent one. Not only do men start off with bigger and denser skeletons, but women, who are smaller-boned, have the added disadvantage of suffering an accelerated loss of bone around and just after the menopause, when levels of bone-friendly estrogen plummet and activity levels fall. At this time, they can lose as much as four per cent of their bone in a *year*. Bone loss speeds up in the first five or six years following menopause and then tails off, often ceasing altogether in much later life. Although the average white woman loses about a third of her total bone mass over a lifetime, some unlucky women can have as little as half their original quota when they get to 70. Such women often have no idea their skeletons are in such a desperate state until they actually fracture a bone. From that point on, life may be wrecked by a succession of painful fractures. One in every five women who break a hip dies within a year due to surgical complications or pneumonia brought on by her immobility. Those who "escape" with their lives are not necessarily as lucky as they seem, however, since many never walk freely again.

THE BENEFITS OF STRESS AND STRAIN

The scandal is that osteoporosis is largely a preventable catastrophe. There is an alternative old age. Within the genetic givens, much can be done to maximize peak bone mass and to keep the skeleton strong. Ideally, prevention starts well before the menopause, and it involves taking exercise not hormones. Fitness is key throughout life, benefiting the bones every bit as much as the heart, lungs, joints, and muscles. A century ago, osteoporosis was very unusual – and not just because people didn't live to ripe old ages; they often did. Pathologists examining elderly skeletons report that thinning bones were uncommon. But then so were automatic doors, automobiles, shopping baskets, elevators, and escalators. To get through life, people struggled with heavy loads that burdened their bones and walked long distances that kept their muscles strong. Now that life has become labor-saving, our bones and muscles are no longer needed and they are literally wasting away. To counter this, therefore, we need to import more physical effort into our daily lives. One analysis of the various studies which have been conducted worldwide concluded that exercise alone could prevent over half of hip fractures.[1]

Give up smoking. The habit brings the age of menopause forward by two or three years, interferes with estrogen metabolism, and is toxic to the bone-building cells. Heavy (pack-a-day or more) smokers add ten years to the age of their skeletons, doubling their risk of hip fracture and tripling their risk of vertebral (spine) fracture. Even "passive smokers," who inhale secondhand smoke, compromise their bone health by having an earlier menopause, which deprives them of bone-conserving estrogen.

Anything that stresses the bones can help stall the bone-wasting process, particularly "weightbearing" exercise that places a strain on the skeleton, which then answers the strain by putting down more bone. The top U.S. women ice skaters, for example, have leg bones that are 20 per cent denser than average. Strength training helps the non-athlete by building up muscle, which keeps the bones stable and balance steady. Encouragingly, not a great deal of activity is necessary to make a difference. In its marvellously adaptable way, the body soon adjusts to the demands put on it. In one experiment, women in their 50s and 60s who squeezed a tennis ball as hard as possible in each hand for just 30 seconds a day measurably increased their grip strength and bone-mineral density in as little as six weeks. Other studies confirm that virtually any sort of exercise, from vigorous housework to mowing the lawn or carrying the groceries, can slow down bone loss and so protect the hips from fracture and may even help reduce the risk of further fracture once the bones are known to be fragile. Although it pays to get the exercise habit young, older women who have had sedentary lifestyles in youth can still build new bone through exercise. In one study at Washington University in St Louis, a group of women over 55 spent an hour walking, jogging, or stair climbing. They also took calcium supplements. After nine months they had not only not lost bone, they had gained five per cent.

Meanwhile, the control group, which took extra calcium but didn't exercise, didn't show any improvement.[2]

Other indicators that strain the skeleton also benefit the bones. Being moderately overweight for your frame is one. When it comes to the bones, as with so much else, moderate midlife weight gain is not the unhealthy event it is often made out. After

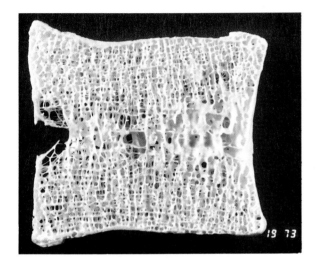
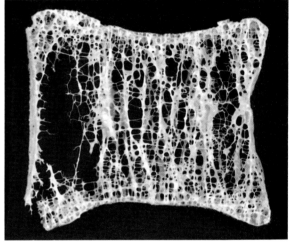

Cross-sections through, LEFT, the spinal vertebrae of a young woman with a strong healthy skeleton and, RIGHT, that of an older woman already suffering the bone-wasting disease, osteoporosis. Although the risk of this common condition climbs as a result of lowering hormone levels at menopause, over-vigorous exercise, crash dieting, and anorexia can have a prematurely dramatic effect on bone by robbing the body of estrogen. Scans show that some women in their 30s have a "bone age" of women several decades their senior.

Keep active – strength-training will particularly help build bones, as will any weight-bearing activity that taxes the big muscle groups, from climbing stairs to carrying the shopping. Jogging, skipping, rebounding (trampo-lining), and step aerobics give bones the best general work-out; cycling and swimming do least and walking falls some-where between, though walking up and down hills qualifies as excellent exercise for the bones. Don't overdo it though: very heavy exercise can cause estrogen levels to drop to a point where bone loss can actually be accelerated.

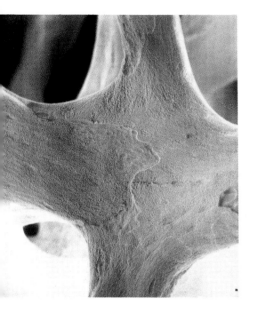

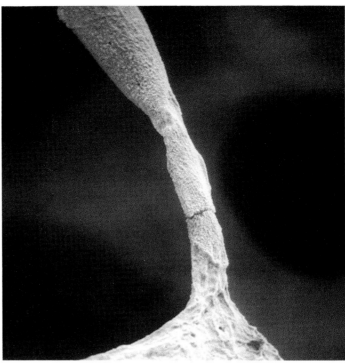

Close-ups of the individual trabeculae that make up the bone, magnified 220 times, point up the difference between the robust thick plate of normal bone, LEFT, and the fragile twig-like bone of osteoporosis, RIGHT; the fault line in the centre marks the point where the body's repair mechanisms have failed to mend one of many tiny internal fractures that will eventually threaten the strength of the whole.

menopause, the majority of estrogen produced derives from the fat cells. The more fat you have, the more estrogen you have to protect your bones. Moreover, while extreme overweight disinclines to activity, when heavyweights do move they stress their bones more than featherweights and so get less osteoporosis. Pregnancy also appears protective: women who have had children are less at risk of future fracture than childless women, due probably both to the extra loading on the skeleton and to boosted levels of estrogen, which rise as pregnancy progresses.

THE CALCIUM CONTROVERSY

Nearly all (99 per cent) of the body's calcium lies in the bones, but because the mineral is also essential to heart function and blood clotting, and these functions take priority over bone-building, insufficient calcium in the bloodstream leads to raids on the bone stores. Although much promoted in midlife, calcium is now widely considered most important during adolescence and early adulthood, when bone is being built up. Once into one's 30s, and certainly once past the menopause, calcium still makes a measurable difference, particularly if one's intake is exceptionally low. Many chronic dieters come into this category. In one survey in Sydney, Australia, three-quarters of the post-menopausal women interviewed were getting less than the 800 milligrams of calcium considered the bare minimum for bone health, and American surveys have found that a quarter of post-menopausal women do not consume so much as *half* this amount, since they make a habit of avoiding not only high-fat milk but all dairy produce. The National Osteoporosis Foundation recommends that adult women should aim for an intake of 1000 mg of the mineral a day (for post-menopausal women not taking estrogen, the recommendation is 1500 mg).

Some experts consider a daily calcium supplement to be a sensible move in view of the fact that the body's ability to absorb the mineral decreases after around the age of 45 in women. Taking calcium can act as an insurance against possible dietary shortfall, they say, it can't hurt (unless you are prone to kidney stones: check with your doctor), and it may have the added advantages of lowering blood pressure and keeping the colon healthy. A glass of skim milk at bedtime may be all that's required.

There is growing evidence that calcium can boost bone density in later life. Up to now studies have concentrated on the immediate menopausal years with negative results – due, it's theorized, to the much bigger impact of estrogen loss. A study at Tufts University in Boston has now shown clear benefits for women who are six or more years beyond menopause – that is, just beyond the period of rapid bone loss associated with plummeting levels of estrogen.[3]

Ensure your diet is adequately high in calcium, bearing in mind that dairy products provide half of all dietary calcium and that low-fat or skim milk, which has the virtue of being low in fat, actually has more of the mineral than whole milk.

The pro-supplement camp advises taking a calcium supplement at bedtime, washed down with a glass of skim milk or calcium-fortified orange juice (each of which contributes a further 300 mg). There are many different forms of calcium – calcium phosphate is poorly absorbed, while chelated calcium, calcium citrate, and calcium gluconate have a better uptake. Chewable calcium tablets dissolve quickly in the stomach, making them well absorbed – as do chewable calcium-containing antacid tablets (Tums), which are just as effective. Some now consider the best supplement to be calcium citrate malate (available only in fortified citrus juices), which trials at Tufts University, in Boston, have shown to be more effective than the most commonly used calcium tablet; a couple of glasses of juice a day should do it.

- Go easy on cereal fiber, especially bran. In addition to several other important minerals, bran binds calcium with it in the intestine and sweeps it out of the system. Researchers in Scotland have found four times the degree of bone-mineral loss in women on high-fiber, high-bran diets. They advise women to get their fiber from fruit and vegetables, and beans and lentils, instead.
- Cut down on salt by avoiding processed foods, by not adding salt to cooking (or only the merest pinch), and by not having it on the table – a strategy that may also benefit your blood pressure. Excessive salt causes sodium to be excreted in quantity from the kidneys and it takes calcium with it.
- Be conscientious about vitamin D, keeping your intake of oily fish high, especially in the sunless winter months. Check with your doctor before taking extra, however. Vitamin K also plays a role in bone health, and may cut calcium losses by as much as half (you'll find it in broccoli, Brussels sprouts, and dark green, leafy vegetables).
- Don't get too thin.

Also critical in later life is one's intake of vitamin D (found in free-range eggs, milk, butter, oily fish, margarine, and cod-liver oil). It is also synthesized by the body in response to sunlight. It is the main agent responsible for calcium absorption and has a range of hormone-like effects on the body. As vitamin D is added to many fats by law, true deficiency is rare: but still the fracture epidemic increases.

HORMONE TREATMENT

While diet may play a part, there is no doubt now that the drastic drop in levels of estrogen at the menopause is the prime ravager of skeletal strength. Fortunately, the process can be stalled and even (slightly) put into reverse. True, once bone has been lost and the spine has warped, there is no power yet known to science that can straighten it out again. But it is now established medical fact that, as well as relieving miserable menopausal problems, hormone replacement therapy (HRT), which restores a woman's estrogen to pre-menopausal levels, halts and in some cases even marginally reverses the process of bone loss. Until recently, no one quite knew why estrogen replacement has this dramatic effect, but in 1992 researchers in Indianapolis discovered that estrogen suppresses a protein that stimulates the development of the bone-destroying cells; when hormone levels drop, it seems these cells go on the rampage.

The earlier that hormone treatment begins, and the longer that it is maintained, the more effective it is likely to be. At least five years is considered advisable, and ten preferable. At the time of writing, however, the average length of taking HRT in the United States is well under a year. While HRT offers substantial protection as long as use is continued, some experts have found a rebound loss on stopping treatment equivalent to (or even worse than) going through the menopause. Nevertheless, the net result remains beneficial. In a long-term study that compared the expected number of hip fractures in women who had taken hormone replacement therapy with women who had not, the expected number of fractures was cut by up to two-thirds in the HRT group. Although there are still wide areas of disagreement, few doctors now seriously doubt that HRT can postpone the risk of fracture for about the length of time it is taken. When taken indefinitely, as some are now advocating, it could even delay a hip fracture beyond the normal life expectancy.

It all sounds wonderful, but many women balk at the idea of taking hormones on an indefinite basis just on the off-chance that they are the one in two or three at risk. After all, two out of three women will *not* go on to have bone problems. Hormone replacement therapy does have side-effects and has not been cleared of causing breast cancer when taken long-term, although, by the same token, it does seem to protect against heart attacks and, possibly, stroke (see pages 329–33).

RISK FACTORS

The most-quoted "risk factors" for osteoporosis are so general – white or Asian, female, slim build, sedentary, etc. – as to be completely unilluminating. However, some specific factors particularly predispose to the condition. Early menopause, due to premature lack of protective estrogen, is the chief one. This includes both early natural menopause (before the age of 45) and surgical menopause brought on by removal of the ovaries (oophorectomy). Additionally, a subset of all women who have had only their womb removed (hysterectomy) will go on to have a premature menopause, even if the ovaries are left intact.

Several causes of estrogen deficiency during the fertile years could also line women up for bone problems later on. One is prolonged amenorrhea (absence of periods), as is often suffered by keen sportswomen, athletes in training, ballet dancers, crash and chronic dieters, and sufferers of anorexia nervosa. A recent wrist fracture or indeed any type of fracture, especially if the fall was only minor, should raise suspicions, as should back pain that has come on suddenly for no apparent reason. Treatment for conditions such as asthma and other lung diseases, rheumatoid arthritis, Crohn's disease, and multiple sclerosis can also be sinister for the skeleton. One study by rheumatologists found bone density to be "significantly lower" in those who had taken steroid drugs for more than six months, leading them to conclude that "the use of low-dose steroids in these patients may not be as safe as other workers have suggested." Thyroid problems can also interfere with the body's bone-building metabolism, as can chronic liver and digestive complaints such as celiac disease.

BONE SCANNING

Most of the aforesaid risks apply only to a minority of the population. However, if you are white or Asian, female, and over 50, you are significantly at risk. Fortunately, for the price of a new pair of jogging shoes you can now have your risk reliably assessed and so discover whether you stand to benefit by taking action at the menopause. State-of-the-art Dual Energy X-Ray Absorptiometry (DEXA) scans can detect unusually thin bones well before there is any chance of serious fracture. In addition to tipping the balance for those who are still undecided about hormone replacement, screening can also have a bearing on important decisions, such as how long to stay on the therapy – allowing women who might otherwise take it for just a few months or even years, and then stop, the opportunity to reconsider.

Scans have their critics. Although bone mass correlates quite closely with bone strength, it doesn't always predict the likelihood of fracture. Thin bones *are* more likely to crack than thick ones and there is a "fracture threshold" below which they crack quite easily. One American study of over 8000 women found that the risk of hip fracture was "strongly associated" with a lowered hipbone density reading, and that, for every degree that the density reading was below normal, the risk multiplied two-and-a-half times.

Bone scans are both painless and non-invasive, using less than one-twentieth of the radiation in a chest X-ray and one-eightieth of the "natural" cosmic radiation to which one is exposed on a transatlantic plane flight by virtue of the thinner atmosphere. They are also extraordinarily accurate: while conventional X-rays can only detect a change in bone mass when as much as 40 per cent of the bone has

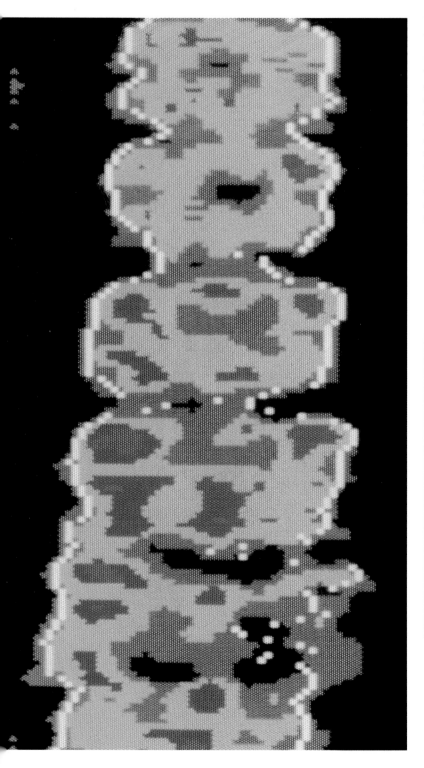

Sophisticated DEXA (Dual Energy X-Ray Absorptiometry) bone scans give precise information about differing mineral densities of bone in key sites that are especially susceptible to fracture. The color coding ranges from red (most dense) through yellow and blue to green (least dense). Compare the scan taken from a normal spine, BELOW, with that of a woman suffering from osteoporosis (brittle bone disease), LEFT. Although scans cannot predict the rate of loss, studies have found that women with low bone density in their spine, wrists, or hips do have a higher risk of fracture, and that this can be minimized by exercising regularly in midlife and by taking hormone replacement therapy at menopause.

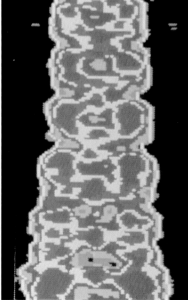

already been lost, the new machines are able to detect losses of as little as one per cent. Here is Mary Roach writing up her scan for American *Vogue*:

> I lie on my back while the quietly humming machine casts an X-ray gaze back and forth above my hip, one of the places where bone loss shows up first. . . . After a few minutes, the machine prints a computer graphic of my left hip socket. It's like an X-ray on paper, with varying shades of gray reflecting the differing densities of the bone. On the next page is a graph showing how my measurements stack up to the norm for my age. I'm already low. The technician is several years older than I am, yet her bones are considerably denser. She does martial arts for two hours every day. I play badminton on alternate weekends.[5]

While women who start off with good strong bones will probably maintain reasonable bone density, those who have flimsier bones can only deteriorate and should do everything they can to protect themselves. Experts, who have screened hundreds of thousands of American women, agree that women in the lowest 30 per cent of bone-density distribution for their age and frame are at significant risk of a major fracture and should seriously consider hormone replacement therapy for the sake of their skeletons. Women with risk factors for osteoporosis who are not otherwise considering taking prolonged HRT would therefore be well advised to seek a scan. If they are among the 15 per cent of women lined up to suffer a hip fracture, such a measure could prove not just bone-saving but life-saving too.

Seriously consider a scan at menopause if you are not otherwise intending to take hormone replacement therapy, and be guided by your doctor/gynecologist as to whether you should then consider estrogen therapy.

If you are taking hormone therapy, and your bone mass has been shown to be low, consider a repeat scan after two years. Research has shown that, on estrogen doses previously thought universally protective, a minority continues to lose bone and may require a higher dose of estrogen.

GUT

WHEN godliness counted for something, inner cleanliness was next to it. A hundred years ago, people blamed everything from bad breath to arthritis on their bowels, looking on them as literal sewers of ill health. Life-threatening toxins, generated by food that had become "stuck" in the bowel, were thought to poison the system as they leaked into the bloodstream. Aging, even death itself, was seen as the result of a sort of toxic constipation. While several health fanatics took the drastic step of having their colons hacked out, there is no evidence that they derived any benefit to their health. Even so, these ideas linger on in modern ideas of inner cleanliness that range from stern toilet training and colonic irrigation to laxative abuse, candida "overgrowth," and esoteric massage treatments said to encourage lymphatic drainage by removing the clutter of cellular waste via the bloodstream.

A QUESTION OF MOVEMENT

Theories of internal toxicity live on too in the obsession with regularity – a preoccupation that often becomes more marked with age, even though, according to a poll of nearly 2000 hospital patients, constipation is actually more likely in younger women than older ones. Contrary to popular expectation, the bowels do not slow up with age. If they "fail" to open as frequently as they once did, this is probably caused not so much by lack of movement on their part as on ours. Activity stimulates the important process of peristalsis (the squeezing motion of the smooth intestinal muscle, which literally pushes food residues along the colon and ultimately out of the body) and keeps the system healthily regular.

In 1991, the medical journal *Gut* published results of a South African experiment which found transit time through the intestine dramatically accelerated when people went out running or bicycling for an hour a day compared with when they just sat around for the same period of time. Although they were eating an identical diet, food raced through the system in just two-thirds of the time: 36 hours compared to 51.

FIBER – MUCH MORE THAN ROUGHAGE

As well as being stimulated by exercise, peristaltic waves are jolted into action by the arrival of food in the stomach, which is why gastroenterologists make such a big point about eating breakfast. The bowels like to function in the early morning if given the chance and plenty of fiber.

There is now overwhelming evidence that fiber is much more than mere bulk that simply sweeps all before it and pushes it out of the system. We now know that it is actually broken down in the colon in a way that may offset the potentially damaging impact of the typical high-fat Western diet. Soluble fiber (fruits, vegetables, cereals, oats) can actually lower the bad, low-density type of cholesterol by binding with the cholesterol-containing bile acids. The theory is that once cholesterol is bound in this way it cannot be absorbed and dumped on the artery walls but is instead swept through the system and excreted. As one enthusiast claimed, upping your soluble fiber intake is "a great way of selectively channeling fat through the feces."

Fiber metabolites also stimulate the bowel wall and encourage peristalsis. Modern fiberless foods stay in the bowel an abnormally long time, lacking the stimulation to push them on through. Where paleolithic-type food sped in and out of the body in a mere 24 hours, modern meals dally for three or four days, or even longer. When Sunday lunch is not excreted until noon on Thursday or even Friday, the balance of the 400 different types of bacteria in the bowel may change in an unhealthy – perhaps even, eventually, cancerous – direction, since the longer any carcinogen is in contact with the lining of the bowel the greater its potential for harm. This perhaps explains why women, who have longer transit times, are more susceptible to colon cancer than men and why exercise, which speeds up the passage of food through the gut, appears to protect. Recently, researchers at Harvard Medical School published the results of a 23-year study in which those individuals who burned more than 2500 calories a week *through any kind of physical activity*, even if it was just walking a couple of miles (a few kilometres) a day, halved their risk of colon cancer compared to their sedentary peer group.

> **B**e conscious of proper bowel care. Eat plenty of fiber as part of a diet generally rich in fruit and vegetables and low in fat. Eat a leisurely breakfast. Get enough exercise. When you need to go to the bathroom, don't ignore it, and do not strain when there, since this can weaken long-term bladder control.
>
> In addition to eating plenty of fiber, lower your consumption of red meat to a maximum of twice a week and eat more chicken and fish. Barbecuing and grilling until the meat chars has been associated with a higher incidence of colon cancer, so cook meat only lightly.

The floating principle is often quoted as a measure of bowel health, with buoyant stools said to pass the test while the more compacted type that sits in the bottom of the bowl fails. However, consistency is now thought a better guide: the perfect stool is smooth and soft, has no cracks, and slips from the body without straining. Stools that have cracks or consist of lots of lumps call out for more fiber until they are soft, entire, and easily passed. But go easy on the bran: it binds with calcium and takes it out of the body, leading, according to one study, to measurable drops in bone density (see page 166). As other studies suggest that calcium may protect against colon cancer, enthusiastic additions of bran could be actively damaging in more ways than one.

LAXATIVE ABUSE

Instead of upping fiber to keep themselves regular, many women swallow laxatives, so at a stroke emptying their systems and ridding themselves of unnecessary extra calories. Surveys suggest that laxative abuse is much commoner than most doctors suspect. In an article for British *Vogue*, Judy Sadgrove confessed:

> I used to worry about the handfuls of laxatives that I gulped down almost daily in my teens and twenties, when I was either starving or stuffing myself. Vomiting was alien to me. But senna pills were easy to swallow, relatively cheap and the effects were grat-ifyingly violent, suitable punishment for my terrible greed. No one knew what I was doing, despite the explosive bouts of diarrhoea, just as they didn't really know the ex-tent of my disordered eating. I was deeply ashamed of it all. And it took many years to give it all up – dieting, bingeing and laxatives.[1]

This scenario continues into mid and late life for surprising numbers of women. As they get acclimatized to the laxatives they are taking, the effects become less dramatic. The sense of urgency slackens, cramps no longer grip the abdomen, and the bowel may not completely empty. The long term consequences can be serious, since, after a while, the ingestion of large quantities of stimulant laxatives can upset the body's biochemical balance. Far from being the passive transit pipe that is often assumed, the colon is an active organ which, among much else, allows crucial salts and water to filter into the system. Laxative-led food bypasses the process, leading to possible potassium and other mineral deficiencies. Even a lesser laxative habit, pursued not out of a desire to be thin but a misguided belief in the virtues of regularity, can cause gastrointestinal disturbances which lead to chronic constipation rather than relieve it.

COLONIC IRRIGATION

The craze for colonic irrigation owes much to our cultural fear of constipation. Devotees of this enema *par excellence* believe that their colons become encrusted with unexpelled, impacted fecal matter that becomes a breeding ground for unfriendly bacteria. These are said to provoke all manner of low-grade illnesses, from continual infections and dragging depressions to headaches, acne, allergies, general fatigue, and, in a word, anything modern medicine doesn't have an answer for. Giving laxatives doesn't resolve the problem, they say, since the waste simply shoots through a tunnel in the middle of the colon.

Colonic irrigation or "colonics," as it's also called, involves pulsing up to 35 gallons (130 liters) of warm water into the colon via the anus, using clear plastic tubing. Its advocates enthuse for hours about the marvelous physiological and psychological high it engenders, but conventional medics dismiss it as bizarre and potentially meddlesome. It is totally unnecessary for anyone who is healthy and unconstipated, they insist. The digestive system is designed to clear itself, they say, and toxins are *not* released into the bloodstream. In fact, there is a danger of peritonitis (inflammation of the lining of the abdominal cavity) if the tubing is carelessly inserted. Some also worry about the long-term effects of working against the normal flow and, specifically, pushing up against the ileo-cecal valve where the small intestine joins the colon.

CANCER OF THE COLON

Colon cancer is the third-biggest cause of cancer death in American women (after lung and breast cancer). It has one of the worst outlooks of any kind of cancer, with 50 per cent of American sufferers surviving after five years. This grim record, which hasn't budged in more than half a century, is almost entirely due to late detection, with the tumor only found when acute abdominal pain sets in, chronic intractable constipation is at last accurately diagnosed, or blood gushes out of the rectum. By this time, the cancer is likely to have spread beyond the colon to the lymph nodes and liver. If a tumor is detected in the early stages, however, five-year survival goes up to more than 90 per cent. With earlier detection, over two-thirds of the lives that are now lost could be saved.

> **A** marked change in bowel habit, abdominal pain, "indigestion" for more than a week, intractable constipation, precipitous diarrhea, weight loss, or any bleeding from the rectum should always be checked out. It may turn out to be due to hemorrhoids, an anal fissure (small tear in the bottom), or irritable bowel syndrome, but diagnosis should always follow rather than replace a proper internal investigation, especially over the age of 40.

As with cervical cancer and endometrial cancer, an estimated 90 per cent of colon cancers have an easily identifiable, generally slow-growing, pre-malignant stage – in the form of growths called polyps or adenomas. Thought to be present in one in ten people over the age of 50, and one in three over 70, these growths are not sinister in themselves, but around ten per cent of them are believed to be the springboard for future malignancies.

SCREENING FOR COLON CANCER

The United States has a long tradition of screening for colon cancer, arguably subjecting some of its citizens to unnecessarily frequent internal investigations. Nevertheless, records show that, while colon cancer is increasing, the mortality rate is going down.

In fact, it is believed that even a single screening of the entire population at the age of 55 using an instrument called a flexible sigmoidoscope, which covers the lower part of the colon (where three-quarters of all cancers and polyps originate), could cut bowel cancer deaths by a third. One trial, reported in the *New England Journal of Medicine* in 1992, found that patients who had had one or more of these investigations in the previous ten years were 70 per cent less likely to die of colon cancer than unscreened individuals.[2] Since polyps take between two and 19 years to become cancerous, if ever, a one-off screen makes good preventive sense and could also identify the five per cent of high-risk individuals who need more frequent monitoring. Recent research suggests that such individuals might also benefit from low-dose aspirin therapy: the equivalent of one tablet a week appears to halve the risk of a polyp developing into a tumor, according to a trial at Emory University School of Medicine in Atlanta.

A non-invasive test to trace hidden blood in the feces is also routinely used in the United States and is presently under trial in several European countries. Preliminary results show that over half of all colon cancers have been picked up at the earliest possible stage, while still confined to the colon and completely curable by surgery, compared to the dismal seven to ten per cent found when no such tests are used. But they must be repeated on a yearly basis. In 1993, in the largest trial to date on over 46,000 volunteers, scientists at the University of Minnesota found that annual use of the test resulted in a 30 per cent reduction of deaths from colon cancer, whereas those who used it two-yearly had little survival advantage over those who did not use the test at all.[3]

While bright red blood on the surface of the stools or the toilet paper is very common and usually the innocent result of a bleeding hemorrhoid or a small tear in the anus, blood that is darker red or mixed in with the stool, or the passing of quantities of mucus, can be an early warning of a cancer, or of a polyp, and should always be fully investigated. Do not be unduly alarmed: such signs are unlikely to be

A self-screening test, known as a fecal occult blood test (available from physicians/pharmacies) can detect minute traces of hidden blood in the stool, which could indicate the presence of a tumor or polyps. A few give an immediate result, but most require laboratory analysis or medical interpretation. As false negatives are common, they need repeating quite often, and many specialists consider their annual use advisable past the age of 50 – when the incidence of colon cancer rises – especially if you have a family history of bowel cancer, if you have a personal history of ovarian, breast, or endometrial cancer, if you suffer from colitis or inflammatory bowel syndrome, or if you have had previous polyps diagnosed.

For optimal prevention, have a flexible sigmoidoscopy at the age of 50 or 55, and be guided by the specialist as to the best intervals for subsequent screens. The U.S. National Cancer Institute recommends rescreens at three-to-five yearly intervals, though some experts believe that, if the colon is clear, a rescreen may not be needed for a decade or more. If polyps or suspicious tissue is present, however, shorter screening intervals will be recommended, especially if you come into the higher-risk categories given above. For such individuals, calcium supplementation (up to a gram a day) and low-dose aspirin therapy should also be given serious consideration.

If you have one close relative over the past three generations (i.e. a grandparent, parent, or sibling) who had bowel cancer, the risk of your getting it rises between two and four-fold. If, however, you have two or more such relatives, your risk rises even further. The identification of the gene responsible for the inherited form of this cancer in the summer of 1993 is sure to lead to the development of a "gene screen"; in the meantime, talk to your physician about colonoscopy (a more extensive test) from age 35.

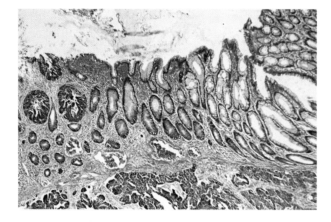

Bowel cancer is one of the three biggest killers of Western women, but with less embarrassment and appropriate screens, two out of three deaths could be avoided. As many as nine out of ten colon cancers have an easily identifiable, generally slow-growing, pre-malignant stage – in the form of growths called polyps or adenomas, as shown by the thickened strands of densely colored cells to the right of the image, BELOW. Present in one in ten people over 50, these growths are not sinister in themselves, but around one in ten is thought to be the springboard for a future cancer. A one-off screening at 50 or 55 using an instrument called a flexible sigmoidoscope, with further screens as advised, could prevent the progression from polyps through to cancer, as indicated by the very dark spherical areas on the far left of the image, LEFT.

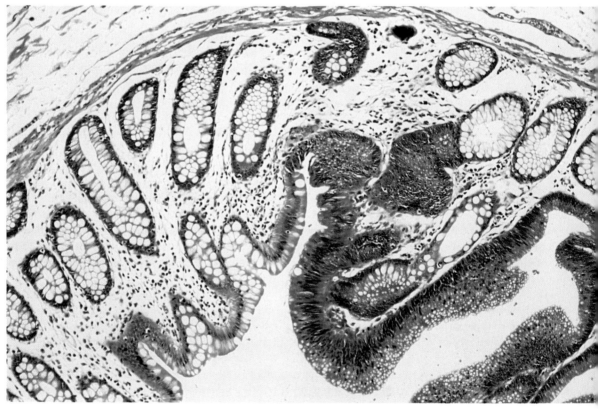

sinister, especially below the age of 50, since only six per cent of colon cancers occur in people under this age. But they must be checked out.

With the right sort of diet, many cases of colon cancer could be avoided altogether. It is, for example, ten times more common in rich South Africa than in the rural center of the continent, and there is now compelling evidence that a high-fat, low-fiber, unnaturally carnivorous diet multiplies the risk. In 1980, 90,000 women aged between 34 and 59 years old completed a dietary questionnaire; six years later, when 150 cases of colon cancer had been documented, the women who ate beef, pork, or lamb every day had over twice the incidence of colon cancer than those who ate these meats less than once a month. Eating fish and chicken (minus skin) actively lowered the risk.

BLADDER

In an age of no-holds-barred familiarity with nearly all bodily functions, an embarrassed silence hangs over incontinence. Women discuss their sex lives in lurid technicolor, talk about their periods, bemoan the miseries of the menopause. But the fact that they leak or wet their pants remains a closely guarded secret.

Surveys show not only that more women suffer bladder control problems than men, but also that they suffer them sooner and more severely. This is not, as is often thought, a scourge of advanced old age but one that affects a surprising number of women in their 40s and even 30s. One survey established that at least a third of women over 35 have an episode of incontinence twice a month or more.[1] According to Help for Incontinent People, a national advocacy group, half of American women between 18 and 45 have occasional incontinent episodes. Such "episodes" range from an imperceptible dribble on coughing or sneezing to almost continuous leaking or a complete emptying of the bladder on failing to get to the bathroom on time. Four out of ten sanitary towels sold in the United States are thought to be bought to absorb leaking urine, and the advertising encourages this with its promises of protection "to keep you dry all day, every day."

One of life's last unmentionables, incontinence wrecks life for millions of women from the midlife on. A Dutch study found that nearly half of all women suffering stress incontinence lose urine during intercourse and most had stopped having sex for fear of urine escaping. Women suffering this problem alter their lives in numerous ways. One Australian physiotherapist ascribes the marked reluctance of women in their 30s, 40s and 50s to sign on for aerobics classes and games of tennis and squash, and their preference for swimming over other forms of exercise, to the fact that they can "keep the secret of their leakage safe" that way.[2]

Incontinence is often thought to be beyond the reach of medicine. Women delay seeking medical help for years after the onset of their problem. When asked, they often say it is the price they have to pay for being mothers. Yet incontinence is not a normal part of growing old nor is it an inevitable consequence of childbearing. It is a sign that something is wrong. With proper evaluation and appropriate treatment, possibly involving medication and surgery, it can always be helped and sometimes cured completely.

THE GOING RATE

In normal climatic conditions, people produce about 1½ quarts (1.5 liters) of urine a day. A well-behaved bladder can store about just over a pint (about half a liter) before the urge to go becomes uncontrollable. Signals to empty come on even earlier, though the timing varies widely. People who think the opportunity to go should never be missed, and have got into the habit of emptying the bladder before it is even half full, will find their holding capacity progressively diminishing as the urge to go comes on sooner and sooner. The commonly held fear that urine will stagnate and become infected unless the bladder is frequently emptied is groundless unless there is already an infection: the bladder is designed to store urine and no possible harm can come from holding on to it.

As the bladder fills, nerve endings in the muscle monitor the degree to which it is being stretched, and relay that information to the brain. When the bladder is fairly full, the urge to go is felt – but it can usually be easily postponed. The urethral sphincter at the base of the bladder clamps shut, the detrusor (bladder) muscle relaxes, the urge to go subsides, and one is able to "hold on." When convenient, the signal to go is transmitted, the bladder contracts, the sphincter at the base of the bladder relaxes, and the urine travels down through the urethra and out of the body. Although the bladder generally retains effective function into advanced old age, it does become less reliable, and the urge to go tends to become more frequent.

If frequency of urination is a problem, a few simple life-style changes may help.

- Restrict fluids to a quart (liter) a day, but be sure to drink this amount to prevent dehydration. Urine that is concentrated, orange in color and strong-smelling suggests you are not drinking enough.
- Try cutting down on caffeine (in coffee, tea, and cola-type drinks) since it irritates the bladder muscle and can make frequency and urgency worse. Try limiting alcohol too, as it acts as a diuretic and increases the volume of fluid in the body.
- Timetable bathroom visits – initially going every 60 minutes and emptying the bladder as completely as you can, regardless of the desire to go. Put off the urge to go between scheduled visits as long as possible by contracting the pelvic floor, pressing hard up on the perineum with your hand, sitting on a rolled-up towel, playing mind games, or using a breathing technique, such as that given on page 224. Increase the intervals by ten minutes every two weeks with a final goal of three-hour intervals.
- Lose weight if necessary to reduce the load on the pelvic-floor muscles. Overweight women often find shedding the extra considerably improves control.
- Check out all prescribed drugs with your doctor for possible side-effects.

THE PELVIC-FLOOR MUSCLES

Although the bladder muscle, or detrusor, is outside our voluntary control, it is influenced by a critical set of muscles, the pelvic floor, which loops around the vagina and anus and supports the bladder and uterus. When the pelvic-floor muscles contract, they stimulate the urethral sphincter to squeeze shut and so stop urine escaping. They also tighten reflexively whenever there is sudden downward pressure on the abdomen – such as when coughing, sneezing, bursting out laughing, jogging, dancing, jumping, lifting, or making love – and so prevent leaking. If this type of pressure is put on already weakened pelvic-floor muscles (as is common after childbirth) or the muscle fibers deteriorate (as they can after menopause), sudden stress can cause the bladder neck to open and urine to dribble or gush out – hence the term "stress incontinence."

Stress incontinence is the major cause of leaking in women. Luckily, the pelvic-floor muscles respond to exercise just as readily as any other muscle in the body. However strong they are, every woman should exercise them several times a day as her best way of retaining control of her bladder. These exercises are known in the United States as Kegel exercises because they were developed by Dr. Arnold Kegel half a century ago to help those of his patients who were complaining of leaking urine.

Unseen and for the most part unheeded, the pelvic-floor muscles not only help keep a woman continent but intensify sensations of pleasure during intercourse. Although Kegel exercises are now taught as routine at antenatal classes, many Western women have amazingly inert pelvic floors. In parts of the world where mothers teach their adolescent daughters to use their pelvic-floor muscles for sexual stimulation, stress incontinence is said to be virtually unknown.

CAUSES OF STRESS INCONTINENCE
It is a telling reflection of our priorities that women who obsessively practice sit-ups in an attempt to get their postnatal belly back into shape commonly neglect their pelvic floor, an equally critical muscle from the point of view of long-term quality of life. Although childbirth is often blamed for stress incontinence in later life, the way that it is managed is more likely to be responsible. If labor itself is unreasonably prolonged or forceps are used to help the baby out, there may be lasting consequences for bladder control, since the nerves that supply the muscles of the pelvic floor can be damaged.

Locate the pelvic-floor muscles when you are next on the toilet by squeezing up hard to stay the flow of urine. If your muscles are in good shape you should be able to stop the flow completely, not just slow it to a dribble. (While this is a good test of pelvic-floor control, it should never be used as an exercise since stop/starting in this way can sometimes exacerbate an underlying problem.) You can also feel the pelvic-floor muscles by inserting a couple of fingers into the vagina and squeezing tightly up around them; the tighter the grip the stronger they are. If you cannot stop the flow or feel your vagina tensing around your fingers, you will need help to identify these muscles. Ask to see a continence advisor. It may be just a little one-to-one help that is required. Alternatively, the use of a pocket-sized electrical stimulator, which uses an electrical current to exercise the muscles passively via an electrode placed in the vagina, can wake up the muscles sufficiently for you to be able to feel them working and then reproduce the contraction yourself.

Once weakened, the pelvic-floor muscles can be further compromised by strenuous physical effort, such as lifting and carrying heavy objects or particularly (an occupational hazard for most women) small children. Obesity is also a hazard; the extra weight pushing down on the pelvic floor gradually stretches and weakens it until it may start to give way and urine leaks out. Chronic constipation is probably the commonest aggravating factor, particularly when combined with straining to open the bowels. Weak abdominal muscles do not help either. Research has shown that incontinence is associated with a general weakening of abdominal muscle tone.

Undetected diabetes and smoking increase the risk of incontinence. A survey of 606 adult women carried out at the Medical College of Virginia and Virginia Commonwealth University found that incontinence problems rose by nearly 30 per cent in smokers regardless of age or number of offspring – a compelling reason to stop if the other risks seem remote.

Although frequency and urge incontinence (needing to go more often and getting less and less advance warning) are thought to be problems of older age, they afflict younger women too. They are often exacerbated by the dramatic fall in estrogen levels at the menopause, which thins the urethral lining and probably also has an impact on the nerves at the bladder base. Deprived of their estrogen, the tissues of the urinary tract, like those of the vagina, can become dry and so more easily irritated and infection-prone. But while the estrogen element of the hormone replacement prescription can sometimes help prevent urgency and frequency problems, and reduce the likelihood of certain infections, it cannot restore lost pelvic-floor tone.

REGAINING CONTROL

The easiest time to take back control over your bladder is when problems first arise, and leakage starts. A rigorous program of Kegel exercises can help two-thirds of

---

If episodes of incontinence are affecting your life, see your doctor; there are many forms of effective help available. If your problem is dismissed or ascribed to "age," and no help is offered, do not be put off; ask to be referred for a thorough urodynamic investigation. It will help the specialist enormously if you know how much the bladder will hold "at best" (usually after a night's sleep), how often you empty the bladder, day and night, and how much urine is produced over 24 hours. Use a measuring jug and make out a chart: simply keep a piece of paper with you at all times so that you can record the time and amount passed on each bathroom visit over a three-day period.

women with mild (infrequent) stress incontinence. It will also act as a safeguard against future trouble if you still have good control. But be aware that, though it is very effective as a preventive measure, women whose stress incontinence is pronounced may require more active treatment. So do not be disillusioned if it doesn't work. It's a good first step, and there are many other avenues to explore.

If you have no trouble locating your pelvic-floor muscles, progress to the exercises detailed below. You will find that the muscles respond beautifully to exercise, swiftly regaining their strength and tone. As they become stronger, you will be able to manage many more repetitions without tiring. This all translates into more control, which can be noticeable in as little as two weeks, and make a real difference within two to three months.

Although better tone is unlikely to cure stress incontinence, it can bring about marked improvements. Further control can be gained by using weighted vaginal cones. When placed in the vagina for 15 minutes twice a day, the cone stimulates the muscles to contract in order to stop it from falling out, so producing a "weight-training" effect. The idea is to use the heaviest weight that you can retain, while remaining on your feet and carrying out non-strenuous activities, graduating to progressively heavier weights as the pelvic floor muscles strengthen.

Do not ignore your symptoms or, worse, get into a pattern of going to the bathroom at every opportunity "just in case." This just reinforces the problem. Instead, try the bladder-retraining program detailed earlier and so increase your ability to hold on. A study coordinated by the University of Virginia in association with the National Institute on Aging in Bethesda, Maryland, took 123 incontinent women of 55 years or older and split them into a treated group, who performed the

---

Practice regular Kegel (pelvic-floor) exercises, and add in a daily abdominal toner to keep these important supporting muscles strong as well. Use cones too (see above) if leaking is already a problem.

First, locate the pelvic-floor muscles. Next, provide yourself with lots of visual prompts that will help remind you to do the exercises: wind brightly colored rubber bands around the faucets in the kitchen and bathroom; stick small adhesive red dots over mirrors, the frame of the television or computer screen, and the driving mirror in the car. Whenever they catch your eye, do a set of the exercises, aiming to do at least five sets of ten a day. If stress leakage is already a problem, carry them out 10 to 15 times a day for three months; you may find it helpful to get a watch with a beep and do them on the hour every hour. It only takes half a minute, but it's half a minute well spent.

Initially do a number of short, sharp contractions and follow with longer, more sustained ones – squeezing up strongly, holding for a count of five, and releasing gradually.

As the muscles get stronger, increase the intensity of the exercise, and the demands on the muscles, by changing your posture. Start by doing them lying down with your buttocks raised on a pillow, then progress to lying horizontal, then sitting, then standing, and finally, squatting, when you will find you have to squeeze up much more forcefully to counteract the downward pull of gravity.

Finally, visualize the muscles as an elevator ascending a building floor by floor in four stages, from the basement up. Contract the muscles to their utmost right up into the abdomen (the top floor) and then let the elevator descend slowly floor by floor. The challenge is to release your grip gradually, without crashing all the way down to the basement.

drill, and a control group, who didn't. The number of incontinent episodes more than halved for three-quarters of the treated group, with 12 per cent completely cured after six months; the amount of urine lost was greatly reduced too.[3]

MEDICAL HELP

If these self-help measures yield no results, or if leakage is regular, copious, and provoked by minimal stress (bending down, for example), ask your doctor to refer you to a specialist, since proper evaluation is essential. If the bladder neck has dropped as a result of pregnancy, all the pelvic-floor exercises in the world will not help – whereas a surgical procedure will often result in an instant cure, simply by returning the bladder neck to its correct position.

While many surgeons will operate only after a woman has completed her family because subsequent births can undo the operation, bladder-support pessaries can serve as a useful interim measure. These are inserted into the vagina like tampons, but instead of absorbing fluid they act as an internal support, gently propping up the bladder and reducing the chances of sudden stress-induced leakage.

DRUGS AS A POSSIBLE CAUSE

Although medication can make a life-enhancing difference to many women, drugs can also be a cause of incontinence. Diuretics (fluid tablets) are sometimes prescribed for high blood pressure and/or heart problems, and are also taken by a surprising number of women in a misguided effort to control their weight by combating fluid retention. They can increase the volume of fluid and lead to urgency, frequency, and even out-and-out incontinence. Some other drugs can also have these effects – another reason for seeing your doctor about incontinence.

REPRODUCTIVE TRACT

FROM medical time immemorial, the internal female organs have been shrouded in fear and distrust. Hidden inside the abdomen and, until this last half century, inaccessible to view, the womb and its associated organs – ovaries, Fallopian tubes, cervix – have always been seen as on the edge of mutiny, malignancy, or at the very least malfunction.

Women share the suspicion. A woman's body, wrote Simone de Beauvoir in *The Second Sex*, is a burden "worn away in service to the species, bleeding every month, proliferating passively, it is not for her a pure instrument for getting a grip on the world but an opaque physical presence; it is no certain source of pleasure and it creates lacerating pains; it contains menaces; woman feels endangered by her 'insides'." A similar contemporary conviction of danger is evident in the numbers of women lining up for elective hysterectomies or obediently going along with the bias that, still persisting in some infertility investigations, subjects them to invasive probings while their partners, who are equally likely to be "at fault," do not so much as have their semen counted.

HYSTERECTOMY: HOW NECESSARY?

The womb particularly is the source of medical suspicion. It comes from the Greek, *hystera,* and is the origin of the word hysteria, a condition in which severe mental derangement was thought to result from disturbance of the uterus. Until quite recently, the uterus was thought not to be tethered in place, like the other organs, but capable of wandering at will and, most fearsomely, of rising upward and suffocating sanity. There are many documented instances of 19th-century lunatic asylums employing gynecologists to hysterectomize their raving female patients in the belief that removing the womb would return their reason. Even today, the womb continues to be blamed for mood swings, murder, and mayhem and to be removed as a result.

Despite some better alternatives, hysterectomy is still one of the most common operations in the Western world. By the age of 55, one in three North American women are without a womb. In the United States and Canada, which have the highest hysterectomy rates in the world, physicians' wives are most likely to be on the receiving end. This figures. Doctors think they are doing women an enormous favor by removing their uteri. The advantages were summed up in an editorial in a medical journal, *The Lancet,* as recently as 1987 as "greater reliability at work, availability at all times for sexual intercourse, and saving on sanitary protection."

Of course, the operation is sometimes essential. If cancer has been diagnosed, a woman really has very little choice about whether her womb, and probably also her ovaries, are removed. Whether she gets better at all may depend on her having the operation as rapidly as possible. Some other gynecological conditions, such as very large fibroid tumors, also make a hysterectomy a near inevitability. Yet two-thirds of these operations are performed for much more casual reasons, such as heavy menstrual bleeding. In one hospital survey, the uteri removed at hysterectomy were closely examined for signs of the trouble that had led to the operation; over half showed no abnormality at all.

LESS RADICAL OPTIONS

It is getting harder to defend hysterectomy as a solution for conditions such as unexplained heavy bleeding (the most common reason), endometriosis, or fibroid tumors, as newer, less radical options, such as endometrial ablation and laparoscopic ("keyhole") surgery, promise to solve the problem while leaving the ovaries, cervix and body of the uterus undisturbed. Thought to be suitable for about half of the hysterectomies currently carried out every year, these procedures are – in the right hands – minimally invasive.

> If a hysterectomy is proposed for anything other than cancer, explore the alternatives. If you plan to go ahead, and the ovaries are being left in situ, be aware of the probability of an earlier-than-usual menopause; be on the alert for signs of it and have regular blood tests to check FSH levels. If your ovaries are also removed at the time of hysterectomy, you would be very strongly advised to take hormone replacement therapy at least up to 50, the average age of menopause.

IF IN DOUBT, TAKE IT OUT?

Doctors would argue that preserving the reproductive status quo is not a good thing, however. Once it has done its job, the womb is better out than in, they say, along with the cervix and ovaries – all potential sites for cancer. Advocates of this "nice tidy midlife housecleaning," as it has been called, include the gynecologist, Mr. John Studd, who, asked by the writer Johanna Roeber in a feature for British *Vogue* how he saw women's health developing in the next 20 years, prophesied thus.

> A lot of women will elect to have a hysterectomy when their families are complete at 40 or 45, in the way women are choosing to become sterilized now. That operation will remove their ovaries, cervix and endometrium, the three major sites of gynaecological cancer. They will then take hormone replacement therapy and continue it indefinitely. It will be regarded as a very safe process – everything out and then HRT – very sensible.[1]

Hysterectomy is not the slight operation that this quote implies. The complication rate is high, even for major surgery. And the intensity of pleasure during sex may also be affected, since studies suggest that more intense orgasms are associated with strong contractions in the uterus, and some women report a marked decrease in their level of sexual pleasure once their wombs are removed.

PREMATURE SURGICAL MENOPAUSE

Longer-term complications of hysterectomy can be much more serious. Removing working ovaries along with the uterus (a procedure known as oophorectomy) brings on a sudden and dramatic menopause. Instead of the slow winding down that happens when the ovaries are allowed to fail in their own time, the supply line is abruptly cut, and menopausal problems – for example, hot flashes and night sweats – can come on with a vengeance. The lack of estrogen that leads to these problems will also insidiously eat away at a woman's bones and skew her blood-fat levels in a less favorable direction, perhaps damaging the health of her heart and predisposing her to stroke.

All women undergoing a premature menopause as a result of having their ovaries removed should protect themselves from such untimely catastrophes by taking hormone replacement therapy at least until they reach the average age of menopause at around 50. The great advantage is that, since there is no longer any womb whose endometrium (lining) needs protecting, estrogen can be given on its own without the addition of progestin, the side-effect hormone. This means no headaches, no periods, no bloating or PMS-like symptoms, and no possibly compromised benefit to the heart (see Hormone Replacement chapter for a fuller discussion).

A woman who has both her ovaries removed in her early 40s (the most common time for the operation in the United States) and does not take compensatory estrogen for at least ten years will have the bone age of a 60-year-old when she comes to the normal age of menopause. Not only will her chances of fracturing a bone increase, she will have also sent her risk of premature heart disease skyrocketing as much as fourfold. The absence of estrogen at such an early age can be considered "good" only in the respect that it lowers her breast cancer risk. But the threat of heart disease is infinitely more of a risk to her life.

Even women whose ovaries are left behind are at risk of an earlier-than-usual menopause, quite possibly the result of damage to the ovarian blood supply at the time of the operation. A subset of women who undergo hysterectomy without also having their ovaries removed have their menopause several years earlier than women whose wombs are left intact – in the mid-40s rather than at around 50. A quarter of these women will have ovarian failure within two years, and by five years half will be menopausal.

Since a hysterectomy removes the most obvious sign of menopause – the cessation of bleeding – and since these women are often a decade or more away from the natural time of menopause, and haven't given much thought to it, they may not realize that sudden overwhelming sensations of heat, scary palpitations and tightness in the chest, joint pains, and vaginal dryness and discomfort have anything to do with the change of life.

CANCER OF THE OVARY

In about half of all hysterectomies, one or other of the ovaries is taken out too, a procedure known as prophylactic oophorectomy. In a recent survey, the vast majority of gynecologists said they prefer to remove the ovaries in post-menopausal women; many preferred not to remove them in women under 45, and opinions differed on the best course of action between 45 and 50. In the last instance, a woman's preference should get the casting vote.

The factor most likely to tip the balance in favor of removal is a family history of ovarian cancer: the lifetime risk of death from ovarian cancer for a woman with a mother or sister who had the disease before the age of 50 closes the odds from one in 70 to one in 13. If two first-degree relatives have had the disease, the risk may be as high as one in three. Other, less compelling risk factors include not having children and/or (perhaps) having taken fertility drugs,[2] having a late menopause (women having their menopause over the age of 50 have more than twice the risk of a woman going through menopause at less than 45), and being substantially overweight. Taking the contraceptive pill for more than five years cuts a woman's risk by two-thirds, a benefit that appears to persist throughout her life, and female sterilization is also proving protective.

As screening tests for ovarian cancer improve, there will be less rationale for removing the ovaries. In the meantime, however, there are few early warning signs beyond vague sensations of abdominal distension and bloating and the need to urinate more often – all of which can be due to many other causes. Unlike cervical cancer (which has an easily detectable and treatable pre-malignant stage – the preventionist's dream) and endometrial cancer (where bleeding in the early stages alerts the post-menopausal woman's suspicions and complete cure can usually be expected), ovarian cancer does not yet have a reliable and generally available screening test. The annual pelvic examinations many women are careful to have are not sensitive enough to pick up small tumours. For these reasons, ovarian cancer kills twice as many women every year as cancer of the cervix and uterus combined and carries a worse outlook than cancer of the breast. If a tumor is found early – which is usually a happy accident during investigation for some other problem – the outlook is very good: nine out of ten women with early cancers of the ovary are still alive five years later. Unfortunately, less than one in five ovarian tumors are picked up at this early stage in the United States.

Efforts to find acceptable screening techniques include evaluation of an abnormal protein, code-named CA-125, which is produced by the tumor and finds its way into the bloodstream in most women with ovarian cancer. Raised levels are not necessarily sinister, since only five per cent turn out to have a tumor. A further screen using ultrasound can help to distinguish the minority with abnormally large and irregular ovaries, who are then candidates for further (usually surgical) investigation. In the United States, the National Cancer Institute has launched a 16-year project, involving nearly 4000 female volunteers, to evaluate the validity of this screening technique, but results are not due in till well into the next century. As some

15 per cent of ovarian tumors do not produce the protein, and around half only do so at a fairly late stage, it will never be a failsafe test. But it is likely that, over time, scientists will develop a "bank" of five or six of these tumor "markers" which will make it possible to pick up nearly all ovarian cancers, rather in the way that a blood test can now alert a pregnant woman to the increased possibility that her baby has Down's syndrome.

Advances in ultrasound technology point a different way forward, especially when a vaginal probe is used, as this gives clearer pictures which can detect cancers at an earlier stage while still confined to the capsule of the ovary. Even so, there are limitations to its usefulness because benign swellings, which are 50 times commoner than ovarian cancers, look for all the world like tumors on a grayish ultrasound scan. It has been estimated that, in order to be sure they are not malignant, at least 50 of these innocent lumps would have to be removed for every one cancer. This is obviously unacceptable. A fairly recent refinement, color Doppler, helps differentiate harmless cysts from malignant tumors by highlighting areas of increased blood flow. The biggest drawback of the method is that it is dependent on the skill of the operator. When perfected, it is likely that screening would be targeted at women over the age of 45, since this is where 90 per cent of cases occur.

> **I**f a close female relative (mother, aunt, or sister) has had ovarian cancer, and particularly if her cancer was diagnosed before the age of 50, ask your physician about the availability of screening tests.

CERVICAL CANCER

Traditionally, cervical cancer is a cancer of older women. It is a particular scourge in developing countries, where it is the commonest female cancer, with very high rates recorded in China, Latin America, and the Caribbean. In North America and Western Europe it is rarer – but still not rare enough, since, theoretically, no woman ever need get this disease, let alone die from it. Despite the fact that an excellent screening test exists – the Pap smear – many women never get one, or allow years and years to pass between one test and the next. Some women, by contrast, tend to have their Pap smears unnecessarily often – sometimes as frequently as every six months, even though they may be in low-risk, monogamous relationships and have no history of any abnormality. According to one study, these over-frequent smears are putting such pressure on the laboratory staff who process them (all smears have to be individually evaluated) that the "false negative" rate is as high as 30 per cent in some centers. Experts consider that the risk of missing potentially problematic cell changes could be as low as five per cent if lab staff had the time and the training to examine each smear properly. According to the U.S. National Cancer Institute, once a woman has had three clear consecutive annual smears, the test "may be

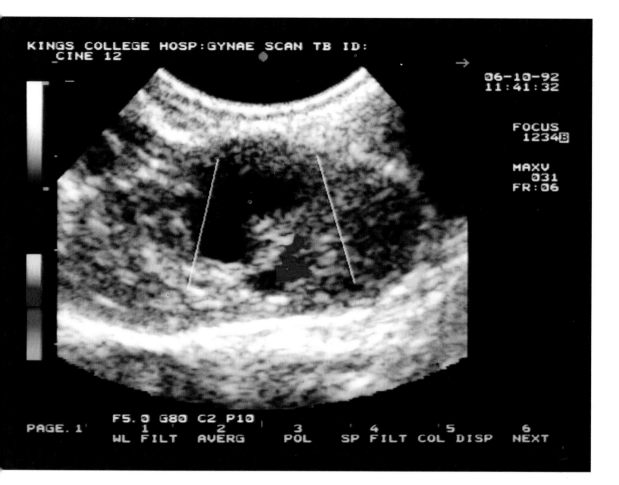

KINGS COLLEGE HOSP:GYNAE SCAN TB ID:
_CINE 12

06-10-92
11:41:32

FOCUS
1234B

MAXV
031
FR:06

PAGE. 1   F5.0 G80 C2 P10
           1   2   3   4   5   6
           WL FILT AVERG   POL   SP FILT COL DISP NEXT

Ultrasound scans hold most promise for the early detection of ovarian cancer – especially with a new refinement, color Doppler, which helps differentiate harmless cysts from malignant tumors. Dark and light gray patches on the screen come to life as splashes of color reflect the velocity of blood in the vessels, an important clue since all tumors need to establish a good blood supply in order to thrive. In this example, the red streak indicates an invasive early tumor. Because it was removed before it had the chance to spread beyond the ovary wall, the patient had an excellent chance of complete recovery. In one trial, color Doppler screening brought the number of false alarms down from 50 to just three per cancer identified, so eliminating many unnecessary operations.

Have two- to three-yearly Pap smears. At age 65 you can stop for good, provided you have had three consecutive negative smears, the most recent one no more than three years previously. Continue to have annual smears indefinitely if you have had treatment for abnormal cells or have had the genital wart virus.

• As many as one-fifth of all Pap smears are poor samples that may prevent early life-saving diagnosis. Guard against having one of them by going to a specialist center that regularly performs smears and by always asking to see a copy of your smear report so that you can see exactly what its recommendations are.

• If you are a smoker and have had a positive smear result, or treatment for premalignant cells, you can help yourself enormously by giving it up. In addition, eating a diet high in fresh fruit and vegetables may be protective, as may taking a 400 mcg folic acid supplement. Research is currently assessing the impact of giving women with positive smears extra vitamin C and beta-carotene, since it is thought these anti-oxidant vitamins may help reverse suspicious cell changes.

performed less frequently at the discretion of her physician . . . Screening every two or three years has not been found to increase significantly the risk of finding an invasive cervical cancer above the risk expected with annual screening."

As with any form of screening, a woman's best protection is to become an informed participant in the process. Smears are notorious for their "false negative" rate, meaning that they may miss an abnormality. This is more of a risk when the smear is taken by an inexperienced doctor or nurse as they are more likely to miss the critical endocervical or "transformation zone" cells, which must be on the slide before a reliable reading can take place. If the smear report states "no endocervical cells seen" or if abnormalities are found, press for further investigation, if only for your own peace of mind. Smears are not a cast-iron indicator of the degree of abnormality. In some trials, up to a third of the mildest grade of cellular abnormality, CIN 1, have actually turned out to be moderately abnormal CIN 2 or severely abnormal CIN 3 on closer investigation by colposcope. This is important because, although none of these cells are yet malignant and may never become so, CIN 3 cells are several years closer to becoming cancer cells than CIN 1 or CIN 2 cells; yet women diagnosed via a smear as having CIN 1 are routinely put at the end of the colposcopy line, if they are referred at all.

Most women find the discovery of lurking abnormal cells profoundly disturbing. "I was well and I felt well. I couldn't believe it," recalled one woman in a survey which revealed that 45 per cent of women felt differently about their bodies as a result of their positive smear result. Most of these women were in the prime of life, and this was their first intimation of mortality. They felt scared, vulnerable, and no longer able to take their good health for granted. Feelings of defilement – feeling "old and moldy" as one woman graphically put it – were common, as were sensations of something happening that was frighteningly outside their control. This is ironic, since smears offer a degree of control that is the envy of other screening practices. In fact, the detection and treatment of cervical abnormalities is one of the great success stories of modern medicine. Providing a woman has regular follow-up checks, the likelihood of going on to develop invasive cancer after lazer treatment is infinitesimal (which cannot, alas, be said for a breast tumor detected by mammography). For the great majority of women, it is a once-and-for-all experience, which although unpleasant and even traumatic at the time, soon fades into the background of their lives, merely leaving them with the necessity of having an annual smear – hardly a great price for having been spared a potentially deadly cancer.

A woman who smokes may be able to protect herself further by giving it up. Some preliminary trials suggest that giving up smoking could persuade mild or moderately abnormal cells to return to normal. It seems geographically improbable that smoking could have a toxic effect on such a distant part of the body, but the link could be the result of the action of some as yet unidentified component of the smoke on Langerhans cells, key immune cells in the cervix that are dramatically reduced in smoking women.

G et to know yourself "down there" – how it looks, how it feels, what is usual and unusual for you. Report anything untoward, whether pain during intercourse, continuing sensations of distension and bloating, a change in bowel habits, any non-menstrual bleeding premenopause, or any bleeding at all once past the menopause.

PRACTICALS

AFTER around 30 years of taking health and high spirits for granted, the way we live starts to rebound on how we feel: a couple of glasses of wine at night muddies mental clarity next day; late-night coffee snatches sleep; food either stokes energy or steals it; a bout of exercise raises our spirits and energy levels, while a sedentary weekend silts up the system and makes us feel a hundred years old by Monday morning.

As the connections become clearer, self-awareness can be our biggest ally. In 1992, at her 20th Wimbledon, and ninth final there, and fitter than many contestants half her age, Martina Navratilova attributed her longevity in a game famous for its short life-expectancy to a rigorous diet tailored exactly to her metabolic needs – no sugar, very little fat, no dairy foods, no alcohol. The champion knew what suited her, and was sticking to it. "If I eat a steak now," she told one reporter, "I know I'm going to feel sluggish the next day." Finally defeated after three hard-fought sets against Monica Seles, it did not escape notice that her victor hadn't even been born when Martina started out on the international tennis circuit.

At a less exacting, everyday level, getting the best from one's body means taking account of what it likes – pacing oneself, having the sense to take time out, eating optimally, building half an hour's activity into day-to-day life. For all the wonders of drugs and miracles of surgery, the recipe for lifelong health and vitality increasingly seems to lie in our own hands. Much of what we call aging comes down to poor nutrition and inactivity.

Genes count for a lot, of course, but many studies show that healthier life choices lead to longer, more active, illness-free lives – whatever our inherited advantages. In 1972, scientists at the University of California assessed the health of over 6000 inhabitants of Alameda County, California, and compared it with the way they lived. The results clearly showed that people who got enough sleep, ate breakfast, stayed lean, avoided snacking, took regular physical activity, never smoked, and either drank moderately or abstained from alcohol were rewarded with better health and longer lives. The physical health of those in their mid-50s who followed six or seven of these good health habits was equivalent to that of individuals 20 years younger who followed three or less. What's more, the margin widened with age, so that those aged 65 to 74 who followed all seven good health habits had the level of health, and the same likelihood of dying, as those aged 45 to 54 who ignored most of them.

According to longevity analyses at Duke University, we can add as many as 15 *vigorous*

We do have a choice about how old we get how soon. Healthier life choices lead to longer, more active, illness-free lives, whatever our inherited advantages. The good news is that huge efforts are not required; in fact many of the strategies proposed in the pages that follow are not only painless but pleasurable, as exemplified by the four-handed massage and the shiatsu foot massage, shown here – the first is said to be uniquely tension-dissolving, the second to work long-distance on the body's organs and internal systems via pressure points on the skin.

years to our lives by living healthfully (stopping smoking, watching fat intake, exercising regularly, and enjoying only a small amount of alcohol). These healthier life choices are discussed at length in the chapters that follow, with action notes in boxes through the text for easy reference. When even one or two of these better health habits are put into practice, the surge of well-being becomes a driving force for further improvements. Research has shown that people who give up smoking or take up exercise (the biggest favors you can do your body) are more likely to make healthy changes in other areas of their lives; exercisers, for example, are nearly twice as likely to stop smoking as non-exercisers and much less likely to eat unhealthily or drink to excess.

The heartening news is that healthier life choices need not entail huge upheavals. We do not have to go jogging at five am, spend half of every day at the gym, or rattle with vitamin pills. A gentler strategy will serve us just as well, better even. More is not necessarily better, and a little counts for more than used to be thought. In 1989, scientists at the Cooper Aerobics Institute in Dallas reviewed over 13,000 individuals who had visited their institute for a health check and had been followed up for eight years. When they grouped them according to fitness, they noticed a startlingly clear relationship between the number of deaths and the individuals' state of fitness. Tellingly, the greatest number of deaths occurred in the group which did no exercise at all. But, although progressively better fitness led to progressively increasing life spans, by far the biggest difference in survival was between the group that did no exercise and the group that did a little, with an "only marginally continued reduction in death rates in the most-fit individuals." And this effect became *more* noticeable when the health records of the more senior participants were examined, with the gap widening markedly after 40 and increasing with age.[1] In the words of Dr. Ralph Pfaffenbarger, one of the experts involved, "Each stair climbed and each leaf raked contributes to health."

Behavioral psychologists believe that it takes around 100 days for a new behavior to become habitual. This means setting out with a conscious commitment to sustain for at least 15 weeks the new ways that we hope to forge into habits. By then, the healthier way of life will have become *our* way of life. We won't think twice before taking the stairs rather than waiting for the escalator, shopping for different foods, unapologetically taking half an hour out of the day to relax and wind down. We won't pine for a cigarette, or miss an evening without alcohol. We *will* feel odd if we haven't had a brisk walk, or challenged the body with the usual stretches, or taken the time off that recharges our energies.

It's never too late to start. People who talk about aging gracefully often preach the virtues of acceptance – but acceptance is one thing, resignation another. If you have noticed that your legs ache and your back hurts, that you puff a bit going up the stairs, that your shoulders feel a little stiff in the morning, that your neck doesn't turn quite so fluidly when backing up the car as it once did, that you feel listless and lacking in energy, don't accept it. Do something positive before you find these limitations permanently circumscribing your life.

RE-ALIGNING

HELEN Gurley Brown, founding editor of *Cosmopolitan* magazine and one of America's most elegant and vocal elder women, once said that good posture and real jewelry are the only things that can improve on Nature once a woman gets to a certain age. As the pulling power of pretty fades, a good line and upright bearing bring riches beyond rubies with the passing years. Good posture carries off clothes to best effect, lends ease and freedom to movement, and counteracts the dejected downward slant of the shoulders that is in every way aging. It is what, quite literally, enables us to grow older gracefully. It is the link between fitness and fashion, the point at which the aesthetics of health and those of beauty meet.

But what is good posture? The old stand-up-straight school of deportment – belly in, chest out, shoulders back – encourages an unnatural rigidity that looks false and feels worse. Ease and freedom are the aims. The goal of comfort to a point of near effortlessness was summed up by *Vogue* more than 70 years ago as "an utter lack of rigidity, an appearance of having been dropped into one's clothes and remaining there by accident." This state of grace is achieved when joints, muscles, ligaments, and tendons are doing the minimum necessary to keep the body upright, and no more.

Few of us achieve such ease. We draft in the neck and shoulder muscles when we merely want to raise a finger, tighten the throat to wiggle a foot. Overuse of one part ricochets through the rest, pulling the whole out of line. Teachers of the Alexander Technique, perhaps the best known of all the re-aligning approaches, compare this to driving a car with the emergency brake on. The worst of it is that we are mostly quite unable to help ourselves. Only too miserably aware of the *result* – the aches and pains, the physical distortions, the insomnia and snappy moods – we are nevertheless generally oblivious to the *cause*, the tensions that created them.

GRAVITY – EARTH'S LOWEST COMMON DENOMINATOR

As we get older, our postural quirks become more visible. Years of gravity pulling us toward the earth makes us shorter and more compact. The head and neck retract into the chest. The spine shortens and stiffens as each vertebra presses down on the next. The back sways and the belly bulges. With less room between the head and the heels, the organs get squashed, and breathing and digestion may suffer. Habit also exacts a price, with the repeated unequal pull of muscles on joints creating noticeable asymmetries.

As undue pressure is put on the spine, back trouble and joint pain are virtually inevitable. Eight in ten people suffer an episode of back pain so severe before the age of 55 that it forces them to see a doctor. While doctors often prescribe acceptance, no one should ever have to "learn to live with" avoidable discomfort – and much of the discomfort of midlife and later is avoidable.

Only when we are aware of the uneven and unnecessarily protracted degree of tension in our muscles can we hope to free ourselves from our lifelong patterns of misuse. Once we start to use our bodies as economically as Nature intended, aches and pains disappear, and movement becomes easier, freer, and less tiring. As the body regains its plumb-line, it lifts, expands, extends, may grow taller. In one experiment carried out on students in the 1950s, the students were found to have grown measurably after a course of lessons in the Alexander Technique. People who have been Rolfed also commonly claim gains in height of up to an inch after having their malleable connective tissue "reshaped."

GETTING THE ENERGY FLOWING

As the muscles loosen their grip, a reservoir of locked-up energy is freed throughout the body. A spring returns to our step. We feel more lively and efficient because we have more energy at our disposal. The Oriental traditions of medicine have mapped this energy, known as Qi, through meridians, or pathways, every bit as specific as the vessels that carry the blood. When the energy gets stuck or stagnates, they say, an imbalance results that can cause illness; health and well-being are restored by getting the energy flowing freely again. At the heart of the ancient movement philosophies, from yoga to the martial arts, is the belief that much of the energy potentially available to us is locked away in clenched muscles, pinched ligaments, and stiffened joints. (Rheumatologists and orthopedic physicians maintain much the same, albeit in radically different language.) Regular practice of yoga postures or a martial art such as t'ai chi extends the muscles, frees the joints, and returns us the energy that is ours.

THE SIXTH SENSE

The process that keeps the body in a happy state of alignment is known as proprioception. Muscle spindles lying alongside the muscle fibers supply the brain with a continual flow of information via the nerves and spinal cord, and in return receive the instructions necessary to make the minimal adjustments that will keep us balanced.

We can tune into this process, also sometimes called the sixth sense, by developing our inner awareness. Some of the world's most ancient movement philosophies can help us in this quest. The slow-motion movement patterns of t'ai chi and some of the martial arts, for example, seem almost to be executed in a heightened state of consciousness.

Also calling on the sixth sense, the core of F. M. Alexander's technique was to prolong the space between intention and action. In that split second, he said, we have the choice as to whether to allow our sixth sense to operate unhampered or fall in with the old habits. If we can resist the force of familiarity (Alexander called this effort of will "inhibition"), then change becomes possible. The good news is that, with practice, we can tune more and more easily into our sixth sense. As we become mindful of what the body is doing, how it feels from moment to moment as ligaments

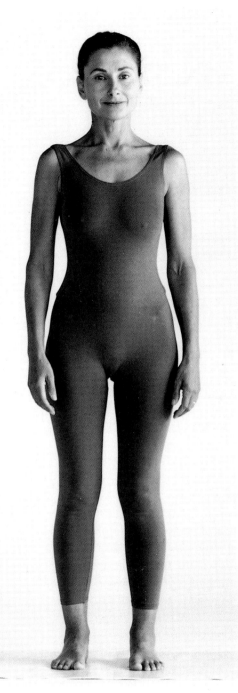

At least once a day, release unnecessary tensions: lie flat on the floor with your head supported on a folded towel, so that your chin is at right angles to your neck rather than poking up or tucked too far in. Check that you are straight. Now take a few deep breaths and draw your knees up, as shown. Try the breathing practice on page 224. Stay there, enjoying the stillness for 10 to 15 minutes, lightly mindful of your back spreading on the floor, your neck being free and your feet flat. Undo stresses on your spine, and ease any backache, by rolling your knees slowly from side to side, while keeping your shoulder blades flat on the floor. Enjoy the stretch and twist. Roll over onto one side to get up.

It's not what you wear, but the way that you wear it . . . The principles of right alignment, as demonstrated by yoga teacher Maxine Tobias, focus on relaxing upward. Encouraging the body to lengthen and widen helps counteract the compressing forces of gravity and habit. To begin with, concentrate on keeping the back long, the shoulders wide and free, the neck soft, and the back of the head up.

lengthen or muscles tighten, we find we do increasingly have a choice about how we react – whether we tense up and allow ourselves to become compressed and contorted, or retain our length and sense of inner space. Such freedom can have a profound knock-on effect in other areas of our lives.

Seek out help with your posture – try any of the methods mentioned in this chapter, give it time and if it doesn't work for you, try another.

Visualization techniques can also help you lengthen and straighten. Here is a version of one that Kate Gyllenhaal, one of New York City's most popular personal trainers, prescribes to her clients. Imagine that you have a paintbrush planted on the crown of your head, with the bristles uppermost; keeping your neck free and throat soft, grow upwards and move your head as though painting small circles on the ceiling. Reverse directions and repeat.

Once you get the idea of right alignment, stick little adhesive dots around the house at eye level (on mirrors, the frame of the TV set, etc) and use them as cues to realign yourself. As you catch sight of them, don't change anything before noticing what your body is doing. Stay with the slump for a moment. If you move too swiftly out of your habitual patterns you will remain unaware of them.

IMPROVING SHAPE BY WORKING BACK-TO-FRONT

The muscles of alignment are situated at the back of the body – which explains why those of us who struggle to improve our shape by sucking our tummies in, pulling our shoulders down, or (worse) pulling them back cannot hope to succeed. The flexor muscles at the front of the body are not designed to stabilize the trunk. By contrast, the "anti-gravity" extensor muscles – which run along the back of the neck and down the spine and backs of the thighs, knees, and calves – are richly supplied with non-fatiguable red muscle fiber that will obligingly work for hours without tiring. As we get out of the habit of using these muscles, the fibers may weaken or even die off. Staying well aligned for more than a few minutes then becomes an effort. This is why years of misuse make it so fatiguing to sit with the legs uncrossed, or to stand evenly balanced on both feet instead of lopsidedly lurching onto one, or to hold oneself at approximately 90 degrees to terra firma. Muscles need training for the job again.

Fortunately, once you start thinking and working back-to-front, the underused muscle quickly comes back into commission and the sense of effort disappears. Once the body lengthens, there is more space between the hips and the ribs, and the stomach naturally flattens. As shape improves, clothes look and fit differently.

Re-alignment methods may have different philosophies and starting points but the goal is always the same: a free, supple, lengthened body that resists the near-universal tendency to contract which causes most of the discomforts wrongly associated with aging. Often, re-alignment techniques focus on "relaxing upward," encouraging the body to lengthen and widen, the principle being that the continual downward pull of gravity makes it imperative to stretch in the opposite direction. This may be achieved actively by certain yoga positions, by playful exploratory sequences (Feldenkrais), by slow deliberate movement patterns (t'ai chi), by ropes and pulleys (Pilates structural reintegration), by manipulative hands-on techniques (Mezière's method, Rolfing) or by giving oneself a set of mental directions (the Alexander Technique).

When lifting or bending, plant the feet firmly apart, bending the knees and hinging from the hips, so that the back stays long and level and merely changes its plane. Take care not to pull the head back. Always hold an object you are lifting close to you and lift it by straightening your knees. Avoid lifting and twisting simultaneously.

● Make sure chairs offer adequate support, and cross your legs at the ankles rather than the knees. Crossing the knees is a near universal habit and a *very* hard one to break, since it sets up a vicious circle by weakening the lower back muscles to the point where any attempt to sit unpropped becomes very tiring. (Stick adhesive dots on walls facing your most-used chairs to help you break this pattern.)

● Work at surfaces which are the right height for you and so enable you to keep your back long, neck and shoulders free.

● When driving, your knees should be slightly higher than your hips – a lumbar support may help.

● Avoid wearing high heels on a continual basis, since these shift the balance of the entire body forward onto the ball of the foot, causing the back to arch, the belly and chest to come forward, and the tendons at the back of the leg to shorten to a point where wearing flat shoes may become uncomfortable. Heels so high or thin as to make you wobble are even worse, because the knees, hips, and back are put under enormous strain as they try to stabilize the body – a task that is the proper job of the foot. For everyday wear, choose shoes that outline the shape of the foot and allow room for it to spread. Wear heels only for short periods, and alternate with flats.

Common to all these methods is the emphasis on economy of effort, because only the relevant muscles are brought into play. As the smallest movement becomes easier, the big efforts also become less taxing and the whole system is spared. Even the breathing pattern changes, becoming deeper, smoother, and slower – down from 18 breaths a minute to just 12 in one experiment conducted on students of the Alexander Technique by the medical scientist David Garlick at the Laboratory for Musculoskeletal and Postural Research in New South Wales, Australia. The parodox is that, in doing less, the body becomes capable of more. Devotees of yoga treasure those mystical moments when the posture previously achieved with much strain suddenly becomes easy. As the body comes into a right relationship with gravity, the limbs seem to float effortlessly away from the trunk as though they could stay there indefinitely.

WHOLE-BODY AWARENESS

As the physical effort diminishes, mental involvement increases. We exchange the fragmentary perception of ourselves that is overly focused on the part we can see ("the front" we present to the rest of the world and study so remorselessly in the mirror) for a whole-body awareness that takes in the back as much as the front, internals as much as externals. As a result we feel more harmonious in ourselves. So many of us know every last detail of our reflected selves – the intricate tracery of lines there, the saggy old gooseflesh here – while the sensations we receive from the inner workings of muscles, joints, ligaments, and tendons remain a mystery. Swapping the savage self-criticism we too often level at our outsides for an appreciation of the inner workings of our bodies can only lead to happier feelings about our physical selves – a wonderful change for women who have been tortured by perceived inadequacies since their teenage years. Being attuned to our internal sensations is also the cornerstone of exercising effectively once into the midlife and beyond. Turn to page 213 for a description of a survey that proves the point.

A bed should offer good support, though orthopedic mattresses are both unnecessary and expensive. Firmness is a matter of personal preference – if your bed is too soft, consider changing the mattress or put a board between the bed base and the existing mattress. To avoid neck strain while sleeping, a pillow should support the head in the same way as the folded towel does in the resting posture on page 197.

MOVING

Go on, take a running jump. Given good nutrition and adequate healthcare, it's the closest you'll get to the fountain of youth. Such is the upswing in life expectancy and well-being enjoyed by the fit that every other recipe for longevity, from ginseng to hormone replacement therapy, fades into insignificance alongside. In fact, scientists investigating links between physical fitness and longevity in Harvard University graduates recently came to the conclusion that if the whole population were to become reasonably fit, the impact on the public health would be equivalent to eliminating all cancer.

THE SURVIVAL OF THE FITTEST

The growing mountain of evidence coming out of medical establishments everywhere confirms that the fittest really do survive. Yet, for all this, the attitude has not entirely disappeared that it is somehow unseemly for women past a certain age to be going to the gym or working with weights or even breaking into a run. The belief that one's body is "not what it used to be" and that one should graciously accept the limitations age imposes stretches back to the last century, when people were thought to start life with a finite store of energy that progressively ran down as the years passed. The wise were sparing of their energies, since once they were used up, only senescence awaited. "It is the duty of all persons who have attained the climacteric to avoid excesses and undue exercise," warned the physician Bernard van Oven in 1853, "to watch at all times for the insidious approach of disorders; never to reject any slight ailment, but to regard them as forerunners of more serious derangements; to seek to repair the most trifling irregularities of function and give rest to any organ of the body which shows debility or fatigue."[1]

Although it soon became clear that activity releases energy for everyday living instead of swallowing it, the old attitudes died hard. In the 1930s, the American magazine *Today's Health* frowned upon the unedifying spectacle of middle-aged people indulging in sports better befitting the young. "These people lack either the sense or the courage to admit that they are growing older and that former activity is becoming increasingly fatiguing," the magazine claimed. "Progressive decrease in bodily exertion is what they need." Sixty years later, we know that such a progressive decrease condemns you decades before time to enforced immobility and a whole string of health problems. The link is so striking as to make the ill-effects of a sedentary lifestyle almost indistinguishable from those of aging itself.

BUILDING ACTIVITY INTO DAILY LIFE

To achieve sufficient fitness to lead an active, independent life (independent of cars, buses, elevators, and escalators, that is, so that you can later be independent of walking frames and wheelchairs), the secret is simple. Keep active. The trick is to

Activity is an essential part of life, not an extra that takes place in parenthesis. Carrying the shopping can be every bit as good as a session of weight training, and a four-mile (six-kilometer) bicycle ride to and from work adds up to an energetic twenty minutes of step aerobics. If we continue to move and use our bodies well in their everyday environment – walking, lifting, running up and down the stairs, chasing children around the garden, as ex-model Bonnie Berman is doing here on her rural retreat on Long Island – we will be able to find the strength, energy, and endurance to do what we want and need to do.

think not so much in terms of *exercise*, the formal work-out that happens only on Mondays, Wednesdays, and Fridays between 12:00 and 1:00, as *activity*, a generally heightened level of operating that spills into the whole way you lead your life. These days, when physicians preach the virtues of exercise, they are not only referring to the vigorous, sweaty type that makes most of us want to run a mile – if only we could. They are talking about a modest amount of activity that is within virtually everybody's reach: a brisker-than-usual walk to the bus stop, a 20-minute bike ride to the grocery store, walking up the stairs at work instead of taking the elevator, a game of ball on the beach . . . Impressive cumulative fitness gains, they say, can be achieved without so much as setting foot inside a gym.

The American College of Sports Medicine puts it clearly: "Physical fitness means being able to do medium-to-difficult daily activities, such as raking leaves, shoveling snow, and cleaning windows, without becoming fatigued, and being able to maintain that ability throughout life." Fitness requirements also change over time. At 80 it may mean being able to get out of the house and along the road to the store; at 60 it may be continuing to play tennis or taking up yoga; while at 40 it may be building up the stamina necessary to combine bringing up the children and advancing a career.

SELF-IMPOSED IMMOBILITY

While superfitness, athlete-style, is unnecessary for most mortals, the pity is that so few of us purpose-build even a little activity into our daily lives. Frighteningly low levels of physical fitness are apparent throughout the Western world. About two-thirds of Americans between 45 and 64 take little if any activity, and of these one third take no activity at all. When researchers at the American Academy of Physical Education set a random collection of women aged between 60 and 64 a series of physical tasks, they found that a quarter could not manage to walk a quarter of a mile (400 metres) comfortably and a fifth had difficulty with heavy housework; furthermore, these proportions "increased dramatically" after the age of 65.

As habits harden in the fourth and fifth decades, the immobility that was once self-imposed and voluntary becomes superimposed and involuntary. Sedentary muscles waste quickly and tire sooner, leading to an ever more immobile lifestyle. Deprived of the free-flowing blood supply that comes from being worked through their full range of movement, the joints quickly stiffen up as the supporting cartilage deteriorates. The heart and lungs become lazy as they get accustomed to supplying a much diminished volume of blood to undemanding muscles. Blood composition changes too: the "bad" clogging LDL cholesterol rises and the "good" scouring HDL cholesterol drops. Even the bowel becomes indolent and refuses to move.

If this is depressing, the good news is that it doesn't take *that* much exercise to put the situation into reverse, even after a lifetime's sitting around. The body – any body – responds gratefully to use. Within weeks of building activity into your life, fat stores decline while muscle tone builds and the metabolic rate rises. Resting heart rate falls as your ability to deliver oxygen to the working parts of your body improves, and blood pressure may also drop (if it was high to begin with). According to one report, as little as eight weeks is "sufficient to produce worthwhile and demonstrable biochemical adaptations," and within months women in their 50s or 60s can equal, and even outperform, women in their 20s and 30s.

Since research reveals that the biggest gains in health are to be made from changing a sedentary lifestyle to a moderately active one, with further but less dramatic improvements when the already moderately active lifestyle is moved up a gear, you do not have to live, breathe, eat, sleep on your stationary jogger. While it used to be thought that the heart and lungs could only benefit if the heart rate was pushed up to a breathless 80 or 85 per cent of maximum, it now appears to be as beneficial, and safer, to work at lower levels for longer – say between 65 and 75 per cent – and to do so for at least 30 minutes three times a week. That's just an hour-and-a-half a *week*.

To obtain maximum benefit from your exercise, keep it brisk but not so hard that you have to stop after only a few minutes. Use the "talk test" to keep the intensity of your workout within safe limits: if you would not be able to talk while on the go, steady your pace.

Alternatively, take your pulse, either at your wrist or at the carotid artery on the temple. To find your target heart range, subtract your age from 220 and, using a calculator, divide by 0.6. Repeat the calculation, this time dividing by 0.9 instead of 0.6. Your target heart range falls between the two figures, and can be checked during activity by finding the pulse, counting for six seconds, and adding a zero. If you find this tiresome, a heart monitor can be worn in the form of a belt around the chest or connected to a watch on the wrist. Pre-programmed to your target heart range, it beeps if you stray above or beneath and costs little more than a pair of good trainers. Some medications, such as beta blockers, will keep your pulse artificially low and invalidate the use of your pulse as a guide to safe levels of exertion. Discuss other safety precautions with your physician before starting.)

Keep a watch on your pulse rate after stopping exercise. As you get fitter, it should return more quickly to normal, and will gradually get lower as the heart muscle gains strength and can send more blood around the body with each beat. If it takes longer than five minutes for your pulse to settle after a session, slow your exercise pace.

THE DISUSE SYNDROME

The paradox at the heart of things physiological is that, while mechanical engines wear out with continued use, the human one improves. The body is designed for vigorous activity and not for a lifetime of sitting around. The adage "if you don't use it you lose it" is supported by fitness surveys worldwide and has given rise to the new term, "the disuse syndrome." This was coined by Dr. Walter Bortz, former president of the American Geriatrics Society, with full acknowledgement to the debt owed to Charles Darwin.

In his *Origin of Species* in 1859, Darwin noted the gradual changes that evolve in the anatomy of a creature according to persistent patterns of use or disuse, singling out for his purposes the domestic duck, which, living in the unnatural state of readily available on-the-spot food supplies, becomes fatter and more indolent than its wild cousins. "I find . . . the bones of the wing weigh less and the bones of the leg more, in proportion to the whole skeleton, than do the same bones in the wild duck," the great naturalist observed, "and this change may be safely attributed to the domestic duck flying much less, and walking much more, than its wild parents."[2]

Darwin's sitting ducks are today's modern mortals. With our electric can-openers, automatic garage-door openers, and television channel changers, every last vestige of effort is swiftly and surely being removed from our lives. At a number of smart eateries, electronic pepper mills are removing even this daily grind. The change from relative activity to near total inactivity is so fast and so recent that the consequences can only be guessed at as the do-nothing generations come of age.

Already, there are grim signs of increasing ill health in midlife. In the United States, over half of women between 55 and 64 have high blood pressure, and nearly 20 per cent have signs of the creeping sugar intolerance that presages adult-onset (Type II) diabetes. (According to research at Harvard Medical School, as much as 25 per cent of this potentially lethal later-life condition can be attributed to a sedentary lifestyle, independent of diet or weight, in both men and women.) Furthermore, 58 per cent of American adults have blood cholesterol levels of 200 mg/dl or higher.

It is now recognized that many of the changes – physical, anatomical, biochemical – that have traditionally been associated with age can more properly be laid at the door of disuse. Stiff joints, flimsy bones, failing muscles, narrowed arteries, high blood pressure, and low lung capacity are often found in those who are inactive, yet they are absent, or much diminished, in their more active contemporaries – at every age. In fact, the health divide between the fit and unfit becomes more apparent as individuals get older, with 70-year-olds more unalike in health terms than 20-year-olds.

These days, physical incapacity strikes increasingly often in *unripe* old age. Well before the menopause has its pernicious effect on the bones, for example, lack of exercise pares away at the skeleton. The crippling bone fractures and warped widow's hump that await us in our 70s and 80s are already implicit in the way we live our 30s and 40s, and are not, as is often implied, merely an unfortunate consequence of plummeting hormone levels at the menopause. Surveys have found strong evidence of bone thinning in the hands, spine, hips, and wrists of inactive pre-menopausal American women in their 40s.

Other future frailties have their roots in our sedentary middle years. Unless we remain active, muscle starts wasting fast from the mid-20s on, imperceptibly but progressively weakening the body. The negative changes in blood-fat chemistry that pave the way toward later heart disease are often already well established by the middle years. This fact led the U.S. Centers for Disease Control to declare a sedentary lifestyle "the greatest single risk to the collective hearts of America." It's as though a certain level of activity is required to fend off the degenerative processes we equate with age; if we fail to meet this level, then all these processes are accelerated. We have come to accept that the so-called age-related complaints and catastrophes that strike in the sixth, seventh, and eighth decades – heart disease, stroke, high blood pressure, diabetes, stiff joints, arthritis – are bad luck rather than bad management. And indeed they sometimes are. But anthropological surveys point to a large number of communities and populations around the world that show no increase in blood pressure with age and smaller fall-offs in muscle and bone mass. We do have a choice about how old we get how soon.

LESSONS FROM OUTER SPACE

Many of the most striking insights come from the new specialty of space medicine. In space, where zero gravity reduces muscular exertion close to zero, astronauts are susceptible to a range of health problems uncannily close to those suffered by sedentary earthlings. Calcium pours out of their bones, which become weakened and porous. Muscles start wasting, providing less support and stability and affecting balance. The blood becomes stickier and more liable to clot. Blood pressure and resting heart rate rise. Aerobic capacity falls. Even depression and insomnia set in.

When the concept of manned space flights first became a possibility, and the effects of space on the physical health of astronauts had to be assessed, scientists put volunteers to bed for three weeks, prohibiting all movement, in order to simulate the effects of zero gravity. On carrying out detailed anatomical and biochemical tests, they found such a wide array of ill-effects that their minds have been concentrated ever since on providing astronauts with intensive exercise programs to preserve their bone density and muscle strength, even if they go into orbit for just a week.

The increasing recognition of the importance of activity in every sphere of life is revolutionizing medical practice. These days patients having major lifesaving procedures are up and out of bed just hours after coming around from their anesthetic, and even heart attack patients are persuaded to get up and going as soon as they are out of intensive care. Whether catching one's breath after childbirth, recuperating after an illness, or receiving therapy for back pain, staying stuck in bed a minute more than necessary is now recognized to do one's health no favors. A few weeks' "bed rest" sounds benign but in fact it measurably thins the bones and reduces the circumference of the leg muscles – with an estimated four per cent of total muscle strength lost for every day spent in bed. Though the effect does drop off, as much as 25 per cent can be gone after just a few weeks.

While fitness is always assumed to be particularly beneficial for middle-aged men – for whom the specter of heart attack looms larger – women, who have traditionally not been the subjects of medical surveys in this area, may benefit even more strikingly. Records kept at the Cooper Aerobics Institute in Dallas show that while physically fit men are 53 per cent less at risk of dying before time, physically fit women are 98 per cent less at risk – even when risk factors, such as cholesterol levels, blood pressure, weight, smoking, and heart disease history, are taken into account. Although the numbers of women taking part in the survey were too small to draw definite conclusions, physically fit women also emerged as fully 16 times less likely to die from any form of cancer (for men the figure was four), and only half as likely to succumb to breast cancer, a rising scourge which now afflicts one in nine of all American women.

PSYCHOLOGICAL SPIN-OFFS

Scientists at Harvard University recently did some elegant arithmetic showing that an active lifestyle can extend lifespan by fully two years. But being fit is not just about warding off death or striving after nebulous future health benefits. It hugely enhances the here and now. Psychological spin-offs come in the form of a pervasive sense of well-being, calm, and contentment, a clearer mind and sharper concentration, more energy during the day and longer, deeper, unbroken sleep at night. These effects have repeatedly been shown to be as valuable in the treatment of mild depression as psychotherapy and drugs, and a much better answer to insomnia than sleeping tablets. Women who start exercising in midlife after two decades spent sitting in offices often say they haven't felt this good since high school.

In addition to psychological well-being, mental functioning appears to improve as the body is put through its paces. A number of small studies have shown that active individuals score higher on short-term memory tests, have longer attention spans and faster reaction times than sedentary individuals, and also possess wider vocabularies, more creativity, and better powers of reasoning into the bargain.[3]

FITTER NOT FATTER

It is not just health and mood that stand to benefit from moving up a gear in your daily life, but shape as well. In the United States, it is estimated that a quarter of white women and nearly half of black women are overweight. The conventional explanation is that we are eating too much. But, contrary to popular belief, we are actually taking in fewer calories than at any time since 1800. It's inactivity that's to blame. Increasing age is known to shift the body's fat/lean (muscle) ratio in favor of fat, but inactivity accelerates it. And many reducing diets merely compound the problem by raiding the body's muscle stores – leaving an even more unfavorable fat-to-muscle ratio and a lower resting metabolic rate. Activity, by contrast, revs up the metabolism while building and maintaining muscle mass. It makes an infinitely better long-term solution to the spreading middle and ballooning thighs than yet another soul-denying diet.

STAYING WITH IT

To gain the advantages that an active lifestyle offers, activity must become a way of life, for life. The change in attitude that's required has been compared to "the difference between going on a diet and changing the way you eat for ever more," by Dr. Adrienne Hardman, senior lecturer in the department of sport science at Britain's Loughborough University, when interviewed for British *Vogue* in April 1992. "There's no point in doing very vigorous exercise for 18 months to get fit enough to run a half-marathon," she pointed out, "if you let it lapse at the end of it. You can expect no credit from past exercise, however vigorous. Only current and continuing exercise is going to confer benefit." This point was underlined by Dr. Ralph Pfaffenbarger's study on Harvard graduates, which established that it was ongoing physical activity in adulthood, not college athleticism, that was associated with a longer life expectancy.[4]

To ensure that the chosen activity is kept up, it is obvious that it must be enjoyable. U.S. surveys show that over 30 per cent of would-be exercisers soon drop out. Those who stay the course have chosen a fitness regime they really enjoy. Americans spend half a billion dollars a year on treadmills and slightly more than that on exercise bikes. But after the first few weeks, 85 per cent of this equipment is consigned to attics and storerooms. Enthusiasms pass quickly if the chosen activity only offers more of the same. It must have its own intrinsic satisfactions, say sports psychologists, who also hold that the motives that drive someone to start exercising – often a desire to look better – are unlikely to provide sufficient motivation to keep them at it. Unrealistic goals, such as shifting the flab in the few short weeks before summer, are associated with failure, whereas feelings of enjoyment, achievement, competence, and happiness with self arising out of one's chosen activity become positively reinforcing.

The boredom factor leads many women to start exploring other forms of movement – oriental disciplines from yoga to t'ai chi, different forms of dance, martial arts such as aikido and tae kwon do. Compared with the snappy aerobics classes filled to the brim with younger exercisers, these often ancient "mindful" disciplines promise something beyond mere fitness. Common to them is the sense of the path or journey whose focus is not just on achieving technical excellence but on what one learns as one travels towards that goal. Women who practice martial arts, for example, often find that the paradoxical result of these fighting sessions is one of calmness and reduction of conflict in their own lives and relationships. The concentrated discipline of the forms offers a safe place in which to fight their own inner battles and to let go of those feelings of aggression, anger, guilt, and self-doubt that can come up with such force in midlife. In one study carried out by Dr. James Rippe at the University of Massachusetts Medical School, 135 sedentary volunteers were given either mindful or mindless exercise to do. While it took the t'ai chi and yoga group just four weeks to report less stress and better moods, the aerobic group took 14, even though the pace of the exercise was more intense.

FITNESS WALKING

Now that it has become clear that a stratospherically raised pulse rate is not necessary to give heart and lungs a boost, all sorts of unexpectedly pleasurable forms of activity happily start to qualify as healthy. Numerous medical surveys show that you can literally walk (albeit briskly) away from heart disease, blood pressure problems, circulatory disorders, insomnia, incipient diabetes, nervous tension, and depression.

Trials on previously sedentary middle-aged women, for example, confirm that a vigorous walk three or four times a week can increase the bone-mineral content of the lower spine and protect against fracture, slow the resting heart rate, and cause a beneficial rise in the "good," HDL cholesterol. In one trial, 28 formerly sedentary women aged 42 walked briskly for (11 miles 18 kilometers) – the equivalent of about 2½ hours – a week, while 16 didn't and served as controls. A year later, the walkers had healthier lungs and hearts, with an 11 per cent increase in their uptake of oxygen. Although their total levels of cholesterol were unchanged, the proportion of "good" HDL, now thought particularly important for female heart health, had risen by 27 per cent.[5]

Even a leisurely stroll is infinitely better than taking no exercise at all. A study at the Institute for Aerobics Research in Dallas, Texas, recently established that a regular habit of walking *at any speed* can increase protective HDL cholesterol and lower the risk of heart disease by about a fifth.

Even a straightforward movement such as walking demands good technique to get most from it. As people get out of condition, they become lazier in the quality of their movement, taking short, uneven, flat-footed steps, which lock the hip joint into a limited range. Try walking, or even jogging, feeling "tall." Lengthening the stride while pushing off energetically from the heel will use a fuller range of movement at the hips and knees. Once the hip joint opens out, the foot and ankle also come into play. Try it and you will feel the difference. Remember, too, to keep the hips centered as the stride lengthens, stopping short of the unnaturally pronounced stride of the race or "power" walkers, which puts a rotational twisting force on the hips and can strain the pelvis.

Walking must be maintained at a brisk pace – 3 to 4 miles (5 to 6.5 km) per hour – to be beneficial. Find a 1 mile (1500 meter) long route and time yourself along it: if it takes more than 20 minutes on foot, your pace is too leisurely. As you get fitter, aim to do it in 15 minutes and then in 12 minutes. To keep up the pace buy a pedometer, which measures the speed at which you are going. Or, just as good, find an energetic dog that needs to be exhausted twice or three times a week.

Clothes should be comfortable and unrestricting. Well-fitting walking shoes made of durable material with thick, flexible, shock-absorbing soles are essential. If buying trainers for the purpose of getting fit, indicate to the salesperson whether you are likely to be walking or running, since they tend to be differently constructed. Because feet swell during the day, it's best to buy shoes in the afternoon and to have on the socks you intend to wear them with.

Walking is not recognized as a sport, or even a valid form of exercise, because it is such a normal part of our lives, yet it is fast becoming the biggest component of the modern exercise message. In the United States, there are now all sorts of variations on a good walk, from power (race) walking to water walking, which entails vigorous width-to-width striding in waist-deep water. The appeal of walking is obvious: to start off with, it produces less strain on the joints than jogging (where the impact each time your foot hits the ground can exceed three times your body weight). And, so long as you stick with the correct technique, it carries no danger of the well-publicized impact injuries that can accompany many aerobic-type activities. For all its apparent ordinariness, fitness walking can improve shape, exerting a fairly strong pull at the back of the thighs and buttocks, typically soft areas for many women. This may explain why weeks of walking tightens this area more effectively than virtually any other form of exercise.

NEVER TOO LATE

Keeping up activity levels becomes even more important the older we get. In one study, elderly people who were also regular runners reported ten times less disability than an equivalent group who did no exercise at all. Reassuringly, a past life of sedentariness need not cause permanent harm, as long as activity levels are stepped up. No one is too old to twist and stretch. In fact, studies unanimously suggest that the benefits of activity intensify with every passing year. Even the very elderly, who have long ago resigned themselves to an ever decreasing range of movement, can find themselves looser and more limber, stronger and more physically confident, within weeks of starting a movement program.

When Tom Hickey at the University of Michigan set 100 men and women between the ages of 75 and 98 a 12-week program of low-intensity aerobics, to be carried out twice a week for 40 minutes at a time, they emerged from the experience with lower blood pressure, better flexibility, balance, and mobility, less joint pain, and a more positive outlook. Programs like this are, sadly, the exception. In "rest" homes up and down North America and much of Europe, the old are usually dumped into "easy" chairs from whence they rarely rise. Yet, with a little encouragement, they could enjoy more physical freedom than they have for years – as unaccustomed muscles and seized-up joints are put back in working order and the body that was once written off goes further than it could before.

THE JOYS OF YOGA

A regular stretching program or a form of movement, such as yoga, is one of the best ways of guarding against late-life seize-up, because it encourages the circulation of synovial fluid, which then lubricates the joints and protects them from damage. This is a particular boon for women, who are about three times more likely than men to develop osteoarthritis as they get older.

The extraordinarily nimble forms of the current generation of great yoga teachers, many now in their 70s and 80s, turn the received view of advanced age upside down. Still enjoying a vigor and suppleness that many children couldn't match, they show that the process of getting older need not be a one-way journey to immobility and physical decrepitude.

Unlike many forms of exercise, which seem exclusively designed for young, fit bodies, yoga can be continued even into extreme old age, as the postures can be adapted around the restrictions that age sometimes places on the muscles and joints and can even be performed, if necessary, in a chair. An imaginative and sensitive teacher is what's required, especially if you already have joint problems, since some of the postures will need to be modified to avoid undue strain. As long as such safeguards are observed, individuals who have resigned themselves to an ever more limited range of movement will be amazed to find themselves twisting in new and unaccustomed directions, stretching further, feeling looser and freer, than they have in years.

When 83-year-old Vanda Scaravelli was interviewed by *The Times* in 1991 and

Radha Warrell demonstrates a new fluid form of yoga, known as Astanga Viniyasa, which brings postures together into sequences that melt into each other in a dynamic flow. Forty-three when this photograph was taken, her long lean shape and evident flexibility demonstrate the benefits of daily yoga practice. Less obviously, such a discipline also uncovers unsuspected strengths and abilities, bringing physical self-confidence of the sort that often diminishes with age.

photographed practicing her particular brand of yoga, she commented, "Regular stretching makes people feel elated. It gives them comfort and encouragement to discover it is possible to modify and control their bodies." She should know: she holds classes for 70-year-olds and turns herself inside-out and upside-down for an hour every morning.[6]

STRENGTH TRAINING

Yoga postures also strengthen the body, helping to maintain muscle bulk and strength – or to build it up again once lost. Increasingly, the adoption of a strengthening program is seen as the key to keeping youthfully strong and independent even in advanced old age and now forms one of the core recommendations of the American College of Sports Medicine for individuals at every age and stage of life. In a now-famous strength-building program run by scientists at Tufts University on ten nursing-home residents aged between 87 and 96, scientists were able to show that the subjects' leg muscle strength nearly tripled and the size of their muscles also grew demonstrably after just eight weeks of training.[7] For these elderly people, however, the measurements were academic. What mattered for them was that their increased muscle mass translated into more independence of movement, enabling them to do more with less help and to get around more easily. Strength training is arguably even more important for women than for men, since women start off with less muscle and have bones that are especially susceptible to fractures if they fall. Strength training keeps the muscles strong, resists the gradual weakening of the body, and leaves you in better shape whatever your age. (For more about muscles and joints see pages 155–60.)

Unfortunately, many exercise classes still include potentially dangerous exercises. Watch out for bouncing stretches, forced toe touches, deep knee bends, straight-leg sit-ups, double leg-raising movements, rapid neck movements, and jogging on your toes rather than using the whole foot.

THE RISK/REWARD RATIO

People who have not exercised for some time often hesitate to begin, apprehensive of suffering impact injuries and shin splints or worse. Ever since Jim Fixx, father of the jogging boom and the man who urged people to get out and run for their lives, dropped dead in the middle of his daily 10-mile run, the stay-at-homes have had a cast-iron reason for staying right where they are.

The possible risks of exercise are no reason for staying put. While running marathons may endanger the joints, the gentler options described here pose little threat. The consensus among physicians and fitness experts is that when the possible dangers of moderately strenuous exercise are set against the possible benefits, the benefits far outweigh them even if you are very unfit – as long as you listen to how your body is responding. The golden rule is never to overrule your own reactions. Sobering statistics suggest that it is those who don't listen to what their bodies are telling them who place themselves in mortal danger.

In an important survey into deaths during exercise in Rhode Island, Professor Paul Thompson found that over three-quarters of the victims had had danger signs, such as chest pain and difficulties with breathing, well before they died but had chosen to ignore them. Thompson went on to draw an important line between short-term safety and long-term health. "If you were to ask me what is the safest way to spend the next *hour* then I would say: sit down and relax. But sitting down is probably the most dangerous way to spend your *whole life*. The benefits of a lifetime of physical activity far outweigh any risks of exercise."[8] The moral is to be aware: to exercise with, not against, your body and, if you cannot easily go further in any movement, not to force it. Find a level of exertion that pushes you a little, and continue at that intensity until it becomes easy, whereupon move up a gear and push yourself that little bit further.

Keep the risk of joint and ligament strain low by warming up for ten minutes before exercising. Walking around slowly for five minutes will get the blood flowing to the muscles and prepare them for more vigorous action. Gently persuade the muscles to extend with the few basic stretches shown on pages 216–19 to increase blood flow through the body. Cool down after exercise by slowing the pace to a walk for five minutes and then do the stretches in reverse.

● Avoid exercising in extreme heat or humidity. This is particularly important over 65, when it becomes more difficult to dispell excess heat from the body. Keep liquid intake up too: sensations of thirst become less acute and dehydration can be a real danger.

● Tune in to how you feel both while you are exercising and afterward, remembering that any pain is a signal to stop and rest and to avoid movements that reawaken or aggravate the pain in future. If the problem persists, seek professional help. You should also stop exercising immediately and consult a doctor if you develop difficulty breathing and/or experience faintness, light-headedness, dizziness, nausea, confusion, chest pain, leg pain, or extreme fatigue.

FITNESS TESTING

What matters is to get out there. Don't wait for tomorrow, next week, the end of a pressing work deadline. If you choose to walk or swim your way to better health, you don't need anybody's permission. Fitness testing, as offered almost universally now by clubs and gyms, is not a necessary prelude, though it can instill additional motivation by offering achievement-oriented individuals a starting point against which future progress can be gauged. It's satisfying to see your resting pulse-rate drop and maximal oxygen uptake rise after several weeks of training, but it's not mandatory.

Fitness assessments often start with a simple test to establish that you are fit enough to take the test. This is because, for a small proportion of people, tests designed to establish a safe upper level of exertion may stress their bodies dangerously, particularly the ECG stress test, which works you to exhaustion on a treadmill or exercise bicycle as it monitors the response of your heart on a graph. While this is the truest test of cardiovascular fitness – and an excellent screen for middle-aged men – there is such a high number of false alarms when the same test is carried out in women before the age of 50, as to render the test inadvisable, unless you have symptoms of heart disease or strong risk factors, since further tests of heart function become much more complicated past this point.

There are other ways of measuring fitness and monitoring progress. Maximal oxygen uptake (VO2 max) can be estimated by taking serial pulse-rate measurements during a test on a stationary bicycle. Average values range from 25 to 45 milliliters per kilogram (.45 to .82 fluid ounces per pound) per minute. Since the starting point is as influenced by your genetic make-up as by your state of fitness, the first measurement is not unduly important; what matters is to exercise and watch your capacity to take in and utilize oxygen shift in an upward direction. With regular exercise, you could be recording rises of up to 30 per cent. Other tests that tend to be routinely offered include indices of flexibility and strength, but the results of these, though of interest, can be misleading, as technique counts for as much as genuine flexibility or strength.

FITNESS SCHEDULES

The Minimal program here gives the minimum amount of exercise that is necessary for heart and lung fitness and that will, additionally, help keep bones dense, muscles strong and joints free. The Optimal level takes it further. If you are over 45 and not particularly fit, or have not exercised in a while, start on the minimal program and move on to the Optimal program when you feel ready (usually after at least six months).

Minimal

Heart/lungs/body conditioning/fat burning
Start walking at least three times a week, rather more briskly than normal, allowing your arms to swing along by your sides. Keep up this pace for at least 15 minutes, by which time you should have covered 1 mile (1.5 km) – a pedometer is an invaluable pace-maker. Make sure you are not so out-of-breath that you cannot carry on a conversation. Gradually increase time, distance, and speed by adding five minutes every two weeks, until you are walking briskly for 45 minutes and covering distances of 3 miles (5 km) or more at least three times a week. Gradually increase speed until you average 4 miles (7 km) an hour. Wearing a stereo headset and listening to rousing music will help keep your pace healthily brisk.
Also worth trying Rebounding (mini-trampolining, which is excellent for bones), swimming, step aerobics beginners' classes.
Flexibility Follow the daily program of simple yoga-inspired stretches on pages 216-19 to move joints through their full range of movement; ideally use this as a warm-up before walking too. Also worth trying: yoga, Medau, most forms of dance, t'ai chi, tae kwon do.
Strength/bones Follow the basic strengthener/bone-builder program shown on pages 220–1 three times a week. Gain bigger benefits by using weight-training machines, aiming to work out, under supervision, for 15-20 minutes three times a week.

Optimal

Heart/lungs/body conditioning/fat burning Aim toward either five hours of very brisk walking a week at a speed of 5 miles (8 km) an hour or 3½ hours' jogging or running, i.e. 11 miles (18 km) a week. Don't start off jogging. Follow the minimal walking program for the first three or four months, then add little 100-yard (100-meter) jogs, gradually shifting the jogging/walking ratio until you are jogging longer than you are walking. Aim for 30 minutes' jogging at a stretch, varying it according to inclination with swimming, bicycling, energetic dance, or step aerobics routines. But pace yourself. It may take several months to get there.
Flexibility Seek out a yoga teacher, trying different disciplines and teachers. Stick with whichever appeals most and aim to complete an hour's yoga practice most days.
Strength/bones More and more often is not necessarily better, as the body needs time to recover between sessions. Even so, the weights you are using should work the muscle to a point of exhaustion after less than ten repetitions. If you can do ten easily, the weights are too light or your technique could be incorrect. Check with your instructor.

BASIC STRETCHES

These yoga-inspired stretches will invigorate your system, mobilize your joints and warm up your muscles before more vigorous exercise. The program was put together by yoga expert Maxine Tobias, right. Now in her late 40s, she has been teaching for 25 years, practices for two hours every day, and values the discipline for the way "it works so completely on the body and mind, the internal organs and systems, keeping all functioning healthily." Try to do these daily, breathing through any tightness but stopping if you feel pain or discomfort. Go into each pose on an out-breath, hold as long as comfortable, breathing easily, and, as your body loosens, stretch a little further. Perform each pose several times to each side.

I. Start with a whole body stretch. Lying on your back, and keeping spine from arching and ribcage flat, stretch buttocks toward heels. Now bend knee and, either catching big toe or looping belt around foot, raise leg to ceiling.

2. Maintaining space between hip and waist, rotate thigh and lower foot onto block, firm cushion or book; stretch foot toward head, keeping opposite hip as flat and pelvis as centered as possible, arms stretched out.

3. Sit on floor, or on a couple of telephone books if more comfortable, with back long, soles of feet together and heels as close to pubis as possible. Loop belt around feet and let knees drop toward floor. Use belt to lift spine.

4. Now kneel over books, as shown, and stretch arms up over head, lifting side ribs and keeping shoulder blades down, neck and throat soft, lengthening from coccyx to crown of head.

5. Bending one elbow behind head, take other arm down and back and grasp belt as shown.

6. Once shoulders become more flexible, do away with belt and catch hand instead.

7. Sitting on telephone books with one knee bent, as shown, lift spine by pressing elbow against knee and twist around toward the bent leg.

8. If you can, bring arm down and around to catch hand or wrist. If you cannot catch, leave elbow against knee, as earlier, and concentrate on keeping as much length along spine as you can.

BASIC STRETCHES (*CONTINUED*)

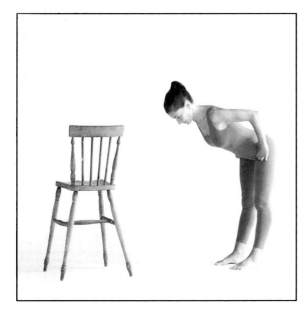

9. Standing with feet hip width apart, bend knees and hinge forward from hips, keeping back and neck long.

10. Rest hands on seat of chair, being sure to let movement come from hips, rather than reaching forward from shoulders. Bend knees and lift buttock bones up.

11. Now straighten knees, not by pushing back into calf, but by lifting muscles at front of thighs.

12. Once you've mastered movement from hips, drop right down.

13. Kneel on all fours with hands a little more than shoulder width apart, fingers well spread.

14. Come up onto balls of feet and lift hips high, bending knees, extending hips back, keeping arms and legs straight and head relaxed.

15. Finally, maintaining action at hips, push thighs and shins back till heels return to floor.

16. Returning to all fours, push back, separating knees, and lengthen forward as far as you can.

BASIC STRENGTHENERS

These rather more demanding poses will improve balance, firm muscles, and stimulate the crucial bone-building metabolism to keep the skeleton strong. They will also help keep you in terrific shape. Try to practice the sequence every day, and remember to perform the standing poses to each side.

1. Standing with feet about one yard (one meter) apart, raise arms to shoulder level, palms down; turning one foot in and the other out, line up front heel with arch of back foot, and extend spine sideways while moving hips back. Rest hand on floor or a couple of books and revolve body toward ceiling; look at upstretched hand without throwing head back and press down hard on outer edge of back foot.

2. Standing as before, with feet turned as before but wider apart, bend front knee and bring buttock down so shin is perpendicular and thigh parallel to floor. Press weight into back heel.

3. Stretch sideways and bring hand to rest on floor (or block or books) behind front foot. Revolve trunk upward and stretch upper arm over head.

4. Starting as before, but with feet wider apart and arms stretched over head, turn feet as before. Now turn the entire body to the front foot, stretching up through spine and bending knee to make right angle; keep back leg strong and straight, pressing heel down, and stretch all the way up to fingertips.

5. This sequence will strengthen the back and improve posture. Lying on front, as shown, press legs, thighs, and pelvis down into floor while raising head, neck, and shoulders, keeping neck long and not throwing head up.

6. Now raise fronts of thighs off floor, pushing pelvis down, and keeping neck long and throat soft throughout.

7. Rest for a few moments, then turn arms so palms are flat on floor. Bend knees, and raise feet so knees leave floor.

8. Now raise head and neck, concentrating on keeping your neck long, and breath steady.

9. To strengthen tummy muscles, lie on floor with lower legs supported on chair, as shown, arms crossed over chest. Breathe in and, as you breathe out, raise head and shoulders, keeping neck long, and pull forward with elbows until you can feel muscles working. To increase the pull, cross hands behind head.

TAKING TIME OUT

Relaxation is yin to the yang of exertion, not opposite but complementary, the one vital to the other. Much more than merely a flop-out tacked onto the end of an exercise session, or a state of collapse at the end of a busy day, relaxation becomes increasingly sidelined in the rush of modern life. Giving ourselves the opportunity to recover from the cumulative stresses and tensions of the day is essential for our physical health and our emotional well-being, our productivity, the joy we have in our relationships. The French have a phrase for it: *reculer pour mieux sauter*, go back so you can jump further. But going back or even just staying still comes hard to modern over-achievers whose impetus is ever onward. If life is not as it should be, the natural tendency is to intensify the effort.

In our do-more get-further go-faster world, women especially feel driven, compelled not only to be perpetually doing, but *seen* to be perpetually doing. Ignoring Robert Louis Stevenson's apposite caution that "extreme busyness . . . is a symptom of deficient vitality," they vie for the vitality award. In a world where energy itself is perceived to be "youthful," and the woman with boundless energy commands admiration and envy, the admission that one needs time to recoup is itself aging. No one can afford to be caught napping. Pride prevents us from taking a break.

We pay for our pride in myriad ways. Woody Allen described death as Nature's way of telling us to slow down. Other signs there to be taken notice of *this* side of the grave are psychological (snappiness, loss of sense of humor, failing short-term memory, muddled thinking, feeling hounded) or physical (a back that aches, a hip that hurts, a neck that twinges, shoulders that feel stiff). As in so many other areas of health, self-awareness is our biggest ally. Only when we know what fatigues and what refreshes can we hope to pace ourselves effectively.

Be conscious of how your body reacts to stress, noting which muscles are tensing and tightening. What is happening to your fists, your shoulders, your throat, your jaw, your forehead? Are you clenching your jaw or gritting your teeth? Has your stance changed? Are you leaning forward? Backward? Are you balanced or askew? Observe all this and then come back to the center, releasing your muscles, dropping your shoulders, and breathing out smoothly and evenly as you regain your postural balance. Compile a mental checklist of your three or four most obvious idiosyncratic responses and run through them every time you feel stress rising up to overwhelm you. You'll be amazed how different you feel.

Explore different ways of unwinding and see what works best for you. Self-hypnosis or relaxation tapes, taking a walk in the early evening, performing a series of yoga stretches, stroking a cat, or spending time in the garden can all provide the perfect means of cutting off. Schedule breaks in your day and use the time for yourself, rather than checking off items on the never-finished list of things to be done. Book a regular weekly massage and, if you can, have the masseur come to you so you don't undo the benefit traveling home afterward.

ANTI-STRESS STRATEGIES

As the years pass, a degree of self-knowledge mercifully comes to our rescue. We get better at recognizing when tired is too tired, tense too tense, the life flame flickering dangerously close to burnout. Taking heed, we learn to make ourselves inaccessible, to say "no," to retreat and recoup our energies as only we know how. It may be as simple as eating regularly and not expecting the engine to run indefinitely on empty, or taking half an hour out in the middle of the day to unwind and touch base. Over the years we develop our own strategies. The actress Bette Midler visits art galleries, shoe supremo Manolo Blahnik builds walls with his bare hands, fashion designer Alison Lloyd (Ally Capellino) bakes bread, Cher strings bead necklaces.

Whatever our outlet, we have to be ruthless in our commitment to unwinding, realizing that taking time out actually becomes *more* essential as life fills up. Nan Talese, executive editor of a New York publishing house, mother of two, and a typical nonstop woman, discovered the truth of this for herself when she took a five-day spa break from the fever-pitch of everyday life and wrote up her experience for American *Vogue*.

> Years ago, I would have considered this concentration on my body the most out-rageous self-indulgence, but as I watched insects march between bright green blades of grass and reveled in the brilliant white and magenta of the marguerites banked against the hill, the necessity of space and self no longer seemed luxurious – it was essential. Women particularly are called upon to give endlessly as if they were magic cornucopiae; they offer attention, sympathy, advice; they are asked to plan social occasions for others and to carry them off with style; they must remember wounds that need to be healed and tend to egos that have been bruised, and often forget to replenish their resources. Time unfilled cannot replenish: discipline, quiet, and exercise can.[1]

Spas are wonderful. Flotation tanks that let one drift off into sensory nothingness and massages are well-deserved treats too, but they depend on forward planning and other people. An anytime–anywhere method is also required, to be put into effect as and when needed.

LEARNING TO BREATHE

Many people find that breathing techniques work brilliantly for them. Because breathing acts as a bridge between the conscious and unconscious minds, it is one of the few bodily processes that can be both voluntarily and involuntarily regulated. We cannot consciously slow down the beating of our hearts, and so lower the pace at which the blood thunders through the vessels, or change the rate at which nerve impulses are relayed to the brain – but we can alter the rhythm of our breathing and, by so doing, steady the racing heart, slow the transmission of over-excitable nerve impulses, and calm the mind.

Learning to breathe seems unnecessary. After all, we all do it hundreds of thousands of times a day – too often, in fact, since most of us do not breathe sufficiently slowly and use only the shallowest part of the chest – not thinking, for example, of taking the air right down into the abdomen or expanding our lungs at the sides and in our backs. (Did you even *know* that you could make your ribs move right around by your spine?) Yogis claim that the average chronic underbreather expells just a quarter of the full gallon (four liters) of air that the lungs can hold at maximum, leaving a lot of stale air behind. A breathing technique encourages fuller use of the lungs and is one of the swiftest ways of quietening the mind and calming the system. Once learned, you've got it for life. Get instruction in yoga *pranyama* (breath of life exercises). The Alexander Technique and many exercise disciplines also include breathing exercises, as, less explicitly, does chanting or singing.

Lie with one hand lightly resting on your chest and the other over your navel. Breathing quietly, take air deep into your lungs and feel the lower hand rise as the abdomen fills; the upper hand should remain quite still. As you breathe out, let the lower jaw drop and make an "Ah" sound. Breathe in this way four or five times and let the breathing become lighter. Once mastered, the technique can be used sitting or standing, and the hands are no longer necessary.

Alternatively, sit in a comfortable position with your back straight and lightly supported and, starting with an outbreath, count each breath from ten down to one, focusing only on your breathing. The technique sounds simple, but it is extraordinarily difficult; after two or three breaths, random thoughts rush in to distract you, forcing you to go back to ten and start all over again. With patience, concentration improves and, with it, inner peace.

Meditation also uses the breath as a path to the ultimate goal – liberation from the ego. In order to meditate effectively, a technique generally needs to be taught. Without instruction, most people flounder around, abandoning their practice once the early enthusiasm wears off. Sanskrit mantras may reek of Eastern mysticism but they do provide a useful anchor to which the mind can continually be brought back. A word outside one's own language, which has no distracting connotations and which, being monosyllabic, often has a special resonant strength, can deepen the meditation.

The sound and light machines that are such a feature of California's so-called Mind Gyms combine hypnotic rhythms of flashing lights and sychronized pulsating sounds to much the same effect. When users are attached to EEGs, the same change in brain activity can be seen as in regular meditators, with the beta waves of ordinary cerebral activity changing into longer, slower, alpha waves, and

"Flopping" is not the best route to relaxation. An all-absorbing outdoor activity, as Grethe Elgort is enjoying here, or light rhythmic exercise such as walking can be much more energizing. The principle is known as "active rest" and research suggests it speeds recovery and rebuilds energy faster than traditional do-nothing methods.

even, at a deeper stage of relaxation, the consciousness-changing, creativity-enhancing theta waves. The difference is that meditators don't have to leave home in order to get there.

ACTIVE REST

Although "flopping" is the only way many women consciously "relax," it is usually not the best way of overcoming tiredness. A physical discipline, such as yoga, or a light rhythmic activity, such as walking, can be much more energizing. Even though the prospect may be tiring, the reality is nearly always invigorating: the movement releases new energies that weren't available before and the mind becomes stiller as the body works. This paradoxical phenomenon is known as "active rest" and research dating back to the beginning of this century suggests that it speeds recovery and rebuilds energy levels faster than the traditional do-nothing method.

In the early 1900s a Russian scientist called Sechenov carried out a series of experiments which established that fatigue in a subject's arm disappeared more swiftly if the other legs and arms were working than if they were resting. This "Sechenov phenomenon" has since been confirmed by other studies showing that light, rhythmic activity helps remove the waste products of fatigue, so speeding recovery, perhaps because the brain is better able to process the relevant "recovery message" when other muscles are firing.

A quiet exercise discipline, such as yoga, can unravel
mental as well as physical tensions leading to more clarity
of mind and enhanced concentration.

EATING

NONE of us chooses to look a minute older than we must. Yet even as we slather on yet another miracle cream or sit pulling faces at the mirror wondering what might be done to stay the sagging flesh, our bodies may be aging unnecessarily fast as the typical self-destruct modern diet surely, and silently, adds years onto every vital organ and system. A few basic changes in our eating habits, however, can put the situation into reverse.

While there is still no magical elixir for youth, the evolving biochemistry of nutrition is bringing us closer than we've ever been to an anti-aging strategy that actually *works*. It does not demand that we go to great trouble or expense or swallow endless supplements. All we need do is make sure that we get enough of the right types of foods. Getting *enough* seems strange in the manifestly overweight West. But it is becoming clear that even the best-fed can be undernourished. This "affluent malnutrition" is quite different from the out-and-out malnutrition of the past. Thankfully few of us are in danger of suffering the grisly end-stages of scurvy or the agonies of beri-beri. But more subtle food deficiencies may be quietly accelerating many of the "normal" degenerative processes associated with aging: allowing fatty deposits in the bloodstream to sneak into the arteries; weakening the cell membranes so dangerous chemicals can seep in and spark a malignant mutation; disarming the immune system's vigilante cells so they cannot recognize, much less shrug off, health-threatening infections.

EATING OURSELVES SICK

With six of the ten leading causes of death in the West known to be linked to diet, it is becoming clear that you can – literally – eat yourself sick. In the United States now, diet-related causes account for a third of all cancers and half of all heart attacks – and lead to more ill health than smoking, drugs, and accidents put together.

In the 1970s, when diet was first widely recognized to play a big role in the development of the major degenerative diseases, we were mostly told what we *shouldn't* be eating. This was the era of saturated-fat phobia, of cholesterol consciousness, of the alcohol abolitionists and of the red-meat police, of forever being told what we couldn't have and why. Now the experts are changing tack, telling us what we should be eating rather than what we shouldn't, recognizing that what we include in our diet has more impact on our present sense of well-being and future state of health than what we leave out. Keeping anti-oxidant levels high, for example, is now thought by some experts to be as important as keeping cholesterol levels low.

If a poor diet can promote cancer, a good one may prevent it. Orangey-yellow fruits and vegetables and dark green leafy vegetables, such as cabbage and broccoli, are potent sources of beta-carotene. This non-toxic precursor of vitamin A is turning out to be one of the most important weapons in our own natural anti-cancer arsenal. Surveys suggest it may also reduce the chances of a heart attack by as much as half.

PROTECTIVE FOODS

The latest discoveries in diet fit a pattern that is set to become the new shape of preventive medicine. A steady accumulation of evidence from well-respected research establishments, such as the American National Cancer Institute, suggests that achieving a healthy balance in the major food groups (protein, fats and carbohydrates, the so-called "macronutrients") and in certain key elements within those groups (the minerals, vitamins, and enzymes or so-called "micronutrients") can give substantial protection against the big diseases otherwise lined up to carry us off. As the research findings come in, a remarkable consensus is emerging – with the sort of diet that appears beneficial from the point of view of cancer also turning out to be good from that of heart disease or cataracts.

The new nutritional blueprint was summed up by Sir Richard Doll, the British epidemiologist who first made the link between smoking and lung cancer in 1954:

> Whether the object is to avoid cancer, heart disease, hypertension, diabetes, diverticulitis, duodenal ulcers or constipation, there is broad agreement among research workers that the type of diet that is least likely to cause disease is one that provides a high proportion of calories in whole grain cereals, vegetables and fruit; provides most of its animal protein in fish and poultry; limits the intake of fats and, if oil is to be used, gives preference to liquid vegetable oils; includes very little dairy products, eggs and refined sugar and is sufficiently restricted in amount not to cause obesity.

The cascade of healthful effects that can accrue from such eating patterns comes from making lifelong changes. This is not a "diet" to hop on and off again, but a permanent course of action, which demands reprogramming all our previous eating habits and assumptions about food, and which, more positively, offers the opportunity to explore all those foods that we may have unwittingly excluded before. This is radically different from the artificially restricted "diets" we so often carve out for ourselves when we want to lose weight. The egg diet, the grapefruit diet, the grape-and-water diet, the champagne diet – and the 1001 grimly monotonous variations thereof – keep us short of the essential vitamins, minerals, and fatty acids that provide the raw materials for every metabolic process, from thinking and breathing to building up bones and fighting off infection. As we age and both the metabolic rate and the quantity of food required drop, each calorie should be more nutritious than it was when we could afford to eat more of them. This less-of-more equation is achieved by eating across an unlimited range of healthy foods: any amount of fruits, vegetables, poached or steamed fish, wholegrains.

The impoverished nutritional state of the chronic American dieter compares poorly with that of the average Japanese citizen. In Japan, a still buoyantly healthy country with a third of our heart disease and a half of our cancer, the consumption of 30 different foods a day is held to be a desirable goal for health – on the principle that one is sure to be getting something of everything.

The message now is that you *can* eat your way to more energy, better health, and a longer life. Those amazing stories of the Central European hill-people living to a hundred on a diet of sheep's yogurt may be over-simplified, but there is a wholegrain of truth in them. Already certain foods are coming to qualify as preventive medicine. The buzz words in scientific circles now are *cardioprotective* (protecting the heart) and *chemopreventive* (preventing cancer), and they are being applied to an ever-lengthening list of foods.

Carrots, sweet potatoes, and cantaloupes appear to guard against cancers of the lung, stomach, and breast; broccoli and Brussels sprouts contain indole compounds that may block the growth of some tumors; herring, mackerel, and sardines help keep the heart healthy when eaten twice a week; a few cloves of garlic may raise levels of the "good" HDL cholesterol that keeps the arteries clear; while a tablespoon of oatbran or an apple a day helps lower levels of the "bad" LDL cholesterol that gums them up.

> If you are planning to lose weight, cut right back on fat and processed or packaged foods. Aim for a slow weight loss of not more than one pound (half a kilogram) a week. This has the double benefit of helping you lose weight while also overhauling your diet in such a way that it forges lasting new eating patterns and enables your weight to stay at a permanently healthy low. Remember that it takes a hundred days to forge a new habit, so you can afford to take plenty of time, and don't be disheartened if it doesn't come naturally to you at the beginning.
>
> Eat breakfast: this vanishing meal is crucial to the regularity that keeps the digestive tract in good working order and helps keep weight stable. It is well known that obese people rarely eat breakfast and have only a light lunch, with the calories building up logarithmically from there on.

THE PALEOLITHIC DIET

As scientists set about isolating the nutrients responsible for these astonishing effects, the evidence is all pointing the same way – namely, back tens of thousands of years to the diet enjoyed by our paleolithic ancestors, the hunting–gathering–fishing folk who lived by the banks of rivers, alongside estuaries, and near the seashore and speared the odd animal when they were in luck. Modern scientific research confirms the obvious: the diet we evolved on suits the human system best. If we can only mimic the paleolithic way of eating – with daily handfuls of nuts, seeds, berries, fruits, regular fresh fish, and an occasional meat feast – we may yet beat the "diseases of civilization" that plague the developed world. Indeed, such diseases are still virtually unknown among those few surviving hunter–gatherer populations whose way of life and eating habits most resemble those of our early ancestors.

A recent analysis of this "paleolithic diet" in the *New England Journal of Medicine* pointed up some big differences between primitive and modern diets. Gaining their information from detailed examination of both skeletal and fossilized fecal remains, the researchers concluded that the fat content of the early hominid diet was just half the modern one (21 versus 42 per cent) and the vitamin C intake was more than seven times higher – 440 milligrams versus 62 milligrams – due to the much higher intake of fruit and seeds and berries. Although dairy products rarely featured on the prehistoric menu, their calcium intake was double ours, thanks to their penchant for mineral-rich wild fruits and vegetables. While the early humans ate a lot of protein (34 per cent compared with our 12 per cent), most of it came from fish and wild game whose meat would have been less than five per cent fat, and mostly unsaturated. This is quite different from today's intensively reared beef and lamb, which is bred to be between 25 and 35 per cent fat for additional flavor and succulence. Because plant foods remained unprocessed before being eaten – at most pounded, scraped, or baked – the prehistoric diet was very high in fiber.

While human lifestyles have changed dramatically since the Industrial Revolution 150 years ago, our genetic make-up has remained constant for millions of years. One group of anthropologists has claimed that almost 99 per cent of our present genetic material developed in our prehuman ancestors, with just one per cent appearing after the human and great ape lines separated some seven million years ago. It is only in the last 5000 years, for example – a mere eyeblink in evolutionary terms – that the cultivation of crops and domestication of animals have allowed us to consume dairy products and grains on a regular daily basis, and it has been an even briefer millisecond since we started lounging around in chairs and overeating.

While most may manage without mishap on such relative innovations, others remain genetically programmed to a more primitive nutritional pattern. Controversy rages in medical circles about the true incidence of out-and-out food allergy, but there is no doubt that thousands of people made miserable by a hypersensitive "irritable" bowel have found blessed relief after leaving wheat and dairy products out of their diets.

WHO's healthy diet

Since the modern combination of sloth and surfeit will spell disaster for many, the wise will make a nutritional nod in the direction of our evolutionary development by following a diet that is biologically compatible with it. The eating patterns of our early ancestors clearly underlie the World Health Organization's recent blueprint for health, *Diet, Nutrition, and the Prevention of Chronic Diseases*, which recommends that individuals eat fish as often as meat; include a complex starchy carbohydrate with each meal; crunch their way through 400 grams (nearly a pound) of fresh fruits and vegetables every day (*excluding* potatoes), preferably raw; and enjoy one ounce (30 grams) of seeds and nuts on a daily basis.

The WHO guidelines are echoed by the U.S. Department of Agriculture, which advises all Americans to have five to nine servings of fruit and vegetables a day. Most people eat nothing like this amount, of course. One survey found that, on any typical day, four out of ten Americans don't eat a single fruit, one in five doesn't have a vegetable and over three-quarters eat no high-fiber cereal or whole-grain bread.[1]

Eat at least five helpings of fresh fruits/vegetables (not counting potatoes) a day – for example, at least two pieces of fruit, one green or mixed salad, one root vegetable, and one green vegetable.

• To meet the fruit requirement, make a big bowl of fresh fruit salad every morning, keep it in the fridge and eat it through the day. The vegetable requirement can be checked off in the same way by slicing raw vegetables and keeping them in the fridge too.

• When you cook vegetables, steam, microwave, or stir-fry till just tender but still crunchy. Or boil in the minimum amount of water, very briefly.

• Salads made from raw vegetables are a healthy option, but bear in mind that dark-green leaves are the most beneficial. Iceberg lettuce is the least nutritious of all greens. Romaine lettuce, for example, has eight times as much beta-carotene and six times as much vitamin C as iceberg, and kale has a staggering 27 times as much beta-carotene and 30 times as much vitamin C.

• The World Health Organization recommends a daily intake of at least one ounce (30 grams) of nuts, seeds, and pulses such as lentils. Being the packages of tomorrow's fruit and trees, these are literally packed with nutritional richness and make delicious additions to salads.

THE FATS OF LIFE

The lack of fresh fruit and vegetables in the modern diet is paralleled by a superabundance of fat. At present, fat accounts for 37 per cent of total caloric intake in the United States, so most of us need to cut down considerably just to get down to the WHO's *upper* limit of 30 per cent. Indeed, many researchers are now suggesting that 30 per cent may not be low enough and that 25 per cent would be a better goal. (The lower limit is 15 per cent.) High fat intakes have been repeatedly associated with heart disease, breast and colon cancer, and, of course, obesity; a gram of fat has twice the number of calories a gram of protein or carbohydrate has.

Cutting down on non-essential fat, by following the guidelines given here, will soon lower the total amount you eat. What's needed is to seek out unprocessed food wherever possible rather than its packaged alternative. Cookies, cakes, chocolates, pastry, French fries, and potato chips contain enormous amounts of saturated fat and are responsible for about a quarter of the average total intake. Processed meat is another common source of excessive fat. While lean organically reared red meat with the fat trimmed off it contains just five per cent fat, meat products, like hamburgers, sausages, and pâtés may contain ten times as much. Fat is much cheaper than meat, and with modern technology, colorings, and flavorings, can easily be disguised to look and taste like meat in these products.

Despite the big drive to "know your number" (i.e. cholesterol count), cholesterol in food appears to be less of a concern than saturated fats. Although some foods, such as egg yolks, shellfish, and liver, put cholesterol directly into the system, their impact is small compared to the effect of saturated fats. Women who entirely edit eggs and shellfish out of their diets in the belief that these will hike up their cholesterol levels are depriving themselves of a marvelously rich protein source along with health-enhancing essential fatty acids and doughty free-radical fighters such as zinc.

In the light of increasing evidence that keeping levels of the beneficial (HDL) cholesterol up is more important for women than keeping the harmful (LDL) cholesterol down (see pages 145–6), women should also think twice about wholesale replacement of saturated fats by polyunsaturated fats, since the latter lower HDL cholesterol along with the LDL. A better strategy would be to vary the oils and fats one eats and to include some monosaturated fat, such as olive oil, which lowers LDL while keeping HDL levels stable. This perhaps explains why those countries that use olive oil as their main cooking fat have low rates of heart disease despite sometimes high overall cholesterol levels.

Replace high-fat foods with their lower-fat alternatives – for example, in place of butter or margarine use a low-fat spread – and/or use less of them. If you love the taste of butter, keep it soft, spreading it as thinly and cutting the bread as thickly as possible. Think: more bread, less spread.

- Replace full-fat milk with low-fat or skim, which has less than half the saturated fat, and *more* calcium.
- Seek out low-fat cheeses and yogurts in place of the full-fat variety.
- Replace hard cooking fats with liquid vegetable oils, which are low in saturated fats (olive, rapeseed, sunflower, safflower, corn, or soyabean).
- Always shop so you know what you are eating – the simpler and less adulterated, the better. Processed foods, such as cookies, cakes, creamy sauces, and meat products are abundant sources of the worst type of saturated fat and also contain a lot of hidden sugar and salt.

Although the popular perception of fats and oils is that they are uniformly damaging, some are actually vital to health and should be eaten – albeit sparingly – in as wide a variety as you can. Always buy good-quality single-source oils (those that name the plant rather than simply having "vegetable oil" on the label). Low-quality oils have often been hydrogenated to prolong their shelf-life; they tend to be found in the form of semi-solid margarines and shortenings. The "trans-fatty acids" that result from the hydrogenating process lower "good" HDL cholesterol levels and have been linked with an increased risk of heart disease. A second drawback to the hydrogenation process is that many of the essential fatty acids which are so critical to health are removed, along with anti-oxidizing vitamin E.

Think in terms of eating, as well as avoiding, fat. Some plant and fish oils furnish essential nutrients that cannot be found anywhere else in Nature. Rather than sticking through thick and fat to one margarine, or vegetable oil, vary them – but always use them sparingly. Use safflower or sunflower oil for cooking, sesame oil for stir-frying, a shake of filbert or walnut oil over raw or lightly steamed vegetables, and olive oil for pasta and salads. Eat regular helpings of oily fish for their unique complement of heart-healthy eicosapentaenoic acid and docosahexaenoic acid.

MEAT AND FISH: A BALANCING ACT

While meat is an unparalleled source of vitamin A, the B vitamin complex, zinc, iron, and numerous key trace elements, animal proteins may be detrimental to the long-term health of the digestive tract when eaten more than a couple of times a week (see page 177), and often contain high quantities of saturated fat as well. Die-hard carnivores should hold back from indulging on a daily basis and, rather than making meat the focus of the meal, should treat it as a side dish, with greater emphasis on grains and vegetables.

There is already good evidence of the life-saving effects of eating fish. Inland cultures have long histories of health problems, from dwarfism to blindness, that have never troubled coastal peoples, who have abundant sources of iodine, zinc, and vitamin A. Fish, uniquely, supplies a class of fatty acids essential to heart and brain function. This is thought to be thanks to our early evolutionary history, when the first life forms emerged from the primeval sea. In a rare long-term study on the effect of diet on disease, thousands of middle-aged Dutch men with no history of heart disease were closely questioned about their diet and followed up for 20 years. At the end of the study, those men who ate at least one ounce (30 grams) of fish a day (that's the equivalent of just two fishy meals a week) suffered half as much heart disease. This effect was ascribed to the eicosapentaenoic acid (EPA), one of the "omega 3" essential fatty acids, in which oily fish like mackerel and sardines are extremely rich. Although this study was carried out on overweight, middle-aged, overstressed men, women would do well to take note, since by the present count they are more than twice as likely to die from circulatory diseases as from all cancers *combined*. Eating oily fish may be especially important in midlife, when the arteries are already likely to be clogged, since their essential fatty acids have a strong anti-thrombogenic action on the blood and may prevent a clot from forming in an already narrowed artery.

THE SIMPLE TRUTH ABOUT COMPLEX CARBOHYDRATES

To complete the balance of the diet, some form of complex carbohydrate such as a baked potato, wholemeal bread, pasta, or pulses, should be given prominence. Over

Fish has long been believed to be "good for you." Now its unique complement of heart- and brain-healthy essential fatty acids is known to be vital for health. Eating fish – especially oily fish such as mackerel, herring or sardines – may be particularly important in midlife, when the arteries are likely to be clogged, since they have an action on the blood that could prevent a clot forming in an already narrowed blood vessel.

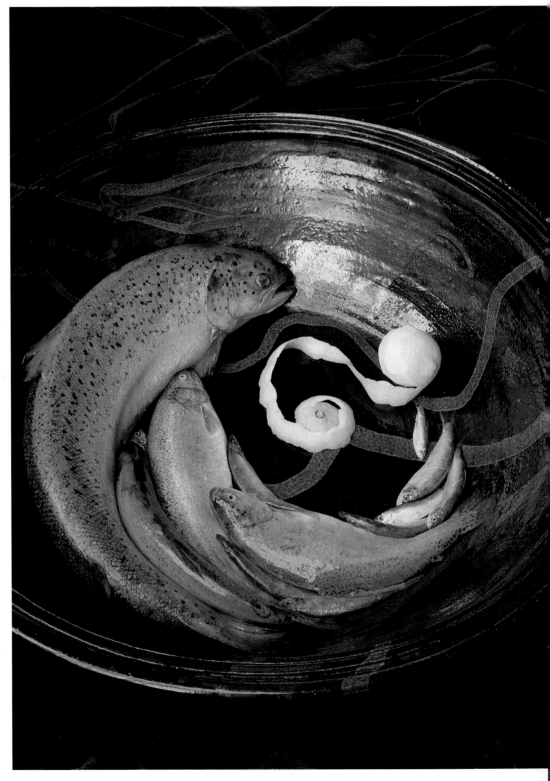

Look on meat as an occasional treat rather than an everyday food. Free-range (also known as "biologically reared") chicken, beef, and lamb are lower in saturated fat and higher in important minerals such as zinc and iron than more intensively farmed animals. Buy it as lean as possible and broil, steam, stir-fry, or bake in stock rather than frying, roasting, or barbecuing. Get lean cuts of meat and trim away the fat; discard chicken skin. Try having at least one "vegetarian" day a week.

Aim to eat fish twice a week, concentrating on oily fish (mackerel, herring, salmon, trout, sardines, pilchards and anchovies, especially with the bones mashed in, tuna, and red mullet). Experiment with monkfish, squid, bream and octopus, and also with shellfish such as lobster, crab, prawns, shrimps, langoustines, oysters, mussels, and clams, all of which are high in zinc. They are a useful second source of the mineral selenium, too, low levels of which have been linked to high rates of cancer.

the last hundred years, our intake of starchy foods – bread, potatoes, wholegrains, cereals, pasta, rice, roots, fruit, and vegetables – has fallen by about two-thirds, as increased wealth has switched us on to foods laden with fat, sugar, and much more protein than needed.

As the idea of the staple food as the staff of life has disappeared, so that satisfying sense of satiety that fiber supplies as it bulks out in the system is also disappearing. One big reason for the epidemic of overweight now sweeping the United States is almost certainly the "unwitting overeating" that is so easy on a highly refined diet. As well as decreasing hunger, the slow metabolism of fiber-rich foods helps the blood sugar stabilize. It also pushes cholesterol levels down because the fiber binds with the cholesterol-containing bile acids in the digestive tract and sweeps it out of the body. Switching to a high-fiber diet will do more to keep the colon clean than any number of "detoxifying diets" or grape-and-water fasts.

Vital nutrients, such as vitamins, minerals, and essential fatty acids, are contained in great abundance in fiber-rich foods. What's more, this bounty is held in a tightly woven molecular matrix, which ensures their slow release into the system, thus giving each nutrient the best possible chance of being absorbed unimpeded into the bloodstream.

When refined foods and, indeed, supplements are metabolized, by contrast, the nutrients are released in an all-out rush and have to compete for absorption. As some are known to fight with each other – iron and calcium are two – the result is sometimes a compromise of sorts.

at fiber-rich foods themselves rather than helping yourself to fiber via bran supplements, as these contain phytate, which hinders the absorption of certain key nutrients, such as calcium, zinc, and iron, from the digestive tract. The U.S. National Cancer Institute recommends eating ¾–1 ounce (20–30 grams) of fiber a day. Achieve this by making a fiber-rich food central to the meal: instead of having a huge steak and small potato on the side, have two baked potatoes and a few strips of meat; or instead of overwhelming a modest nest of spaghetti with a rich sauce, hold back on the sauce and load on more pasta – wholewheat, of course. And always eat wholewheat bread.

SUPERNUTRIENTS – OR PSEUDONUTRIENTS?

It has been the eternal dream that some magical ingredient could stay the passage of time, reversing the ravages of age. Plundering nature, humans, ever hopeful, have gorged themselves on everything from the root of the ginseng plant to the vitamin-rich jelly that the short-lived worker bees feed the grub destined to become their long-lived queen; all, sadly, to no effect.

Nevertheless, there are now tantalizing suggestions that diets rich in certain micronutrients (vitamins, minerals, essential fatty acids, and trace elements) can bring a host of benefits to health – reducing the risk of certain cancers; slowing the development of degenerative diseases such as coronary heart disease, Parkinson's disease, and cataracts; and perhaps even lessening the damage to lungs caused by carcinogens in cigarette smoke or ozone in polluted air. While some of the wackier claims have yet to be substantiated by hard medical evidence, every major cancer organization now has several ongoing vitamin studies. America's ultra-cautious National Cancer Institute, for example, has over two dozen trials going on all around the world, looking specifically at the possible prevention of a number of different cancers. With results due from the late 1990s, we should soon know for certain whether these vitamins and minerals live up to their early promise or prove merely to be pseudonutrients.

If their value is proved, our approach to cancer prevention is sure to be revolutionized. Manipulation of the diet could allow us direct access to, and influence over, our body's biochemistry without drugs – a radical departure from pharmacology's avowed aim of keeping millions of Americans on lifelong drug treatment for their high cholesterol levels.

FREE RADICALS: THE TROUBLEMAKERS

The protective effect of these nutrients is thought to derive from their anti-oxidizing action. Oxygen may be a life-giving gas, but it has a distinctly malevolent side. The actual process of oxidation – a sort of controlled burning in which molecules and proteins are chemically combined with oxygen to release energy – is essential for burning food and fueling physical and mental activity. But, in the process, a number of damaging potentially dangerous by-products known as "free radicals" are formed. While normal molecules consist of paired electrons, with the energy of one counterbalancing the other, free radicals have lost their stabilizing other half. Exhibiting the sort of behavior that led one scientist to describe them as delegates away from their wives at conventions, free radicals split up previously stable pairs, leaving a dangerous, unpaired electron that then goes on to attack and injure the essential components of cells throughout the body in harmful chain reactions. As cell membranes are damaged, they become more susceptible to potential toxins. The genetic code within the cells may become scrambled, provoking the sort of mutations that could some day lead to cancer.

The oxidative process thus forces the body to play with fire. It is both essential to the continuation of life on earth and responsible for initiating a process that will eventually destroy us. Increasingly, gerontologists believe that free-radical reactions underlie the deterioration that is the hallmark of aging in all individuals, healthy as well as sick. Like it or not, they say, we are all gradually oxidizing away in the manner of fats going rancid or apples turning brown when deprived of their protective peel and left to the air.

Whether the damage manifests itself in new lines on the face or dangerously narrowed arteries, the good news is that we can slow the rate at which the oxidization, and hence the damage, occurs. Our bodies are fortunately well-equipped to deal with these free radicals (which are also created in the body in direct response to ultraviolet light, ozone, tobacco smoke, vehicle emissions, and pollutants.) Our main line of defense is a group of nutrients or nutrient-derived enzymes that neutralize free radicals in their tracks by mopping up the unstable electron. There is growing evidence that when the diet is rich in such anti-oxidants, destructive free-radical energy is harnessed.

ANTI-OXIDANTS: A TEAM EFFORT

The most important food-derived anti-oxidants are beta-carotene (the non-toxic part of vitamin A), the vitamins C and E, and the mineral selenium, with manganese, copper, and zinc playing supporting roles. Vitamin C, which dissolves readily in water, has been shown to inactivate free radicals in the watery environment inside cells, while vitamin E, soluble only in fats, prevents damage to the unsaturated fatty acid molecules in cell membranes.

These nutrients work together. When scientists induced breast tumors in rats, and then gave them extra selenium, there was only a small drop in tumors, and vitamin E alone had no effect, but when they gave both together they had a strong inhibiting response.[2] Mice aren't men or women, of course. But a Finnish survey of human subjects has shown that individuals with low blood selenium levels had nearly six times the risk of succumbing to a fatal cancer than those with high levels; if selenium and vitamin E levels were both low, the risk was nearly 12 times higher. Another trial by the same research team established that healthy women had ten times the chance of going on to develop breast cancer if both their blood selenium and vitamin E levels were low.[3]

Alongside vitamin E and selenium, beta-carotene – the parent molecule of vitamin A, which colors vegetables yellow and orange – is turning out to be one of the most important weapons in our own natural anti-cancer arsenal. Animal studies have shown that it is hard both to induce and to transplant tumors into experimental animals that have sufficiently high levels of beta-carotene in their blood – results which tally with human surveys showing low levels of the vitamin among sufferers of cancers of the lung, stomach, and esophagus. One staggering analysis found that smokers with high levels of beta-carotene were *less* likely to develop lung cancer than non-smokers with low levels. Since beta-carotene is found in abundance in fresh fruit and vegetables (especially the yellow/orange variety and deep green leafy types) it is hardly surprising that the experts are now placing such emphasis on eating plenty of fruits and vegetables – the fresher the better, since some of the nutrients are destroyed by long storage.

Intriguingly, the exact same nutrients as appear to protect against cancer seem important for preventing heart disease and stroke. An ongoing study at Harvard Medical School among over 20,000 male doctors, half of whom were given a daily beta-carotene tablet and half of whom were given a dummy pill, found half the incidence of these diseases in the first group, and the same results are now emerging for women. Vitamin E also appears to defend the heart against some of the worst consequences of 20th-century living. In late 1992, Meir Stampfer, one of the world's top epidemiologists and associate professor at Harvard's School of Public Health, announced the results of a survey of 87,000 nurses, all of whom were free of heart disease at the start of the survey, but 552 of whom suffered heart attacks over the next eight years.[4] When a number of lifestyle variables were analyzed, those who had taken vitamin E supplements of more than 100 IU "at some time" were found to have reduced their risk by a third, while those who took it for more than two years had just half the risk – exactly the same reduction as has been achieved for estrogen replacement therapy. Stampfer himself confessed that the results surprised him.

> I'm skeptical by nature but I was even more skeptical going into this study. It just didn't seem plausible that a simple maneuver like taking vitamin E would have such a profound effect. So even though there was really a lot of sound scientific basis for the hypothesis that anti-oxidant vitamins can reduce heart disease, I expected to show that this was not a true association.

As Dr. Stampfer acknowledged, the effect can be explained scientifically. It seems that vitamin E can disrupt the chain of events that progressively blocks the coronary arteries with fatty plaques high in cholesterol, since the LDL-cholesterol

Eat more oranges: there are tantalizing suggestions that eating foods that are rich in certain vitamins and minerals can bring a host of benefits to health – above and beyond their ability to prevent deficiency diseases. Vitamin C, for example, is a free-radical "scavenger" second to none, which appears to protect against age-associated damage to the system – ranging from cataracts to cancer.

component can only enter the cells lining the arteries once it has oxidized, whereupon it draws other cells to it, precipitating an avalanche of biochemical reactions that culminate in a thickened lining to the artery. The hypothesis that vitamin E renders LDL cholesterol resistant to oxidation tallies with a recent Swiss study showing that Europeans with high levels of vitamin E in their blood are less likely to die from heart disease than their peers with low levels, even if they have high levels of cholesterol and/or high blood pressure.[5]

Following findings like this, many of the cardiologists who scoffed at the outrageous claims made for this vitamin are now covertly scoffing supplements instead, in the belief that it offers a more direct route to arterial health than concentrating on lowering their cholesterol levels does. When presenting his results, Dr. Stampfer was asked whether he took vitamin E. "Every day for years," he replied. Some are taking vitamin C too, following evidence that its free-radical-scavenging nature also helps prevent the oxidation of LDL. In addition, a UCLA study found that men who took vitamin C supplements were less likely to develop heart disease.

FOUR APPLES A DAY . . .

Research into these nutrients remains in its infancy. But the preliminary signs are strong enough to have pushed nutritional experts to recommend that we increase the amount of anti-oxidant foods that we eat, since there is a big difference between the small amount of vitamins necessary to stave off the outright deficiency diseases – scurvy, beri-beri, rickets – and the relatively large amount required to prevent the degenerative changes now increasingly being looked upon as another kind of (chronic) deficiency disease. The amount of vitamin E that appears necessary to give anti-oxidant cover for the heart, for example, is seven times the American recommended daily allowance. Equally, while we need just ten milligrams of vitamin C each day to prevent scurvy, significantly more is required in order to rout free radicals.

THE QUESTION OF SUPPLEMENTS

Where feasible, it makes more sense to acquire anti-oxidants by sticking to Nature's sources – although some, such as vitamin E, are hard to get in sufficient quantity from food alone. It appears that it is the combination of nutrients acting in concert that bolsters the protective effect, and the complex ways in which they work together are only beginning to be understood. While some nutrients compete for absorption when combined in a supplement, those naturally contained in foods tend to be more compatible. This more holistic approach also enables us to capitalize on those still unidentified nutrients that are likely to be important for health. Already an array of exciting new compounds are coming under the microscope – from sulforaphane in broccoli to taurine in wholegrains – that derive from exactly the same sources: namely, fruits, vegetables, nuts, seeds, fish, and wholegrains.

Predictably, as positive results come in, pressure is increasingly being exerted by the purveyors of lucrative vitamin supplements to encourage us to pop pills rather than change our lifestyles. Four out of ten Americans take regular supplements, and vitamin E even has its own public relations company! Health "food" stores are stocking up with an ever more insane array of worthless remedies, which escape the tight controls of efficacy, safety, and product promotion that the U.S. Food and Drug Administration imposes on conventional drugs. Mostly this does no harm, since few vitamins are truly toxic and most are excreted if excess to the body's requirements.

PROCEEDING WITH CAUTION

Although side-effects from swallowing vitamins are extremely rare, even on big doses, some vitamins, especially A and D, can be harmful not healthful. (Some early Arctic explorers poisoned themselves by eating polar bear's liver, which is very high in vitamin A.) Others can irritate the intestines by their excessive presence or cancel the absorption of other important nutrients. Eating fruit and vegetables that are high in beta-carotene avoids any risk of vitamin A poisoning, since enzymes in the wall of the intestine convert beta-carotene into the vitamin only if body supplies are low.

Supplements taken in moderation as additional insurance are unlikely to harm, provided you keep within the safe doses given on the following pages. Understand, too, that for all the infectious excitement, this new area of medicine is far from mapped. Insights are fragmentary and certain knowledge elusive, with those surveys which show no effect getting least publicity. Few people, for example, are aware of the big American survey of over 10,000 people that, try as it might, found no relationship whatsoever between blood anti-oxidant levels and cancer risk *at any site*.[6] Even though the positive associations at present outweigh the negative ones, caution is required. Studies in animals have shown that when cancers are induced, either too little or *too much* selenium can enhance the effects of the cancer-producing agent; individuals who megadose on the mineral could therefore actually be doing themselves a big disservice.

Avoiding processed foods and not adding salt at the table (and preferably not in cooking either) will cut your salt intake by at least a quarter. If you are among the one half of the population that is sensitive to salt, this strategy will help keep your blood pressure low and your heart healthy, thereby cutting the risk of heart disease and stroke. In place of salt, experiment with herbs, spices, garlic, and lemon/lime juice – all of which are not only non-damaging but positively good for you. After just a month of this salt-free approach, the palate previously deadened by sodium will regain its sensitivity, enhancing your enjoyment of the foods you eat.

NUTRIENT	WHAT IT MAY DO
vitamin A	Anti-oxidizing effect may protect against heart disease, cancers of lung, bladder, and colon, and degenerative damage to the brain. May boost immune system. Keeps skin strong and vision clear.
beta-carotene	Anti-oxidizing effect may protect against cancers of the lung, breast, pharynx, skin, bladder; may help prevent heart disease; may have beneficial effects on the immune system.
vitamin C	Anti-oxidizing effect may protect against cancers of the cervix, breast, and colon; has beneficial effects on cholesterol. High doses may reduce risk of cataract. Vitamin C neutralizes nitrites in meat, so preventing formation of potentially carcinogenic compounds which could lead to stomach cancer. May protect against and/or reduce severity of colds.
vitamin E	Anti-oxidizing action helps keep arteries healthy, probably by preventing LDL ("bad") cholesterol from gaining entrance and gumming them up. May protect against cancers of the breast, lung, cervix, gastro-intestinal system, liver, and skin, especially if selenium levels are also sufficiently high. May help relieve hot flashes and other menopausal problems. Protects against neurological disorders, and boosts immune system.
calcium	May help keep the skeleton strong in later life, especially when combined with exercise and vitamins D and K. (Major bone-strengthening influence occurs in early adult life, however, when bone is being laid down.) May protect against colon cancer. May help lower blood pressure.
selenium	May help prevent a range of cancers, especially when twinned with fairly high vitamin E levels. Thought to be important to immune response and many other systems that can be compromised with age.
omega-3 fatty acids	Probably important in keeping the heart healthy, by lowering triglyceride levels, preventing atherosclerosis, and keeping the blood fluid and less likely to clot. Said to be helpful for relieving the stiffness and pain of rheumatoid arthritis. May also be good for brain function.
soya	Linked to lower risk of several different cancers, especially breast cancer, perhaps by dismantling a potent type of estrogen.
indoles	May help protect against breast cancer by lowering levels of biologically active estrogen, and may also have a more general anti-tumor effect.

WHERE TO FIND IT FIRST	SUPPLEMENT (SAFETY) RANGE
Dairy (whole milk) products, fish, liver, margarine, eggs, carrots, orangey-yellow fruits, and dark green leafy vegetables.	Concentrate on food sources and, if wanting to supplement, take beta-carotene. The pure vitamin is toxic in high doses, and could even cause brain or liver damage. Vitamin A supplements can be dangerous if planning to conceive or if pregnant.
Any yellow/orange or deep green fruit or vegetable, in particular carrots, kale, spinach, and watercress, sweet potatoes, pumpkins, papayas, mangoes, broccoli, apricots, peaches, orange-fleshed melons, pink grapefruit.	Turns into vitamin A when you eat it, but only if body stores of the vitamin are low. Beta-carotene is non-toxic but very high quantities of carrots can turn the skin yellow and may interfere with the menstrual cycle. If desired, take supplements up to 25 mg a day. Absorption is enhanced by eating beta-carotene-rich vegetables with a dash of butter or oil.
Most fruits and vegetables especially citrus fruits, blackcurrants, parsley, strawberries, red and green peppers, leafy green vegetables, broccoli, cauliflower, tomatoes, berries, melons, beansprouts, fresh potatoes.	It is much better to eat fruit and vegetables as they offer so much additionally, but large doses (up to one gram) of vitamin C can be taken without fear. Much bigger doses may cause mild diarrhea and are not worth taking, since the extra is just passed out of the body in the urine. Requirement for vitamin C rises threefold if you smoke.
Main sources: vegetable oils (peanut, soya, corn, palm) or cold-pressed seed oils (safflower, sunflower), wheatgerm. Secondary sources: nuts (especially almonds), seeds, wholegrains, legumes, leafy vegetables, lettuce, egg yolks.	Keep within 200 IUs; excessive doses can lead to diarrhea and cramps. Those who have a high polyunsaturated fat intake, take a lot of exercise, or smoke may need more of the vitamin. It's hard to get more than 25 IUs from food alone – even on a vitamin-E-rich diet.
Milk (whole, low fat, or skim), cheese (particularly parmesan), yogurt, green vegetables (especially parsley, spinach, broccoli), tinned salmon, sardines (especially with the bones mashed into them), soyabeans, brazil nuts, almonds, sesame seeds.	Supplement first from food and then up to one gram a day (1500 mg post-menopausally) by taking chewable tablets or calcium citrate malate (found in fortified citrus juices). Avoid eating bran at the same time you ingest calcium, as it prevents calcium from being absorbed. If you have a tendency to kidney stones check with your doctor before taking extra. Megadoses can cause constipation and interfere with absorption of zinc and manganese (also important nutrients). Phosphate-containing (junk) foods, such as soda drinks, increase the calcium need.
Brewer's yeast, garlic, onions, broccoli, cabbage, tuna, fish oils, shrimps, prawns, mushrooms, radishes, wholegrains, brown rice, eggs, liver, kidney, heart.	Eat a wide range of selenium-rich foods and keep supplementation to a minimum; there is a fine line between enough and too much. The latter leads to nausea, diarrhea, and nerve damage and may even predispose to cancer.
All fatty fish, especially mackerel, herring, halibut, haddock, sardines, tuna, red mullet, salmon, trout. (Note: wild salmon and trout are richer in these fatty acids than farmed fish.)	Supplements seem nearly as good as the real thing; take up to four 500 mg capsules a day.
Soya milk and dairy substitutes, soyabean meat substitutes, tofu.	Only available in the foods themselves.
Cruciferous vegetables: bok choy, broccoli, Brussels sprouts, cabbage, cauliflower, kohlrabi, turnips, rutabaga.	Only available in the foods themselves.

DRINKING

Having learned the tricks of fermentation and distillation in prehistoric times, man has enjoyed the magical firewater ever since – and woman too, albeit rather less freely. Where social embargoes once prevented a woman from enjoying alcohol, now medical censure has taken over. The demeaning specter of drunkenness and moral disintegration that kept the pioneer mother from the bottle has given way to the equally fearful prospect of liver damage, breast tumors, and damage to the unborn child.

It is hardly surprising then, that these days, the pleasures of alcohol come distinctly guilt-edged for the well-informed modern woman who knows that she is "especially vulnerable" to its ill effects. She has read that she may be increasing her risk of getting a tumor in her breast if she enjoys as little as two glasses of wine a *month*, and has become culturally conditioned to fear for the health of her liver every time she so much as raises a glass to her lips.

It was not always thus. In the relatively recent past alcohol frequently featured in medical prescriptions. Red wine was regarded as a healthy drink stuffed with iron and vitamins to fortify the adult and disinfect the child's drinking water. Light beers were looked upon as a soft drink suitable for anyone over the age of ten. But in the course of this century, safe limits have taken a distinctly downward course – diving from the advice *"jamais plus d'un litre par jour"* ("never more than a liter a day") in turn-of-the-century France to just two glasses of wine a night, in our own time – at most. The Department of Health and Human Services now defines moderate drinking as no more than one drink a day "for most women."

The horrors of heavy drinking are legion. Immoderate drinking wipes 15 years off life-expectancy and doubles the risk of dying before time from such avoidable catastrophes as cirrhosis of the liver, stroke, cardiovascular disease and malignancies of the breast, mouth, larynx, throat, esophagus, and liver (particularly when combined with smoking). The biggest risk to health from moderate drinking, meanwhile, is the risk of its getting out of control: around one in seven social drinkers develops a drinking problem, defined by America's Council on Science and Health as that point "when an individual is unable to stay within moderate limits," and at least five per cent become alcoholics. The difficulty lies in distinguishing that point at which drinking stops being an enjoyable social activity and becomes a covert form of suicide.

THE GRAY AREA
While the hazards of heavy drinking are well established, the six out of seven people who drink regularly and will *not* develop any dependency or health problems are given no clear guidelines and are thus left with a general apprehension that any amount is probably somehow, and in some way, insidiously damaging to health,

when in fact there is evidence of some benefits from moderate amounts of alcohol. The difficulty dates back to the 1920s, when scientific investigations revealed that, while heavy drinkers had a shorter life expectancy than moderate drinkers, moderate drinkers were enjoying longer lives than abstainers. Not only does this puzzling association continue to hold, it is backed up by epidemiological (population) surveys showing that the wine-producing countries of southern Europe (France, Spain, Italy, Portugal, and Greece), whose people enjoy wine on a more or less daily basis, have healthier hearts and longer lives than the more abstemious races of northern Europe. Interestingly, the women of southern Europe seem to do especially well. French women, for example, are the longest-living of any of the 12 member states of the European Community, notching up an average of over 80 years. (The life expectancy of U.S. women is 78.8 years, with nearly half of American women using alcohol.)

The truth seems to be that, unlike smoking, which is a damaging activity at any level, light drinking may actually improve some aspects of your health. This is a hard message to get across in a society burdened by murderous drunk driving, rising liver disease, and alcoholism – and most doctors prefer not to try, worrying that the subtleties of the message will be lost on us and that they will be accused of supplying heavy drinkers with the excuse to drink more. It may go against the medical and cultural grain to give positive drinking data, but it is actually possible to be quite precise about what "moderate" means, even though individuals of similar size and the same sex metabolize alcohol differently. With the exception of breast cancer, where the situation is still far from clear, enjoying one or two drinks a day may well benefit your health. For women, the harm starts, and then escalates, after two drinks.

THE MEASURABLE EFFECTS OF ALCOHOL

At one to two drinks a day, blood pressure remains as low as (or even lower than) when no alcohol is taken. At this level, liver damage is very unlikely, there is a direct protective effect on the heart and cardiovascular system, and there are no measurable ill-effects on the brain (such as loss of short-term memory or a reduced capacity for learning and absorbing new information). Indeed, research carried out at the National Institute of Alcohol Abuse and Alcoholism suggests that the little-but-often drinking pattern does not interfere with cognitive function at all: alcohol appears to tease brain cells for a few hours or so and then glides back out, allowing them to return to their normal state.

Larger amounts of alcohol, however, not only reduce subsequent performance when sober, but are also thought permanently to alter the structure of cells in certain areas of the brain, having measurable effects on memory and on specific cerebral skills, such as mental arithmetic.

It is on more than two drinks a day that the trouble starts. Experiments on college students in Maryland carried out by the National Institute of Alcohol Abuse and Alcoholism found that memory falters after just two drinks – and is still reduced

5½ hours later. Many professional women know that even a couple of drinks at night take the edge off mental clarity in the morning. Worse, women who drink chronically at risky levels can suffer subtle changes in brainpower that may lead to their performance at work falling off imperceptibly over time: they begin to delegate more than is wise and instead of coming up with new ideas they continue to live on past credit.

At three to five drinks a day (21 to 35 units a week), the physical risks rise too. At these levels, damage to the liver and other organs, such as the heart, brain, and pancreas, can develop, and blood pressure rises. Digestive disorders such as ulcers become more common, and cerebrovascular catastrophes such as stroke are increasingly likely. The concern is that many women regularly drink this much. Research recently carried out in four medical practices revealed that, over a six-month period, more than a quarter of women seeing their physicians were drinking in this "hazard zone." These women thought of themselves as regular social drinkers, and many were unaware that the sexes differ markedly in the amount of alcohol they can safely consume.

If you already drink, one drink a day is probably not too much. To enjoy the benefits of alcohol, while keeping the risks low, try not to exceed 14 units – that's 14 small glasses of wine or single measures of spirits or glasses of beer – a week. Avoid straying into the "increasing risk" zone (15 to 35 units), and keep well out of the high-risk one (more than 35 units a week).

● Have at least two alcohol-free days each week to give the liver a rest and avoid the dangerous slide into dependency.

● Keep a tally of how much you drink. If you are regularly exceeding two drinks a day, look critically at how and when you drink. Perhaps by trimming a few – cutting out the lunchtime drink or the one before dinner – you can eliminate harm, and remain in control.

● If you are regularly drinking in the increasing-risk or high-risk zone, stop drinking for two months in order to give yourself the chance of getting back to a more sensible pattern. If you find this hard or impossible, you need help.

SEX DIFFERENCES

Alcohol is no respecter of gender. Even after allowing for differences in weight and size, women feel intoxicated sooner, reach drunk-driving limits earlier, and get drunk more quickly than men. They also tend to develop drink-related disorders at a younger age. These differences are thought to be due in part to the fact that women have lower levels in their stomachs of a crucial enzyme, called gastric alcohol dehydrogenase, which deactivates alcohol before it reaches the liver and bloodstream. In metabolic tests this enzyme appears about four times less active in women than men. In addition, a woman's higher ratio of body fat results in a higher blood-alcohol level. This means that women can drink only about half to two-thirds as much as men before risking effects on their health.

Of all the body organs, the liver is most sensitive to alcohol because it bears the brunt of detoxification. The first signs of overload can be raised levels of liver enzyme, called Gamma GT. A positive GGT reading can be a powerful motivating factor to bring drinking into line (as can raised blood pressure), but since about half of heavy drinkers do not show raised levels and many non-drinkers also have elevated readings it is not a failsafe guide. The first structural signs of liver damage are fat deposits in the cells, followed by inflammation, and cell death. If drinking continues, more severe, possibly life-threatening, damage called cirrhosis (when scar tissue replaces liver tissue) is almost inevitable.

Studies have repeatedly shown that, compared with a man with a similar drinking pattern, a woman is more likely both to damage her liver and to do so more severely. The risk of damage becomes "significant" at three or more units of alcohol a day. (Men may get away with up to six before their risk starts to rise.) Not only are men only half as prone to liver disease, but also when they stop heavy drinking their liver disease often ceases to get worse, whereas in women the condition is likely to continue to deteriorate even if they become models of abstention for ever afterwards. Interestingly, this risk is marked only in pre-menopausal women, so the menopause may actually confer some protection in this respect.

ALCOHOL AND BREAST CANCER

Liver damage is frightening, but at least quantifiable. The still-unclarified anxiety for many drinkers, even those who drink only moderately, is the possible effect of alcohol on the breast. The first stirrings of anxiety sprang from studies on more than 100,000 women conducted jointly by the Harvard School of Public Health in Boston and the U.S. National Cancer Institute, which showed that women drinking up to three drinks a week had a measurably higher risk of developing breast cancer than non-drinkers, while at the so-called "safe" level of two drinks a day the risk rose to between 40 and 70 per cent. This suggests that, from a lifetime risk of just under ten per cent, regular light drinking was found to increase the chance of developing a breast cancer to between 14 and 17 per cent. While a few studies have found no such elevated risk, most confirm this effect – though in some it only appears significant in lean women with a BMI (body mass index) of less than 22 (see page 84) or in women who began drinking before the age of 30, regardless of present-day consumption.

Who knows what this actually means for women? At present, even the experts don't, though there are plenty of hypotheses. It is thought that alcohol could contribute to the development of a cancer by shortening the latency period, so bringing the timing of a tumor forward, or that it could enhance the passage of cancer-causing substances across the cell membranes in the breast tissue or upset hormone metabolism. Nutritionally minded doctors have suggested that alcohol does its damage by depressing levels in the liver of vitamin A, which plays a key role in the maintenance of normal growth and control of cell differentiation. It could also be that alcohol increases the amount of estrogen in the body, a known risk factor for breast cancer. Research at the University of Pittsburgh has found that post-menopausal women who drink moderately have higher estrogen levels. This is thought to be because alcohol stimulates the conversion of the male hormone androgen into estradiol, the form of estrogen doctors prescribe to control bone loss and prevent heart disease.

> **I**f you know yourself to be at risk from breast cancer, by having a strong family history, for example, preliminary studies suggest that you may be able to keep the risk low by abstaining from alcohol, or by limiting your intake to less than two units a week. A small study run by the U.S. National Cancer Institute in 1993 suggests that drinking over the time of ovulation is especially risky, as it increases estrogen levels by 30 per cent.

ALCOHOL AND HEART DISEASE

The confusing conundrum is that, while women who drink a little on a regular basis may increase their risk of breast cancer by about 40 per cent, they will be *decreasing* their risk of heart disease by about the same amount. Some scientists, not all in the pay of the liquor industry, say a woman may be better off drinking moderately than abstaining because the risk of heart attack outweighs the risk of cancer. Certainly many more women die of heart disease every year than die of breast cancer, common though the cancer is.

Alcohol's much-disputed protective effect against heart disease has been confirmed by more than 30 studies on hundreds of thousands of individuals all over the world. These have shown with extraordinary consistency that a moderate consumption of alcohol (and even surprisingly high levels of consumption, in some cases) reduces the risk of heart disease when compared with complete abstention. Of several explanations for this so-called "J-shaped" curve, the most persuasive is that people who become ill or find they have heart disease tend to clean up their lifestyles and give up alcohol: joining the ranks of the teetotalers, they tip the scales against the non-drinker. But even when studies discount existing illness, or remove former drinkers from the equation, the relationship still holds – to a point where the prestigious British medical paper *The Lancet* has seen fit to suggest that "alcohol taken in moderation may be one of the most efficient drugs for protection for CHD [coronary heart disease]".[1]

One explanation for this protective effect is that alcohol has a known impact on blood fats – raising the advantageous HDL cholesterol component, a known risk factor for heart disease. More persuasively, light and moderate amounts of alcohol make the blood less sticky and likely to clot, by reducing the activity of the platelets, in a way similar to that of low-dose aspirin, while also fractionally expanding the diameter of the body's coronary arteries, so enabling more blood to get to the heart muscle. In one study, published in *The Lancet*, just drinking at the weekends (7½ units a week) or even less frequently (2 units a week) was found to lower the likelihood of blood cells clumping together.[2]

Predictably, most of the research has been carried out on middle-aged men. But a New Zealand research team found the protective effect even more marked in women, and the biggest study carried out so far on middle-aged women also confirms the effect. In an American study, published in the *New England Journal of Medicine*, 87,526 nurses were questioned about their diet and drinking habits and in particular were asked whether they had greatly increased or decreased their drinking over the last ten years. When they were followed up for four years, and when the results were analyzed, a 40 per cent lower risk of heart disease was found among women drinking between one and 16 units a week, and a 60 per cent lower risk among women drinking more than 16 units a week.

"Although the data is sparse, the consistency of an apparent protective effect of moderate alcohol consumption on the risk of coronary heart disease in women is remarkable . . ." stated the authors in their report. While acknowledging that the breast cancer question complicates the issue, they pointed out that in the United States heart disease causes 38 per cent of deaths in women, far more than breast cancer (four per cent) or stroke (ten per cent). "The net effect of moderate alcohol intake might therefore be expected to be beneficial but more data are required."[3]

WINE AND FOOD

Several studies have suggested that wine – especially red wine – may be more closely linked with this protective effect than beer and spirits, thanks to its high concentrations of procyanidins, powerful anti-oxidants which are particularly plentiful in red wine, and phytoalexins, natural anti-fungal agents found in the skins of grapes, which raise HDL cholesterol levels while rendering the blood less sticky and liable to clot.

> Reduce possible harm by enjoying wine or beer *with* food, as is the Mediterranean custom, rather than on an empty stomach. Food in the digestive tract may slow the absorption rate by as much as 50 per cent, thus resulting in a lower blood alcohol level than when no food is taken. It may also have more beneficial effects on blood fats.

Alcohol give precious little nutritionally beyond a lot of unnecessary calories (six drinks swallows a third of an entire day's calorie requirement). In addition, heavy drinking, in the order of four or more drinks a day, can dangerously deprive the system of many important nutrients such as protein, potassium, magnesium, zinc, vitamins B1, B6, and B12, and folate.

HIGH-RISK INDIVIDUALS

In the future, doctors are almost certain to be able to identify those individuals of both sexes who are especially likely to suffer breast cancer and liver damage if they drink. It is already known that people with certain genetic markers on their white blood cells, known as B8 or DR3 HLA antigens, are more likely to get liver damage than people without. In the future, these individuals will probably be warned to be particularly careful about the amount they drink.

Alcoholism may also be inherited: in one study, between 20 and 30 per cent of the daughters of women alcoholics were found to have become alcoholics themselves. The same link has now also been found among identical girl twins. According to psychiatrist Kenneth Kendler, who carried out research on over 1000 pairs of identical and fraternal female twins at Virginia Commonwealth University in Richmond, Virginia, women who have parents or grandparents who were alcoholics are quite likely to have inherited a genetic tendency to immoderate drinking in their own turn. They should, therefore, be especially watchful about their drinking habits. He told British *Vogue* in 1993 that "a family history of alcoholism makes women vulnerable in the same way as a family history of heart disease or breast cancer."

If you have a close relative who has or had a drinking problem, you may well be at an increased risk of alcoholism. Be vigilant and, if you find it hard to control the amount you drink, try abstaining entirely.

Expectant mothers should also abstain. The very obvious defects of fetal alcohol syndrome – growth deficiencies which persist through childhood, mental and developmental delays, and poor coordination and muscle strength – are associated with big binges and large amounts of alcohol, and are usually seen in outright alcoholic mothers who didn't manage to check their drinking in pregnancy. The recently identified and less obvious fetal alcohol effect, however, has made it clear that a woman does not need to be an alcoholic to damage her unborn child. While two big studies suggest that no measurable harm is done to the baby by having one drink a day in pregnancy, especially if the woman also refrains from smoking,[4] most experts consider there is not yet enough evidence to enable them to specify a "safe" level. The advice during pregnancy is therefore not to drink at all. Women contemplating pregnancy should preferably give up drinking as soon as they give up contraception, since it is at the time of conception and in the first few weeks of pregnancy that damage to the fetus is most likely. Experimental work even suggests that alcohol may affect the genetic material of the egg during the final stages of maturation just prior to being expelled by the ovary for fertilization.

Abstain from drinking entirely if pregnant, planning to conceive, or breastfeeding. And, of course, don't drink if you will be driving, swimming, boating or engaging in any activity that requires skill or alertness.

ALCOHOL IN LATER LIFE

For the rest of us, the enjoyments and probable benefits of small amounts of alcohol persist throughout life. No one over the age of 60 should allow themselves to be bullied into giving up alcohol for "the sake of their health" unless they are already drinking immoderately. Studies among elderly patients have shown that a glass of beer or wine taken with the evening meal increases sociability, reduces the need for mood-altering drugs, improves sleep, and may even lead to functional improvements. Again, it is a question of degree. In excess, alcohol is especially likely to cause confusion and to affect memory in later life, since older people may metabolize alcohol more slowly than younger ones and are also more likely to suffer side-effects from medication. Balance is the key.

Avoid alcohol if you are taking benzodiazepines (tranquilizers, sleeping pills), MOA-inhibitors for depression, or antihistamines. Since many other medications may also interfere with the body's ability to metabolize alcohol, check with your doctor whether or not you can drink when prescribed any drug.

SMOKING

THE message has got through – people *are* starting to stop – though the bad news is the habit is proving slower to lose its grip on women. Girls are taking up smoking in greater numbers than boys; and women entering their 40s and 50s are more likely to be current, rather than former, smokers, whereas for men the opposite applies. If the sex gap continues to narrow, more American women than men will be smoking by the middle years of this decade.

Of course, by now everyone knows that smoking is a lethal habit. In May 1992, a joint research effort by the American Cancer Society, the Imperial Cancer Research Fund, and the World Health Organization concluded that the risks of smoking had, in fact, been considerably *under*estimated and that between a third and a half of all smokers can expect to die prematurely from their habit. The half of premature smoking deaths that occur in middle age will deprive its victims of an estimated 24 years of life – that's a quarter of a *century*. Increasingly, smoking can be seen to be taking its toll both in midlife (as those who started smoking earlier succumb earlier) and in women. In the United States, lung cancer overtook breast cancer in 1985 to become the leading form of cancer death in women.

EXTRA RISKS FOR WOMEN SMOKERS

As with alcohol, it seems that women are more susceptible to nicotine. They need fewer cigarettes to get comparable levels of the drug in their blood and they metabolize it less rapidly. Women's lives also tend to be more restricted than men's by their smoking habit: their contraceptive choices become limited after the age of 35, and they expose themselves to more social disapproval by smoking when pregnant or around their children. In addition to sharing exactly the same cancer and heart disease risks as male smokers, women smokers also run some nasty additional health risks of their own and may suffer some smoking-related diseases more severely. The miserable chronic obstructive lung diseases (chronic bronchitis and emphysema), for example, appear to set in earlier. One study of nearly 6000 smokers at the National Heart, Lung, and Blood Institute found more damage in the lungs of women aged 35 to 44 than in the lungs of men of the same age. With an already shortened life expectancy, these relatively young women had only the prospect of steadily worsening health ahead if they persisted with their habit.

Smoking also affects a woman's reproductive system in myriad ways. In addition to the established risk of cancers of the liver, lungs, respiratory passage, throat, and esophagus that all smokers run, female smokers have a three times higher risk of cancer of the cervix. It seems geographically implausible that the smoke a woman takes in through her mouth could damage such a distant part of her anatomy, but some as-yet-unidentified component in cigarette smoke is known to obliterate key immune cells in the cervix, called Langerhans cells, which alert the immune system to the presence of viruses and other infective agents that could one day lead to cancer. Not only are women smokers more prone to cancer, but those with abnormal Pap smears who continue to smoke are more likely to go on to get invasive cervical cancer than women who manage to give up.

Quite apart from the well-documented damage to their offspring, women who smoke may have considerable trouble conceiving at all. Toxins in cigarette smoke have a direct effect on the hypothalamus, the part of the brain that stimulates production of both the hormone that kickstarts the ovaries into action each month and that necessary for continuing a pregnancy. According to the 1990 U.S. Surgeon General's report, smokers have nearly three times more fertility problems that non-smokers and also run higher risks of miscarriage and stillbirth.

Women smokers may also run a higher-than-average risk of incontinence. A survey of 606 adult women at the Medical College of Virginia found a significant statistical association between smoking and the development of all forms of urinary incontinence, thought to be caused by the repeated coughing weakening the pelvic floor and leading to leaking.

PREMATURE AGING

Smoking ages a woman prematurely in at least three ways. It puts lines on her face, it accelerates biological time, bringing forward her age of menopause by about two years, and it ages her skeleton. Of these, the first is, of course, the most readily apparent. Smokers *look* older than non-smokers. After 25 years, women who smoke a pack a day will have added about ten years to the look of their faces. Smoking appears to decrease blood supply to the skin, cutting off its normal supply of oxygen. It also unravels the springy network of collagen and elastin fibers that lend the skin its elasticity; and it gives skin a yellowish leathery tinge and puts deep wrinkles around the eyes and mouth.

In an experiment carried out in California, the left eyes of over 1000 men and women were photographed and the crow's feet around them measured. When the resulting "wrinkle scores" were lined up against age, sex, smoking habits, and degree of exposure to the sun and wind, the smokers were found to be much more wrinkled than non-smokers, even if they had stopped smoking at an age before the lines had become apparent. Also, the degree of wrinkling could be linked with surprising accuracy to the number of cigarettes smoked. The most heavily wrinkled eyes in each age/sex group belonged exclusively to smokers. Dr. Harry Daniell, the physician who ran the experiment, concluded that there was a "more substantial association between wrinkling and cigarette smoking than between wrinkling and outdoor exposure, even among subjects living in an area with long, hot cloudless summers."

Surveys on the timing of menopause have found that smokers tend to cluster in the late 40s, compared with the average age of 51, and that "passive" smokers (non-smokers who live in smoking households) may also have their menopauses earlier. This helps explain why smoking has such bad effects on bone. Research using bone

Taking an active role in one's own health, rather than being a passive recipient when things go wrong, means making certain lifestyle changes – for life. And the earlier you start, the better: don't wait for age to impose limitations that make you wish you had taken better care of yourself. Eating fresh whole foods, staying active, not smoking, drinking moderately, and taking the appropriate opportunities afforded by screening have immediate pay-offs as well as future benefits, since healthy habits boost present energy and improve the quality of the here-and-now – as exemplified by Bonnie Berman enjoying the healthy outdoor life with her children on Long Island.

density scanners at the University of Wisconsin at Madison suggest that women smokers between the ages of 20 and 40 already have more fragile spinal vertebrae than non-smokers, so putting them at greater risk of osteoporosis. When twinned with their earlier-than-necessary menopause, which robs them of two or three years of protective estrogen, the risk of a deforming vertebral fracture triples, and fracture of the hip also becomes more likely. On the positive side, one study suggests that a woman who gives up smoking in midlife could reduce her risk of hip fracture by as much as half.[1]

THE ANTI-SMOKING MESSAGE

So what's to stop a woman stopping? The answer seems to be "plenty." Anti-smoking propaganda is rarely aimed directly at women, even though they are susceptible to some of the direst effects of tobacco smoke. This is partly a hangover from the 1950s, when the possibility that smoking might lead to cancer was seen primarily as a problem for men – not because women didn't theoretically share that risk but because in number and manner of smoking they were at least a quarter of a century behind – and partly due to campaigns urging women to give up in order to keep their unborn babies healthy and safeguard the well-being of the family. As with so many other areas of health promotion, these reinforce the impression both that a woman's health is not really important for its own sake and that she is not, perhaps, at very great risk anyway. Once a woman is past childbearing and childraising, the neglect becomes even more marked, with surveys showing that older women are less likely to receive medical advice about giving up smoking than any other group. In a survey of nearly 2000 northern Californian citizens who were aged between 50 and 65, 40 per cent of the women smokers said that their physicians had never even raised the subject with them.

FINDING IT DIFFICULT

While some smokers find giving up easier than expected, few find it easy. A 1992 poll revealed that, of those who had tried to give up, 43 per cent had lit up again within a month – a relapse rate equivalent to that for heroin addiction. Difficult as it is for everyone, study after study has shown that women have even more difficulty giving up smoking than men. Perhaps it is because their motivations for smoking are different or because they are more accustomed to failing and so do not embark on the next attempt with much expectation of success (confidence in being able to stop is a big marker of success). Many women have unaddressed anxieties about becoming fat, and frighteningly unable to control what they eat, or fear that without regular infusions of nicotine to keep them calm they will turn into explosive powder kegs, flying off the handle at the slightest provocation.

Surveys show that, almost without exception, women are "negative-effect smokers," lighting up to assuage feelings they'd rather not have. Men, being "positive-effect smokers," are more likely to smoke when relaxed and at ease. The observation that women light up because they are feeling bad is supported by surveys showing that women with a history of depression are not only more likely to start smoking, but are also only half as likely to be able to stop, suggesting that smoking serves as a form of self-medication.

As smoking sheds its social acceptability, and awareness of the dangers of passive smoking grows, the self-esteem of the woman-smoker is destined to drop yet further. As smoking ceases to be a "normal" habit, and becomes a dangerous anti-social one that threatens other people's airspace and, indeed, health, the image of the woman-smoker has taken on a sort of deviant status. Now not only careless of her own health, the woman who smokes draws ever-increasing social opprobium for jeopardizing the health of her children and those around her, so failing in her primary role as caretaker of the well-being of others.

Look on ceasing to smoke as an investment in your own health and well-being – not just something else you should be doing for the sake of children or spouse, but a route to the better health that you deserve.

● It may also help if you look on it not as a single event but as a *process*, composed of: thinking about stopping, preparing and deciding to stop, actually stopping and (the hardest part) staying stopped.

● The cravings will be most intense during the first week and will gradually subside over the next two weeks. Counter them by wearing a patch, chewing gum, cleaning your teeth or embarking on activities you do not associate with smoking.

● Look on lapses as slips rather than excuses to return to smoking full-time. Be aware that the desire to smoke still assails ex-smokers even many years after giving up – but it gets much less frequent and easier to resist.

WEIGHT GAINS, HEALTH LOSSES

Because women smoke for different reasons, they also relapse for different reasons. While men are likely to relapse in social situations, women tend to falter when stressed, depressed, bored, or, very commonly, panicked by the weight they are putting on. Terror of gaining weight keeps many women on the weed. Though this fear is mercilessly exploited by the tobacco companies, with their "long, slender" lines, "Slims" and "Lights," it remains almost wholly unaddressed by health educators, who have the responsibility for encouraging women to stop, even though research at Johns Hopkins Hospital in Baltimore has shown that women are more likely to relapse as a consequence of gaining weight they cannot shed than because of unbeatable nicotine addiction.

Research confirms that the fears are real. A survey at America's National Heart,

Lung, and Blood Institute found that over a third of the women gained ten pounds (4.5 kilograms) or more one year after quitting, compared with a fifth of the men. Arguments that this additional weight is as bad as smoking for one's health (if not worse) are specious, however. Although very overweight women are more prone to diabetes, high blood pressure, and the ill-effects of immobility that increased size often imposes, even these fade into insignificance compared with the health risks of smoking. Indeed, it has been estimated that for an average-sized woman to bring her risk of suffering a heart attack up to that of a pack-a-day smoker, she would have to gain around 140 pounds (64 kilograms).

There are several good physiological reasons why people gain weight when they stop smoking. Once rid of the habit, the artificially raised metabolic rate slows down to normal. In addition, newly stopped smokers do snack more on high-carbohydrate foods. Like smoking, eating carbohydrate raises levels of a mood-improving neurotransmitter in the brain called serotonin. Carbohydrate cravings therefore appear to be the body's way of readjusting its neurochemistry in order to maintain a serotonin "high." This hypothesis is supported by research showing that treatment with a serotonin-releasing agent, dexfenfluramine, helps keep carbohydrate cravings under control and weight steadier. Nicotine replacement in the form of chewing gum or patches may also have this effect. A study in Switzerland, which compared weight gain in volunteers who had been given either nicotine or dummy patches, found that those with dummy patches put on more than nine pounds (four kilograms) after giving up while those wearing the nicotine patches did not.

WAYS OF STOPPING

To date, nicotine replacement is the only medically proven method of giving up smoking, with long-term success rates of nearly 50 per cent when combined with counseling and support (though only about half this when used with no therapeutic back-up). Skin patches can maintain constant blood nicotine concentrations over a 24-hour period. They can have side-effects, however, ranging from disturbed dreams to indigestion and rapid heartbeat, and thus are unsuitable for those who have heart conditions or ulcers. A nasal spray, which better imitates the fast buzz that comes from smoking, is currently under development.

When using nicotine gum, it is important to follow instructions to the letter. The correct, intermittent manner of chewing advised by the manufacturers not only ensures a steady absorption of nicotine from the lining of the mouth into the bloodstream and on to the brain, where it supposedly extinguishes the need to light up, but also prevents unpleasant side-effects, such as a sore mouth or throat, hiccups, nausea, and indigestion.

Other ways of stopping include acupuncture, hypnotherapy, group support, and aversion/behavioral therapy, all of which can be helpful provided the will to give up is there. For those who decide to go it alone, a research study at the School of Health at Loma Linda University in California, which looked at reasons for relapsing in over 2500 people trying to give up, may provide some helpful pointers. Successful quitters were more likely to have stopped in one go, thrown away their cigarettes, studied the hazards of smoking, avoided smokers, used prayer or meditation, and let lots of people know what they were doing. Unsuccessful quitters, meanwhile, were more likely to have attempted to stop by putting their cigarettes in an awkward place, switching brands, cutting down, quitting as part of a bet, and relying on relaxation techniques.

Target a time to quit, preferably within a month from now, and then do it. If you can predict the times when you'll be under high and low pressure, pick the latter – such as immediately after a period if you suffer from PMS so you have a clear two weeks before tensions set in again. Women trying to give up smoking often suffer stronger withdrawal symptoms in the week before their period.

- On the appointed day stop all at once, rather than cutting down. Use the run-up to make inroads in your habit: delay the first cigarette of the day, cut down on "less essential" cigarettes, and put them out after smoking half to two-thirds (the most dangerous components in the tar are concentrated in the last third). Be conscious of how few cigarettes you really need. Chant, "This cigarette is making me feel crummy, I am losing the desire to smoke" – a method claimed to brainwash smokers into disliking the physiological effects of cigarettes. Increase motivation by asking an anti-smoking pressure group to send you their literature. Let the notion of stopping become increasingly attractive; feel how powerful you will be by breaking your dependence on cigarettes.

- Be positive not fatalistic. Much of the damage can be undone. Even women who have smoked heavily for years can reduce their risk of heart attack to the same level as women who have never smoked within just a year of giving up. After ten years of non-smoking, the risk of dying is nearly equivalent to that of a woman who has never lit a cigarette.

- Make public your decision to stop. Ask for help from family, friends, and colleagues at work.

SCREENING

MODERN women have one big health advantage unknown to earlier generations: screening offers an unparalleled opportunity to catch a lurking problem before it becomes health- or life-threatening. Regular checks can reveal unsuspected tumors, potentially problematic cells that might one day become cancer, above-average blood pressure, the beginnings of glucose intolerance, and rising pressure in the eyeball (glaucoma) which might eventually lead to blindness. They can also help a woman make appropriate health choices. A bone scan at menopause, for example, may tell her whether to opt for hormone replacement therapy and how long to continue, and a colon screen at around 50 whether she is one of the at-risk minority that requires more frequent checks and perhaps a change of lifestyle or diet.

FINDING A BALANCE

All this is to the good, but even so a balance is required, especially in midlife when a woman can come under particularly strong pressure to submit every last bodily nook and cranny for scrutiny. Advertisements and articles call out to her to have her breasts X-rayed, her cervix smeared, her bones scanned, her abdomen and pelvis palpated, and her ovaries and uterus investigated. She will read that she should be testing her feces for "occult" blood and having her blood fats analyzed for a dizzying number of different "markers." In this brave new world of biopsies and blood tests, it can seem as though there is always something lurking in some dim dark recess that must be caught before irreparable harm is done.

It was not always thus. Midlife woman used to be written off as beyond help or hope when medicine could offer her nothing beyond platitudes about submitting gracefully to whatever Nature threw at her. But now that she is the focus of concerted (often commercial) pressures to have every last part of her body probed and scraped, she can feel she is passing up a life-or-death opportunity if she does not take part – despite lack of clear evidence of benefit for many types of screening and the measured recommendations of the official bodies in both the United States and Europe. In the U.S., where women come under much greater pressure to undergo all forms of screening than in Europe, women face a barrage of unnecessary (and often unnecessarily invasive) tests and screens. In 1992, when the American Medical Association ran a survey of over 1000 randomly selected physician members, 84 per cent said they routinely ordered extra tests and screens over and above those they professionally thought appropriate, mainly in order to protect themselves from possible charges of negligence.

A judicious use of what's available is the right approach. While screening *is* an important element of every woman's health care, it behooves the midlife woman to be wary, to know that the pressure to screen does not always operate in her own best interests and that more is not necessarily better. In certain circumstances, which are actually quite well defined, screening *can* make a life-or-death difference. No woman over 50, for example, should skip her regular mammogram or bypass an (at least) three-yearly Pap smear. A colon check at around the same age is also strongly advised. Well-informed women making best use of the formidable new technology will have these tests and then get on with their lives. Recognizing that even exhaustive checks will never entirely eliminate the possibility that something is brewing somewhere, they will not throw vigilance to the winds either. Some doctors are concerned that women having regular breast X-rays might be lulled into complacency by the negative results and so miss signs of the so-called "interval" cancer which appears between screens. This is the reason most often given for the shock results of a huge Canadian study, in which more than 50,000 women aged between 40 and 49 either were given regular mammograms or received no such attention.[1] The news that women found to have cancer through screening had a worse outlook than women who chanced to find a cancer themselves or had a doctor discover it, was especially devastating for the right-on right-living woman in her 40s who believed that, by having mammograms often enough, she was eliminating the threat of breast cancer from her life.

Scans should never be a substitute for vigilance. Check out any changes that you don't like the look or feel of. These include lumps that weren't there before, sores that don't heal, changes in bowel or bladder function, and bleeding from any orifice – mouth, vagina, urethra, anus. You should also notify your doctor if you have an indigestion-like pain for more than three weeks; it could have a number of causes and should be fully investigated.

FALSE POSITIVES AND NEGATIVES

When considering screening, it is important to know in advance what a test involves and how much information it can supply. Many cannot give a definitive "yes" or "no." They point the way forward to further investigation – whether it is colposcopy after a suspicious Pap smear; a repeat mammogram, high-resolution ultrasound scan, or biopsy after a breast X-ray; or a thallium scan or angiogram after a positive ECG. Many tests result in a "false positive" – which means that they appear to have found a problem that then turns out to be a false alarm. In fact, when lesions detected on X-ray are biopsied, only 10-30 per cent of them turn out to be cancerous. False positives are even more common if the woman is pre-menopausal, when it can be harder for the radiologist to distinguish between the dense white of a tumor and a milk-producing gland. Before they heave their huge sigh of relief, women who have had a suspicious mammogram may suffer days, or even weeks, of agonizing anxiety. This is why it is so important both to go to reputable screening centers with

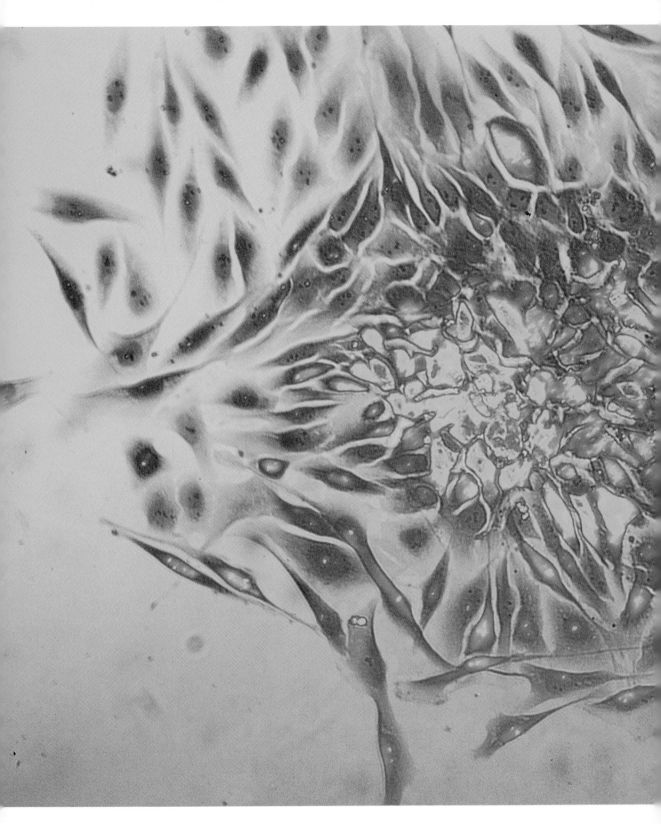

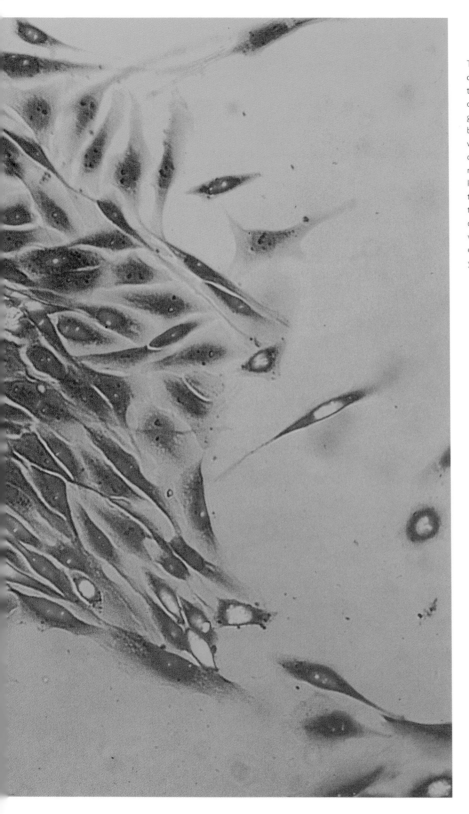

The rationale of screening is to spot a disease before it becomes health- or life-threatening. This clump of human breast cells (magnified several hundred times) is growing in a laboratory test-tube, but it is behaving exactly as if inside the body, with single cells breaking away from the center and spreading outward. Regular mammograms (soft tissue X-rays), which lead to early detection and hence treatment, have been proven to detect this process soon enough to reduce the chance of a breast tumor spreading in women over 50, where they reduce death rates by a third. Their value in younger women is much less certain.

accredited staff and to make a point of asking beforehand what the provision will be in the event of a "positive result."

It is not only false positives that complicate the picture. Some quite well-established tests are notorious for *failing* to pick up an existing problem (a "false negative"). The resting electrocardiograph (ECG), for example, though still routinely used to detect underlying heart problems by supplying a tracing of the electrical activity of the heart, is famously bad at predicting impending coronary catastrophe. In one study, more than half the people dying of heart disease had passed their ECGs with flying colors less than 12 months previously.

Cervical screening has been long held as the gold standard of screening, since, unlike mammography, it can detect unruly cells that have not yet become – but may one day turn into – cancer. Even better, these cells can be smartly obliterated in minutes by a high-powered lazer in a hospital outpatient's department. With regular screening, no woman should ever get invasive cancer of the cervix. As even the more aggressive forms of cervical cancer take several years to develop, a smear taken every few years should offer real protection. Yet such is the false-negative rate (as much as 50 per cent in some surveys) that women should let no longer than three years elapse between smears.

HISTORICAL FACTORS

In addition to using the screening schedule on the following pages, always allow yourself to be guided by your own physician, who knows your personal and family history. Family history determines susceptibility to illness to a greater extent than most people realize, and than egalitarian enthusiasts of the healthy lifestyle would pretend. An astonishing number of otherwise well-informed people are hopelessly unfamiliar with their family histories. If there is a tendency in your family to heart disease, to breast, ovarian, or colon cancer, or to certain types of eye disease, make sure you know about it, since earlier/more frequent screens may be advisable.

> **B**ecome familiar with your family history. Find out what chronic illnesses your parents and grandparents suffered from and what they died of. Inquire particularly about blood pressure, early heart attack, late-onset diabetes, and any form of eye disease or cancer.

FROM THE RIDICULOUS TO THE SUBLIME

If orthodox screening methods have considerable shortcomings, they are as nothing compared with the alternative "health" scene which, at worst, carries out a crazy range of elaborate and expensive tests, from taking hanks of hair and subjecting them to mineral "analysis" to swinging pendulums over a list of supposedly allergy-producing foods. Such tests commonly uncover whole areas of unsuspected ill health, which then create casualties out of previously well-enough individuals. These tests are not analyzed here for they are of unproven benefit and may well turn out to be harmful – to your wallet and psyche if not actually to your person.

In the not-so-far-off future, many of our present screening tests are likely to seem cumbersome, if not primitive. Already blood tests are giving leads about likely malignancy at various body sites, and may lead to a more targeted approach to screening. As the ambitious international genome project approaches its aim of mapping every single one of the 100,000-odd genes that constitute our make-up, scientists consider it merely a matter of time before genetic screening for inherited *susceptibilities* becomes commonplace. In as little as ten years' time, specialist centers may be able to give us a comprehensive profile that will pinpoint our predisposition to a range of preventable calamities from clogged arteries to cancer – all on the basis of a single blood test.

Dozens of biotechnology companies are already racing to find the genetic "markers" for such common degenerative diseases as adult-onset diabetes, heart disease, cancers of the breast and ovary, and various forms of mental illness, from Parkinson's to Alzheimer's disease. The finding of the inherited gene for colon cancer in the summer of 1993 will almost certainly lead to a blood test by the late 1990s, so that those found to be carrying the gene can be intensively screened for early signs of cancer. While all the answers are unlikely to be this definitive – many major killers are the result of the combined influences of many genes working in close interaction with an individual's environment over a lifetime – such screens could represent the ultimate in preventive medicine. They could supply the motivation to give up smoking (or not to start), to change one's diet, to get vaccinated against a triggering virus, to take a medication that would modify one's risk (for example, the anti-estrogen drug tamoxifen in the case of breast cancer), or even to have the suspect part of the body removed (such as the ovaries once one's childbearing days were done).

Already at the Human Nutrition Research Center at Tufts University, Boston, scientists are taking blood from the umbilical cord of newly delivered infants and examining it for evidence of the rare genetic misprint that sends blood fat levels soaring. By identifying susceptible individuals at this early stage, the theory is that preventive nutritional and lifestyle strategies can be embarked upon and the heart kept healthy right from the start.

The new genetics will almost certainly refine the screening processes we do have, allowing doctors to better distinguish those women who are likely to benefit from those who won't. It is already known, for example, that women carrying a gene capable of causing a rare genetic disorder called A–T (ataxia telangiectasia) have a six times higher risk of breast cancer and that this risk may be raised yet further by X-ray or radiotherapy. In the future, a test given to women before undergoing mammography or treatment for breast cancer could identify these women, and they could then be directed toward alternative diagnostic techniques, such as high-resolution ultrasound, and receive different therapeutic measures too.

RECOMMENDED SCREENING SCHEDULES

WHAT	WHEN
blood pressure	At least once every two years; more often, according to doctor's advice, if you take the contraceptive pill, have a family history of high blood pressure or heart disease, are diabetic or extremely overweight, or smoke.
blood/fat analysis	Both total and HDL (high-density lipoproteins) cholesterol should be measured at least every five years. If the first is high or the second low, more frequent testing may be necessary.
blood glucose	No formal intervals. Women who are at high risk (family history of diabetes, sugar in their urine or gestational diabetes when pregnant, giving birth to a very large baby) should have a three-yearly blood test. Everyone should be aware of warning signs (see right).
bones	Women at risk of developing osteoporosis should consider getting a scan around the time of menopause to help them in making decisions about HRT. Women taking HRT might consider a repeat scan to check the bones are responding to the dose they have been given – up to 15 per cent don't.
breasts	Clinical examinations (by a doctor or nurse) yearly up to the age of 50. Mammograms every 12 months thereafter, with clinical examinations as appropriate. The decision to get mammograms or not prior to age 50 should be made in consultation with your doctor. Women with a first-degree relative (mother, sister) with breast cancer should start mammograms at the age below that at which the relative had it. Certain types of biopsy-result for benign breast disease may indicate a need for earlier/more frequent scans, as may a history of persistent breast cysts. Check with your physician.

WHY

To check for hypertension, which can be completely symptomless. High blood pressure is a recognized risk factor for heart disease, stroke, and many other problems. Borderline and moderately raised pressures can often, and should where possible, be brought down by lifestyle changes (see page 367–8) rather than drugs.

High cholesterol levels may contribute to the development of heart disease, especially if other risk factors (family history, raised blood pressure, smoking, extreme overweight, diabetes) are present. A fairly high result (between 6 and 8) can provide a strong motive for making healthy changes to the diet; above 8 may put you in line for medication.

Diabetes can be lethal if left unchecked and is the third-leading cause of death in later life, contributing hugely to heart attack, stroke, and kidney disease, so it is essential that it be detected early and brought under control. Half of all adult diabetic individuals are not aware that they have the condition. Once diagnosed, lifestyle changes, such as losing weight, adapting one's diet, and taking some exercise, are often sufficient to control it.

Low bone density at menopause should prompt serious consideration of hormone replacement therapy.

To pick up cancers at the earliest possible stage, when they are less likely to have spread and require less extensive surgery to take them out. Experts disagree about the advisability of mammography before 50 as it is harder to distinguish a tumor from healthy tissue on X-ray and studies show little evidence of benefit.

WHAT TO WATCH OUT FOR

Wide fluctuations, especially when taken by a doctor. In studies, a quarter to a third of patients diagnosed as having high blood pressure are later found to have normal pressures (so-called "white coat hypertension"), so a suspect reading needs repeating at least once, preferably twice.

Disagreement about the relative importance of raised cholesterol in women (which tends to be higher than men after the age of 50) and what value lowering it has; U.S. doctors tend to screen for, and treat, raised cholesterol more aggressively than European doctors, but the climate of opinion is changing – especially as regards pre-menopausal women.

Signs of possible glucose intolerance, which include fatigue, dehydration, and blurred vision, unremitting thirst, a frequent need to urinate, and persistent infections, such as cystitis and yeast infections. Reliable self-tests can now be bought over the counter. Diagnosed diabetics need annual eye tests.

Great variation between machines. Avoid ultrasound. The best scan is known as DEXA (Dual Energy X-Ray Absorptiometry). Ideally, have spine and/or hip density measured in preference to any other site. When booking, make sure a full family history and risk evaluation will also be carried out so that informed recommendations can be made.

False positives. Even in expert hands, five out of six suspicious mammograms turn out *not* to be cancer. Go to an experienced, accredited center for maximum expertise, minimum radiation dose, and speedy assessment in the event of a suspicious result. Be aware that a cancer can occasionally be missed on mammogram and may also appear between screens; if your instinct tells you something is wrong, or different, get it checked out.

RECOMMENDED SCREENING SCHEDULES *(CONTINUED*

WHAT	WHEN
cervix	Every two to three years up to age 65; thereafter, smears can be discontinued if there have been three consecutive negative smears no more than three years previously and no history of cervical abnormality. Women who have had treatment for abnormal cells or have had the genital wart virus should continue to have annual smears indefinitely.
colon	Yearly use of a fecal occult blood test from 50 (ask your doctor to supply you with this) and, ideally, a more invasive procedure known as sigmoidoscopy, at age 50 or 55, with repeat screens as advised by your physician. The procedure is especially worthwhile if you have a family history of colon cancer (see page 175) or have already had a polyp diagnosed.
ears	If you think that you are not hearing as well as you should be, ask your doctor to check your ears. He or she may refer you for audiometry, which can detect deficits of hearing across the entire range of frequencies.
eyes	Individuals with a family history of glaucoma (ten times higher risk) should be screened every one–two years from 35, and at least yearly on reaching the age when the parent developed it. Everybody else needs a glaucoma check every two years from 40; checks for near-sightedness, cataract, and macular changes can be carried out at the same time. Diabetic and hypertensive individuals may require more frequent eye checks.

WHY	WHAT TO WATCH OUT FOR
To pick up premalignant changes – graded CIN 1, 2, and 3 according to degree of abnormality – which may one day become cancer. Such cells can nearly always be permanently obliterated by lazer.	False negatives and inconclusive results. As many as one-quarter of smears may miss an abnormality and one-fifth are poor samples that may prevent early lifesaving diagnosis. Guard against having one of them by going to a specialist center that regularly performs smears and by always asking to see a copy of your smear report so that you can see what its recommendations are.
To detect changes that may one day become cancer. The use of a sigmoidoscope (a long flexible tube) can enable the specialist to view the lower two-thirds of the colon and to detect polyps, usually benign growths which occasionally turn cancerous. Individuals with a strong family history may require a more extensive investigation, known as colonoscopy.	A marked change in bowel habit, abdominal pain, intractable constipation, precipitous diarrhea, weight loss, or bleeding from the rectum. Always check these out. Never accept a diagnosis of "irritable bowel" until you have been fully investigated.
The sooner a problem is picked up and the quicker a hearing aid is fitted, the less danger of becoming isolated and cut-off. Sometimes all that is needed to restore auditory sharpness is to have the wax removed from the ears (though once the ears are syringed you may have to return regularly for further treatments).	Warning signs: suspect hearing loss, and see your doctor, if you regularly find yourself asking people to speak up, fail to hear the telephone or doorbell ring, or find yourself saying "pardon?" more frequently or leaning forward and tilting your head to hear better. Having others comment that the television or radio is too loud, and that they are having to shout to be heard also indicates the need for a hearing test.
To catch early changes, which can be corrected before further damage sets in, or to detect changes that require further monitoring.	Any change in sight. If you are aware of pain in the eye, blurred or distorted vision, spots before your eyes, colored haloes around lights, or flashes of light, see your doctor, optician or ophthalmologist as soon as possible. Many degenerative eye diseases have early warning signs and are most treatable at this stage.

HORMONALS

THESE days, women have unparalleled control over their once ungovernable hormones. Indeed, in the last decade, the manipulation has taken on an almost magical element. If biology is destiny, the fast-moving world of medical science has shown us that destiny can be redirected. The menopause can be not only postponed, but actually reversed. Using donor eggs from younger women, hormones can be given to make the post-menopausal uterus as warmly receptive as the wombs of women several decades younger. While some gynecologists set time limits, preferring to treat only those women whose ovaries have come to a premature halt, others are happy to give normally menopausal women an extra decade of fertility. There are some strange contradictions, however. As women in the United States and Europe become the world's first-ever generation of sexagenarian childbearers, pregnant women fully a quarter of a century younger are still being looked upon as obstetrically geriatric. For all the medical brow furrowing and dire warnings of fetal abnormality, studies on the hazards of these later pregnancies, which are examined in some detail in the Fertility chapter that follows, suggest that the pessimism is much overdone.

Even before menopause, millions of women manipulate their biology in formerly unthinkable ways. Since the historic moment on May 9th, 1960, when the world's first contraceptive pill, Enovid, was released for prescription sales, millions of women have exchanged their "natural" menstrual cycle, with its ebb and flow of hormones and ovulation at mid-point, for an unchanging hormonal state in which ovulation is bypassed entirely. Many doctors now consider that the off-duty ovary, far from being "unnatural," as critics charge, acts more in the way Nature intended than the one that works overtime. They point out that, while modern (Pill-less) women menstruate 300 to 400 times, taking time off only to bear and (briefly) breastfeed their 2.4 children, women in traditional societies – who are pregnant or breastfeeding for most of their reproductive lives – ovulate a mere 30 to 40 times in the entire stretch between adolescence and menopause. The price of our newfound reproductive freedom is fibroid tumors and tumors in the womb, and cysts and tumors on the overstimulated ovary. Not only does the Pill protect from these hazards, but the benefit persists for years after the last one is swallowed.

The 35-year cut-off stands corrected. Following a ruling by the Food and Drug Administration in October 1989, healthy non-smoking American women can now continue hormonal contraception right up to their menopause. As evidence of the benefits of hormonal contraception comes in, the rationale

These days, stunning advances in reproductive and medical technology are enabling women to stop (or even to wind back) their biological clocks, whether it's by extending their childbearing years into their 60s or by abolishing menopause.

for taking the Pill in later reproductive life is increasingly persuasive, yet just one in 100 women does so. The other 99 are deterred by their own fears or by their doctors' often outdated objections, when they might find it the perfect transitional solution to the sometimes difficult years leading up to the menopause. Once there, they can if they like switch over to hormonal replacement therapy, and so achieve a near-enough seamless menopause.

As the gospel of hormone replacement has spread – the modern doctrine of salvation by pill, patch, or implant – the menopause has become the big bogey of modern medicine. While the benefits of hormone replacement *are* considerable, women need to keep a sense of proportion and to realize that menopause is not everything it has been cracked down to be. The oversell of HRT, thanks to unimaginably big commercial interests and evangelizing gynecologists and their patients, has made modern women more menophobic than at any other point in history. To make the most of what modern science can offer us, we need to keep an open mind. Listening to women who have been through menopause, and out the other side, can take away some of the needless apprehension. Making sure we are informed, and keep informed, in this extraordinarily fast-changing area of medicine will also give us a realistic idea of what hormonal therapy can offer. Only when we are fully informed are we in a position to choose, being neither panicked by menopausal despair into the drug companies' enthusiasm for hormone replacement for all, nor unduly swayed by romantic but unscientific back-to-nature arguments that might deprive us of its considerable benefits.

Technology can help too. A bone scan and an evaluation of family history and heart-disease risk factors can enable us to make an informed personal choice. If our bones are found to be good and dense, and our risk of heart disease minimal, we may confidently decide to experience our menopause minus the mask of hormones without worrying that we are dooming ourselves to a life-threatening condition in the future. Or, if the results are equivocal, we can decide to go with medicine some or all of the way. Neither decision is irrevocable. The course can be changed at any point – even a decade or two after periods stop. Nothing that can be read here or anywhere else is a substitute for a good gynecologist, of course. Finding the right professional to partner us on our journey through the later fertile years, over the menopause, and out the other side should be one of midlife's top priorities.

SEXUALITY

FOR most of this century, older women have not been seen as sexual, let alone desirable. With the notable exception of older French women, who continue to enjoy an allure other women can only envy, the limits of legitimate passion have been set much lower than the age at which such passion generally stops. Onscreen lovers are nearly always under 40. Only recently has it become clear that continuing sexual activity into later life is the rule rather than the exception. Previously, surveys never asked older women about their sex lives because they just assumed they didn't have one. In an era in which sex was still linked with procreation rather than recreation, the menopause by definition disqualified them.

Some women, no doubt, give up less-than-satisfying sexual relationships thankfully at the earliest opportunity, welcoming the menopause at least in the respect that it offers the excuse to stop doing what they've wanted to stop for years. Others, however, find that their sexual desire strengthens with age. There is a huge variation in appetites and activity, just as there is at earlier ages, with both remaining much more stable over time than used to be thought. Surveys reveal that accustomed sexual patterns persist into the seventh and eighth decades; those who enjoyed sex considerably in youth and midlife remain sexually active as they get older, while those who felt only moderately interested during midlife are more likely to give up later on.

For some women, sex simply goes on getting better and better. In good relationships, where men and women, wise with the years and rich in shared experience, have learned all about each other, there is often an ease and familiarity that compensate for the earlier electricity. As they become more comfortable with their sexual selves, and are freed both from the fear of pregnancy and the often crucifying self-consciousness of early adulthood, many women feel increasingly self-assured. They know what they like and how to express it. Attending to their own pleasure and sexual needs instead of being preoccupied with those of their partner, they throw off the obligation to be the good citizen. It is no coincidence that a large proportion of women who change sexual orientation do so in midlife as they come into full possession of their own private sexuality; this may be quite different from the public sexuality which they are accorded by others or which is safely expressed in their closest (heterosexual) relationships.

THE SPECTER OF THE INSATIABLE OLDER WOMAN

Keeping your sex life going is fine if you are half of a well-adjusted couple. But for the many women out there on their own from midlife on, a new sexual relationship is exposing. It demands a degree of physical self-confidence that not all older women have. Sexual desire, that "intense body hunger" as one woman described it, goes against the social stereotype that men have stronger sex drives than women and

The era of the ingenue starlet is drawing to a close; these days, the hottest actresses in Hollywood are 30-plus – Michelle Pfeiffer, TOP LEFT, and Demi Moore, LOWER LEFT, are two, along with Sharon Stone, Geena Davis, Melanie Griffith and Ellen Barkin. Many (Streep, Sarandon) are in their 40s. Along with such raunchy and implausibly middle-aged rock stars as Debbie Harry, ABOVE, and Tina Turner, CENTER, they are extending the limits of legitimate sexuality by overturning the received idea of how women are supposed to act, and react, once the first flush of youth is over.

raises age-old comic clichés about women's sexual appetite increasing voraciously with age while men's capacity to satisfy it wanes. The image of the terrifying hag raging out of control – Lilith, Medusa, the Hindu Goddess Kali, Hurricane Betsy, the black widow spider devouring her mate even as she copulates – can be traced back to that enduring, thousands-year-old myth that the insatiable carnality of older women would devour the energies of any man who came into their clutches, enfeebling him, while sex with virgins would rejuvenate him and enhance his vigor. While Joan Collins is said to have struck a blow for the sexuality of older women, her portrayal of Alexis Carrington fits the mold exactly. Her sexuality is so dangerous that it's positively toxic, a literal *femme fatale* guaranteed to frighten off anyone coming within kissing distance.

THE AGE OF DISQUALIFICATION

Alexis apart, women in their 40s are at last being accorded a sexuality they were not in the recent past. When interviewed for British *Vogue* in 1987, Charlotte Rampling, an actress known for playing the passionate parts rather than the decorative love interest, said she was pleasantly surprised by the number of roles still open to her when she got to 40. "There used to be an attitude that after the age of 40, women shouldn't be seductive or want a man to want them. Now a woman of 40 can be very desirable. We've been given another ten years." But ten years is all. The menopause is still the great divide.

Culturally, older women remain at a tremendous disadvantage. Ceaselessly exposed to young, nimble bodies in suggestively sexy poses, it is easy for them, being possessed of quite different bodies, to feel that sex is not for them anymore. Sex, so natural and healthy in young people, is seen as naughty, dirty, and even deviant in older ones. Modern society, which prides itself on being so free-thinking and liberal, is actually more censorious in this respect than traditional societies: one study of 106 such communities showed an acceptance of continued sexual activity and strong sexual interest in aging women that is quite absent from our culture.[1]

Our own cultural taboos are likely to be intensified for many women by their feeling of being sexual objects rather than subjects, spectators of their own performance and, of course, appearance. If, as Suzanne Lowry suggested in a piece she penned for British *Vogue*, a woman doesn't like to gaze on her own flaccid flesh, soft tummy, and crepey thighs, who else can be expected to?

> I remember a very lovely friend of mine in her late 40s, involved with a much younger man, describing the shock and revulsion she felt seeing what she thought of as her worn, old body in conjunction with what she perceived (probably with equal exaggeration) as a young, beautiful one. It amazed her that he wanted to be with her at all, and she found it very hard to accept that he thought her attractive.[2]

For all her independence of spirit, a woman's idea of her own sexuality is often conditional on the effect it has on another. Having been conditioned all her life to regard sexuality and sexiness, arousal and allure, as one and the same, the persistence of strong desire in the absence of the necessary feedback that she is desirable is bound to disturb. She may feel, as did one of Doris Lessing's heroines, "like a doll whose sawdust is slowly trickling away." In her book, *La Force de l'Âge*, written at the age of 52, Simone de Beauvoir described how this other perspective impacts on a woman's sexual self-confidence:

> A woman is usually more narcissistic in love than a man; her narcissism is directed at her body as a whole. She has a delightful awareness of her body as something desirable, and this awareness comes to her through her partner's caresses and his gaze. If he goes on desiring her she easily puts up with her body's aging. But at the first signs of coolness she feels her ugliness in all its horror, she is disgusted with her image and cannot bear to expose her poor person to others.[3]

The sense of disqualification becomes especially acute if a woman's partner rejects her for a younger version, or if the end of one relationship forces her to start over again. To be over 50, single, *and* sexual in our culture is especially tough since surveys show that after this age marital status becomes the crucial factor in determining whether a woman's sexual activity continues. While married and otherwise attached women commonly continue having sex into their 60s and 70s – with a recent survey showing that at around 50, seven-eighths of women regularly engage in sex with their partners; at 60, seven out of ten do; and at 65 about half – single women are less likely to forge new relationships or to have affairs once into their 50s.

Even within long-standing sexually active relationships, it is generally the male who finally rolls away uninterested. When the male partner loses his libido, his self-confidence, or his ability to have an erection, he literally pulls out and all sexual activity comes to an end. A study carried out at the University of Arizona in the 1980s found that lack of a secure relationship and a sexually active partner spelled the end of sex for women, whereas for men it was "performance anxiety, ill-health of self or the spouse, fatigue, boredom, overindulgence in food and drink, and excessive involvement with outside activities."[4]

> If you or your partner experiences any sudden drop of sex drive in a previously active relationship, question the medications you both are using: some antihypertensive drugs can have a marked effect on libido, especially on a man's ability to "achieve" and maintain an erection, and a change of drug can often help.

A WOMAN'S LIBIDO
Where illness, impotence, or lack of interest puts a stop to sex, a woman's libido may well outlast her partner's. Surveys reveal that over three-quarters of women over 70

still feel erotic desire, but that few express it. Certainly, the indications are that after the age of 50 more women masturbate than don't. Back in the 1940s, Kinsey found about half of widowed, separated, or divorced women in their 50s masturbated to orgasm an average of once every three weeks, and about a third of women masturbated within marriage. A more recent Consumers' Union survey in the United States showed that over a third of all women continue to masturbate into their 70s. Yet many women feel embarrassed or unhappy about taking their pleasure this way, as though they are not entitled to any sort of sex life, even on their own, while others say they feel overwhelmed by a sense of grief for their lack of a partner even as they climax.

STAVING OFF THE MENOPAUSE

While the older woman is keenly aware of an imperative to retire gracefully from the sex scene, an equally strong pressure now exhorts her to "keep it up" on the grounds that plentiful sex and penetration will stave off some of the worst excesses of the menopause. This means that from the age of 50, a woman must wrestle with two quite opposite cultural assumptions. One is the idea that she should no longer be doing it at all; the other is that she should be doing it all the time – if only for the benefit of her own anatomy.

Frequent intercourse with a man has become the *sine qua non* of female health, a youthful "activity" that women must keep up – like jogging – in the interests of better vulval and vaginal tone. Regular penetrative sex is touted to help keep the genitals juicy, compensating for the absence of estrogen. Lots of orgasms are also *de rigueur*, being said to improve the circulation and muscle tone in the pelvic area. Penetration by the penis keeps the vagina dilated, say the sexperts, and even sperm are thought beneficial.

These are not new recommendations. In the 1920s there was a popular philosophy that good regular doses of penetrative sex could fend off the menopause itself and, perhaps more to the point, keep a woman serviceable and receptive to her husband's advances so she could continue to grant him favors in bed. "I have found that the physical signs of age are most noticeable in married women whose husbands practise withdrawal and who themselves never complete the sex act," observed one doctor, quoted in Marie Stopes's *Contraception – Theory, History and Practice*, first published in 1923. "Especially is this noticeable just before or during the menopause." The common practice of coitus interruptus was much frowned upon as it denied a woman the seminal and prostatic fluids from which was absorbed "some substance, hormone, vitamine [sic], or stimulant which affects their internal economy in such a way as to benefit and nourish their whole systems."

These attitudes persist today, perpetuating the agist assumption that penetrative sex is the only sex worth having, when research actually indicates that it is the whole process of intercourse, and especially the earlier stages of arousal and excitement, that keeps the vaginal mucosa functioning, rather than mere mechanical poking. The continued emphasis on the wonders of penetrative sex leads to feelings of failure and frustration as people get older and the mechanics of intercourse become harder to sustain, especially for the man.

PROBLEMS OF DRYNESS

The idea that all women are doomed post-menopause to pleasureless, painful sex has a strong hold on our collective conscious. We are warned that without regular infusions of estrogen to keep the vagina moist and welcoming, it will soon shrivel into a thin, short, desiccated shadow of its former self in which the sides may even gum together for lack of lubrication. Walking will become uncomfortable, sex unbearable, submitting to a Pap smear a higher form of torture. Though dyspareunia (pain during intercourse) does become more common after the menopause, probably due to both lack of lubrication and the prolonged penetration often necessary for older men to reach orgasm, it is not one of later life's inevitables. The over-emphasis on the role of estrogen "deficiency" neglects the importance of the emotions and psyche. One respondent to a questionnaire produced in order to gain information for a leaflet on the menopause, put the point succinctly when she reported: "I thought that the menopause was the leading cause of my dry and irritable vagina. My doctor thought it was lack of hormones, but with my new lover, I am reborn. Plenty of lubrication, no irritation." The distinction can be a difficult one, however. "It was hard to decide which came first," admitted another honestly, "not wanting to have sex or not wanting it because it hurt."

Do not be panicked into sex for genital self-preservation. The vaginal cells never lose their ability to respond to estrogen, and even quite advanced stages of vaginal atrophy can be reversed after a few weeks on treatment. A decade or more after pain and dryness may have forced a woman to forgo intercourse, estrogen replacement can soon restore the lining, depth, and secretions of the vagina.

See pages 375–6 for practical ways of dealing with post-menopausal vaginal dryness, irritation, and infection.

As with the other tissues of the body, different women respond differently to the withdrawal of estrogen from their vaginas. In general, since the vagina needs estrogen to keep it lubricated and elastic, the post-menopausal vagina will feel less full and lubricious than formerly. Penetration or deep thrusting may hurt, but they equally well may not. The vagina itself may become so dry and itchy it feels like sandpaper inside, or it may remain slickly receptive, especially when genuinely aroused. Without sufficient arousal, sex by definition becomes uncomfortable, since the clitoris, which becomes more exposed as the labia shrink, needs to be well lubricated before touching becomes bearable, let alone pleasurable. While some post-menopausal women suffer dryness in the vagina (together, often, with dry eyes and mouth and repeated vaginal/urinary infections), many women either never experience it or only find it a problem many years after the menopause. The U.S. Consumers' Union survey revealed that over a third of women in their 60s and nearly a quarter of those in their 70s still had sufficient natural lubrication to enjoy sex. Add on the quarter of women who don't have sufficient natural lubrication *before* their periods stop, and the proportion of women suffering sexual trauma due to menopause can be seen in a truer light.

When vaginal dryness is a problem, estrogen cream, pessaries, or the newly introduced hormone-releasing vaginal ring (not yet available in the U.S.) can be very effective, allowing easier intercourse and restoring desire and, with it, pleasure to a previously happy and active sexual partnership. But if the relationship was previously unhappy, and sex unenjoyable, no amount of the so-called female sex hormone will compensate for the lack of desire that keeps the vagina dry. Estrogen makes the mechanics of sex easier, not necessarily better.

Hormone treatment

Disregarding this simple truth, hormone replacement therapy has become the modern-day equivalent of rhinoceros horn. Enthusiastic claims for its "tonic" effect fly in the face of an almost total lack of evidence that estrogen fires the libido and adds zest to a lusterless love life. Sexual desire is driven by testosterone – the so-called "male" hormone. While testosterone levels tend to fall in older women, the decline is far less dramatic than that seen in estrogen. According to some specialists, however, the receptors that pick up testosterone in the bloodstream develop an increasing resistance to the hormone, so that even small decreases in testosterone levels might be magnified.

In menopause clinics up and down the United States and Europe, some gynecologists are now slipping pellets of testosterone into the estrogen implants they are giving to their post-menopausal women patients to hike up their flagging libidos. They are doing this despite an alarming list of untoward side-effects, of which the recipients are often unaware. These range from increased hair growth on the face and body and a deepening of the voice, which may be permanent, to enlargement of the clitoris, which can become so supremely sensitive that some women have reported orgasms when zipping themselves into a tight pair of jeans. A growth in face and body hair may not be welcome to a woman worried already about her fading feminine charms, yet she is rarely asked whether she wants to trade more interest in sex, which is at best disconcerting and at worst unmanageable, for a hirsute sprouting on her chin. If she decides she doesn't, and the implant has already been buried in her abdomen or buttock, she will have to wait the requisite six months before the hormone is all used up or submit to surgery in order to have it removed. Already the hormone is suspected of turning a woman's blood fats into a more "male pattern" and so, possibly, of predisposing to heart disease.

With disadvantages like these, the benefits would have to be considerable. Yet anecdotal reports suggest that relationships rarely benefit from this heightened sexual energy, since testosterone is linked more to auto-eroticism (masturbation, fantasies) than to a heightening of shared sexual experience, and may even drive a woman to look elsewhere for satisfaction. But there is no predicting responses. Some women have found it brings a new dimension to their sex lives which they would not be without and return enthusiastically for more. Others find themselves no longer turned on by their present partner and assailed instead by disturbing fantasies and a near-continual desire to masturbate. Lesser doses, however, are proving less problematic: at London's internationally renowned Kings College Hospital menopause clinic, implants given at half the usual dose and replaced every six to nine months have been found to abolish side-effects in the great majority of women.

It's not just women who are on the receiving end of such treatments. These days, sexologists are also giving testosterone to men to bolster their sex drive, administering it in the form of pills, injections, or, a new development, "scrotal film," a soft patch the size of a credit card which delivers the hormone through the testicular skin. Many justify it by talking of an "andropause" or "viropause," in which 40- and 50-something men suffer a virility crisis and need testosterone to reverse a loss of drive in all directions. The current thinking among all but those doctors giving these hormones the hard sell, however, is that, unless a man's testosterone levels are analyzed and found to be exceptionally low, there is rarely much benefit to be had by adding more. In fact, there is some evidence that large amounts of testosterone can upset various chemicals in the body, especially blood fats, disposing to the formation of clots and a risk of heart attack, and may give rise to prostate problems. What is certain is there has not yet been sufficient research to allow anyone to pronounce it safe. The prospect of biochemically reprogramming a 60- or 70-year-old male to respond like an excitable adolescent also poses some real practical problems: since the hormone cannot prop up a limp erection, frustration is almost inevitable as the now-rampant male is prevented from performing as lustily as he'd like.

PHYSIOLOGICAL EFFECTS OF AGE

For all the fuss about hormones, physiological changes are *less* likely to affect a woman as she ages than a man. The arousal phase becomes slower, the skin flushes less luridly, and the breasts do not become quite as engorged, though they often retain full sensitivity. Muscular contractions at orgasm may become weaker (though this is unlikely if the pelvic-floor muscles are kept well toned) and the blood flow to the vagina diminishes slightly. While sensations become less intense, they are often more prolonged, allowing for more leisurely enjoyment.

By contrast, as many as 30 per cent of men are impotent by the age of 60, and the other 70 per cent are coming to terms with marked delays in "achieving" erections. The loss of the once easy faith in their sexuality can lead to loss of confidence on all sorts of levels, and a high degree of frustration on the part of their partners. Yet the cultural assumption is that men continue to be ardent lovers, and that it is women whose libido fizzles first. "We struggle away to achieve a weak erection and the whole point of lovemaking now is to see if he can maintain that for any length of time let alone ejaculate," lamented one woman in a newspaper article.[5]

Medicine hovers by, ever ready to help. Erections can be assisted by drugs that lower the arousal threshold. Cylindrical implants can be placed in the penis and inflated and deflated on demand, and bypass surgery can be performed on vessels to divert blood to the penis. Such measures can sometimes transform life for men who thought sex had given up on them. But with more understanding, many are quite unnecessary. Too many men measure their performance against those of the young bucks they used to be. This, compounded by the anxiety that their partner is using the same invidious standard for comparison, is bound to have a deflating effect. With more time, the older man can actually make a much better, less urgent, lover.

CHANGING FOCUS

Here, as with so much else, information is empowering. If both men and women become more aware of the possible changes that happen over time, they will not be thrown into panic or pressured by unrealistic performance standards, and they will accept that, with increasing age, penetrative sex with ejaculation is less likely. There is abundant evidence that those people still enjoying rich, satisfying sex lives in their 60s and 70s have learned to diversify their approach, moving the focus of sex from penetration and orgasm to other, non-genital aspects of arousal, which, once incidental, become more and more central. As orgasms get more elusive and cannot be counted upon, other pleasures develop more importance along the way. Snuggling, hugging, kissing, oral sex, and mutual masturbation are much more than second-best options introduced when physiology fails. To a generation brought up to believe the gospel of the simultaneous multiple orgasm as the peak of sexual delight, however, adjusting to the idea that intercourse will not mean orgasms every time forces couples either to become more resourceful or to drown in introspective anxieties about their own, or their partner's, erections and orgasms.

Women need to know too that no great harm comes to a man if he has an erection but doesn't ejaculate every time they make love, as happens to most men around two out of three times past the age of 60. To the often noted pressure to come themselves, women now have to accept that their partner may not have an orgasm either and to accept this rather than taking it personally. Since women are always seen as

---

There is more to sex than penetration. Other intimacies can be as satisfying and more pleasurable, especially since they are less likely to fail and provoke anxiety and frustration.

responsible for turning men on, however, it can be hard not to blame oneself for "failing" to arouse him.

Janet Spencer-Mills spoke for many women when she described in British *Vogue* her struggle coming to terms with her partner's impotence :

> I began to doubt my own body, my own attractiveness. Maybe it was the way I smelt, or the fact that I had a scar on my stomach (that old demon came back to haunt me in spades). Maybe I was too old. Maybe, and this was a damagingly pervasive thought which I never had the courage to table, maybe his preferences were not being met by even the large à la carte menu of pleasures we had written between us. I wondered if there were dark indulgences he dare not mention, dare not ask for.[6]

THE RETIREMENT OPTION

If sex is no longer satisfying, there is an alternative. Anthropologists and historians tell us that the idea that a long-term relationship should be fervently passionate is a 20th-century myth, quite alien to all other societies and all other centuries. Certainly it puts impossible pressures on many marriages and long-term partnerships. These days if sex does not hold much magic, it is hard to retire gracefully and to feel good about it. For women particularly, there is now no end in sight to conjugal duty. The sexual revolution has created a new bind whereby women (and, indeed couples) who, 50 years ago, might have been quite happy living in companionate relationships where sex had become infrequent or non-existent, now feel guilty for their less-than-invigorating sex lives. After 30 years of fighting for a woman's right to feel comfortable about having sex when and as she wants it, it is an irony that still, in these supposedly liberated times, a woman does not feel comfortable about *not* having sex when she doesn't want it.

The publicity given to the pharmacological route disguises the fact that many women and men get to the midlife and beyond and give up sex. In one survey fully half the women questioned believed that they could stay in a relationship without having sex, and one in five had spent six months or more in a relationship without intercourse. Loss of coitus need not mean loss of intimacy. Sensuality, which is lifelong, may instead become more diffuse; a touch, a hug, a hand to hold, and all the countless demonstrations of affection that constitute closeness can be of themselves so satisfying that penetrative intercourse is hardly missed.

The relatively new idea that penetrative sex is critical to human health and happiness originated with the great sexologists of the late 19th century – Freud and Havelock Ellis – and has become received wisdom in our own time, despite a resounding lack of evidence that not having it is physiologically damaging in any way to either sex. The consensus now is that lack of sex is only a problem if it is causing a problem. No self-respecting sex therapist would advocate putting more sex back into relationships that have established a status quo both halves are happy with. When disparity in desire is leading to frustrations and resentments, however, therapy can sometimes help couples reach a negotiating point, though it demands considerable effort, time, mutual love and understanding.

CONTRACEPTION

CONTRACEPTION has thankfully come on apace since the beginning of this century when ways of limiting one's family included "sitting upright the moment after ejaculation has taken place and coughing violently,"[1] and the possibilities are widening all the time. Nevertheless, lack of ready information can lead women to feel that their options are becoming ever narrower. The so-called "contraceptive gap," coined to cover the years from 35 to menopause, aptly describes the yawning gulf in services and information for older women. Commonly, as women who have "completed" their families hover between options, they conceive yet another, positively the last, baby. Doctors report that the over-35s often display a curious apathy towards contraception. Some have forgotten the fear of unwanted pregnancy, believing it a hazard of adolescence and not a complication that could overturn their own lives. Others have simply stopped believing that they could have a baby. Family planners say they regularly come across women who have an overdeveloped sense of their declining fertility, believing their ovaries to be senile and their eggs ancient, when in fact fall-offs in fertility, though an undoubted biological reality after 35, are highly individual, with many women continuing to ovulate just as efficiently at 40 as they ever did at 20. In one telling survey only five per cent of childless women between the ages of 40 and 44 said they believed that they could still conceive.

Relaxed attitudes to contraception are common in the late 30s and 40s. Some use the notoriously unsafe "rhythm method," not realizing that it becomes even unsafer in later reproductive life, when periods are veering away from the classic 23-to-30 day norm. Because anovulatory (non-egg-producing) cycles are more common in the 40s, this haphazard approach may work for a while. But the complacency can be abruptly shattered by a positive pregnancy test.

> **I**f you think you have taken a risk, "emergency" post-coital contraception can be effective within 72 hours of intercourse. Of the two options currently available – four high-dose contraceptive pills taken two at a time exactly 12 hours apart, or having an IUD fitted – the IUD is the more effective because, unlike the Pill, it is virtually guaranteed to prevent implantation of the fertilized egg.

Counter to popular belief, unwanted pregnancies get more, not less, common with age. A greater proportion of older pregnancies end in abortion than younger ones (even when therapeutic terminations, performed because the fetus is damaged,

285

> he hormone dose in the present Pill is now so low
> that the margin of error is also lower. In 1990, a sur-
> vey revealed a surprisingly high rate of accidental
> pregnancies in women on the Pill, with a third of all the preg-
> nant women claiming to have been using the method at the
> time of conception.
>
> It is now also known that missing some pills is riskier than
> missing others. The most dangerous omission is the last or the
> first pill (or pills) in the pack, since prolonging the seven-day
> break could allow sufficient hormonal change to induce ovula-
> tion. If you miss one (or more) of the first 14 pills in the pack,
> take the most recently delayed pill, use another method of
> birth control for the next seven days; if you miss one of the
> last seven pills, take the pill as before and use another method
> of birth control for the next seven days *and* start the next
> packet immediately – in other words, skip the pill-free week.

are taken into account). Even in 1988, 41,000 babies were born to women of 40 or older, as against 24,000 terminations; compare this with women in their early 30s, who gave birth to 804,000 babies, and had 181,000 terminations.

When older women *do* use contraception reliably, however, they are often more conscientious than younger ones, which helps to explain why failure rates for methods such as the diaphragm and the condom dive with age. In one study, condom failure was as high as 15 per cent in women in their 20s but fell to less than a half of one per cent for women in their 40s. Similarly, the failure rate of the progestin-only ("mini") pill, which must be taken at the same time each day, is between two and five times lower in women over 30 than in women under 20, and ten times lower past the age of 40. However, it may not always be greater diligence that's responsible; frequency of sex often falls off, as may fertility.

OUT-OF-DATE ATTITUDES TOWARD THE PILL

Women who have had time off from 100 per cent effective contraception while having their children are often ten years behind in their thinking. Unaware that formulations have changed, they "remember" that the Pill made them sick or overweight or depressed, and have anyway had it repeatedly drummed into them that they should be off it by the age of 35 (which is now usually only true if they smoke or are considered at exceptionally high risk of heart disease). In a telling survey conducted in 1993 for the pharmaceutical company Schering, nearly a third of the 1000-plus women who were interviewed agreed with the assertion that "it is dangerous to take the Pill after 35."

As a result of such mistaken thinking, women entering midlife will often rule out the one contraceptive that is utterly reliable (as long as they are utterly reliable people, that is), on the grounds that it heightens their risk of having a heart attack or stroke. They are unaware that such a risk fades into insignificance compared with the greater hazards of pregnancy and childbirth or abortion. In October, 1989, the Fertility and Maternal Health Drugs Advisory Committee to the Food and Drug Administration, an organization known for its entrenched conservatism in matters medical, reviewed the mass of evidence on Pill-taking and age. As a result, it removed all age limits on the use of the combined oral contraceptive by healthy, non-smoking women.

Not surprisingly, women are wary about continuing on the Pill. After all, this is the *fourth* time that the upper age limit for the Pill has been changed. To begin with, it was prescribed irrespective of age. Then, in 1977, following an increase in deaths in women over 35 from heart attacks and stroke, the upper age limit was set at 35. In 1981, when the data were reanalyzed and the risk was realized to pertain only to smokers, the limit was raised to 45. Now, given the all-clear up to menopause, women are holding back. One survey revealed that while Pill use has steadily increased for women in every age group under 30 since 1976, it has steadily decreased for women in every age group over that age. In its most recent report, only one in 100 40-year-olds was taking the Pill even though its suitability up to the age of 45 is now well established.

THE MODERN PILL
So what's changed? Firstly, the modern micropill is a mere shadow of its former self, delivering as much estrogen in a week as was swallowed in a day back in 1960 when it was first launched. And this with no loss of efficacy: when taken as directed, the combined pill has a protection-from-pregnancy rate second only to abstaining entirely. As novel delivery systems are developed to mimic the release of the body's own hormones more closely, the dose may drop yet further.

Secondly, the hormones not only are being given in smaller doses but have fewer side-effects and health risks. This particularly applies to the progestin half of the combined pill. (The combined pill is the one commonly referred to as the Pill.) Since natural progesterone is destroyed in the stomach it cannot be given by mouth, and artificial "progestins" have to be given instead, which are similar but not identical to the progesterone hormone produced by the body. Because these progestins are synthesized from the male hormone testosterone, some of the male characteristics linger on, giving so-called "androgenic" side-effects, such as excess hair and acne, weight gain from increased appetite, and (in some women) depression and changes in libido. Most progestins also raise blood sugar and change blood fats in an undesirable, more "male" direction, lowering the beneficial, HDL cholesterol and raising the detrimental LDL. Since the mid 1980s, however, a new generation of progestins (desogestrel, norgestimate) have changed the picture. While these newer agents are not devoid of the side-effects of their forebears, they appear to be a significant improvement. In addition, the ill effects on the metabolism and blood fats

Crystals of naturally occurring estrogen, the synthetic
form of which is contained in the modern "micro" Pill.
Now delivering as much hormone in a week as was
swallowed in a day back in 1960 when first launched,
its lower dose makes it an ideal contraceptive choice
for many women in later reproductive life. In fact, as
surveys bring several life-preserving benefits to light,
the Pill is increasingly appearing to be a viable way of
defending one's health rather than an assault on one's
body. Provided that a woman doesn't smoke or have
one of the other risk factors listed in the box
opposite, she can now safely stay with it till
menopause.

seen with the older progestins are far less dramatic with the newer generation of hormones.

Thirdly, the research is encouraging and comprehensive. These days, women balancing the risks and benefits for themselves can be confident that no medication taken by so many on such a regular basis has been studied so closely for so long by so many people in white coats. (This was scandalously *not* the case 30 years ago when the Pill was launched after trials on just 123 Puerto Rican women.) Indeed, as surveys on literally hundreds of thousands of women have brought several life-preserving *benefits* to light, the Pill is increasingly appearing a way of defending one's health rather than an assault on one's body – with the few remaining gray areas pertaining more to its use in younger women than in older ones. In 1989, when Professor Martin Vessey's department at Oxford University published the results of their massive follow-up on over 17,000 women, half of whom had taken the Pill and half of whom had never used it, women who had taken the Pill were clearly shown not only to be no more at risk of premature death than women who had never taken it, but in fact slightly *less* likely to die early.

Women who do not smoke and who wish to continue taking the Pill past the age of 35 should see their doctors and have a full medical and family history taken. Cardiovascular risk factors, which include a family history of a parent or sibling having a heart attack or stroke under the age of 45, marked obesity (BMI of 30 or more), diabetes, high blood pressure or abnormal levels of blood fats should be carefully investigated. Women who are only moderately overweight or who have only moderate elevations in blood pressure, or well controlled diabetes, may be able to stay on the Pill. Ideally, they should be followed closely by their doctors who may test their blood fats, clotting factors, blood sugar and/or blood pressure at regular intervals. Women with multiple risk factors are at high risk for heart disease, and another method of birth control is probably advisable.

Even if you don't smoke and you have none of these risk factors, do consider the new, safer, lower-dose options. As the risks of cardiovascular disease rise with age, any additional risk, however slight, is best avoided. The safest policy is to switch to a formulation containing one of the new progestins if you are not on one of them already. In the United States, these are Ortho Cyclen-21/28, Ortho Cept, and Desogen.

HEALTH ASPECTS OF THE PILL

The protective effect is mainly attributed to the fact that Pill-takers are much less likely to die from ovarian cancer, and this applies not only while taking the contraception but up to 15 years after Pill-taking stops. Following a huge American trial which found a protective effect after just six months of Pill-taking – the effect intensifying with duration of use – statisticians have worked out that for women between 50 and 84, just seven ex-Pill-users in 1000 will get ovarian cancer, compared with 33 non-users. Since this is one of the most lethal of all female cancers, it is a benefit well worth having. Cancer of the endometrium (lining of the womb) is also halved, thanks, it is thought, to the Pill's ability to suppress ovulation (see the introduction to this section).

Fears that the Pill would cause cancers of the breast and cervix are also being laid to rest – particularly for women in later reproductive life. The risk of breast cancer, possibly the most feared of all theoretical Pill-related risks, now appears potentially significant only at the younger end of the age spectrum, with a recent overview of 35 studies showing no association between breast cancer and Pill-taking after the age of 25. In fact, there is even a whisper of a slight *protective* effect. The association between the Pill and cervical cancer is unclear at this time. While it was once thought that the Pill increased the risk to the cervix, it is now uncertain whether it has any effect at all. The earlier, stronger association is thought to be due to the fact that, historically, Pill users have tended to have more sexual partners and to be more likely to smoke – both potent co-factors for cervical cancer in their own right. Until the issue has been settled once and for all, women on the Pill should err on the side of caution and make certain that they get Pap smears at regular intervals.

It is telling that, while heart attack deaths were three times higher in the Pill group in the Oxford survey, all but one of the 18 women who died had been recorded as smokers at the start of the study. It is now recognized that smoking is a much more dangerous activity than taking the Pill and that the two together are especially risky. Smoking while on the Pill is dangerous for your heart at any age. This is because the extra estrogen, which increases blood clotting, also has a beneficial action on those substances that help dissolve the clots – and smoking prevents this beneficial action. Thus, smoking and taking the Pill become more dangerous than just taking the Pill or just smoking. The two got confused because in the early days most women who took the Pill (which was seen as an avant-garde, risky thing to do) also smoked (which had an equally avant-garde, risky image).

OTHER BENEFITS
For women who don't smoke, and don't have the strong cardiovascular risk factors listed in the box on page 289, the Pill can be the perfect solution to the contraceptive, menstrual, and menopausal problems that beset women in their 40s, offering both contraception *and* hormone replacement (unlike standard hormone-replacement preparations, which do not contain enough estrogen to be reliably contraceptive). In the 40s, when ovarian activity and estrogen levels are often already on the blink, some women experience mood swings, joint pains, hot flashes, and vaginal dryness along with erratic and often very heavy periods. The Pill can smooth these problems out while conveniently regularizing the menstrual cycle. A telling number of female doctors in their 40s who have no need for the contraceptive properties of the Pill are nevertheless taking it for its considerable benefits. The Pill can also be a particular boon for women who suffer from premenstrual syndrome, which tends to peak in the lead-up to the menopause, and may even strike for the first time.

As estrogen levels may drop for many years before stopping completely thanks to an increasing tendency to anovulatory (non-egg-producing) cycles, the onset of menopausal-type bone loss can precede the last period by half a decade or more. Pill-taking can postpone this problem so that bone density is improved prior to menopause.

Now that the Pill can, in most cases, be safely continued into the 50th year, its regular-as-clockwork monthly bleeds make it impossible to know whether or not the menopause has happened, especially as the additional estrogen masks menopausal signs such as hot flashes.

Experts advise coming off the Pill at 50 and using an alternative method for three months, after which time a blood test can be taken; if high levels of follicle-stimulating hormone (FSH) confirm the menopause, you can either switch to hormone replacement (lower estrogen dose and a different type) or forget about hormones and contraception entirely.

If you are not using hormonal contraception, you can assume you are menopausal if you are under 50 and two years have passed since your last period; if you are over 50, just a year without periods qualifies as "safe."

THE PROGESTIN-ONLY PILL

Once a woman is over 35, many gynecologists prefer to steer her toward progestin-only methods of hormonal contraception, as the absence of estrogen removes even the slight risk to the circulation. The progestin-only pill, or POP, works by changing the cervical mucus, making it more impenetrable to sperm and, in some cases, also preventing ovulation. Although there is no stopping for periods – the pills are taken continuously – bleeding can be irregular. In fact, a disrupted menstrual cycle is the commonest reason for discontinuing; 40 per cent report their periods unchanged, 40 per cent report them being more erratic and/or heavier and more prolonged, and a lucky (when they have got over the panic of possible pregnancy) 20 per cent have no bleeding at all.

Some gynecologists are wary of progestin-only contraception. By suppressing ovarian activity in a small percentage of women, they fear that the progestin-only pill may deprive them of some of their bone-preserving and heart-protecting estrogen, since much of the hormone derives from the developing follicle in the ovary. Others disagree strongly with this hypothesis, however, pointing out that the trials that would prove or disprove this point have simply not been done.

OTHER FORMS OF HORMONAL CONTRACEPTION

Other ways of giving progestin include delivery by injection, implant, ring, and IUD. Injectable contraception (also known as Depo-Provera or DMPA) drew feminist fire in the mid 1970s following the finding that beagle bitches given huge doses of contraceptive were very likely to develop breast cancer. Although it was quite quickly shown that beagles had a very high likelihood of developing breast

> **I**f you are taking the progestin-only ("mini") pill, you only have a three-hour leeway for error, compared with 12 for the Pill. For maximum efficacy, set your time for taking it well before having sex. (For example, if you usually have sex at night, take your pills in the morning or mid-day rather than when you're preparing for bed.) Women who are taking progestin-only contraception long-term and do not have periods (and all women taking Depo-Provera) may be at risk of developing osteoporosis and should talk to their physicians about the need for a bone scan in order to check on the skeleton.

cancer with or without the extra progestin, the huge publicity that had accompanied the first studies was typically absent from the later reports, which remained confined to the back pages of obscure medical journals. The Food and Drug Administration, which has closely examined the evidence, has now, after a 14-year moratorium, unreservedly declared the method safe. The World Health Organization added its voice to theirs in June 1993.

Certainly there is much to commend it; the injection is given every 12 weeks, the failure rate is just 0.1 per cent (meaning that out of 1000 women using it for a year only one will become pregnant), and side-effects are slight, though it can take up to a year for fertility to return after stopping. On the down side, periods are erratic, irregular, or nonexistent (often a plus). Unlike pills or the IUD, it cannot be removed, which means any side-effects may last for the duration of its action. One report from New Zealand caused consternation with its suggestion that "partial estrogen deficiency" caused by cessation of ovulation – which, unlike other forms of progestin-only contraception, applies to all women – was resulting in a greater osteoporosis risk for long-term users;[2] but since no bone-density measurements were taken at the start of the trial, further research is needed to establish whether there is a possible risk to the skeleton and, if so, whether it persists on stopping therapy.

Progestin-only implants are popular in the United States, and are used to provide maintenance-free contraception for up to five years. Comprising six flexible rods, each about the diameter of a pencil lead, they are inserted surgically in a fan shape under local anesthetic into the upper arm, where they continue to be visible underneath the skin. A slow-release progestin (levonorgestrel) seeps into the bloodstream. Fertility returns promptly once the implant is removed. The effectiveness of the method, Norplant, is better than the POP, even though the hormone dose is lower. The biggest problem, as always, is menstrual irregularities, with mid-cycle bleeding, unpredictable spotting, and straggled-out periods. Sometimes this settles down, but it can continue for the full life of the implant. A refinement, Norplant 2, which uses two rods in place of six, is under research and

Crystals of progesterone. This steroid hormone is destroyed in the stomach and must therefore be given in its synthetic form, progestin. Once a woman is over 35, many gynecologists still prefer to steer her towards progestin-only contraception – in tablet (the POP or "mini" pill), injectable, or implant form – in order to rule out even the slight risk to the circulation associated with estrogen. Recently, a new generation of these synthetic hormones has been introduced which minimizes the metabolic side-effects of the Pill, and may therefore be especially appropriate for women over 35.

may be available by the mid to late 1990s. Biodegradable implants would have the obvious advantage of not requiring removal, but they are at an earlier stage of development.

The long-awaited vaginal ring is made of soft silicone rubber which, once inserted into the vagina, finds its own place (unlike the diaphragm, which has to be correctly positioned) and sits there comfortably, while slowly releasing its hormone. At the moment both a progestin-only and a combined hormonal ring, using the lowest-ever dose of estrogen, are in the final stages of clinical trial. Both must be replaced every three months, but within that time they can be removed and replaced by the woman herself for stretches of up to three hours at a time. The idea of the ring has been well received, but following a report in 1993 in which the method was seen to cause thinning of the protective epithelial (surface) tissue, red patches on the vagina and cervix and (sometimes) gross inflammatory changes,[3] all projected launch dates have been postponed. Obviously, these unexpected findings require further investigation to rule out the possibility that the red patches could lead to ominous cell changes or facilitate the transmission of diseases, such as AIDS.

IUDs

After being litigated virtually out of existence in the United States, following fears of infection leading to sterility, the intra-uterine device (IUD) is making a cautious comeback. It is still highly popular in Europe especially in women over 30, for whom it gives the highest level of satisfaction after sterilization. Even so, many women are terminally put off the mere thought of an IUD thanks to one terrible device, the Dalkon Shield. This caused so many cases of miscarriage and infection, sometimes leading tragically on to infertility, not to mention 10,000 lawsuits, that it was removed from the market in 1974. The aftermath virtually halted the distribution and promotion of all IUDs in the United States from then on. Even today, many people have an image of murderous barbed-wire-like contraptions, when in reality IUDs are small, delicate devices. Some contain copper, and the newest ones release hormones. Both types work by changing the biochemical milieu of the uterus and making it unreceptive to the fertilized egg, so preventing it from implanting there. Some researchers believe that they may also prevent fertilization from actually taking place at all.

Although still painful when being fitted (a problem that can be eased by the use of a local anesthetic), the new generation of IUDs have fewer side-effects and, being smaller, are less likely to provoke painful periods and heavy bleeding. Organon's desogestrel-releasing IUD (still at clinical-trial stage) and Leiras's new levon-orgestrel version (soon to be available in the United States) are particularly likely to suit older women, since the "side-effects" of these IUDs include very much lighter periods after the first three months of fitting, so helping to counteract the very heavy bleeding, or "flooding," that can be such a problem in the run-up to menopause.

In their first year of use, IUDs have a ten per cent accidental expulsion rate and a 15 per cent removal rate – usually due to abnormal bleeding and pelvic pain. Some gynecologists now use vaginal ultrasound to double-check their position after fitting, and claim many fewer problems as a result. The dreaded risk of pelvic inflammatory disease, which has given IUDs such a bad name, rises directly in line with the number of partners a woman has and, because of the rare but real risk of subsequent infertility, makes it a better option for monogamous women or for those who have finished their families.

The risk of infection is known to rise with every IUD change, which can introduce bacteria into the uterus. One study found six times as many cases of pelvic inflammatory disease occurring in the first 20 days following fitting as at any other time. In view of this, the consensus now is that IUDs should be refitted as *infrequently* as possible. Many devices fitted after the age of 40 can remain in place until the menopause, with any resulting slight loss of effectiveness matched by the decline in fertility that occurs with age. With check-ups carried out at the same time as the routine Pap smear, it could, with luck, be the last contraceptive decision an older woman ever has to make.

IUDs should be kept in place for their full life span. There is no need to refit them every couple of years or so as is still common gynecological practice. The majority need changing every five years at most (Nova T), and many of the newer versions can safely be left for eight (Copper T 380 and levonorgestrel-releasing devices).

NATURAL FAMILY PLANNING AND BARRIER METHODS

A substantial number of women are reluctant to take hormones, however ingeniously delivered and whatever reassurances of safety they receive. For them one option is natural family planning. Based on meticulous observation of physiological changes through the cycle, it *must* be taught on a one-to-one basis by a qualified teacher. Even with exemplary instruction, however, the method gets less appropriate as menopause approaches, when the menstrual cycle tends to become erratic.

A second option is the ever-widening range of barrier methods. These may seem pedestrian compared with the advanced hormonal formulations presently available, but at least they have come on from 12th-century Arabia, where a woman would be instructed to take the testicle of a wolf, rub it with oil, wrap it in wool, and insert it into the vagina. The rather more streamlined, modern-day versions have gained new acceptability now that the fear of AIDS has transformed the criteria for what women look for in a contraceptive.

When it comes to protecting oneself against the small but real risk of fatal illness, condoms have no equal. Women who have been put off by memories of early fumblings are often pleasantly surprised when they rediscover the condom. After so many years, it can be a welcome change to be relieved of sole responsibility for contraception. Innovations such as the female condom (Femshield) and the bikini condom, which is designed for use by women, have had a mixed reception, however. The consensus among those who have tried them is that to carry these bulky and rather inelegant options off, you need a good relationship, a sense of humor, and a certain confidence in your body – qualities that many women have in more abundance at 40 than at 20.

> **L**ubricants should be specifically formulated for sex. Oil-based lubricants, such as baby oil, Vaseline, petro-latum, cooking oil, and massage oil, can destroy con-doms and diaphragms. In addition, some vaginal medications, such as those prescribed for thrush and vaginal infections, may affect condoms. Check with your doctor.

When used conscientiously, as in one study of long-term users, the diaphragm, or Dutch cap, has a failure rate of just two per cent a year (although first-year failure rates are as high as 20 per cent). It also gives valuable protection against sexually transmitted disease, including cervical cancer and the grades of pre-malignancy that may lead up to it. A relatively new throw-away method, the sponge, is doused in spermicide and inserted high into the vagina. Although it promised to be an improvement over the diaphragm, it has proved disappointing when put to the test, with studies suggesting that if 100 couples were to use the sponge for a year, as many as 25 pregnancies could result.

STERILIZATION

After the age of 30, sterilization replaces the Pill as the most widely used method of birth control. By 44, one partner in nearly half of all couples has been sterilized – and, it's usually the woman, despite the fact that vasectomy is both simpler to perform and often more easily reversible if required. In skilled hands, both of the procedures are simplicity itself – especially the new, no-scalpel vasectomy which has been pioneered in the Far East and which is performed through a one-millimeter puncture in the testicle skin.

Even female sterilization is no longer the big operation it used to be. Now a relatively slight, 20-minute procedure, a tiny incision is made under an augmented local or light general anesthetic and the Fallopian tubes are either tied (ligation), sealed (coagulation/diathermy), or closed off with clips and rings. Since the last option damages less of the tube, it is usually the method of choice. Some hospitals are now using a lazer to create scar tissue which blocks the Fallopian tubes; while this is undoubtedly quicker and simpler, the long-term effects have yet to be evaluated. Once sterilization is complete, the egg released each month by the ovaries cannot travel down the Fallopian tubes and so disintegrates and is reabsorbed by the body, with no untoward effects on health.

In the 1970s it was thought that sterilization could injure the blood vessels and so compromise the flow of blood to the ovaries. This was in turn suspected of causing hormonal imbalances that could lead to a "post-sterilization syndrome" characterized by shorter menstrual cycles with heavier, more prolonged bleeding, more premenstrual tension, loss of libido, vaginal dryness, and such tenderness about the uterus it could even lead on to hysterectomy. Since then, techniques have improved considerably, and surveys give little support to the belief that the procedure leads to menstrual problems, psychological difficulties, or subsequent surgery. Some women find their periods become heavier but this is likely to be due less to the operation than to coming off the Pill, since the Pill has the effect of obliterating the natural menstrual cycle and putting an artificial one in its place. Pill periods are lighter, briefer bleeds with less discomfort and cramping; post-sterilization periods are those Nature always meant you to have.

> **A**fter sterilization, some discomfort and tiredness are to be expected, together with some cramping (especially if clips and rings are used). Minor complications, which are very rare, include injury to surrounding organs or blood vessels (more of a risk with diathermy/coagulation) and pelvic infections; any major complications arise out of the general anesthesia rather than the operation.

Vasectomy is performed by sealing the vas deferens tubes which carry sperm from the testes to the penis. It does not stop sperm from being produced, but these are absorbed into the body instead of entering the seminal fluid, which continues to be ejaculated minus sperm, again with no ill-effects on the system. Erections are maintained as normal and sensation during orgasm is unaffected. The operation is performed under local anesthetic on an outpatient basis or in a doctor's office. Some bruising or tenderness is likely. Fertility is not immediately obliterated, as in women, but diminishes with each ejaculation until the sperm count reaches zero (usually ten to 12 ejaculations). It is essential that a man has his sperm counts as scheduled, both so that he knows when contraceptive-free intercourse is safe and so that the doctors can ensure that the most common reason for vasectomy failure, recanalization of the tubes, has not taken place.

Although vasectomy is a simple outpatient procedure, many men, being fearful that the procedure will somehow unman them, hesitate to undergo the operation. This fear has been played on by sensationalist reports that vasectomy provokes a "male menopause," causing fatigue, loss of libido, and every other conceivable midlife malaise. One doctor recently described the operation as being like "tying a knot in the barrel of a gun," so feeding the paranoia many men feel at having this sensitive part of their anatomy interfered with. Endocrinologists (hormone experts), however, reassure that the operation causes absolutely no interference with male hormone production and hence libido.

More worryingly, in 1993, the *Journal of the American Medical Association* published two papers showing a link between vasectomy and later prostate cancer, with a past history of the operation raising the risk some ten per cent. Other studies, however, have failed to find any connection. Just a year earlier, for example, the World Health Organization published a report based on the findings of 23 international experts and concluded, "It is unlikely that there is any causal relationship between vasectomy and the risk of cancer of the prostate or testis." And one huge American study indicated that men who undergo vasectomy are actually likely to live *longer* than men who do not.

A FINAL OPTION

Since successful reversal of sterilization is not always possible, it must be looked on as a final option. It is appropriate only for those who have given the matter serious thought over several months, are positive they have had all the children they will ever want, and have considered the widening range of contraceptive methods. American studies suggest that people who give less than a month's consideration to the operation before going ahead are more likely to regret it than those who have considered it for longer. Although microsurgery techniques for rejoining the Fallopian tubes have made reversal more feasible, the success rate is still far from certain, since the tubes are just a hair's breadth in thickness, and natural scarring after surgery to attempt a reversal can quickly reclose them. The chances of reversing vasectomy are generally higher – but fertility may not always be restored, especially more than ten years after the operation, both because of the formation of anti-sperm antibodies, which attack and destroy the man's own sperm, and because the tubes themselves deteriorate.

FERTILITY

As little as a decade ago, a woman expecting her first baby at 25 was quite likely to find herself described as an "elderly primigravid." Terrorized by tales of premature labor, uncontrollably high blood pressure, and fetal abnormality, expectant mothers in their late 30s or early 40s were routinely treated as though they had one foot in the grave. It is hardly surprising to find one 36-year-old woman complaining in *Vogue* in 1981 that she was made to feel as though she had "a disagreeable and possibly contagious illness."

The cultural pressure on women to squeeze childbearing into their 20s, when they are theoretically at their peak of biological readiness, is a fairly new neurosis. Before the 1950s, and the advent of dependable birth control, new mothers were often old mothers as women continued adding to their families well into their 40s. In those days, siblings commonly spanned a generation and a woman finishing her family late in life could find herself both new mother and grandmother at the same time. Currently in the United States, less than ten per cent of all babies are born to women over 35 and only one per cent to women over 40.

TAKING THEIR TIME

Although the average age of giving birth is lower than it was, the trend among professional middle-class women is now markedly older or, as obstetric euphemism has it, "reproductively mature." With established careers, later or second marriages, and the help of some stunning new science, more and more women are tuning out the ticking of the biological clock, and waiting longer before starting to have children. In 1990, four times as many first babies were born to American women over the age of 30 as were born in 1970, and the number of first-time mothers in their 40s doubled.

For all the talk of ticking clocks, many women in their early 30s feel no urgency to reproduce. Contrary to the image of 30-somethings being panicked into pregnancy, many women feel happy taking their time before they embark on motherhood – fully confident that with good health, access to diagnostic antenatal screening tests, and competent management by their doctors, they have been given several years of grace and can look forward to healthy babies and reasonably straightforward births.

Many doctors are getting more relaxed too. In 1986 the American College of Obstetricians and Gynecologists went counter to the prevailing "wisdom" when they came right out with the suggestion that there might actually be a health *advantage* for women having their first baby in their early 30s, on the grounds that the average woman is in better physical shape at 30 than she was at 20, is more likely to have established routine medical care, and is less likely to be alarmed by the physiological changes of pregnancy.

MOTHERHOOD – ENJOYMENT AND ENDURANCE

There is little evidence that older women take longer to "bounce back" after childbirth. Motherhood is exhausting at *any* age, especially for first-time mothers – and arguably even more draining in early adult life when women are less likely to have lined up help. A research group at Leicester University in England found that first-time mothers were particularly likely to be overwhelmed by fatigue, taking an average of 11 months to get back to normal, compared with just seven months for mothers who already had children. This finding led the researchers to conclude that the degree of fatigue may be more strongly linked to the baby's position in the family than to the mother's age.

Anecdotal evidence, however, does suggest that it takes longer for older women to get back into shape physically and that they are more likely to suffer problems as a result of a weakened pelvic floor. Having often more tightly structured lives, they may also find it hard to accommodate a demanding, unpredictable new individual who doesn't appreciate the rules.

"Life was thrown into chaos," remembered the late writer Angela Carter in British *Vogue*. Having had her first baby at 43 she regretted the loss of an independence she had long grown accustomed to. "I missed time on my own. There was definitely a sense of never going to be alone again."

Although the sense of the body's aging can be exacerbated by the sheer hard slog of rearing a small child, many older mothers report that they feel more relaxed than with previous offspring and, surveys suggest, are less likely to describe the baby as "difficult." Other factors operate in older parents' favor too. They are more likely to be in stable relationships and to have more money and clearer ideas about what they want for their children. Having often found fulfillment in their own work lives, older mothers are less likely to see motherhood as a "sacrifice" or to try to live out their ambitions through them.

One study found that five-year-old children who could read fluently on entering school tended to have older-than-average parents, and other studies have also found that such children tend to do better educationally. It is theorized that this is perhaps because older mothers, having completed more of their own life's agenda, are happy to devote more time and energy to their children.

THE MYTHOLOGY OF DANGER

Medically, later childbirth is not as fraught with danger as it's often painted. Care has improved dramatically, and with improved management of complications of pregnancy, childbirth has become safer for all women irrespective of age. In the United States, maternal deaths have come down from 22 per 100,000 births in the late 1970s to eight in the late 1980s. In addition, the ever-widening range of antenatal tests and scans can give a good picture of the baby's structural and genetic health and give parents the chance to decide what to do in the event of an abnormality.

Of course, women who choose to delay their families have to take certain established risks into account. Higher rates of miscarriage, infertility, complications

Every older mother's dream: a healthy, happy baby. Here, the author's daughter, Clemmie Stebbings, with sister Romilly, at two days old. The veritable barrage of ante-natal tests and screens that now confronts every expectant older mother can transform the experience of pregnancy from one of happy anticipation to one of nailbiting apprehension. Yet the good news is that the risk of many birth defects actually bears no relation to the mother's age. Certain chromosomal and genetic abnormalities do become more common with advancing maternal age, but pediatricians now judge that, if expectant parents availed themselves of the appropriate tests (see chart, page 308–9), up to two-thirds of all serious handicaps could be predicted in advance.

of late pregnancy, and a few genetic conditions do become increasingly significant, and these are examined in more detail later. But other so-called risks such as anemia, incompetent cervix (which leads to late miscarriage), premature and long labors, and uterine dysfunction are no more likely to affect older women than anyone else.

In 1990, a U.S. study reviewed the outcomes of delayed childbearing among several thousand women in their 30s and 40s and found "no evidence . . . that they had an increased risk of having a pre-term delivery or having an infant who was small for gestational age, had a low Apgar score or died in the perinatal period." Publishing the paper, the *New England Journal of Medicine* concluded that the data represented "very good news for women in their 30s who are contemplating their first pregnancy . . . What should be emphasized is the fact that the few pregnancy-related problems in nulliparous women who are 35 or older are readily manageable in 1990. Given sound genetic diagnosis and counseling, together with appropriate prenatal care and the judicious management of labor and delivery, the increasing number of women postponing their first pregnancies can look forward to excellent outcomes."[1]

Despite these positive findings, the mythology of danger lives on and may even influence the way pregnancy and birth are managed. Several surveys have found that older mothers are more inclined to have medicalized pregnancies, that their labors are more likely to start with an induction and end with a Caesarean, and that their offspring are more likely to be admitted to special-care units soon after birth. This sounds like damning evidence of an adverse age effect, but when one American researcher actually looked at the reasons behind these interventions he found no evidence of burning medical need. It was increased concern for the older mother, he concluded, that often led the doctors to act.

Keep your fitness up during pregnancy and, if anything, work at improving your flexibility and physical strength. It really makes a difference, if not to the nature of the birth itself (contrary to expectation, fit women are not necessarily rewarded by easier births), then to the time it takes to feel oneself again afterward. Walking, yoga and swimming are excellent forms of exercise in pregnancy and there are many good classes and books.

• Practice Kegel (pelvic floor) exercises (see page 182) daily throughout your pregnancy to keep these crucial bladder-control muscles strong – and continue after delivery too.
• After delivery ease gradually back into exercise. Avoid jumping immediately into a strenuous routine, as your muscles (your abdominal muscles in particular) are deconditioned and susceptible to injury.

KIDGLOVE TREATMENT

The expectation of greater difficulty quickly becomes self-perpetuating. Many older women are automatically scheduled for a Caesarean and allowed no trial of labor, or only the very shortest one, on the unproven basis that the tissues are less elastic and so less capable of normal delivery. Tellingly, women who undergo assisted conception techniques, such as IVF or GIFT, also receive more "care" when it comes to the delivery of their babies. However humanitarian the motives, subconsciously singling out certain categories of pregnant women as worthy of "special" attention doesn't do them many favors. No well-informed woman would consciously choose a Caesarean over a vaginal delivery. Surgery raises the risk of complications such as infection, blood loss, and blood clots and can involve a full-scale anesthetic, while soreness from the scar can take the joy off early motherhood. When Dr. Gertrud Berkowitz, associate professor of obstetrics and gynecology at New York City's Mount Sinai Hospital, headed a study that found that 35 per cent of women over the age of 35 had a Caesarean section compared with 22 per cent of those under the age of 30 (already an extraordinarily high figure), she concluded that most of the difference could be avoided if physicians could only be persuaded to drop their "overly cautious treatment of older pregnant women."

The kidglove treatment may have some advantages, however: a study on 8700 women over 35 indicated that the perinatal death rate (when the baby is either stillborn or dies within the first 28 days) was actually lower than average among this age group, due, it was theorized, to all the extra attention that older women receive during delivery and afterward.

INCREASED DIFFICULTIES IN CONCEIVING

It would be silly to suggest that there are no obstacles facing the woman contemplating pregnancy in her late 30s or early 40s. Conception is the first, often unforeseen hurdle – even for the woman who has previously become accidentally pregnant at the drop of a diaphragm. Fecundity is known to start falling off after the age of 30, strikingly so after 35, and to be all but lost in the majority of women by the age of 45. In addition, older couples are more likely to have medical complications, to have suffered sexually transmitted diseases or to have fibroid tumors – all of which may affect their fertility. A somewhat depressing recent study on 750 Dutch women presenting for artificial insemination showed that after the age of 31, fertility drops by 12 per cent per year, and a 35-year-old woman is twice as likely to have her pregnancy end in miscarriage as a 25-year-old.[2]

If attempts at conception are disappointing, try a home ovulation test kit. This works by analyzing urine samples for levels of luteinizing hormone, which surge in mid cycle and trigger the release of the egg, so giving advance notice of ovulation by some six to 24 hours. It's a more reliable approach than the time-honored and more cumbersome methods of temperature-taking or checking the consistency of the cervical mucus.

Overweight women who are having trouble conceiving might usefully shed the extra weight. But aim for a gradual loss; crash dieting could otherwise render your body dangerously low in vital nutrients at the most important time, around conception. Shaping up could be especially worthwhile if your waist-to-hip ratio (WHR) is 0.75 or more (see page 91). In 1993, a Dutch study discovered that the tendency to store fat around the waist, apple-fashion, has more impact on fertility than weight or age, with every unit increase in WHR lowering the likelihood of conceiving by 30 per cent.

If you use contraception before you're ready to get pregnant, choose a barrier method such as the diaphragm. The Pill makes it hard to date pregnancy, and the IUD can increase the risk of pelvic infection, which can interfere with fertility.

The medical and lay press gloatingly reported these results as showing that "fertility plummets" after the age of 30, so satisfying many medical preconceptions. But what the study really showed was that while older women may take longer to conceive, they do – usually – get there in the end. After 12 cycles only half the women over 31 were pregnant compared to three-quarters of the women in their 20s, but by the 24th cycle, 75 per cent were pregnant as opposed to 85 per cent of the younger women. The fact that the great majority eventually conceived, regardless of age, suggests that with perseverance there is a good chance of pregnancy. The delay can be hard to deal with, however, especially for women who have got used to organizing their lives down to the last detail. Fear of infertility after several months' trying may have them resorting prematurely to some of the radical new fertility management techniques.

One reason some women take longer to conceive as they get older is that they are more likely to have anovulatory (non-egg-producing) cycles. Like a car gradually running out of fuel whose engine runs ever more erratically before the car – finally – sputters to a halt, so too the ovaries release their eggs in an increasingly sporadic fashion: sometimes one, sometimes two (non-identical twin births are around 30 per cent more likely at 40 than at 20), and often none. There are ways of assessing the responsiveness of the ovaries, and any couple considering

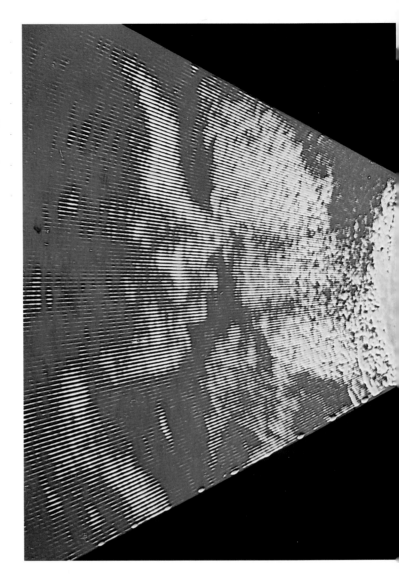

Ultrasound image of the developing baby at seven months' gestation, showing the face and shoulders in profile. As scientific understanding of the normal and abnormal stages of fetal development expands, the identification of high- and low-risk anatomical "markers" may enable older women to skip the invasive diagnostic procedures that can provoke a miscarriage.

assisted methods of conception should make sure their fertility investigation begins with this relatively simple test, before leaping to the more dramatic options of IVF or donor eggs.

The statistics may be encouraging, but women should not defer too long, especially if they have not had a baby before. Those who have become used to exercising choice in all other areas of their lives may have a misplaced belief that this also extends to their fertility. The implicit message behind "birth control" is that, just as all women can choose not to get pregnant, so they can also get pregnant when they choose. Not only is this not true, but a delay of two years for a prospective first-time mother who is in her mid-30s can make a significant difference. Past the age of 40, fertility cannot be relied upon – even for the woman who has a child or children already.

With age, the risk of miscarriage rises – from 15 per cent in the 20s to 30 per cent or

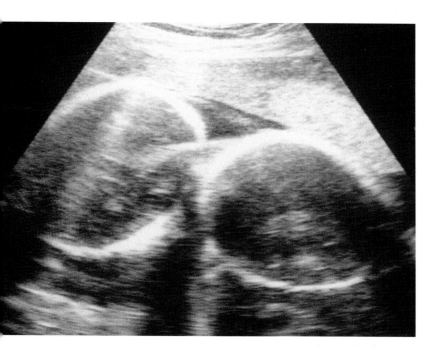

Ultrasound scan showing the heads of twins at 25 weeks. In later reproductive life, an increasing number of pregnancies result in multiple births, due to the ovaries' releasing their eggs in an ever more sporadic fashion. Assisted methods of reproduction, such as *in vitro* fertilization, also carry a much higher chance of twins or triplets if the conception is successful.

more at 40. It used to be thought that this was because the uterus becomes less hospitable. But it is now clear that the age of the egg is more critical than the age of the uterus. In donor egg programs, the miscarriage risk drops to that of the donating woman (see page 311).

COMPLICATIONS OF PREGNANCY

While older mothers don't exactly need to prove themselves on the athletic track, good health is crucial. Specific conditions like diabetes, heart disease, and obesity, which increase the risk of complications, do become more prevalent with age. Any woman contemplating pregnancy who already has an established medical condition, such as high blood pressure or diabetes, should therefore consult her physician first.

Complications that do become more likely as women get older include pre-eclampsia (pregnancy-induced hypertension and protein in the urine), which rises from about ten per cent in the 20s and early 30s to 20 per cent in the late 30s and early 40s. Older women also have double the chance of developing diabetes or a pronounced glucose intolerance, which carries a greater likelihood of complications in late pregnancy and a large baby.

Antenatal checks are a pregnant woman's best protection; in addition to careful monitoring, active treatment is often possible to prevent further complications that could damage the health of mother or baby. With regard to pre-eclampsia, for example, a syndrome which can, if untreated, lead to eclampsia (now the leading cause of maternal death), several trials have revealed that low-dose aspirin can be used effectively in its prevention. While a case for the routine use of aspirin has not been established, some argue that the evidence may be strong enough to justify its use in women at high risk.

THE CONSCIENTIOUS APPROACH

There is much a woman can do before becoming pregnant. Many of the so-called complications of later pregnancy have their roots in the woman's state of health before she so much as conceives. A fit and healthy woman has a good chance of a successful pregnancy, whatever her age, and there is now good evidence that older woman aiming for pregnancy are actually fitter than the average expectant mother. Unlike the olden days, when babies born to women in their 40s were mainly conceived in error, modern-day late pregnancies are often meticulously planned. Women who purposely put off childbearing tend to be healthy non-smokers who approach pregnancy conscientiously.

In 1987, the U.S. Department of Health and Human Services' report, *Trends in Postponed Childbearing*, noted that, compared with 1970, more than twice as many women giving birth in their late 30s were college graduates. This is important: survey after survey confirms that better-educated women have better outcomes when it comes to giving birth. They are more likely to seek care early in their pregnancies, to avail themselves of all the latest information, to attend antenatal clinics, to be well nourished, to gain adequate weight, and to give up (or not to be) smokers. It is established obstetric fact that it is twice as safe to have a baby if you are in a professional or managerial job than if you are an unskilled worker.

If you are planning to get pregnant, take three months to get into shape: stop drinking and smoking, avoid all non-essential medications, including over-the-counter remedies, and attend to your diet. Research increasingly suggests that this pre-conceptual period, together with the first three months of pregnancy, is the most critical for the health of the baby.

Be sure to get enough calcium, iron, zinc, and folate by eating lots of fresh fish, fruits and vegetables, and wholegrains, and continue these good habits into your pregnancy.

The Recommended Daily Allowance (or RDA) for folic acid increases significantly during pregnancy (to 400 mcg/day) as folic acid has been shown to reduce the risk of neural-tube defects (spina bifida, anencephaly). Since the practice of prescribing multivitamins once pregnancy is diagnosed may actually miss the crucial first six weeks of the baby's development, the U.S. Center for Disease Control and Prevention now recommends that all women of childbearing age take a daily multivitamin supplement containing folic acid.

GENETIC ABNORMALITIES

Often it's not so much hazards to the mother as to the offspring that cast a cloud over later pregnancies, transforming the experience of pregnancy from one of happy anticipation into one of nailbiting apprehension. Concern about the health of babies born to older mothers goes back a long way. In 1912 one writer noted that "children of old parents are often delicate and wanting in vitality, as though themselves prematurely old."[3] Since then, late babies have been pronounced at greater risk of schizophrenia, malformations, and all manner of psychological and behavioral problems, from anorexia to truancy from school.

The main age-related fear is that of a chromosomal abnormality. When the egg splits just before ovulation, the 46 chromosomes normally divide into two identical groups of 23. But in older women, with older eggs, the chromosomes become "sticky" and do not always divide perfectly. The most common problem is an extra number 21 chromosome, which results in Down's syndrome. The association of this condition with advancing maternal age is striking. According to several large studies, the chance of a 20-year-old woman having a baby with Down's syndrome is about one in 1350, rising to one in 385 at 35, one in 40 at 40, one in 28 at 45 and a staggering one in eight at 50.[4] The father's age plays no part in this genetically caused abnormality – probably because, however old he is, he produces sperm at an average rate of 500 million every 24 hours, so they are always both short-lived and newly minted, whereas all the eggs a woman will ever have are present from before birth and age along with her.

Non-genetically the news is more encouraging. In a massive study published in 1991, Canadian researchers, who analyzed some 600,000 births over a 20-year period, found that not one of the 43 non-genetic birth defects they encountered, from spina bifida to cleft palate, bore any significant relation to the mother's age. In fact, two showed an inverse association, leading the researchers to conclude, "These findings should be reassuring for women who opt to delay childbearing, have tests for chromosomal disorders if aged 35 or over, and do not have conditions with known implications for pregnancy outcome, such as diabetes, rhesus incompatibility, and alcoholism."[5]

DIAGNOSTIC SCREENING

The chances of a baby's being born without a devastating genetic abnormality have been greatly increased by genetic diagnosis, which can identify couples at risk of specific conditions, such as cystic fibrosis or Duchenne muscular dystrophy, and detect more common random mutations, such as Down's syndrome, at early-to-mid pregnancy. Pediatricians now judge that if expectant parents availed themselves of all the appropriate tests, up to two-thirds of all serious mental and physical handicaps could be predicted, and the pregnancy either terminated or the best of specialist facilities and neonatal care lined up in advance of delivery.

The definitive test is still amniocentesis. It is invasive, however, and carries a one to two per cent risk of disturbing the pregnancy and provoking a miscarriage (the risk partially depending on the still of the operator). A newer procedure, still under evaluation, takes cells at a much earlier stage in pregnancy. This is possible because essential fluid is removed only temporarily, sieved for cells, and then returned to the womb in a procedure called amniofiltration. Another earlier diagnostic test, chorionic villus sampling (CVS), can be carried out as early as the eighth week. It has a slightly higher risk of provoking miscarriage than amniocentesis does, and question marks still hang over its safety.

Detailed ultrasound scans by skilled technicians together with non-invasive biochemical blood tests for Down's syndrome are increasingly eliminating the need for amniocentesis in many older mothers. Neither screen gives a straight "yes" or

ANTE-NATAL TESTS AND SCREENS

WHAT	WHEN	WHAT FOR
genescreen	Before conception	A genetic carrying tendency, the most common being for cystic fibrosis (also Duchenne muscular dystrophy and, imminently, Fragile X, the commonest cause of mental handicap after Down's syndrome)
genetic analysis	3 days after fertilization (IVF only)	Any identifiable genetic disease, from cystic fibrosis and Down's syndrome to muscular dystrophy
ultrasound "Nuchal fold test"	10-14 weeks (preferably 11)	Down's syndrome (possibility)
chorionic villus sampling (CVS)	10-12 weeks (It can be carried out from 8 weeks, but this is not advised)	Down's syndrome; any inherited sex-linked disease; gender of baby (definitive answers)
amniocentesis	As early as 10 weeks in some centers (though there is a risk the cells will not grow and the test will need repeating); generally 12-18 weeks.	Down's syndrome (definitive answer) and other less common genetic defects; gender of baby
Triple marker test/ Triple-Plus test, also known as biochemical tests	16-18 weeks for the Triple test; 13-16 weeks for the Triple-Plus	Down's syndrome (possibility)
alphafetoprotein (AFP)	16-18 weeks	Spina bifida; hydrocephalus (possibility)
cordocentesis	20 weeks	As amniocentesis
ultrasound abnormality scan	18-20 weeks	Spina bifida; hydrocephalus; Down's syndrome; heart, lung, liver, and kidney disorders; cleft lip and palate

WHAT'S INVOLVED	**WAITING TIME**
Slooshing with a mouthwash to test carrier status for cystic fibrosis (the most common inherited disease); if both parents are carriers, the risk of an affected baby is one in four. Other screens are performed by blood test.	2-3 weeks
Where there is a high risk of a baby inheriting a genetic defect, and parents are undergoing IVF, a genetic evaluation can be carried out by removing one cell at the 8-cell stage with no harm to the health of the eventual baby; the sex of the embryo can also be determined.	A few hours
Undergoing an ultrasound evaluation to look for a suspicious fluid-filled space behind the baby's head; preliminary trials suggest that nine out of ten Down's babies can be flagged this way, and that a "positive" result multiplies your age-related risk tenfold, while a negative result decreases it by the same amount.	Immediate assessment
Having a long fine needle inserted into the womb via the vagina or, more usually, the abdomen, and a sample of cells from the developing placenta (identical genetically to the baby) taken for analysis. (The one in 50 risk of miscarriage rises if procedure is carried out before ten weeks or operator is inexperienced.)	A few days
Having a long, fine needle inserted through the abdominal wall, guided by ultrasound, past the baby into the amniotic fluid, and a sample drawn off for culture. A quick, simple procedure, but there is a one in 100 risk of miscarriage. Pilot studies are assessing feasibility of earlier testing.	2-4 weeks
Having a blood test to look for raised concentrations of two hormones (estriol and HCG) and low levels of the protein AFP (see below) can pick up two-thirds of affected babies. (Some clinics just measure the last two.) Even where an increased risk is shown, amniocentesis is required to give definitive answer. New Triple-Plus test also measures levels of an enzyme called neutrophil alkaline phosphatase (NAP) and is said to pick up 85 per cent of affected fetuses. Ultrasound is also needed to judge precise gestational age.	1-2 weeks
Having a blood test for raised levels of alphafetoprotein, which can indicate spina bifida or hydrocephalus (also often identifiable on ultrasound).	One week
As amniocentesis, but blood is drawn from the umbilical vein, with a higher risk of disturbing the pregnancy than CVS or amniocentesis.	2-3 days
A very detailed ultrasound scan, lasting about 30 minutes. When taken by an expert, this can reveal a host of information about the baby's health and gender.	Immediate assessment

"no" answer, however. The blood test works by measuring a number of biochemical "markers" that are present in abnormally high or low concentrations in Down's syndrome pregnancies. When these are fed into a computer, along with a careful estimate of the baby's gestational age (in weeks) and the mother's age (in years), a "result" is obtained which is expressed gambling-style in odds, such as one in 500. According to the odds she receives, a woman will either be "screen negative" and reassured that no further action is necessary, or "screen positive" and advised to consider amniocentesis. Around five per cent of all pregnant women whose risk is found to be higher than one in 250 (a 37-year-old's risk of having a Down's baby) are advised to take this option. While still not a positive result, sensitive counseling is essential to point out to the woman with a so-called "highish" risk of say one in 150 that she is still 149 times more likely to have a chromosomally intact baby than a damaged one. She should also be aware that tests carried out on older women are more likely to yield positive results since the age factor does come into the calculations. A 38-year-old woman starts off in the risk zone. While her risk may lengthen after the test from, say, one in 100 to one in 1000, it may equally well stay high.

The availability of antenatal screens is changing the experience of pregnancy for many women. Before the development of these tests, a baby was assumed to be healthy unless there were evidence to the contrary. The new procedures are shifting the balance toward one of suspicion that the baby may not be all right – a doubt, which, once sown, can only be satisfactorily removed by undergoing a series of tests that will demonstrate that the baby is normal. As a result, pregnancy itself has become a less enjoyable, less carefree state. In one survey, it was found that once the alarm has been sounded, and the specter of anxiety has entered into a pregnancy, women are rarely completely reassured.

Egg donation

An increasing proportion of women hoping for babies in later reproductive life have not managed to conceive naturally and are hoping that the new technological advances will work the miracle they long for. But the chances of the usual methods of assisted conception working are statistically very poor after the age of 41 – unless women are "good responders" and produce plenty of eggs with each ovulation – and plunge to almost zero after 44. Even if assisted pregnancies do occur in the 40s, the prospect of a baby is still far from assured. It has been a consistent disappointment that those longed-for IVF and GIFT conceptions that do occur past the age of 40 are as likely to end in miscarriage as in the birth of a bonny bouncing baby. Now, the advent of oocyte (egg) donation, pioneered in Australia in 1983, has transformed the chances of motherhood for older infertile women. It has opened up a whole decade for aspiring mothers of a certain age and for the one per cent of women who, reaching the menopause before they turn 40, find their chances of natural conception gone forever.

In the decade since it was pioneered, egg donation has become a viable alternative for older women, though often attempts are defeated by the serious shortage of eggs. When eggs can be removed from a younger woman and transferred to the Fallopian tubes, as in GIFT (gamete intrafallopian transfer), or to the uterus by the test-tube baby technique IVF (in vitro fertilization), and the pregnancy sustained with hormones that prime the uterus to receive the egg, the prospect of a successful pregnancy soars to between 35 and 40 per cent for women in their 40s.

In one study by Mark Sauer at the University of Southern California, women who had premature ovarian failure and received donor eggs were found to have near identical rates of pregnancy, whatever their age. There are two apparent reasons for this success: a carefully prepared uterus and a relatively youthful egg. A donated egg from a younger woman, for example, instantly lowers the risk of miscarriage from 50 per cent to between 10 and 15 per cent, while the risk of Down's syndrome also plummets – often allowing doctors to rule out the sometimes risky amniocentesis procedure.

EXTENDING THE REPRODUCTIVE LIFESPAN

With the surprising success of egg-donor programs in the United States, Australia, and Europe, even the menopause is becoming obsolete, and the limits of childbearing – as the author of an editorial in the *New England Journal of Medicine* wrote recently – "anyone's guess." "Perhaps they have more to do with the stamina required for labor and 2am feedings," she suggested, "than with reproductive function."

In fact, the programs are proving almost *too* successful. Because younger eggs from more fertile women have such a good chance of implanting in older women, the ambitiously high numbers of eggs being transferred in some programs are leading to as many as half of the resultant pregnancies being twins or triplets. This is giving cause for concern, since multiple pregnancies are higher-risk pregnancies, especially in older women.

Egg donation is just the beginning. Some scientists believe it will soon be possible to extend a woman's reproductive lifespan well into her 60s by delaying the aging process of the ovaries. By slowing down the rate at which eggs are lost, they say they will be able to postpone the age of menopause some 10 to 20 years. Others talk of removing an entire healthy ovary in the 20s for reimplantation at 40, 50, or even 60 – thus suspending biological time for two or three decades. In an article in British *Vogue*, Sheila Kitzinger expressed horror at the implications of such "advances" and was especially skeptical of the motives impelling much older women toward childbirth – especially when dependent on donated eggs and hormone treatment to get the uterus acting young enough to accommodate them.

> There are some women who will be having these babies only because they want to prove that they can. Having a baby is a symbol of youth. There is a tremendous fear of age and death in our culture that prevents us from celebrating each stage of life. And it is a myth that no woman is emotionally or physically fulfilled until she has had a child.[6]

There are fears, too, that such manipulation could end up killing women through strokes and heart attacks. Certainly, pregnancy places an extra strain on the heart, blood vessels, brain and kidneys, and multiple pregnancies place an even greater load. There are other considerations. In her article, "Last Minute Mother" for British *Vogue*, Anne Merewood quoted Dr Machelle Seibel, director of the Faulkener Center for Reproductive Medicine in Boston, who limits the age of his patients to 46 for both ethical and medical reasons. "This becomes an addictive kind of process. Previously, couples could eventually accept that they were not going to conceive a child. Now we've created an open-ended reproductive lifespan, people can always feel they haven't done enough."

Along the family way: Grethe Elgort with her children, Sophie and Warren. Research suggests that giving birth in one's 30s and 40s has many advantages for both parents and offspring. Older mothers, having often found fulfilment in their own work lives, may be less likely to see motherhood as a "sacrifice" or try to live out their ambitions through their children.

MENOPAUSE

A few generations back, women entering their menopause were as like as not to be grandmothers. Long reconciled to (and thankful for) the fact that their childbearing days were over, they looked old, felt old, thought of themselves as old. Wrung out by the continual round of pregnancy, childbirth, and infant care, most counted themselves lucky to get to the menopause at all, greeting the absence of bleeding with relief once the dreadful prospect of yet another pregnancy could be ruled out. The hot flash was welcomed rather than dreaded as an unmentionable that had to be medicated away.

These days women coming to the end of their fertile lives have never felt less old. As likely to have a clutch of demanding school-age children as a grandchild on their knee, they may just be getting into their stride professionally and have no intention of dwindling into little-old-ladyhood. Even though the timing of menopause has not budged by as much as a month over the last few hundred years and cross-culturally arrives at around 50 (the 12th-century Abbess Hildegard put the age of menopause at 50 in her *Causae et Curae*), the first hot flash does nevertheless seem to hit unseasonably soon.

Certainly, the menopause comes at an earlier point in the life cycle. In the 17th century, when a woman's life expectancy was shorter than the life expectancy of her ovaries, she had only a 28 per cent chance of even getting to the menopause; now 95 per cent do. With life expectancy touching 80 (it was 50 in 1900), the menopause has become the midpoint, rather than the beginning of the end, with as many adult years to be looked forward to after as before.

In the past, a woman could at least look forward to the end of her periods as a release from the twin tyrannies of pregnancy and menstruation. But, with the advent of reliable contraception and discreet sanitary protection, the menopause signals only the point at which it becomes impossible to remain, in one's own mind at least, a perpetual 35. This is an event that cannot be dieted, tinted, or exercised away, although clever gynecological practice can now render the passage from fertility to non-fertility so seamless as to be almost unapparent.

AGE-OLD ANXIETIES

Menophobia has a long history. Freud, who maintained that the ability to bear children was a woman's only consolation for not having a penis, argued that the female psyche suffered such a profound sense of loss and redundancy at the Change that its balance could be forever shaken. Denied their biological *raison d'être*, women became irrational, hysterical, melancholy, neurotic, quarrelsome, difficult, and obstinate. Impelled towards drink and kleptomania, they were prey to all manner of lewd sexual imaginings. The theory may have been new but these were actually well-worn arguments. In the 18th century, the Quaker doctor, John Fothergill, wrote that he had come across many women living in dread anticipation of the physical and emotional havoc to come:

> There is a period in the life of females to which, for the most part, they are taught to look forward with some degree of anxiety. The various and absurd opinions relative to the ceasing of the menstrual cycle as discharged and propagated through successive ages, have tended to embitter the hours of many a sensible woman. Some practitioners in other respects able and judicious, if they have not favoured these erroneous and terrifying notions, seem not to have endeavoured to correct them with the diligence and humanity which such an object requires.

Modern women, so well informed about so much, and so squarely in control of so many different areas of their lives, look upon the Change with no less anxiety. Fearing the unknown, they panic that life's doors are closing on them and worry that their femininity will disappear with their fertility. Even the most insouciant start to fear for their health. The menopause touches some of our deepest fears about aging. And the great wave of publicity given to the wonders of hormone replacement over the last ten years has done nothing to allay our apprehensions. In fact, it exposes us to many more menopausal negatives than ever before. The prevailing image of menopausal woman in her natural unmedicated state – her mood depressed, her temper explosive, her skin creasing, her breasts sagging, her bones crumbling, her heart failing, and her vagina shriveling – is so terrifying, who would want to join her?

While there are real health, even life, preserving benefits to be gained from hormone replacement therapy (see the next chapter), the panic that women feel as they come up to the menopause is overdone. Surveys show that pre-menopausal women have a worse picture of menopause than women who have actually been through the Change and out the other side. When questioned, younger women commonly say that it is all downhill after the menopause, while the great majority of women who have been through it report feeling better once it was over and deny that it was the beginning of permanent decline. When workers at the New England Research Institute in Watertown, Massachusetts, questioned over 2500 postmenopausal women, less than one in five said that they felt regretful or ambivalent about the passing of their fertility; the rest were either relieved or felt neutral that their periods had stopped. Similar studies in Canada, Norway, and Britain have found much the same attitudes expressed.

ENTER THE DOCTORS

At one time, the medical profession was reluctant to provide any sort of help for women going through menopause. It was the Change, and women should expect to change with it. Now they talk of ovarian "failure," "estrogen deficiency syndrome," even "biological sabotage," as though menopause itself were a disorder, like scurvy or rickets, and our hormones somehow delinquent, and reel off such a frighteningly long list of "symptoms" as to spur any woman to sign up for hormones as soon as she reaches her 50th birthday. Many doctors believe quite genuinely that the climacteric is a catastrophe from which women must be rescued. It was after witnessing his own mother's "living decay" that hormone replacement therapy's best-known evangelist, the American gynecologist Robert Wilson, made the menopause his vocation, which was once summed up as supplying women with adequate estrogen from puberty to the grave. "I was appalled at the transformation of the vital, wonderful woman who had been the dynamic focal point of our family into a pain-wrecked, petulant invalid," he wrote in *Feminine Forever*. This ecstatic hymn to the virtues of estrogen switched American womanhood onto an untested therapy that led to an alarming outbreak of womb cancer.

CLASSIC SYMPTOMS, CULTURAL PREJUDICES

Certainly some women suffer intolerably, the unluckiest for years on end. But many menopausal women are more distressed by what society throws at them than what Nature ever inflicts. As a term of abuse, "menopausal" is infinitely more degrading than a hot flash could ever be. This universal stage of life is still such a cultural turn-off that few women share their hormonal vicissitudes with their partners, reluctant to age themselves by explaining why they are suddenly taking showers in the middle of the night and kicking back the bedclothes in February. The myth that women go mad at menopause adds to agist employment practices by fueling the prejudices of would-be employers and amplifies the many apprehensions women already have as they approach this stage of their lives.

There is good evidence that many of the neurotic "symptoms" attributed to the menopause are experienced equally as commonly by men at midlife, and are much more likely to be explained by life events than by ovarian inactivity. When a team of epidemiologists asked over 1000 women and 500 men about their state of health and well-being, with no specific mention of the menopause to alert their suspicions, they found both sexes suffering identically from many classic menopausal "symptoms," ranging from loss of appetite, headaches, depression, and urinary problems to crawling sensations on the skin, low back ache, and irritability. There was no difference in the degree of depression suffered. The only problems which they didn't share were loss of libido (a male problem) and hot flashes, night sweats, loss of confidence, and difficulty making decisions (women's problems).[1] At one conference held in 1991 to inform the public about the effects of menopause, after the gamut of emotional symptoms had been exhaustively discussed by a panel of learned gynecologists and the sanity-saving virtues of estrogen promoted, a woman stood up. "Is there," she asked, "anything my husband could take? He has most of the symptoms you've talked about."

DEPRESSION

The inclusion of psychological problems in the menopausal rag bag has always been controversial. Even though estrogen is known to cross the blood/brain barrier and to have a certain affinity with some of the cells in the brain, scientists still disagree about how much general misery and depression can be attributed to the menopause, how much to the knock-on effects of menopause, such as hot flashes and sleepless nights, and how much to other, unrelated factors. While there is no evidence of greater depressive *illness* in the 40s and early 50s, statistics do show that depressed *mood* is more common at three key hormonal change points: premenstrually, postnatally, and menopausally, with the latter being most marked in the two to three years *before* periods cease. Interestingly, post-menopause there is a sharp drop in depressive illness, which accords well with anecdotal reports of a resurgence of energy and sense of well-being at this time of life.

Although one study showed that estrogen patches helped lift depression in the lead-up to the menopause, when ovarian function was faltering, they had no impact on women post-menopausally, so we should be wary of leaping to hormonal conclusions. There are plenty of instances of doctors treating inadequately investigated women with hormones when they later turn out to have been anemic or suffering thyroid malfunction or a quite unrelated clinical depression, all requiring a very different therapeutic approach.

Surveys have shown that episodes of depression before the menopause are the best predictor of depression during it. They also suggest that single women have fewer problems than women who are married, divorced, or widowed (countering the idea that this must be a time of grief for lost fertility), and that having a career also appears to protect. Contrary to the popular idea of the empty nest, women tended to greet the flying fledglings with relief; there is some evidence that women who have children at home are more likely to suffer menopausal problems.

GLOBAL DIFFERENCES

In some cultures, where the ending of the menses brings new freedom, the menopause is actively welcomed. Research has shown that among Mayan Mexicans, traditional New Zealand Maoris, and Rajput Indian women, the end of bleeding lifts many of the restrictions associated with menstruation and signals the start of a new, freer phase of life, in which they participate alongside men professionally and politically, so actually enhancing their status within society. Tellingly, these cultures have no word for "hot flash" in their vocabularies. While menopausal problems are real enough, they are more likely to be looked upon as incidental or unimportant. Western women will sometimes say the same, especially when their lives are seen to hold just as much interest, promise, and novelty as they did in early adulthood.

"I've come to believe that bodies know whether their times of transition are leading to something positive or negative," mused Gloria Steinem in her autobiographical book on self-esteem. "If I tell you that menopause turned out to be mainly the loss of a familiar marker of time, plus the discomfort of a few flushes and flashes – and that, to me, the ease of this transition seems related to the much-longed-for era of relative peace and self-expression it ushered in – you may think I've gone off my rocker. But consider the results of a 150-nation menopause study: negative symptoms *increased* when women went from more to less social mobility and power, but *decreased* when women's power and freedom grew."[2]

In Western culture, much of the negativity still surrounding the menopause can also be traced to the old idea that monthly bleeding was a necessary curse that freed the body of evil humors. In the Middle Ages, witches were believed to gain their malign and magical powers from the retention of menstrual blood, and one of the reasons for the burning of Joan of Arc was that she did not menstruate.[3] Women were believed to be the longer-living sex because the flow of menstrual blood cleansed impurities and bad humors from their bodies, thus improving their health. At the menopause, however, the blood that previously would have been shed was believed to be building up and stagnating inside, provoking an array of physical and emotional ills, from cantankerousness, agitation, and hypochondria to personality disorders and even insanity.

Nineteenth-century gynecologists "treated" the menopause with leeches to re-induce bleeding, and even cut veins to let the blood out, in sometimes life-threatening quantities. Women said to be suffering "involutional melancholia" or "climacteric insanity" routinely had their wombs removed, and many lunatic asylums included gynecologists among their teams of medical consultants. Even today the marked reluctance of women suffering menstrually induced anemia to take three packs of contraceptive pills end to end (so-called "tricycling") can be put down to fears of "bad blood" building up inside.

In China, where a more positive value is put on the menstrual blood, the menopause presents the opportunity to preserve what is precious. In women, the menstrual blood is the outward manifestation of the *Jing*, or primal essence, which nourishes the physical body and gradually seeps away throughout life until it is exhausted at death. (The male *Jing* is manifested in the sperm.) Since with every menstruation a small amount of *Jing* is lost, which can never be replaced, the menopause is perceived as a benign brake on the aging process.

INDIVIDUAL DIFFERENCES

The cultural differences are illuminating but the menopause remains real enough. The wacky temperature changes so characteristic of this stage of life are real events in which rises of several degrees Fahrenheit (a couple of degrees Celsius) can be recorded. While the four-fold reduction in the levels of circulating estrogen during the menopause can send shockwaves through the system, it equally well may not. There is no one menopause, and women attempting to generalize from their own experience cannot possibly hope to speak for their entire sex. The menopause is a normal life event just as menarche (arrival of menstruation) is. And just as some women have problems with their periods, are made grouchy by the ebbs and flows of the menstrual cycle, or feel sickened by the great estrogen surge at pregnancy, so women also experience the menopause differently.

While some genetically blessed individuals (specialists say the figure is between ten and 20 per cent) sail through their climacteric without so much as changing tack, about the same proportion founder on the rocks. Problems are likely to be more pronounced if menopause comes artificially early due to the ovaries being removed or ceasing to function following hysterectomy (see page 186), certain drugs, or radiotherapy treatment for cancer.

Surveys of Western women reveal that hot flashes are the most common menopausal problem (experienced by two-thirds), followed by night sweats (half) and insomnia and tiredness (a quarter), with complaints such as loss of libido reported by just five per cent. But although more women have hot flashes than don't, not all are incapacitated. Many look on them as a nuisance that is nonetheless manageable. A few even find them pleasant – the light-headedness "like an altered state of consciousness," as one woman put it, and the heat useful for giving a warm glow on cold winter nights.

> **W**omen who have had a hysterectomy, and their ovaries left intact, are at risk of an early menopause, with one in four women going through it within two years of surgery, possibly due to interference with the ovarian blood supply. Menopause should be suspected if problems such as hot flashes occur.

Women having a late menopause, at 52 or 53 or more, often have a smoother transition than women going through it earlier, as do women who move from irregular menstrual cycles to no cycles at all (the so-called "perimenopause") in a matter of months rather than years. While women who previously remained on an even keel over their cycles tend to have fewer ill effects, those who have always been sensitive to hormonal fluctuations, suffering premenstrual syndrome for example, may register menopausal changes more markedly.

The amount of post-menopausal estrogen probably also has an effect. The major source of female hormone post-menopause is estrone, a weak form of estrogen processed from the male hormone androstenedione in the body's fat cells. There is a suggestion that well-covered women, cushioned by their more generous hormone supplies, tend to have less miserable menopauses than skinny women. The arrangement may even be Nature's way of ensuring sufficient estrogen in the post-menopausal years.

TIME OF ARRIVAL

When the menopause will come cannot be predicted either. One clue is thought to be the length of cycle: women who have shorter menstrual cycles (26 days or less) tend to reach menopause earlier than women who have longer cycles (33 days or more). Smoking can also knock one or two years off the fertile lifespan (a phenomenon which, startlingly, also applies to non-smoking women who are living with smokers).

TUMULTUOUS CHANGE: THE PERIMENOPAUSE

What is clear is that you do not have to be menopausal, and to have ceased menstruating, to have menopausal problems. The range of difficulties encountered at the menopause can start well before bleeding stops and, indeed, may be at their worst at this time. It seems increasingly likely that many menopausal trials, particularly such psychological problems as poor concentration, loss of confidence, and indecisiveness, are not caused so much by low estrogen levels as by *lowering* ones. Some women may be barely into their 40s, still busy advancing their careers and even considering a last-minute addition to the family, when, suddenly, like a bolt from the blue, their periods go haywire, their thermostat jumps uncontrollably, and they are thrown into a state of disequilibrium. Women who have never suffered premenstrual tension can feel unaccountably jittery as the ratio of estrogen and progesterone, which is regulated to a large extent by the developing egg follicle in the ovary, is thrown out of kilter by the increasing tendency to anovulatory (non-egg-producing) cycles.

Some women go on bleeding, regular as clockwork, until their last period and then simply stop, suffering little hormonal disruption to their lives at all. Others, however, may have to contend with as much as a decade of unpredictable periods – copious and uncontrollable one month, non-existent the next. See-sawing hormone levels can derail the best-regulated menstrual cycle by creating imbalances that cause the lining of the womb to build up excessively and/or not slough off completely. As with so much about the menopause, this has its mirror image at puberty: just as those first cycles were erratic and unguessable so the last tend to become increasingly sporadic. They may come sooner or later than expected, appear to have stopped and then start again, come so close together that it seems like life is one continuous period or not come for months, flood through the heaviest protection or scarcely leave a stain. Alternately panicked by the twin fears of a possible late pregnancy and an undiagnosed pathological condition, many women find this a time of great unease. Such trials are, of course, masked for women on the contraceptive pill whose bleeds generally remain both manageably light and blissfully regular until the last: an option worth considering for women whose lives are thrown into turmoil by such unpredictability.

Women who customarily keep a tight rein on their lives are particularly likely to find this lack of predictability unnerving, especially where treacherous hot flashes also call attention to their age and menopausal condition. In her book, *The Silent Passage*, the writer Gail Sheehy sums up such perimenopausal perils as the "meanest loss of menopause" for her high-achieving contemporaries:

> These mid-forties dynamos can fax a dinner menu to a caterer, sell a stock, talk supportively to a spouse over a portable phone without missing a step, and remember to take their aerobics shoes to the office along with their satin slingbacks so they'll be able to exercise before appearing glamorous at an evening benefit – all this on the way to argue a case or perform surgery. But they cannot control when they break out in a hot flash or when they bleed.[4]

The turbulence of the perimenopause (years leading up to the menopause, when the hormones are already on the blink) can be smoothed out by taking the low-dose contraceptive pill (see page 290). This protects against pregnancy, regularizes the cycle, and keeps hot flashes at bay. At 50, the advice is to switch to another method of contraception for three months and then to have a blood test, which should be able to establish whether or not you have been through the menopause.

Irregular periods are common as you come up to the menopause, but irregular bleeding (between periods, after intercourse, or after the menopause) should always be checked out. It may involve having a biopsy (sample of womb lining) taken to rule out any malignant change. Beware of pressure to have surgery for heavy periods; there are other, less invasive options (see pages 370). Though inconvenient and worrying, the only risk associated with heavy bleeding is that of iron-deficiency anemia (see pages 359).

A SECOND WIND

The good news is that, once hormone levels eventually settle at their new post-menopausal low, many of these problems resolve. The average time of transition is four years but there are wide variations. The new equilibrium and stability that are attained come as an especial blessing for those women who, in addition to the upheavals of the menopause, have had to endure premenstrual tension all their adult lives. It's only at the point where women recognize that they have been through the menopause (an event which, unlike the shock of the first sight of blood at puberty, can only be known in retrospect) that they start to feel better – not just well again, but weller than well. "I think every woman notices a slight shift in her identity at this time," observed the 60-year-old writer Isobel Colegate. "The change in your internal mechanisms brings about a second wind, a sense of the self you were before puberty returns; the real you."[5]

The term "post-menopausal zest" was coined by the anthropologist Margaret Mead, after a personal and professional renaissance in her 50s following a series of devastating emotional hammerblows in midlife. The writer Gail Sheehy has described how, after years as "a collaborating wife," Mead started buying designer dresses, had a new romantic relationship, seemed in her daughter's eyes "to become prettier," and, at the age of 51, went out to New Guinea and embarked upon a whole new area of anthropological research.

The fact that the recorded incidence of depression rises among females at puberty, to become twice as common as among males, before leveling off again after the menopause, supports subjective reports of a sense of psychological well-being such as many women have not enjoyed since adolescence. It's as though the years of turbulence are rewarded not only by a sense of calm regained at the end of the storm but, more positively and often completely unexpectedly, by a surge in energy and sense of well-being as women regain their mental and physiological balance and leave the menopause behind them. This lends a rather different interpretation to this stage of life than that summed up by the psychoanalyst Helene Deutsch in the 1940s when she wrote that at the menopause "woman is mortified because she has to give up everything that she received in puberty." This idea of well-being without estrogen, though absent from the modern pathological model of menopause, is reflected in the fact that women in their 50s actually make *less* use of medical services than in their younger years and appear to enjoy *better* psychological health.

In *The Second Sex*, which was published in 1948, Simone de Beauvoir defined the post-menopause as a time when a woman regains the health and energy that are her birthright. "From puberty to menopause woman is the theater of a play that unfolds within her and in which she is not personally concerned . . . Often, indeed, this release from female physiology is expressed in a health, a balance, a vigor that [she] lacked before." Not dissimilarly, Germaine Greer, writing nearly half a century later in *The Change*, welcomes the opportunity to be once more that "passionate, idealistic, energetic young individual who existed before menstruation" and to "change back into the self you were before you became a tool of your sexual and reproductive destiny."

There are many parallels between the young girl taken by surprise by her first period and the grown woman experiencing her last. In 1991 a survey looking at adolescent girls' attitudes towards menstruation found that "almost all girls are frightened, worried, or waiting with dread for their first period," looking at it as "unpleasant, hardly believable, frightening and disgusting." So too do grown women await the menopause. Just as many adolescent girls need several years to adjust to their altered chemistry after estrogen first floods into the bloodstream, so, too, does the menopausal woman need time to readjust to not menstruating, in order to let go of those aspects of her fertile self that have for so long been part of her identity – but never her whole self.

See Alphabeticals for more information and practical self-help advice on hot flashes, night sweats, depression, insomnia, menorrhagia, and vaginal dryness.

H O R M O N E   R E P L A C E M E N T

WHERE previous generations of women flushed and sweated it out, having no option but to endure whatever Nature flung at them, modern women can postpone their menopause by five, ten, 15, 20 years, or even indefinitely. Clinical trials the world over show that topping up declining levels of estrogen can obliterate such menopausal miseries as hot flashes and night sweats (and the sleeplessness and irritability caused thereby) in eight out of every ten women, as well as having longer-range benefits for the body.

Historically, many doctors have resisted providing even this much relief, but, under pressure from women and an increasing number of evangelical specialists, the mood has changed and they are markedly more willing to prescribe. The thinking now is that no woman should have to wake up half a dozen times a night drenched in sweat unless she *wants* to – and some do. A sizable number of women hold that Nature should be allowed to take its course. The menopause is a natural event, they say, and not a disease that has to be staved off pharmacologically. They believe that estrogen is a dangerous drug of habituation, which goes against Nature, saps a woman's confidence to live without it, and carries still unclarified risks to the breast and possibly ovary.

Interestingly, the same sort of objections were being raised at the beginning of the century to the concept of contraception, which was seen to be diverting the course of Nature and violating the natural integrity of the body. In her seminal work *Contraception – Theory, History and Practice*, which was first published in 1923, the birth-control pioneer Marie Stopes wrote:

> This "argument" [that contraception "is not natural"] is incessantly brought forward by shallow thinkers and moralists. It is hardly necessary to point out that in this sense, the whole of civilization is "not natural," that tooth-brushes and eye-glasses, chloro-form and telephones are each and all as much a violation of "nature's laws." Sir E. Ray Lankester pointed out very vividly that "Man is Nature's rebel. When Nature says 'Die!' Man says 'I will live!'."

THE HAVES AND THE HAVE-NOTS

It may be politically correct to aim to have a "natural" menopause, but it is also questionable whether it was ever natural to live long beyond 50, let alone the three decades that have now become the norm. Imperfect as the present hormone replacement formulations are, one consistent fact emerges: the haves outlive the have-nots. In one survey of more than 8000 women living in southern California, women who had taken estrogen were 20 per cent less likely to die from any cause than women who had not, while those who had been on the therapy for 15 years had nearly half the risk of dying prematurely when compared with women who had never taken it. Although there are still many gaps in our knowledge, we do know for certain that taking hormones for at least five years can help stall the progressive loss of bone that is near universal in later life and probably also lowers the risk of heart disease. As the therapy improves, these benefits should become more marked, and it will become increasingly hard for women to turn their backs on a medication that will prevent them from suffering life-threatening degenerative diseases. Women have even begun suing their doctors for *failing* to offer it.

In the United States, one in three post-menopausal women currently takes hormones. Twenty years ago, hormone replacement therapy (HRT) was thought likely to increase the chances of thrombosis, strokes, and heart attacks, and cancers of the uterus, breast, and cervix – all areas that have come under suspicion with the Pill. One by one, these fears have been discounted, with the exception of breast cancer, as it has come to be realized that whereas the Pill keeps hormone levels artificially high, HRT *replaces* what is no longer there, restoring it to pre-menopausal levels. The estrogens given are different too – the contraceptive type being considerably more potent than the post-menopausal type, which are more like the hormones a woman used to make before her ovaries stopped functioning. These differences, combined with the altered biochemistry of the post-menopausal woman, have led to the finding that many of the conditions associated with the Pill – and still quoted by many doctors as reasons *not* to give hormone replacement – are actually prevented by HRT. In fact, many specialists now look on it not so much as an answer to uncomfortable menopausal problems but as essential preventive medicine that should be available to all women on demand.

A CHECKERED HISTORY

Hormone replacement has had a checkered history. In the 19th century, a brief fashion for "glandular therapy" led women to take pulverized ovarian extracts to alleviate their menopausal problems. But it was not until the late 1920s that the first estrogens were identified and another 40 years before they were widely prescribed. Promoted as an elixir of youth under the happy slogan "Feminine Forever" and swallowed in high doses by women desperate to fend off the signs of age, estrogen was one of the top five best-selling prescription drugs in the United States by 1975. The elation came to an abrupt halt later that year, however, when those women who had taken the wonder drug were discovered to be many times more likely to develop cancer of the endometrium (lining of the womb). The longer they took estrogen, and the higher the dose, the more likely they were to develop tumors.

Once it was recognized that the estrogen was stimulating the lining of the womb in a dangerous way, another counter-balancing hormone was added to induce a protective monthly bleed. The result is that most American and European women who have not had a hysterectomy are now prescribed seven, ten, or 12 days of progestin along with their estrogen every month. This dual approach is known as combined or "opposed" therapy. After various trials, the number of days that the progestin is taken for has turned out to be critical, with a 12-day regimen categorically found not to increase the risk of endometrial cancer. In 1993 the results of a trial that was carried out at the University of California Medical Center in San Francisco were published which showed just 14 days of progestin every three months to be safe – a pattern which has the additional advantage of only entailing one bleed every 12 weeks.

There has also been a change in prescribing patterns. Ten or 15 years ago, women took the therapy for a few years at most to tide them over immediate menopausal difficulties. As evidence grows of its long-term beneficial effects, increasing numbers of women are now taking hormones on an indefinite basis to protect against several life- and health-threatening hazards of older age. Specialists are also prescribing it earlier, in some cases well before the last menstrual bleed, in the belief that topping up a woman's declining estrogen levels for the year or two *before* her periods stop can lessen those disabling menopausal problems which are often at their worst during this time. For an increasing number of women, the daily pill, the twice-weekly patch, or the six-monthly implant has become a way of life that they have no intention of giving up. Ever.

UNANSWERED QUESTIONS

It is good that late-20th century menopausal women are not bowing to the "inevitable" and soldiering on in silence, yet they must make sure that they are fully aware of the potential risks that this impressive, but as yet not fully tested, drug carries. While the risks and benefits of taking estrogen alone ("unopposed" therapy) are quite well understood, the effects of the more commonly prescribed combined estrogen/progestin regimen are far from fully evaluated. HRT is often represented as medicine's greatest gift to womankind. Male gynecologists confess themselves envious that there is nothing like it for *them*.

When pressed, however, even its most ardent champions will admit that the current therapy is not as good as it will be in 20 years' time – when many outstanding questions will have been answered, new smoother formulations developed, and an "ideal" progestin isolated that protects the womb from cancer while provoking none of its present unpleasant side-effects or metabolic consequences. For the time being, then, hormone replacement is still an evolving therapy, with pharmaceutical companies working continually to come up with better, safer, more effective hormone combinations that have fewer side-effects. Only now is the U.S. Women's Health Initiative, a massive $500 million study of 140,000 women, trying to evaluate the effects of different therapies, with answers not expected until well into the next century. While the Initiative is unlikely to spring any nasty big surprises – and may possibly have some pleasant ones in store – there is no escaping the fact that it is the experiences of the women now taking it that will enable the missing parts of the jigsaw to fall into place. This has led one American public-health expert to describe the present pattern of prescribing as "the largest *uncontrolled* clinical trial in the history of medicine."[1]

The aim of managing one's own menopause comes naturally to a generation of women who have been accustomed to exercising control over every area of their lives, from childbirth to the family's finances. But it demands living with uncertainty, keeping pace with conflicting and fast-changing research findings, and maintaining an open mind when it comes to considering whether to renew one's prescription, knowing that the more you look for facts, the more those facts are likely to elude you.

A VAST ARRAY OF OPTIONS

Although hormone replacement therapy, like the Pill, is always referred to in the singular, there is a mindboggling array of different types, doses, and paths of delivery. Tablets, implants, skin patches, creams, pessaries, suppositories, and soon-to-be licensed rings and IUDs deliver drugs through the mouth and digestive system, across the skin, out of slow-release implants embedded in the fat of the thigh or abdomen, or via the vagina, rectum, or uterus. A method that suits one woman perfectly will provoke intolerable side-effects in another. A dose that magically lifts miserable menopausal problems in one sufferer won't touch them in the next. Every woman both responds differently to the hormones she is given and has different levels of her own post-menopausal estrogen, or estrone, to start off with. If a woman is lucky and/or persistent, she will find an informed and sympathetic doctor willing to consider all the options, to tailor the dose to suit her needs, and to switch approaches when the first or second or third is not found to be working. Such partnerships are, alas, rare: in a recent U.S. survey of 25,000 women, 20 per cent had stopped therapy in the first nine months due to unacceptable side-effects, and unaddressed fears of cancer; a further ten per cent were only taking it intermittently.

Take the time and trouble to find a health practitioner who will partner you through any teething troubles on starting hormone replacement therapy. Menopausal problems usually begin to lift within a week, though it may take three months or so for the full effect to come through. If, after three months, menopausal problems persist, you may need a higher dose for a while which can later be tailored down. If problems "break through" each day after 18 hours or so, they can often be abolished by taking a divided daily dose.

Give yourself three months to adjust to transient estrogen-type side-effects such as leg cramps, nausea, and breast tenderness. If nausea continues, a patch may be a better choice than pills. There is some evidence that side-effects noted during the progestin phase (bloating, PMT-like irritability and depression, headache) are more likely to persist than to settle, and may necessitate a change of hormone type or delivery (now available as a patch and, shortly, as an IUD). A fairly new strategy is to take a much reduced dose continuously over the cycle with no break for bleeding or to take the progestin in divided daily doses, morning and night. The newly approved regime of taking just 14 days of progestin every three months should reduce the number of off-days (you only have a period every 12 weeks too). Taking natural progesterone by pessary or suppository is another option that reduces side-effects.

Women who start out with unreal expectations of what HRT will do for them are heading towards disappointment. While the menopause may be a movable option, aging is not. Recent breathless testimonies from a whole series of high-profile women promising continuing sex appeal and transformed careers can be put on a par with the proponents of a long line of quack remedies. At this level, the estrogen derived from pregnant mare's urine occupies the same historical place as monkey glands or unborn sheep's placenta, or any of the other bizarre rejuvenative practices of the early 20th century.

SIDE-EFFECTS

Women whose expectations are stoked by all this razzmatazz are bound to feel cheated. Their disappointment speaks for itself. Hormone replacement therapy has one of the worst compliance rates in medicine, with about one third of women junking it either because it does not have the hoped-for effect on their lives or because they cannot stand the side-effects. In a telling survey of 400 women who had been specifically advised to take HRT after having their bones scanned, four out of ten had abandoned it eight months later, even though they had been warned that they were at especial risk of fracture in later life; 22 per cent had simply ignored the advice that their doctors had given them, and 17 per cent hated the way that the hormones made them feel.

The truth is that, while most women cope well with the estrogen half of their prescriptions, the progestin given to protect the womb from cancer can make the rest of the body pay for the privilege: bloating, weight gain, splitting headaches, acute pre-menstrual-type irritability and depression (especially in those who suffered PMS pre-menopausally) so severe as to make the winds of Change seem a breeze by comparison. Many women either drop the therapy or stoically soldier on, unaware that a change in type of progestin or in the method of delivery may be all that is needed.

In her partly personal account of the politics of menopause, *The Silent Passage*, Gail Sheehy describes the strange see-sawing of mood that can come from taking estrogen, followed by progestin for half of every month:

> Within days the "blue-meanie" moods lifted. I was able to write for twelve hours straight on deadline and remain calm and reasonable under crisis. Within a few weeks all the other complaints were gone. I was staggered by the potency of the female hormone. But . . . on day fifteen, when I had to add the Provera [progestin] pills to my regimen, I felt by afternoon as if I had a terrible hangover. This chemically induced state was not to be subdued by aspirin or a walk in the park. It only worsened as the day wore on, bringing with it a racing heart, irritability, waves of sadness, and difficulty concentrating.

As Sheehy is the first to admit, not all the side-effects of HRT are negative. Some women find estrogen such a great get-up-and-go hormone that it is only once on it that they realize just how low and lethargic they had felt before. Others find it pleasantly calming, even tranquilizing. Research at UCLA suggesting that estrogen has specific anti-depressant properties accords with the general experience that climbing levels of estrogen (as in pregnancy or just after a period) lift mood while lowering levels (for example, just after birth or before a period) depress it. Other

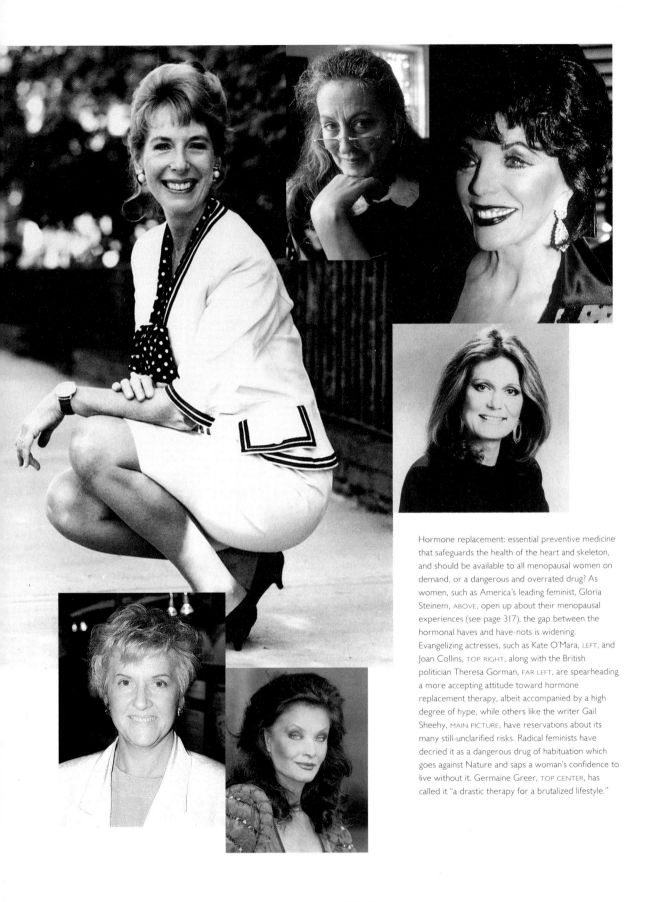

Hormone replacement: essential preventive medicine that safeguards the health of the heart and skeleton, and should be available to all menopausal women on demand, or a dangerous and overrated drug? As women, such as America's leading feminist, Gloria Steinem, ABOVE, open up about their menopausal experiences (see page 317), the gap between the hormonal haves and have-nots is widening. Evangelizing actresses, such as Kate O'Mara, LEFT, and Joan Collins, TOP RIGHT, along with the British politician Theresa Gorman, FAR LEFT, are spearheading a more accepting attitude toward hormone replacement therapy, albeit accompanied by a high degree of hype, while others like the writer Gail Sheehy, MAIN PICTURE, have reservations about its many still-unclarified risks. Radical feminists have decried it as a dangerous drug of habituation which goes against Nature and saps a woman's confidence to live without it. Germaine Greer, TOP CENTER, has called it "a drastic therapy for a brutalized lifestyle."

positive side-effects – positive for some women, anyway – include a near-universal phenomenon of breast enlargement.

Less welcome estrogen-linked side-effects include weight gain, nausea, leg cramps, fluid retention, tender breasts, and sensitive nipples – side-effects not dissimilar to the early stages of pregnancy, when the body is also adjusting to rising estrogen levels. (Women who suffered intermittent breast tenderness premenstrually or severe nausea in pregnancy are more likely to develop these problems on estrogen.) As in pregnancy, these side-effects usually settle after about two months. Yet some women, who have been inadequately counseled by their doctors, panic that the disconcerting new sensations in their breasts signal malignant change, and so they abruptly abandon therapy. In fact, the sensations are simply caused by estrogen-sensitive tissue responding to unaccustomed levels of the female hormone.

PROTECTION AGAINST OSTEOPOROSIS

Against such short-term advantages and annoyances, the longer-term risks and benefits need to be carefully weighed. The most unequivocal evidence in favor of estrogen is that it staves off the crippling bone-wasting condition osteoporosis and consequent fractures of the spine and hip. For most women, at least five years of estrogen given as early as possible in menopause will prevent the normal drop in bone density for as long as it continues to be taken. In fact, bone may even be built up a little during the first year or so of therapy; this effect then levels off with (usually) minimal loss of bone as long as therapy is continued.

Many women at high risk of osteoporosis come off the therapy too soon to have a beneficial effect; at present the average length of therapy in the United States is only nine months. Since research indicates that a minority of women continue to lose bone at doses previously thought protective, a follow-up bone scan three to five years after starting therapy may be advisable for women identified as being at especially high risk of osteoporosis. Combined therapy seems to have similar effects on bone loss, with some progestins shown to have an independent bone-conserving effect, though there is no evidence that they are superior to estrogen alone.

> **W**omen who have had an early menopause (at or before the age of 45) or a surgical menopause (removal of the womb, hysterectomy), and/or removal of the ovaries (oophorectomy) should seriously consider hormone replacement therapy and be aware that, without it, they will be at greater risk of heart disease and of fractures due to accelerated thinning of the bones. They may also require slightly higher doses of hormone than women going through menopause at the usual time.

There is some debate about how long the protective effect lasts after discontinuation of therapy, but any "rebound" loss of bone following withdrawal of the hormones probably mimics the loss that would have occurred at menopause, and therefore postpones first fracture by the number of years it is taken for. Thus, an 80-year-old woman taking HRT for ten years between the ages of 50 and 60 would have the bones she would have had at 70 had she remained untreated.

PROTECTION AGAINST HEART ATTACK AND STROKE?

The value of taking hormones to protect against heart attack and stroke, though often vigorously promoted, is less certain. In the early days, researchers expressed relieved surprise that there was no jump in the number of heart attacks when post-menopausal women were given estrogen, since the Pill was already known to predispose to blood clots and heart attacks. It was only gradually that the hormone was actually seen to be preventing deaths and looked upon as positively beneficial. An authoritative overview of 16 studies recently showed a significantly reduced risk in all but one of them – the discrepancy is thought possibly to be the result of higher hormone doses than are now generally taken. Certainly, there is now plenty of evidence that the arteries behave differently when estrogen levels are restored in post-menopausal women: the blood vessels remain elastic and open, blood flow improves, levels of "bad" (LDL) cholesterol drop and those of "good" (HDL) cholesterol rise.

Angiograms comparing the condition of the blood vessels of women taking post-menopausal estrogen with those who are not on the therapy have found that the former are about half as gummed up. The endocrinologist Professor Howard Jacobs believes that this makes estrogen "one of the best known coronary preventive measures currently known to medicine, against which the benefits of cholesterol-lowering drugs fade into insignificance."

The largest survey to date, carried out on over 48,000 American nurses and reported in 1991, confirmed resoundingly that taking estrogen lowered the risk of heart disease, with nearly half the number of heart attacks among women currently taking the hormones. But there seemed little carry-over protection, with ex-users only about ten per cent better off than non-users.[2] Exciting as it is, this finding has to be interpreted with some caution; since most women surveyed were early users of estrogen, they would have been carefully screened for heart disease risk and only given therapy if their risk was low, so they were perhaps less likely to die of a heart attack anyway.

THE EFFECTS OF PROGESTIN IN OPPOSED THERAPY

Since the great majority of women surveyed in the trial were taking only estrogen, the so-called "unopposed" therapy, it is not yet known how the addition of progestin affects the estrogen benefit. Most specialists now suspect that some of the most widely prescribed progestins (namely norgesterel and high-dose norethisterone acetate) are protecting the womb at the expense of the heart and cardiovascular system, "swapping a rare, almost always curable cancer for an increased risk of heart disease," as the noted gynecologist Mr. John Studd perceives it.

Progestins mostly affect the blood fats in a less-than-ideal way. They raise LDL cholesterol, lower HDL cholesterol, increase internal arterial resistance to blood flow, raise blood pressure, and affect carbohydrate metabolism in such a way that it might predispose an already susceptible woman to glucose intolerance and diabetes, potent heart risk factors in their own right. While an unpublished Swedish study of 23,000 women has revealed no *increase* in heart attack in women taking the opposed therapy, what is sure is that health practitioners who tell a woman that the combined approach will halve her risk of heart attack are being economical with the truth. At the moment, no one knows for sure, since the large-scale trials now being embarked upon have yet to yield their answers.

Women at additional risk of heart disease – through smoking or having a family history of heart disease (in a parent or sibling before the age of 65), high blood pressure or a family history of it, diabetes or a family history of it, angina, or high cholesterol – should ask their physician about taking one of the less androgenic progestins. They should also consider other routes of delivery as these become available, from the patch to the new IUD (presently only available in Finland). They may also wish to explore the possibility of taking unopposed (estrogen-only) therapy supplemented by regular biopsies of the endometrium. Such checks need to be continued for some time after the estrogen ceases to be taken: one study found a raised risk of cancer for 12 *years* following as short an exposure as 12 months.

In North America, many gynecologists will consider leaving out the progestin half of the therapy if a woman suffers intolerable side-effects, unrelieved by a change of prescription, or is at demonstrably higher risk of heart attack, on the grounds that the risk of endometrial cancer is tiny when compared with that of heart disease. In 1993 in the United States, there were approximately 5700 deaths from endometrial cancer compared with well over 100,000 from heart attack. Even should a malignancy occur, they argue, it has a high cure rate when caught early – an eventuality that can be virtually assured by having annual biopsies to check the endometrium. New aspiration techniques and vaginal ultrasound probes now make this an acceptable, if uncomfortable, outpatient procedure equivalent to having an IUD fitted. As with cervical cancer, endometrial cancer usually has a recognizable pre-malignant stage in the form of an abnormal thickening of the lining of the womb known as atypical hyperplasia.

Many doctors outside of the United States see the logic of the American approach, especially as they suspect that many women who feel bad on their 12 days of progestin may be skipping it anyway, and so putting themselves at an unnecessarily increased risk of the cancer through simple lack of surveillance. In one study, additional cases of endometrial cancer arising in women on opposed therapy were attributed to "truancy" from the protective part of the therapy.[3]

Women whose menopause is still ten or more years off are lucky. They stand to benefit from the new "metabolically friendly" progestins (gestodene, norgestimate, and desogestrel), which are currently incorporated in the contraceptive Pill and are now under intensive development for hormone replacement purposes. These have little effect on blood fats, and fewer nasty side-effects. Some doctors are trying to sidestep the progestin problem by giving natural progesterone in suppository form via the rectum or vagina (known as micronized progesterone). Although some women object to the messiness of the method and others feel draggy and drowsy during their progesterone days, the worst of the drowsiness can be avoided by taking it in the late evening.

HRT AND BREAST CANCER

While post-menopausal estrogen has been cleared of causing cancer of the cervix and probably ovary, it may play a part in cancer of the breast – if not turning normal cells cancerous, then perhaps by stimulating a cancer that is already present to develop. Because estrogen functions like a growth hormone, promoting the development of breast tissue, it has always been feared that it could have a potential cancer-promoting effect on malignant cells already in the breast, permitting them to take hold and spread.

Certainly, breast cancer risk is quite clearly linked to how much estrogen a woman is naturally exposed to during the course of a lifetime, with women who go through an early menopause at 45 having half the risk of women who go through a late menopause at 55. (A breast tumor which first appears during pregnancy, when estrogen levels are at their all-time high, has a notoriously frightening prognosis.) It is therefore entirely plausible that prescribing estrogen beyond the menopause should increase a woman's risk of breast cancer by bumping up her age of menopause.

Certain knowledge is hard to come by, since many of the research findings have been completely contradictory. While some show no increase in risk for the first ten or 15 years of use, others show a rise after five years. An analysis of several studies by the U.S. Centers for Disease Control in Atlanta, Georgia, which was published in 1991, found no extra risk for five years of hormone replacement therapy but a 30 per cent higher risk after 15 years.

CONTRA-INDICATIONS

In the recent past many women were barred from taking hormone replacement therapy because they had conditions known to be risky if taking the Pill; they were heavy smokers or they had high blood pressure or a history of a blood-clotting

Many women may choose to take hormone replacement to tide them over the difficult transitional years and then stop. This will help control symptoms when wildly fluctuating hormone levels have their most miserable consequences, will give valuable protection to the bone, and might well have some positive effects on the circulation, though these only appear to be significant as long as a woman continues taking it.

Women with a family history of breast cancer (mother or sister) at a young age, when the relative was estrogen-sensitive, should be guided by their physician both as to the wisdom of hormone replacement at all, and as to the type of estrogen. (Conjugated equine estrogen, Premarin, seems associated with a lower risk than estradiol.) They should also be wary both of starting therapy before their periods stop, since this has been associated with a higher risk of breast cancer in some studies, and of continuing therapy for more than five years.

problem such as deep-vein thrombosis. Now that it's realized that these risk factors do not necessarily apply to hormone replacement therapy, it means that there are very few women who cannot take it. Women who are diabetic, have high blood pressure, or gallstones (all three conditions tend to get worse on the therapy) may be better suited by patches or implants than pills. Usually, absolute contraindications are: present or past cancer of the endometrium or breast (some specialists no longer even consider these causes enough not to prescribe), present severe thromboembolism (such as heart attack), and severe liver disease.

RECENT DEVELOPMENTS

For the many women who view HRT's compulsory monthly bleed as an unacceptable side-effect, there are now some methods that either involve less frequent (albeit heavier) 12-weekly bleeds or do not entail having periods at all. The relatively new drug tibolone (Livial), for example, causes the endometrial cells to atrophy rather than proliferate and so can be given without having to induce a regular protective bleed. Tibolone controls menopausal problems as effectively as estrogen does, though the effects on the bone (which look quite positive) and on the heart have yet to be evaluated. Another method involves giving combined estrogen and progestin continuously, the latter in much reduced doses, with no break for menstruation, so also avoiding a withdrawal bleed. But as bleeding can go haywire before it actually stops for good, close monitoring is essential to establish the ideal hormone ratio.

Before embarking on therapy, a full medical and family history should be taken, together with a vaginal and breast examination. A mammogram, if you have not had one in the last year, is advisable too. Weight and blood pressure should also be checked; if blood pressure is found to be raised, it should be treated and/or monitored closely. Three-yearly Pap smears are advised, though treatment for past abnormalities is no bar to therapy. A three-monthly appointment is essential after the first prescription to check progress and bleeding patterns, and regular follow-ups are also important.

Another path of delivery of HRT is the implant, whereby a tiny pellet is inserted under local anesthetic into the layer of fat of the buttock or abdomen. This five-minute procedure maintains estrogen levels for four to six months at rather higher levels than those usually produced by pills or patches. Implants are good for women whose menopausal problems persist on pills, who have a tendency to gallstones or high blood pressure, or who have bone densities that continue to fall on conventional doses and delivery methods. While implants may be especially protective of the skeleton and heart, there are fears that they may pose additional risks to the breast. As they continue to influence the endometrium long after stopping therapy, additional progestin needs to be given until estrogen levels fall adequately and/or a close eye kept on the endometrium.

The patch is probably the better option for most women. When placed on the lower back or buttock, this circular transparent disk releases its hormone at a constant rate across the skin into the bloodstream much as the ovaries did before they stopped production. (Pills, on the other hand, provide an initial burst and gradual decline over 24 hours.) A progestin tablet also has to be taken for 12 days, though a new progestin patch, which doubles with estrogen for the last ten days of therapy, making a goggle-shape, is hoped to reduce some of the PMS-like side-effects of the oral progestin. Since the hormones do not have to pass through the digestive system, the patch is a good choice for women who feel nauseous when taking tablets and is often recommended if blood pressure is high. About one-third of women have minor skin reactions to the adhesive, which can be overcome by changing its site on a daily basis, and about one in 20 has a more severe reaction which renders the method unworkable. It is not yet known for sure whether delivering estrogen this way is equally beneficial for the bones and heart.

Vaginal creams and pessaries and the soon-to-be-introduced vaginal ring are particularly effective for the urinary urgency/frequency problems linked to lack of estrogen and for reversing vaginal dryness (see page 373 for more details). As the hormone is well absorbed into the general circulation, though not always in sufficient quantities to preserve bone and protect against osteoporosis, it might increase the risk of endometrial cancer unless given in opposed form or in the much reduced doses now known to be effective for treating vaginal dryness and urinary problems. Delivering the progestin component of the therapy via a slow-releasing IUD also seems logical, since this is the only place where the hormone is actually required. A new, low-dose, seven-year levonorgestrel-releasing IUD, though still not licensed for hormone replacement purposes, is creating much excitement in the medical world since it has the requisite effect on the uterus while not disturbing blood fats or breast tissue. Side-effects can still be a problem, however. Further off, nasal sprays are under development.

> **T**he key to stopping therapy, as with sleeping tablets, is to taper off gradually rather than stopping abruptly, so giving the body the chance to adjust to lowered hormone levels. This can also prevent unpleasant re-bound problems, and it allows for restarting therapy, at a possibly lower estrogen dose, if problems then recur.

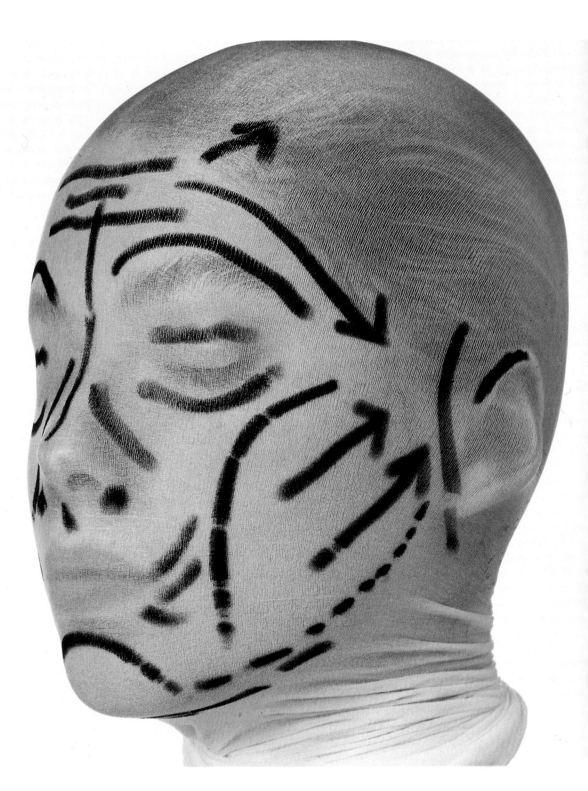

PSYCHOLOGICALS

THE graffiti yells, "Old Age is Real. It Will Happen to You." But who on earth ever believes it? Just as Freud maintained that the human psyche dispatches with death ("No one believes in his own death . . . In the unconscious everyone is convinced of his own immortality"), so at some irrational, deep-down level do we also believe that we are exempt from the ravages of time. We may accept aging as the general lot of humanity but we never expect it to catch up with *us*. "When it seizes upon our own personal life," said Simone de Beauvoir, "we are dumbfounded."

Mostly, women are dumbfounded sooner than men. In spite of the sea change in society's perception of women in their 30s and early 40s, women of 45 plus are still perceived as older than equivalently aged men. Time hangs heavier on their faces and bodies. The process of disqualification in the job, sex, and marriage market starts sooner. Leading roles – and, more importantly, role models – run out, as a 30-year hiatus yawns between "Pretty Woman" and "Life on Golden Pond." To the feeling many women have of being the wrong shape all their adult lives is added the realization that they are now the wrong age as well.

Confronted with their graying selves, some women panic and try to turn back the flight of time with all the artifice open to them. In a memorable quip minutes before she was junked for a much younger model, Ivana Trump declared, "Donald wants me to stay 28 and I've told him it's going to cost him a *lot* of money." The effort to remain a perpetual 28 demands ever larger inputs of time, money, and maintenance: hair tinting and highlights, workouts at the gym, shots of silicone and sessions of liposuction, increasingly skillful applications of make-up and artful arrangements of hair. And even then, as Mrs Trump and Co. remind us, it may not always work.

ATTEMPTS TO BEAT THE CLOCK

The modern doctrine of fixability – that if something is not as one wants, it is just a question of finding the right person to fix it – can become an all-consuming quest as the eternal optimist ages. In some sections of society, the pressure to look young is stronger than it has ever been. The American Society of Plastic and Reconstructive Surgeons (ASPRS) reports that the age of face-lift patients is dropping. More than a quarter are now between the ages of 35 and 50, "with many in the lower end of that bracket." Fritz Barton, MD, speaking for the ASPRS, asserts, "The norm used to be to help older-looking people appear more middle-aged. Now what's happening is that people want to retain their youthful appearance rather than recapture it."

As we age, we can go in one of two directions – both prevalent in the last decade of the millennium. We can sign on for perpetual youth, fighting our lines and wrinkles with the ever-widening array of cosmetic options now open to us. Or we can resist the nip and tuck and make peace with our older selves and our aging faces, as many Europeans have done for centuries.

Women are not alone in their attempts to beat the clock. Men are increasingly candidates for cosmetic surgery. While women may mourn the loss of their youthful looks, men regret their declining strength and vigor just as much. The man whose adult life has been built on a sense of his competence may try desperately to reassert control as a dawning awareness of his own mortality, and the terrifying specter of heart disease, takes hold. He can be seen in the gym, doing circuits and pumping iron, as though by controlling his physiology he will somehow face down other experiences that he doesn't know how to tackle. Or he may be found running headlong from his marriage of many years into the arms of a much younger lover. These denial tactics are as old as time itself and were summarized thus by the psychoanalyst Carl Jung nearly three-quarters of a century ago.

> As a rule, the life of a young person is characterized by a general unfolding and a striving toward concrete ends; his neurosis if he develops one, can be traced to his hesitation or his shrinking back from this necessity, but the life of an older person is marked by a contraction of forces, by the affirmation of what has been achieved and the curtailment of further growth. His neurosis comes mainly from his clinging to a youthful attitude which is now out of season. Just as the youthful neurotic is afraid of life, so the older one shrinks back from death.[1]

THE SHOCK OF THE OLD

The denial tactics are so strong that the recognition that we are aging, held so long and determinedly at bay, can deal a body blow to the image we have of ourselves. Such a recognition is often forced by the visibly changed perceptions of others. In *The Summer Before the Dark*, the novelist Doris Lessing weaves a compelling tale around the invisibility of Kate Brown, a once striking woman who no longer commands a glimmer of the attention that at one time had fallen effortlessly to her.

> No one took any notice of her. She knew now, she had to know at last, that all her life she had been held upright by an invisible fluid, the notice of other people. But the fluid had been drained away . . . For the whole of her life, or since she was sixteen, she had looked into mirrors and seen what other people would judge her by. And now the image had rolled itself up and thrown itself into a corner, leaving behind the face of a sick monkey.[2]

The shock and disbelief women feel when they come up against the reality of their own aging may be continually relived as the self-image, which is ageless, struggles to adjust to the change. In their book, *Look Me in the Eye*, Barbara Macdonald and Cynthia Rich describe this sense of detachment:

> Sometimes lately . . . I see my arm with the skin hanging loosely from my forearm and cannot believe that it is really my own. It seems disconnected from me; it is someone else's. It is the arm of an old woman. It is the arm of such old women as I myself have seen, sitting on benches in the sun with their hands folded in their laps; old women I have turned away from. I wonder now how and when these arms I see came to be my own – arms I cannot turn away from.[3]

Some are catapulted into the recognition of their own aging by the death of a parent, which abruptly shifts them on a generation and forces them to see their own as the frontier one. Others may simply glance sidelong into a mirror and catch a familiar but unfamiliar face looking back at them. In American *Vogue*, Germaine Greer recalled her own adjustment to the aging process:

> Aging is like growing. It isn't a gradual imperceptible process, but happens in leaps and bounds. You can go on for years being the same age. Your face doesn't change much; your weight remains much the same. You never think of yourself as too old to learn the latest craze, can't wait to off with the old and on with the new. Then, crunch. You're polishing a mirror table and you realize your neck has gone. Just like that. You put down your polishing cloth and examine the thing that has appeared like a bracket joining your chin to your neck. A wattle, in fact. You're talking to your sister on the telephone and feeling your chin with your fingertips. Then, you scream. "What's the matter?" asks your sister. "I've found something, on my chin." "A bristle, dear," says your sister. "The first of many."[4]

Judging by the new confessional literature of middle age, a period of coming to terms and of depression, even disgust, with the physical changes of age is common. Writing in British *Vogue*, Suzanne Lowry owned that she "certainly went through a phase of pulling faces and figures in a cruel mirror, suddenly able to see undeniable signs of facial and bodily decrepitude. I worked myself into a state of revulsion against my own body in particular and middle-agedness in general." Simone de Beauvoir, several decades earlier, was even more repelled. "When I was able to look at my face without displeasure, I gave it no thought, it could look after itself . . . I loathe my appearance now: the eyebrows slipping down toward the eyes, the bags underneath, the excessive fullness of the cheeks, and that air of sadness around the mouth that wrinkles always bring."

However careless of their appearance women have been in youth, a time of grief seems mandatory before acceptance can dawn. The youthful looks that were once taken for granted – the unlined skin, the hair, and the figure that in its own time was constantly found wanting – take on new value once they are seen to be slipping away. The physical changes reproach us for never fully appreciating our bodies in their prime: the once unbounded energies that now have such circumscribed limits, the magical powers of procreation that were continually countered with contraceptives and are ebbing away, the eyes that once beheld whatever was put in front of them and now cannot decipher the small print.

A CIRCUMSCRIBED FUTURE

Quite apart from what is culturally seen as "loss" of looks, there are other losses. By midlife, the choices have been made. The life course is mapped. Where once a vista of endless opportunity stretched indefinitely ahead, the future now appears both finite and circumscribed. According to psychoanalytic theory, the recognition that life will never hold Olympic honors, professional qualifications, renewed or firsthand experience of childbirth and motherhood – in short, the realization that we cannot

accomplish or become everything that we would like in the short space of a single lifetime – lies at the heart of the midlife crisis.

In his paper, *Death and the Mid-life Crisis*, the psychoanalyst Elliott Jaques summed up the 30s and the 40s as the time when the brutal discrepancies between the ego-ideal, the wish life, and the actual, come to be most painfully apparent. At the height of the crisis, past achievements seem trivial, present strivings senseless, relationships devoid of meaning. "The route forward has become a cul-de-sac." In this "mid-life encounter with one's own eventual death ... the achievement of mature and independent adulthood presents itself as the main psychological task. The paradox is that of entering the prime of life, the stage of fulfillment, but at the same time the prime and fulfillment are dated. Death lies beyond."[5]

The language of mourning is apt. Adjusting to the fact of one's own aging often takes the pattern that so commonly follows a death: shock and disbelief, followed by yearning for the loss to be reversed, anger and resentment, and finally acceptance. The psychoanalyst/social psychologist Joan Raphael-Leff notes that many women spend their early adult lives waiting for "one day," that magical moment in the fictitious future when, having shed all their unwanted baggage (the excess weight, the imperfect complexion, the lack of self-confidence), their "real" emotional life will begin. The shocking realization that life is half over and that "one day" is here, today, engenders grief about wasted opportunities and potentialities. At the same time, however, it can enable the more questioning woman to free herself from a life spent in rehearsal and to begin living each moment more fully in the present. According to Raphael-Leff, the bereavement process can also be softened by the recognition that, as the years pass, you are not so much losing the old self as adding new ones.

> You contain everything you've always been – infant, little girl, adolescent. As you grow older, so you add to your repertoire, gaining additional points of reference and contact with generations other than your own. Motherhood and grandmotherhood give a second and even third attempt at childhood, a renewed opportunity to work through unresolved unconscious struggles more consciously and to come to terms with those hived-off internal areas.

When seen in this light, the struggle to stay an eternal twenty-eight can be seen as the ultimate denial – since disowning the years becomes by definition a discarding of parts of oneself. Increasingly, hearteningly, there are bulletins back from the breach. As the frontline feminists grow older and the women's movement, formerly so preoccupied with the issues of reproductive health, sexual freedom, contraception, and abortion – younger women's issues all – turns its attention to the perplexities of growing older, we learn that there is life after midlife. Following on from the grief over faded looks, lost opportunities, and waning fertility, there are unexpected new

Germaine Greer, revving up on the eve of her 50th birthday ... "a chronic adolescent" who feels she is growing old without ever having grown up. "At fifty, with a thickening waistline and grizzled hair, jowls that show a pronounced tendency to droop and an intermittent sciatica that shoots down my right leg like lightning, you'd think I was becoming a solid citizen," she confided to the readers of British *Vogue*, "but I am as much of a ratbag as ever."

freedoms. Liberated from the anxiety of matching up to the prescribed feminine ideal, the woman who has consented, if not actually to growing old then at least to not striving to be "young" anymore, escapes from the self-consciousness of prettiness and finds a whole new world the other side of youth and beauty. Arriving there can often be quite a relief.

ENHANCED MENTAL HEALTH AT MIDLIFE

The myth that women go mad at menopause, and stay dispirited and depressed for ever after, has no basis in truth. In fact, the incidence of clinical depression is at an all-life *low* in the 50s, and there is lots of evidence that women are psychologically more robust in later life than earlier. About 30 years ago, doctors in New York assessed different groups of people according to their psychological health, and then reassessed them about 15 years later; the one group enjoying better mental health were women in their middle years. The researchers attributed this to the greater fulfillment and self-esteem that the women, most of whom had work lives as well as home lives, gained through their achievements outside the home, which in turn enriched their family life. The benefits of forging a life of one's own, independent of home and family, continue throughout life and are apparent even in extreme old age.

Far from winding up in an arid backwater, many women's lives often take off at the midpoint. Counselors and psychotherapists talk of a curious crossover in the 40s and 50s, with women moving off in new directions while men tread water – and occasionally go under. In India, a similar observation underlies their centuries-old belief that a baby girl is surrounded by 100 angels and a boy by 100 devils; every year a devil and angel swap sides, so that from the age of 50 a woman is on the devil's side. If a woman can resist the pressure to be ever more accommodating and uncomplaining as she gets older she will come at last into the age of dissent. After years of living around other people's needs, "a sponge for small wants" as one woman described it, she can finally attend to her own. The empty nest provides the perfect opportunity for finding her wings and taking flight. This new confidence and independence of spirit can be intimidating, especially to men, and gives a whole new interpretation to the French idea of a "dangerous age."

Many is the midlife woman who has marveled at how resilient, strong, wise, and clear-sighted she feels as she comes into her full complement of capacities and energies. Erica Jong, writing in American *Vogue*, is an example:

> At 20, I had no sense of power as a woman, no unstoppered delight in my sexuality, no sense of how to dress, and no understanding of men. Trapped in my own wants, desires and neuroses, I could not penetrate anyone's feelings but my own, and I could not break out of the prison of my own self-doubt and self-loathing. I did not know how to listen. At forty-five, I know what I want and who I am; I like myself. I delight in hearing what others have to say.[6]

Jeanne Moreau was 30 before she shot to fame with her 23rd film, *Ascenseur pour L'Échafaud*. Her face already showing the traces of time, Moreau summed up a dangerous siren sexuality which has persisted long after the kittenish appeal of her contemporaries, such as Bardot, has faded. Interviewed by Joan Juliet Buck for British *Vogue*, she said, "Nothing starts at one specific moment. The older you get, the more you realize that everything is the fruit of what you are."

Others echo the theme. "You could say it seems like feminist claptrap," averred Lauren Hutton when interviewed at the age of 47 by Sarah Mower for British *Vogue* on the occasion of her lucrative new contract with Revlon, "but there is something about being the age I am that feels like coming to fruition. Women are extraordinarily powerful. After menopause, that's when women really become dangerous, politically and in their femininity!"

YOUTH CULT

The panic many men and women feel at the midlife – the last-chance feeling that wrecks relationships and undermines confidence – owes as much to the belief that there is nothing to look forward to as to regret for the past. Age in our culture is such a cultural turn-off that even elderly people disassociate themselves from their contemporaries. "Old," they say, is a misfortune that happens to others; it has nothing to do with birthdays. "If you're alert and physically well," they reassure themselves, "there's no such thing as old." The feminist ideal of sisterhood fractures as one elderly woman insists on her otherness from the next, the competitive once-over women give each other in earlier life continuing into ripe old age. In one Canadian study, researcher Jane Aronson found a group of retired female schoolteachers "at pains to distance themselves from other older women." Robustly proclaiming their independence of lifestyle and outlook, they projected their negative feelings onto those who were perceived not to be "coping" so well and derided them for their frailty, fussiness, forgetfulness, and dependence on others.[7]

Some contemporary historians date the present cult of youth from the overthrow of the old order by the American and French Revolutions. The white heat of the technological revolution has intensified the tendency in our own time. The pace of "progress" is now so swift that even yesterday's experience has to be trashed as obsolete. As any job advertisement makes clear, the premium that used to be put on age and experience now belongs to youth and innovation.

VALUING AGE

Yet, when it comes to the eternal verities – seeking justice, advice, or direction in life – people look to age rather than youth for answers. Ministers and counselors, judges, priests, and psychotherapists know that their own age actually widens their appeal, and even cosmetic surgeons are learning the same. Succumbing to the pressure to have their own faces lifted and lines erased, they have found their newly youthful looks bad for business. Virginia plastic surgeon George Weston, quoted in the magazine *Allure* after having the bags removed from his eyes, said he wouldn't be considering further procedures. "I already look too young to have enough experience ... I've had some women come in for consultations and take one look at me and say, 'I've got *shoes* older than you.'"

One of the century's most enduring beauties, Katharine Hepburn, photographed in 1991 at the age of 83 on the publicaton of her autobiography, *Me: Stories of My Life*. With a nice line in self-deprecation and characteristic good humor, she called herself "a weatherbeaten old monument" in the photo session and wisecracked at the inconveniences of age – even though still agile enough to stand on her head for four minutes every day and to plunge into the icy waters of Long Island Sound. "I think everything's quite funny. It just tickles me. Laughing is fun and I laugh at practically everything."

STABILITY . . . OR STAGNATION?

While old people are seen as wise and rich in experience (albeit often an experience that no longer counts for anything), they are also seen as unchanging. The storms of youth and early adulthood having passed, they are assumed to have reached a point that is at best stability and at worst stagnation. In some cultures, however, the whole of the lifecourse is seen as a time for exploration and growth. Indian Hindus, for example, are expected to withdraw from family and public life in the last quarter of their lives and attend to their spiritual selves, moving from a state of activity to one of contemplation. Some even leave home, discarding their possessions, and wander the wider world until the transition from body to spirit is complete. Such journeys in the West are not considered possible, even metaphorically. Here the "formative years" are restricted to childhood and adolescence. Growing pains are expected to pass as adulthood approaches, and any possibility of inner development and growth dismissed thereafter. If people are more contemplative in later life, it is because they have nothing better to do.

This dismissiveness seems a contemporary evil, but in fact it stretches back a long way. In 1906 Professor William Osler, later Sir William Osler Bart, the most eminent physician of his day, gave up an American medical appointment to take up the prestigious Regius Professorship of Medicine at Oxford University. In his inaugural speech, he alluded to the uselessness of everyone over the age of 40. "The real work of life is done before the 40th year," he said. By the age of 60, when everyone was dispensable, "a peaceful departure by chloroform might be what was wanted . . ." The speech, delivered half in jest (he was 57 at the time), was greeted by a storm of protest. But these attitudes were actually shared by many of his contemporaries.

Sigmund Freud, for example, influenced generations to come with his belief that, as they get older, people develop a sort of arthritis of the psyche, getting ever more reinforced in their defenses and neuroses. At the age of 49, he asserted that it simply wasn't worth spending therapeutic time and energy on older patients since "near or above the age of fifty, the elasticity of the mental processes on which the treatment depends is as a rule lacking – old people are no longer educable."[8] This is curious considering that Freud didn't embark on the self-analysis that was the cornerstone of his work till he was 40, went through a midlife crisis on the death of his father, worked until weeks before his own death at 82, and produced some of his most astonishing and outrageous works toward the end of his life. Nevertheless, these ideas have stuck and stuck fast. The acceptable range for psychoanalysis is still set between the ages of 15 and 40.

DEVELOPMENT OF THE PSYCHE

By contrast, other 20th-century thinkers and writers, such as Erik Erikson and Carl Jung, believed passionately that people continue to develop psychologically throughout their adult lives. "It seems to me that the elements of the psyche undergo in the course of life a very marked change – so much so, that we may distinguish between a psychology of the morning of life and a psychology of its afternoon," wrote Jung. Unlike Freud, he was in a good position to judge, since two-thirds of his patients were middle-aged and older.

Increasing numbers of contemporary psychotherapists echo the view that, far from being unreceptive to therapy, older clients are often *more* open to change. In later middle age, life events, such as bereavement, divorce, and impending retirement, can act as a trigger for re-evaluating goals and priorities and give a new urgency to seeking help. No longer hamstrung by the full-time demands of job and family, older people have the time and the commitment and, often, the considerable financial resources necessary to spend time on their inner search. The British psychoanalyst Pearl King, the first person to present a paper at any psychoanalytic meeting on treating the over-40s (fully three-quarters of a century after such meetings first started), says she has found her older patients ("particularly those between the ages of 40 and 65") less likely to resist unpleasant insights and quicker to integrate them into their lives.

> I consider that gradual awareness of changes in the life situation of these middle-aged patients brings a new dynamic and sense of urgency into their analyses, thus facilitating a more productive therapeutic alliance than one manages to establish with similar young adult patients. They are usually conscious of the fact that this is their last chance to effect an alteration in their lives and relationships, before being faced with the reality of the physical, psychological and social effects of ageing to themselves.
>
> This rediscovery of their own identity ... often runs parallel to and is perhaps mediated by the development of new forms of creativity and new ways of *perceiving* people, perceiving *time* and the world around them. With some it is as though they have to learn to exist in a new key or dimension of being, which they feel is very different from how they have lived before. It is as if the centre of their gravity moves from the edge of themselves to their own inner centre. They begin to experience a new sense of tranquillity which is not dependent on the continuity of an intact body, or of family relationships, or of a role in the community, although it may be enriched by these, but which is based on a sense of identity and of their own value and purpose in life. When elderly patients have achieved this, I find they are then often able to get access to new forms of creativeness within themselves, which result in experiences of satisfaction quite different from any experiences during the first half of their lives.[9]

MOVING AWAY FROM MATERIALISM

The advent of this inner centeredness and tranquility was described by Jung as the dawning of a long-postponed spirituality which, combined with a regret at the materialism of early life, heralded the beginning of a new, more reflective phase of life. It is only as worldly passions and desires are shed, he wrote, that a person can get closer to God. Even in our own godless age, surveys suggest that, as people age and the future shortens, the consumer in them disappears. There is a rejection of triviality and a longer perspective, which adds up to much more than fear of the dark. To the advertising industry's enduring frustration, older people are not easily taken in by commercialized images of happiness and personal well-being. In one

Honor Blackman, still a blonde bombshell at an improbable 67. The first, most famous Bond girl, as Pussy Galore in *Goldfinger*, and the original Avenger, she finds the acting opportunities have expanded as she has gotten older and shrugged off the blonde stereotype. "When I was young, I had a huge bosom, was very, very pretty and was never considered for the kind of roles I am now being offered, such as being given the chance to play comedy. From all points of view, this is a very good age to be."

telling project in southern Ontario, two different age groups (25–35 and 65–75) were questioned at length about their possessions and the meaning these held in their lives. In the words of the researcher:

> The most striking observation made of the entire sample was the extent to which the older respondents exhibited a general contentment with their present standard of consumption. Indeed, when asked what they would buy if they suddenly won a lottery, respondents were unable to identify with ease the purchases they would make. They exhibited such difficulty with this question that it became obvious that they did not have an internal consumer "wish list." This strongly differentiated them from the younger group of respondents who were able to produce such a list immediately and with evident, anticipatory relish.[10]

Further questioning revealed that these people were not so much numb to the hard sales pitch as appreciative of the greater *value* of old objects. They were positively disinclined to trade in their superannuated cars and humble dishwashers for newer models, since this would mean displacing existing possessions, which were seen to have served perfectly well. They had even undergone a "kind of increase in value" as a result of their length of ownership, becoming symbols of continuity and thus "an archive" of their own lives.

Ego integrity

The psychoanalyst Erik Erikson, known for his explorations of the lives and psyches of septuagenarians and octogenarians, observed that a definite shift takes place in one's orientation to the world as the years pass by and that, of a series of eight big tasks that present throughout life, it is only in quite advanced old age that one faces the supreme psychological challenge. The achievement of what Erikson called "ego integrity" comes from integrating all life's previous lessons and arriving in the fullness of time to an acceptance of one's time spent on earth as the one and only life cycle. This entails accepting one's parents for who they were rather than blaming them for who they weren't, and instead of forever wishing that they (and so by implication oneself) could have been different, taking on the idea of life as one's own responsibility. Even the most miserable childhood must be respected as the stuff one is made of; for better or worse, it has forged the kind of person one is.

According to Elliott Jaques, the same spirit of acceptance is the hallmark of maturity in all human endeavor:

> Out of the working through of the depressive position, there is further strengthening of the capacity to accept and tolerate conflict and ambivalence. One's work need no longer be experienced as perfect. It can be worked and reworked, but it will be accepted as having shortcomings. The sculpting process can be carried on far enough so that the work is good enough. There is no need for obsessive attempts at perfection because inevitable imperfection is no longer felt as bitter persecuting failure. Out of this mature resignation comes the serenity in the work of genius, true serenity, serenity which transcends imperfection by accepting it.[11]

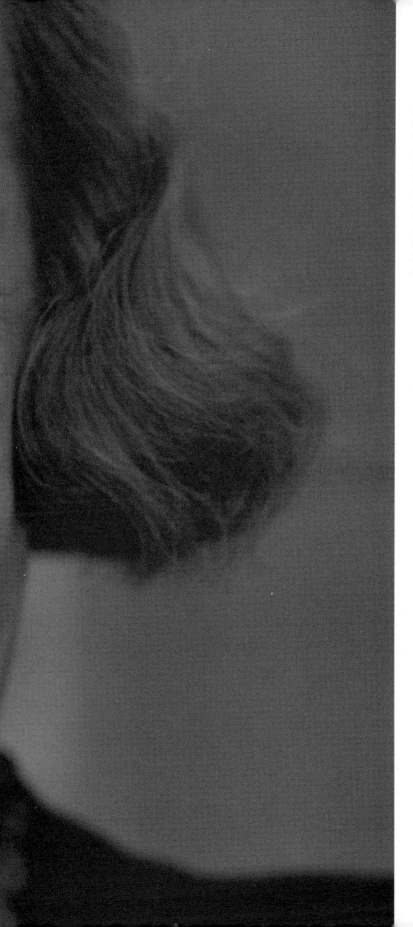

Andrée Putman, one of the most sought after and widely copied interior design gurus on the international circuit. Still turning heads in her 60s, thanks to her commanding height and perfect posture, set off by years of practicing the Alexander Technique, her inimitable style evolved as a result of using her own appearance to exaggerate line and form – a trick, she told *Vogue*, that sprang from "the attitude of someone who never liked herself too much. Too tall, so I went taller with high heels. Broad, athletic shoulders, so I emphasize them with a well cut jacket."

Vivienne Westwood, widely admired within the fashion world for her unflagging originality and ability to spring fresh surprises with each new season. The author of such prescient ideas as underwear worn as outerwear, the crini, tights under jackets, and many of the glorious excesses that were Punk, she is recognized as a fashion genius of the first order whose inventiveness never stales.

The opportunity for self-discovery in life is unending. Even the path to death can be a creative constructive experience – a lesson that life is, literally, not over till it's over.

TAKING THE PRESSURE OFF

The dreary pessimism about later life that underlies so much in our culture is not borne out by reality. When researchers carried out a survey, *The Myth and Reality of Aging in America*, for the National Council on Aging, they found that for every older individual who felt that old age was worse than anticipated, at least three were pleasantly surprised by what they found when they got there.[12] But since so few of us listen to older people, let alone feel there is anything to be learned from them, we cannot draw comfort from what they have to tell us. Instead, taken in by the mythology of impending decline, we get to the midlife and panic, feeling time is about to run out on us. If, on the other hand, we look about us, talk to older people, and listen to what they have to say, we may feel differently. The gerontologist Alex Comfort has pointed out that the prospect of an older age in which intellect, health, sexuality, and activity remain very largely unimpaired for a long time takes the pressure off middle age. Time opens up again, presents new opportunities, and returns a sense of the future. We can afford to take a longer view, and start to conduct our lives with that future in mind. Even though that future is itself inevitably shorter, it may also be sweeter, its quality sharpened by the finite nature of time left to us.

> All that the "proximity to death" does to age is to add value to living, to reduce our tolerance of triviality and to increase our anger with those who, or those attitudes which, cause us to waste a store of time and experience that we cannot afford to dissipate or have destroyed.[13]

CONTINUING GOOD HEALTH

The idea that we all go steadily downhill from the seventh decade has such a strong grip on our collective cultural imagination that, once there ourselves, we expect our health to deteriorate, our minds to muddy, our senses to close in on us, our bones to break, our joints to lock, and our strength to wane. If they don't, we believe ourselves lucky to have escaped the general lot of aging humanity, rather than realizing that continuing health and strength is the general experience of older age, and a valid expectation if we are in the habit of taking reasonably good care of ourselves.

Action and pressure groups campaigning tirelessly on behalf of the neediest, loneliest, most afflicted elderly give the impression that infirmity, confusion, frailty, arthritis, hypothermia, and isolation are the natural consequences of old age and that all old people are the ailing objects of pity and charity. In so doing, they unwittingly reinforce the stereotype that all elderly people are leading isolated lives beset by serious health problems. Yet old age is not the great leveler it is so often made out to be. In fact, stereotypes are even less true at this stage of life than any other, with old people more *unlike* each other in terms of health and strength than at any time of life.

Shakespeare's famous seven stages of life – the last of which consigned the individual to "mere oblivion, sans teeth, sans eyes, sans taste, sans everything" – sums up the prevailing view of age as a time of loss. Yet modern surveys give the lie to this depressing image, revealing that healthy (some call it "successful") aging is much more prevalent than the popular view of decline, disease, and dementia. Not only are lifespans longer, but there are signs that illness is increasingly being compressed into the few years, or months before death, especially for those who have got into the habit of looking after their health. Surveys show that fully half of all Americans in the 75- to 84-year-old age group are free of health problems that require special care or curb their activities. Even in the very oldest group, those aged above 85, more than one-third declare no limitation due to health.

THE MEDICAL MODEL

Just as, in recent years, the normal everyday experience of childbirth has been wrested back from the obstetricians (who, being called upon to attend difficult deliveries, tend to assume all births are fraught with hazard), so our general ideas about later life need to be sharply disassociated from the dismal picture of older age represented by the ailing minority on a nation's geriatric wards. Although they actually represent less than four per cent of the total, they influence how the elderly get treated – as objects of pity by the general public, past hope of salvage by many in the medical profession.

Even today, doctors still have a disposition to look at the afflictions of their older patients as progressive and irreversible, scarcely warranting research or resources. As the medical profession wakes up to the agism rife in its own way of operating, or more often not-operating, countless surveys in both the United States and Europe are revealing that the elderly are regularly denied lifesaving medical treatment, preventive health strategies, and even routine care.

The traditional explanation for such policies is that elderly people do less well despite aggressive treatment. But it is becoming apparent that, with careful assessment, selection, management, and aftercare, even octogenarians do very nearly as well as patients many years younger. In 1992, *The Journal of Cardiovascular Surgery* carried a report from the Medical University of South Carolina, after surgeons there had carried out high-risk triple bypass surgery on 25 octogenarians. Follow-up showed 84 per cent survival after one year and 88 per cent survival after five years – a better record than that achieved after mastectomy for breast cancer.

Just as, once upon a time, the menopausal woman was told that her wretchedness was just Nature's way, and left to endure sweats and hot flashes unaided, now our older citizens are having their problems airily dismissed. Complaining of confusion, depression, dizziness, and joint pain, they are as likely to be lectured on the virtues of living with it as offered any constructive help and asked what else do they expect at 70 or 80? Yet, in truth, none of these problems, though commoner in later life, are the invariable effects of age. Doctors committed to the more sensitive care of the elderly delight in telling the apocryphal tale of the 104-year-old who, on complaining of a stiff painful knee and being told, "What do you expect at your age? Of course you can't expect to be agile," retorted, "My left knee's 104 too and that doesn't hurt."

DEPRESSION – AN ILLNESS NOT AN INEVITABILITY

The prevailing pessimism that hangs heavy over later life means that, just like the aching knee or the weakened bladder, depression in the older person is considered an inevitable rather than a treatable condition, on the grounds that old age is, well, plain miserable. The consequence is that the elderly woman who suffers from depression is probably continuing to do so needlessly – not realizing that her dragging fatigue and chronic lack of sleep are due to an underlying, and treatable, disorder. The theory that depression becomes commoner with age because the biochemistry of the brain tilts it in a direction that lowers mood may explain why so many elderly people feel restored to their own selves again after a spell on anti-depressant therapy.

Once the depression that develops in later life is recognized as an illness rather than a natural consequence of growing older, the idea that we all go steadily downhill psychologically as well as physically is free to be challenged. Misery and loneliness are not the natural state of older age. In those surveys where the aged are invited to rate their own contentment and emotional well-being – rather than, as is so often the case, being spoken for like unreliable children incapable of expressing a view – a surprisingly high degree of satisfaction with life the "wrong" side of 65 or 70 emerges. In one 1991 survey, for example, although 92 per cent of those aged between 25 and 54 agreed with the statement that "a lot of older people feel lonely these days," only 22 per cent of the older people said loneliness was a problem for them. In fact, 81 per cent of those over the age of 75 wanted no more contact with anyone.

GREATER CONTENTMENT

When older people's own priorities and values are taken into account, they actually appear *happier* with their lot than younger ones. In one Irish survey[14] that included these factors, the surprise finding was that those in the older group (average age 73) were "significantly" more satisfied with their quality of life than the younger sample (average age 28). The finding demonstrated, said the researchers, "the basic error of *imposing* a definition of quality of life on the individual rather than eliciting one."

As values and aspirations change with age, different aspects of life become important. When relatively young researchers impose their own values on older individuals, who may have a very different definition of quality of life, the results of their researches are bound to be skewed. For example, an arbitrary higher score is often awarded for more frequent meetings with friends and family, but the subject is not asked if he or she actually *wants* to see friends and family several times a week; the researcher has already decided that more meetings mean greater satisfaction. The Irish survey suggests that, while contact with family usually remains central, friendships and other relationships become less significant, with only 20 per cent of the older group rating them as important to their quality of life compared with 86 per cent of the younger group. In another telling comparison, religion and spirituality were important to 74 per cent of the older individuals but only considered significant by seven per cent of the younger ones. And quality of life was also perceived rather differently, with 48 per cent of the younger group rating "happiness" as most important against just four per cent of the older sample, who looked for satisfaction rather than happiness itself.

What older people throughout the Western world do say they have to struggle with is not primarily failing health and strength, nor isolation, but bias, negative attitudes, and, in many countries, poverty. In today's world, financial investment for old age is as necessary a precaution as keeping fit and healthy. After good health, it is probably the most important single thing separating a good old age from a bad one. The anticipation of poverty, of money running out, is an unrecognized source of anxiety, especially for women, whose longer life-expectancy promises many years of making do. In the U.S. National Council on Aging's survey, *the Myth and Reality of Aging in America*, most of the respondents over the age of 65 said they wished they had planned better for their later lives.

THE AGE OF DEPENDENCE

Eventually, of course, we must all confront failing health, increasing dependency, debilitation, and ultimately death. For women especially, the transition from independent to assisted living comes hard. Many men are in receipt of care for most of their lives, but most women, having been in control of their households and caregiver to the generations below, above, and alongside, are likely to have an especially acute sense of being burdensome and useless. As elderly women are only too aware, self-reliance is the cardinal virtue of late life, allied to the supreme womanly virtues of not grumbling or complaining and bearing all with resignation, submissiveness and good grace. Yearning for security and safety, and yet fearful of imposing, they either contain their low spirits, mask their anxieties, and gamely stifle their need for assistance, or accept help and end up consumed by guilt that they are not living up to society's, and their own, expectations.

The few surveys to have glanced in the elderly woman's direction have found that preserving an independence of attitude can still count for a lot, even when dependent on help for the most basic activities of life. The feeling of being in control of one's life, even when circumstances become very difficult, is increasingly recognized to enhance recovery prospects from diseases as various as cancer and heart disease, and to make a big impact on our own aging – especially as we get very much older and events seem to be taking off and proceeding without us.

One survey of the lives and attitudes of 50 women over the age of 75 came to the unexpected conclusion that a woman's perception of her degree of independence did not necessarily accord with the extent to which she was actually "in charge" of her life, as opposed to dependent on others to organize and structure things for her.[15] The researcher distinguished between two groups of women, one of which she called "active initiators" and the other "passive responders." The first group, though often severely restricted in their mobility and hence ability to care for themselves, did not see themselves as particularly dependent and felt in control of their circumstances. For example, one 89-year-old, despite having poor eyesight, poor hearing, arthritis, and recurrent chest complaints, and being dependent on her children for help with the basic activities of daily life, preserved her sense of independence by cooking for her daughter and helping with the housekeeping, and she organized a large family party to celebrate her birthday. The "passive responders," meanwhile, relied on others to organize their lives and, in spite of a consensus among their helpers that they could do more, saw themselves as highly dependent and acted accordingly.

Interestingly, analysis of these women's past lives revealed that those of the "passive responders" had conformed more closely to the homemaking model, with most of their time spent at home, caring for others. In later life, bereft of their active caring roles, these women seemed to have lost their sense of purpose. The "active initiators," meanwhile, who had invested their time and energies into activities other than traditional "women's work," were more likely to have interests that were not exclusively home and family based. They enjoyed a self-forged identity, above and beyond that of caretaker wife and mother, that led to greater satisfaction in later life, whatever their circumstances and made it possible for them to age with pride and independence, maintaining a positive self-image into ripe old age.

While a new realism about the positive aspects of later life is essential if we are to be free from dread apprehension, at the same time we need to be on our guard against Methuselah-like illusions that decline and even death are somehow optional.

ALPHABETICALS

ACNE

Acne occasionally continues into midlife. At least one in 20 women still suffers after 25, while others may even find their skin becoming spotty again when they start taking hormone replacement therapy, the progestin component of which can sometimes switch sebaceous glands back on again; a change of progestin can often help. Steroid therapy can also provoke acne.

Effective treatments range from antibiotics to drugs that influence the way the skin responds to hormones – but it may take two months for any improvement to show. If excessive oil production is to blame, acne can respond well to tretinoin (Retin-A). When applied in cream, gel, or lotion form, it dries oil from the skin and increases cell turnover, unblocking follicles. It has the secondary bonus of erasing fine wrinkles (see pages 32–4). In the worst cases, another vitamin A derivative, Roaccutane, can be taken by mouth, though the side-effects are considerable.

If spots and pimples re-erupt after years of quiescence, question your cosmetic products. Acne cosmetica becomes more common in midlife, when women, panicked by the signs of age in their faces, opt for ultra-emollient creams and then find tiny bumps breaking out under their skin. Use a light moisturizer that is quickly absorbed, saving richer creams for use only when needed. And go easy on cleansing: scrubbing irritates the skin. Instead, spot-treat blemishes with creams containing sulfur, resorcinol, or benzoyl peroxide.

Make-up products, such as oil-based foundations, popular for their good coverage and often misguidedly chosen to mask the signs of age, may stick fast to the follicles and provoke blackheads and whiteheads (comedones) or out-and-out acne, as can concealer sticks. Simplify your routine, using products labeled "non-comedogenic" or "non-acnegenic," opt for low-oil foundations, and see if the condition clears. A medium-depth chemical peel or dermabrasion can do wonders for acne and post-acne skin, refining the texture and smoothing out the skin tone.

A separate dermatological disorder, acne rosacea, especially affects fair-skinned women between 30 and 50. The cause is unknown. Unlike the big, inflammatory pustules of acne, rosacea spots are small, red, and scaly, likely to cluster around the middle of the face, and not accompanied by comedones. Flushing is common – due to dilation of the small blood vessels – and usually precedes the appearance of the pimples. Since flushing is aggravated by emotional stress, extremes of temperature, alcohol, hot drinks, and hot, spicy foods, avoid these and, if there's no improvement, see your doctor. Antibiotics may be prescribed to clear the spots, as might beta-blockers to reduce flushing. The enlarged blood vessels, or telangiectasia (qv), can be cosmetically treated or zapped by lazer. As rosacea-affected skin is dry and easily irritated, over-the-counter acne-type creams should be restricted to the affected area, otherwise they may magnify the problem. **Also try:** Chinese herbal medicine.

AGORAPHOBIA

Characterized by avoidance of situations that provoke fear and panic – stores, crowded streets, public transportation – agoraphobia strikes most often in midlife, becoming less common in old age. Three-quarters of sufferers are women. Depression (qv) increases the risk of developing agoraphobia by as much as 15 times, and panic attacks by nearly 20.

Full-blown agoraphobia is often preceded by, and may actually be caused by, panic attacks. In these, intense fear is accompanied by palpitations, shortness of breath, and choking. Fear of being away from a safe place in the event of another attack drives the sufferer indoors. Many doctors prefer to treat the phobia by directing treatment toward the panic attacks, often coupling short courses of anti-depressant therapy with breathing techniques to overcome the panicky effects of hyperventilation (literally "overbreathing"). It is now recognized that the additional great gasps of air taken at the onset of an attack upset the body's oxygen/carbon-dioxide balance. This provokes all sorts of unpleasant effects, from shaking legs to palpitations and thudding in the head, so intensifying the fearful feeling of being out of control. This vicious circle can sometimes be broken by breathing out into a *paper* (not polythene) bag, and in again, since breathing in one's own carbon dioxide readjusts the ratio safely and swiftly. Other forms of help include behavioral therapy, psychotherapy, and self-help groups.

AMENORRHEA

In pre-menopausal women, amenorrhea (absence of periods) signals either pregnancy or cessation of ovulation for other reasons, principally crash dieting and/or over-vigorous exercise. The condition is common and should be taken seriously, since prolonged spells can jeopardize the long-term health of the skeleton, substantially bringing forward the risk of developing osteoporosis.

Erratic, infrequent, absent, or very heavy periods are common side-effects of contraception, especially progestin-only contraception, or they may occur when coming off the contraceptive pill after a long time taking it. The general consensus is that these are not significant, though there is some concern that amenorrhea following progestin-only contraception may slightly increase the risk of osteoporosis in later life if ovulation is also entirely suppressed.

In the 40s and early 50s, absent or infrequent periods are common and can herald the menopause. Pregnancy cannot be ruled out, however. For contraceptive purposes, menopause can only be safely assumed to have occurred if a year has elapsed since the last period if you are over the age of 50, or two years if under 50.

ANEMIA

Iron-deficiency anemia is by far the commonest form of anemia and women are much more susceptible than men, with ten per cent thought to be borderline anemics, or worse, thanks to excessive blood (and hence iron) loss during menstruation. The risk commonly rises in the 40s when very heavy periods – so-called "flooding" or menorrhagia (qv) – are common.

Lack of iron causes problems ranging from tiredness and breathlessness to palpitations and weakness in the limbs. If you suspect anemia, see your doctor. Do not dose yourself with supplements: commercial pills are unlikely to contain enough iron and, if you are not anemic, too much iron can be dangerous. The tablets can anyway give rise to indigestion, nausea, and constipation.

Safeguard yourself by eating meat and liver (preferably from organically reared animals), fish, legumes, soyabeans, dried fruits, dark-green leafy vegetables such as broccoli and watercress, almonds, pumpkin seeds, and molasses; and by making sure these iron-rich foods are eaten with vegetables/fruit high in vitamin C, or fruit juice, since this optimizes absorption of the mineral. Avoid drinking tea with iron-rich foods or adding bran, as the tannin in tea and phytate in bran bind up the iron (along with calcium, zinc, and magnesium) and sweep it out of the system.

If you are pre-menopausal and prone to very heavy periods and hence anemia, consider a change of contraceptive, either to the new levonorgestrel-releasing IUD (see page 294) or to the low-dose pill (so long as you are a non-smoker).

ANGINA

The most common sign of possible heart disease is angina, an indigestion-like pain on any exertion that increases the call for blood. As narrowed coronary arteries restrict the supply of blood, the heart muscle is kept short – hence the pain, which varies from mild discomfort to an excruciating vice-like pain, described as like having an elephant sitting on your chest. It may radiate up to the jaw

or along the shoulder and arm, producing pins-and-needles in the fingers. Once the strenuous activity or excitement that brought on the attack subsides, the pain goes away and no irreversible harm is done because the blood can still get through the arteries, even if the normally powerful flow is dramatically reduced. So-called "unstable angina," which comes on at rest and wakes you in the middle of the night or isn't relieved by tablets under the tongue, needs urgent investigation by a specialist as it may presage imminent heart trouble. For reasons that are not well understood, women are particularly prone to angina.

Angina can be controlled and often completely prevented by calcium channel blockers, beta-blocking drugs, or nitroglycerine pills or patches to keep the blood vessels dilated. Nitrate tablets under the tongue can give immediate relief in the event of an attack and can also be used in anticipation of an attack if, say, some unusual exertion is required. Since the drug relaxes all the blood vessels, not just the coronary arteries, flushing sensations or headaches can be side-effects. Long-term low-dose aspirin therapy is increasingly advised (see page 152). Occasionally, severe angina can be treated by a surgical technique called angioplasty, which forces the narrowed arteries open.

Also try: vitamin E, which may reduce risk of heart attack in angina sufferers by 40-50 per cent. Find it in natural sources first (vegetable oils, especially corn and soya, wheatgerm, legumes, egg yolks, nuts such as almonds). Any supplement should provide no more than 400 IUs – check with your doctor first if you are diabetic or have high blood pressure.

ANXIETY/AGITATION

Although anxiety and depression (qv) are often twinned, the familiar high agitation of older age is often quite free of depression, and tends to take the form of specific phobic disorders or a more generalized "free-floating" anxiety, which is characterized by tension in the muscles, apprehensiveness, and general jitteriness.

While psychological approaches, such as cognitive therapy, are more appropriate than drugs, where anxiety is acute or, of course, symptomatic of an underlying depression, anti-depressant medication can often give sufficient breathing space to respond to one of the "talk" therapies. Benzodiazepine-type tranquilizers, however, once much prescribed to allay anxiety, should be avoided: they are now known to create a dependency syndrome that throws a third of long-term users into a frightening withdrawal reaction when they try to stop the drug – provoking redoubled anxiety, often to a point of panic and later phobia, insomnia, and even re-emergence of the original anxiety that led to medication; a mourning reaction in someone treated for bereavement, for example. Such drugs still have a value for very short-term relief of acute anxiety, but long-term users need to have their medication very gradually diminished to prevent rebound attacks. Alternative strategies, such as behavior therapy and relaxation training, are preferable.

B

BACK PAIN

Second only to the common cold as a cause of absenteeism at work, back pain is common at any age and gets commoner as we get older. While bedrest is important acutely, the long-term philosophy must focus on getting people back on their feet and teaching them how to strengthen and use, but not abuse, their muscles and joints. When Danish researchers put chronic low back pain sufferers through a twice-weekly program of rigorous leg and trunk lifting exercises, the exercisers were far better off than patients doing little or no exercise, irrespective of age, duration, or severity of back trouble. But sufferers should always be guided by their physician as to what type of exercise, if any, is appropriate. Women in particular should be sure to get persistent back pain checked out, since crush fractures, due to osteoporotic thinning of the spinal vertebrae, may be the cause.

Awareness is often the key to avoiding recurrence of pain. This involves paying close attention to posture, considering one of the "alternative" realignment techniques listed below, and taking especial care when lifting heavy objects (guidelines are on page 199).
Also try: osteopathy; chiropractic; postural re-education, especially the Alexander Technique.

BAGS UNDER THE EYES

Thanks to the unholy trinity of heredity, gravity, and age, bags under the eyes appear as the skin stretches out and subcutaneous fat breaks through the weakened muscles, causing the baggy tissue to balloon out, sometimes to a point of obscuring vision. Cosmetic surgery, known as blepharoplasty, is the only effective treatment and, when bags are severe, can transform the look of the face.

BREAST PAIN

Also known as mastalgia, breast pain tends to wax and wane over the menstrual cycle, often becoming especially marked just before a period, along with general lumpiness and swelling. It is very common; one survey of working women found 66 per cent affected by sensations ranging from heaviness and tenderness to out-and-out pain which, for some, persisted for fully half the cycle.

The rule rather than the exception, breast pain is not a disease; when examined, hormone levels and breast tissue are invariably found to be normal. Many people, associating *pain* with *harm*, find the discomfort easier to live with once reassured that the breasts are quite normal. Even so,

the discomfort can sometimes be disabling. Self-help measures include wearing a good supporting bra day and night; cutting out coffee, tea, and cola drinks; reducing animal-fats; and taking oil of evening primrose, which trials have found to be effective in half of all women. If no relief is found, drug treatment is often effective but the side-effects can be considerable. Drugs range from the anti-estrogen medication, tamoxifen, to other hormone treatments, such as bromocriptine and danazol.

Filling out a breast-pain chart over three menstrual cycles, using symbols to denote "no pain," "mild pain," or "severe pain" and marking every day according to how you feel, will enable you, and your doctor, to detect a pattern and monitor treatment. Post-menopause, breast pain can sometimes be provoked by hormone replacement therapy, and can often be assuaged by switching to a different type or dose of progestin. Tenderness, caused by the breast reacting to the unaccustomed levels of estrogen, should subside within two to three months. Asymmetric breast pain (in one breast only) should always be thoroughly checked out.

C

CATARACT

Cataract is responsible for much poor sight in later life. The condition generally advances snail-pace over several years, even decades, with opaque flecks gradually clouding the fine-focusing lens inside the eye, so that sight becomes blurred and eventually obscured.

The first signs are trouble in seeing detail, being easily dazzled, seeing better in half light than in bright light and, if long-sighted, an unexpected *improvement* in your sight which may even allow you to give up your glasses. Even earlier signs can be detected by a simple medical examination, which should be a part of every healthcare schedule past the age of 40. This is particularly important for diabetic patients and for anyone with a family history of cataract.

To date, only surgery, which removes the damaged lens and replaces it with an alternative lens, either as an implant within the eye or in the form of a contact lens or glasses, can prevent the slow, insidious slide into loss of sight. Doctors used to leave cataracts to "ripen," but now consider early surgery preferable if the quality of life is suffering. If there are no other changes, such as macular degeneration (qv), surgery has a high success rate, with over three-quarters of patients able to see well enough after their operations to read.

Vitamins C and E may play a part in the future prevention of this disorder. Research at Tufts University in Massachusetts has shown that people with low blood levels of vitamin C are 11 times more likely to develop cataracts than those with high levels, while a further study in Boston found that older people who took multivitamins that included vitamins A and E reduced their risk by 37 per cent.

Some experimental research also suggests that low-dose aspirin may be able both to prevent cataracts from forming *and* to delay their progress, with studies on diabetic rats (who, like humans, are prone to the disorder) showing that regular doses of aspirin, paracetamol, or ibuprofen (an anti-inflammatory drug) halt the progress of the condition.

CHRONIC FATIGUE SYNDROME

Also known as postviral fatigue syndrome (PVFS), "post-viral exhaustion," "myalgic encephalomyelitis" (ME), "epidemic neuromyasthenia," "chronic Epstein-Barr (EB) virus syndrome," and "Persistent Virus Disease" (PVD), chronic fatigue syndrome still mystifies the medical profession. While no virus has yet been identified, immunologists have found specific signs of heightened immune activity suggestive of an infective agent.

The effects are real enough: unexplained exhaustion and fatigue, profound muscle weakness made worse by exercise, impaired concentration and memory, depression, insomnia, irritability, gastro-intestinal upsets, painful joints, giddiness, disturbed vision, and such dragging fatigue that it is not relieved even by sleep. Real, pervasive, and often incapacitating, CFS has been met with almost total lack of help, let alone recognition, from orthodox medicine, and has accordingly become a focus for unsubstantiated claims from alternative practitioners and pill-pushing manufacturers.

Some alternative therapists advise colonic irrigation (see page 173) to spring-clean the colon. Others recommend the removal of amalgam fillings in the mouth, and yet others diagnose a range of bizarre food allergies and prescribe handfuls of vitamins and minerals to rectify the problem. A popular theory is that the candida yeast present in the intestine has somehow penetrated the gut wall causing toxins to leak out into the blooodstream, where they cause pervasive ill health. "Ozone treatment" involves having a pint of blood removed, having it suffused with ozone, and then returned to the body. The basis for this, as with so much else in the field, is wholly unscientific. All of these so-called remedies remain untested (and expensive) and may even make the illness worse. There is no reliable evidence that people with CFS have any vitamin or mineral deficiencies, with the possible exception of low magnesium levels, or that they will benefit from detoxification fasts, which are more likely to weaken their already debilitated condition.

Treatment that may be of help, besides hanging up your jogging shoes and taking plenty of rest, is magnesium supplementation. Injections are given into the muscle once a week for at least six weeks, followed by maintenance monthly injections for a year. (Magnesium levels must be checked first, however, as overdosing may provoke kidney problems.)

CIRCULATION PROBLEMS

As women get older, they are especially prone to cold extremities. This may amount to little more than a bluish tinge to the tips of the fingers, or it may give rise to such frequent and severe pain that it interferes with the quality of life. Sometimes the cause is serious, reflecting damage to the body's blood vessels, particularly those supplying the legs. Although peripheral vascular disease (PVD) has always been predominantly a disease of men, increasing numbers of women are now suffering at all ages – a consequence, it is thought, of smoking. PVD can cause intense pain on walking, which is relieved only by resting and raising the legs. Because it indicates possible obstructions in the arteries elsewhere in the body, the condition is linked to a greater risk of heart attack and stroke.

Another less ominous but more common source of pain, Raynaud's disease, is a particular nuisance for women. It is caused by an uncontrollable spasm in the small vessels which supply blood, usually to the fingers, but the feet, ears, and nose may also be affected. Attacks are usually triggered by cold or, less often, stress. The affected part undergoes a series of color changes, first white as the artery goes into spasm, then blue as old blood stagnates, and finally red as the circulation wakes up again. This is usually the most painful phase and it may be so bad that all sensation is (temporarily) lost. Raynaud's is particularly common in smokers, though it can also be caused by drugs. Preventive tips are to stop smoking, to keep warm and avoid sudden changes in temperature, and to wear warm gloves when outside in cold weather. Although drugs can help keep the blood circulating by dilating the blood vessels, they all have side-effects. In extreme cases, surgery can cut the nerve supply to the blood vessels and so cancel the pain, if not the color changes.

CONSTIPATION

Constipation has come to be seen as the root of all physiological evil, and the daily bowel movement an indispensable criterion of health. Yet, in reality, "normal" encompasses anything from three times a day to three times a week. What is not normal is any significant change in bowel habit, particularly if it comes on suddenly, alternates with diarrhea or is accompanied by pain, bleeding, or weight loss.

Constipation can be a side effect of many drugs taken for chronic conditions. Codeine-containing analgesics, sedative antihistamines, beta-blockers, diuretics, and iron tablets are some of the most common obstructors of regular bowel movements.

The most effective short-term answer to constipation is to use a fecal softener, like dioctyl sodium sulphosuccinate, or a bulk laxative, such as lactulose agar, psyllium, prunes, figs, and methylcellulose, which has the osmotic effect of retaining water in the colon, softening and bulking out the stool. Long-term, the best strategy is to take more exercise (as we slow up, so the bowel also becomes more indolent) and gradually to increase the fiber content of the diet, not just with bran but rather with a variety of foods, such as fruit, vegetables, wholemeal bread, pasta, and brown rice. Constipation that persists on such a diet should be checked out by a specialist.

Stimulant laxatives are one of the most abused forms of drugs among women who believe themselves constipated or use them in a misguided attempt to control their weight. Continued use of these substances – the most common are bisacodyl, senna, castor oil, cascara, aloes, ducusatet – can actually cause gastrointestinal problems including worsening constipation.

Also try: self-massage of the lower abdomen working in a clockwork direction; hypnotherapy.

CORNS

As we get older, the cushioning layer of fat beneath the skin shrinks and the bony joints of the foot become prominent, the skin can get squeezed between the bones and shoes, causing painful calluses and corns. Surgical treatment which removes abnormally overgrown tissue can often work wonders.

The best preventive measure is to make sure that shoes fit well, and, if corns are already a problem, that the heels are not so high as to throw the weight onto the balls of the feet. Soak your feet for ten minutes in warm water once a week and use a pumice stone to shave down the dead skin, slathering on plenty of hand cream afterward.

CYSTITIS

Suffered by fully half of all women at some stage in their lives, cystitis is caused by an inflammation of the bladder lining due to either infection (likely if there is also fever) or irritation of the sensitive cells within the bladder wall. Cystitis can be extremely painful and inconvenient – all sufferers know the constant, wearying, almost uncontrollable desire to pass water, only to squeeze out a searingly painful dribble on getting to the lavatory.

Fortunately, cystitis responds well to short courses of antibiotics (if there is an infection) and to a range of simple self-help measures. At the first signs, drink as much water as you can to dilute your urine and flush germs from the bladder. While avoiding potential irritants, like alcohol, coffee, strong tea, or most fruit juices, try drinking cranberry juice, which will alter the pH of your urine, creating an environment less agreeable to bacteria.

To prevent further attacks, avoid strongly perfumed soaps, all talcum powders, bath oils, and bubble baths, and "feminine" vaginal deodorants. Do not wear tightly fitting underwear, clinging pants, or pantyhose. After each trip to the bathroom wash yourself gently and dab dry. Get into the habit of wiping front to back to avoid transferring germs from anus to vagina. Empty your bladder as soon as possible after intercourse, and wash too. If you find tampons aggravate cystitis, use sanitary pads instead.

Also try: acupuncture.

CYSTS: ON THE BREAST

Though uncommon after the menopause, a tendency to breast cysts may continue in women taking hormone replacement therapy, and can sometimes be averted by a change of hormone type or dose. Pre-menopausally, they are often associated with marked premenstrual breast tenderness and general fluid retention in the breasts. The cause can generally be traced to the duct system, which produces milk in the breastfeeding mother and which at other times, particularly during the second half of the menstrual cycle, manufactures a small amount of fluid. A cyst can appear literally overnight and is often tender or even outright painful. Being felt as a firm lump, it may cause great concern, though women who have recurrent cysts and come to recognize the familiar smooth texture are usually not worried in the slightest, knowing that their tendency to breast cysts, though inconvenient, is not indicative of malignant change. In order to exclude cancer as a possibility, a diagnostic high-resolution ultrasound scan may be advised; or, more commonly, a needle may be inserted into the breast. If the lump is a cyst, the fluid will drain out and the pain and the lump disappear as if by magic.

CYSTS: ON THE OVARY

Ovarian cysts are generally caused by a developing follicle in the ovary that, for some reason, has not ruptured to release an egg. More common pre-menopausally, they are unusual in women taking the combined pill (which reduces the likelihood by 90 per cent) and can be provoked by the anti-estrogenic drug, tamoxifen. Ovarian cysts frequently cause very little trouble unless they grow quite large. Occasionally they can burst, and can result in intensification of the symptoms.

Also try: acupuncture.

D

DANDRUFF

Dandruff is thought to be caused by accelerated turnover of cells on the skin of the scalp, which clump together to form large flakes. Frequent shampooing with an anti-dandruff (medicated) shampoo should control it, especially if the hair is well brushed first to loosen the flakes and the shampoo is left on the scalp for a few minutes to give the active ingredient (generally, tar, zinc pyrithione, selenium sulfide, sulfur, or salicylic acid) a chance to work. If it fails to respond, consult a doctor or a trichologist since it may be due to psoriasis (qv) or eczema, which require different treatment. If flaking also appears on the eyebrows, on the sides of the nose, or around the ears – it could be caused by seborrheic dermatitis, which gets commoner in midlife and which may require medication.

DARK CIRCLES UNDER THE EYES

The skin around the eyes is the thinnest on the body, which is why lines first tend to form there. Because the blood vessels also lie closer to the surface, the darkish blood can lend a bluish/black tint to the skin. It may even leak out of the vessels, causing more pronounced, and permanent, discoloration. Dark circles can usually be well concealed by camouflage creams (see page 100), but a light touch is essential. Pronounced dark circles can be very effectively lightened by a phenol (chemical) peel, though – be warned – this can be extremely painful.

DEPRESSION

Depression gets commoner as we get older, and by the 60s is thought to afflict one in five people. By far the single most ignored disorder among the elderly, it is often overlooked for the reason that older people are expected to be miserable, and their circumstances condemned as the cause, rather than an illness being suspected. This cultural bias feeds the hopelessness all depressives feel.

Depression that seems to descend from nowhere and takes a strong hold over a short period of time is likely to have a biochemical cause and is an illness. Without medication it can linger for months, or even years, whereas with treatment it can start to lift in weeks. Apathy, early-morning wakefulness, weight loss, and lack of appetite, feelings of guilt and self-blame, sadness, irritability, a tendency to cry more often than usual and to take no joy in former pleasures, such as food and sex, are all signs of depression.

Fortunately, depressive illnesses are highly responsive to treatment, with two-thirds of patients benefiting from medication and even more when counseling is also included. Unfortunately, awareness of the possible dangers of long-term tranquilizer use (see anxiety) has led to a fear of any drug prescribed for disturbances of mood. Yet antidepressants, which have an impressive track record, are not addictive and can be phased out over a short period of time without withdrawal problems. But they do take three to six weeks to act and must be taken for at least four months, preferably six, after mood has improved.

Side-effects – dry mouth, drowsiness, blurred vision, constipation, confusion, perhaps dizziness – tend to become apparent before any lifting of mood can be felt and should be interpreted as a sign that the drug is working rather than cause to abandon medication. Most individuals become acclimatized to these side-effects after about two weeks, but if they continue to trouble, a different anti-depressant may be better tolerated. There is a wide range of drugs, and a change will not delay the advent of the mood-improving effect. A new generation of drugs, the 5HT reuptake-inhibitors (fluoxetine, sertraline) are less likely to interfere with clarity of thought, are safer in overdose, and have fewer side-effects – no dry mouth, less of a drowsy hang-over feeling, and less likelihood of a change in blood pressure. Driving is safer too. Nevertheless, side-effects of all mood-changing drugs, including sleeping pills, become more pronounced with age and require cautious dosage.

In addition to correcting the chemical imbalance that underlies biological depression, medication strengthens the ability to cope – restoring sleep, assuaging anxiety, removing suicidal thoughts, and so allowing the fog to lift sufficiently for the individual to see a possible way through. At this point, counseling can be very helpful and cognitive therapy is particularly effective. This practical approach focuses on today's problems and tomorrow's apprehensions rather than looking back for keys in yesterday's childhood traumas. By modifying negative expectations, it can swiftly help "decatastrophize" the future and increase a sense of ability to cope with problems that previously seemed insurmountable.

DIABETES

Unlike the type of diabetes that demands daily insulin injections and strikes in early life, the non-insulin-dependent, "late-onset" form is relatively common with age. It afflicts about one in ten individuals over the age of 65, half of whom will not be aware that they have the condition. Women are particularly at risk. Although often thought of as "mild," this disorder is actually the third leading cause of death in later life, since it contributes hugely to heart attack, stroke, and kidney disease. It is also a leading cause of blindness and limb amputations – making it essential that it is detected early and brought under control.

In the healthy person, the hormone insulin trickles steadily out of the pancreas into the bloodstream, where it enables food to be moved into cells for growth, energy, and healing. Unlike early-onset diabetes, where insulin completely ceases to be produced, the late-onset sufferer still produces insulin but the cells become insensitive to it. This causes excessively high levels of glucose to build up in the blood, which in turn leads to fatigue, dehydration, blurred vision, and, if unchecked, the more serious complications mentioned above.

Late-onset diabetes is strongly linked to obesity and is the main justification for keeping weight within reasonable limits as we age. Having a history of sugar in the urine when pregnant, having developed "gestational" diabetes in pregnancy, having given birth to very big babies – over 10 pounds (4.5 kilograms) – and having a family history of the condition are all additional red flags and good cause to keep weight down, and activity up, to prevent the full-blown condition from developing. They also indicate the need for regular screening checks.

More awareness of the early signs of diabetes, and earlier management, could prevent many of the worst consequences of the condition. In one hospital survey, over a third of 100 newly diagnosed patients had had signs for over a year but had ignored them. Fatigue and lack of energy, unremitting thirst, a frequent need to urinate, and persistent infections, such as cystitis and vaginal yeast infections, should all ring alarm bells and need checking out with a doctor.

While routine screening tests are probably only warranted for those at high risk of developing diabetes, everyone should be on the lookout for signs of creeping glucose intolerance.

Newly diagnosed diabetics should lose weight (where appropriate) until they achieve a near normal Body Mass Index (see page 84), though even modest losses can make a difference. Concerted efforts to give up smoking and to bring high blood pressure under control are also important. A disciplined diet and exercise regime is often all that is needed to stabilize the late-onset form, especially when the diet is high in unrefined ("complex") carbohydrate and low in sugar. Light regular exercise spurs the body to use more glucose and can help lower blood/glucose levels for hours, or even days, at a time. But get a thorough physical evaluation from a physician first, as complications may rule out certain activities, and safeguards must be scrupulously observed.

Also try: yoga (shown to have lowering effects on blood glucose in controlled trials).

E

ENDOMETRIOSIS

This miserable condition, the second commonest gynecological problem after fibroid tumors, occurs when the cells that ordinarily line a woman's womb migrate to the ovaries, Fallopian tubes, vagina, or elsewhere in the abdomen. Once there, the displaced cells grow rapidly and, because they are sensitive to the same hormones that govern the cells inside the womb, they behave identically – building up over the menstrual cycle and being shed. Over time, this leads to internal damage which can cause excruciating periods, pain during sex, and, eventually, infertility since the abnormal overgrowth interferes with the normal transport of eggs from the ovaries to the Fallopian tubes.

Endometriosis usually gets worse over the fertile years and generally resolves after the menopause, unless hormone replacement therapy is taken, which can reactivate it.

Suspected endometriosis can only be definitively diagnosed by laparoscopy. This involves inserting a thin light-tube into the abdomen under general anesthetic so that the doctor can see the pelvic cavity and make a diagnosis. Hormone treatment with high doses of progestin can often keep mild cases under control; other hormonal therapies are also effective but have unpleasant side-effects.

Patches can be excised surgically or vaporized by a carbon-dioxide lazer, a relatively new treatment which can be performed laparoscopically, has the advantage of being minimally invasive and requires just two tiny incisions. In experienced hands, this also dramatically increases the chances of pregnancy. One study showed that of 228 women treated by lazer, two-thirds remained pain-free over seven years, and three-quarters became pregnant.

EXCESS HAIR

With age, the fine, virtually invisible hairs on the chin, above the upper lip, and along the sides of the face may become coarse, darker, more bristly, and more obvious. By the age of 65, four out of ten women have noticeable hair on their upper lips and one in ten on their chins. While these changes are perfectly normal, if unwelcome, any sudden increase of body hair requires medical investigation since it may signal an internal disorder, or it may be a side-effect of drugs.

Body hair may also become thicker, darker, and more abundant with age. Shaving or waxing is still generally the best solution. The inflammation that so often gives the "plucked chicken" look following a bodywax may be prevented by taking aspirin 30 minutes before treatment or rubbing a 0.5 per cent anti-inflammatory hydrocortisone cream over the affected area immediately afterward; and a tendency to pimples caused by ingrown hairs avoided by frequent exfoliation to keep the follicles clear of dead skin cells, which would otherwise clog them up.

The widespread belief that shaving aggravates hair growth has no basis in truth. Studies comparing natural growth versus shaving show no difference in diameter or rate of growth. Shaved hair feels coarser because it is shorter, blunter, and more rigid. When shaving, or indeed tweezing, is blamed for aggravating an existing problem it is because the problem itself has got worse. Odd scattered hairs can be plucked out; for all the dire warnings about vengefully robust regrowth, there is no danger of "stimulating" plucked hairs to grow back darker, coarser and more numerous.

Bleaching is a good alternative that leaves the follicle intact. As post-menopausal skin color tends to be light, the contrast between bleached hair and darker skin is not as apparent as it would be on younger, darker complexions. You can make up your own solution: add 20 drops of ammonia to each fluid ounce (25 milliliters) of six per cent strength hydrogen peroxide solution. Apply immediately on mixing and leave for 30 minutes. If doing this for the first time, patch test a small area on your arm at least 24 hours beforehand, and if there is any sign of irritation reduce the strength of peroxide.

Electrolysis is the only permanent method of hair

removal, but it is painfully slow. Because every hair must be treated individually and most hairs need zapping more than once, even a limited growth on the upper lip or chin can take months or even years to clear. A fine wire needle is inserted into the hair follicle and a current passed down until it reaches the root, loosening the hair which is then tweezed out. Only actively growing hairs will be permanently eliminated, however; resting hairs will grow back. Ask your doctor or dermatologist for the name of a reputable practitioner to avoid complications such as scarring, infection, and spots of permanent skin darkening. Electronic home devices do not work and should be avoided.

The present unsatisfactory, unwieldy methods of removing hair may soon be superseded. Scientists at Cambridge University in England are not only growing human hair in a test-tube, which is a world first, but are also managing to make it fall out by adding a hormone called epidermal growth factor. In time, it could lead to a novel hair removal technique.

F

FIBROID TUMORS

Fibroid tumors are generally harmless bundles of muscle fiber and fibrous tissue growing in the wall of the womb. One in five women over 35 has them, though many are unaware of their existence. No one knows why they form, but estrogen is known to accelerate their growth. Pregnancy and long-term use of the Pill may cause fibroids to enlarge. Following the menopause they tend to subside and cause no further trouble (although hormone replacement therapy may make them worse).

While some fibroid tumors are pea-sized and painless, others can swell to the size of a melon. They are a common cause of heavy, irregular bleeding – known as menorrhagia (qv) – in women in their 40s, and can also cause abdominal distension, painful cramps and/or a near-continual dull ache in the pelvis and back. If they press on the bladder, they can cause urinary frequency and even stress incontinence; if they grow inward into the uterus they may provoke recurrent miscarriage. They are a major reason for carrying out hysterectomy.

Fibroid tumors are not life-threatening, and less than one per cent ever become cancerous. Mostly they cause no problems and only come to light when a woman is being examined for something else – during a Pap smear, a vaginal examination for infertility, a D&C (dilatation and curettage or "womb scrape") or biopsy, an ultrasound scan for ovarian cysts.

There is no good medication for fibroid tumors – and all drug treatments have serious side-effects. Although commonly the rationale for a full hysterectomy or a smaller

operation, called a myomectomy, which can remove them while leaving the womb intact, there are newer, more effective surgical options. Some fibroids can be removed by an electrical current introduced via a small wire loop through the vagina. Others can be removed via laparoscopic surgery, which is also minimally invasive. Very large, troublesome fibroid tumors may still require hysterectomy, however.

Also try: homeopathy, acupuncture, Chinese herbalism.

G

GALLSTONES

This is a common problem in midlife, particularly for women, who are around three times more susceptible than men. Hormone replacement therapy increases the risk of the disease and, some physicians feel, should be avoided if gallstones have already been diagnosed.

The gallbladder sits just beneath the liver and serves as a reservoir for bile, which is produced by the liver and is composed of cholesterol, among much else. If there is too much cholesterol in the bile, it silts up or even compacts into outright stones. Generally this causes few problems (beyond mild discomfort after a meal, belching, bloating, and nausea), but if the stones or sludge pass out of the gallbladder and into the duct leading off it, severe pain (biliary colic) is almost inevitable, along with fever, nausea, and vomiting. Occasionally, more serious, even life-threatening complications can develop, such as jaundice, liver infection, and even destruction of the pancreas (so-called pancreatitis).

Supposedly more common in women who are "fat, fertile, and forty," there is some evidence that more cholesterol accumulates in the bile of overweight women. Keeping weight within limits is an important preventive measure when gallbladder problems have already been identified.

While there is no connection between cholesterol in bile and cholesterol in food, a link has been found with very high calorie diets which are also high in fats. Once gallbladder disease is diagnosed, a low-fat diet will keep symptoms at bay, especially abdominal discomfort and pain after a meal.

Gallstones can be diagnosed by abdominal ultrasound. Cholecystectomy (removal of the gallbladder) is one of the most commonly performed operations in the United States. A new, minimally invasive technique, laparoscopic cholecystectomy, which involves inserting a tiny video camera into the skin to view the abdomen and removing the gallbladder through a couple of tiny incisions, is now the treatment of choice, and any woman advised to have surgery should push to have it performed by this "keyhole" method, provided she is referred to an experienced surgeon. Drugs to dissolve the stones are effective in a small minority of cases. Other methods, such as using shock waves to smash the stones, are intriguing but often unsatisfactory, since the gallstones commonly re-form after treatment.

Also try: acupuncture; eating foods which are high in sulfur (such as cabbage, asparagus, Brussels sprouts, celery, cauliflower, onions, radishes, garlic) in order to stimulate the flow of bile; adding supplements of lecithin, vitamin B12, folic acid, vitamin C, and magnesium to an already low-fat diet.

GLAUCOMA

One of the most common eye disorders in the over-60s, this illness accounts for about 10 per cent of all blindness in the U.S., and the pity is that it is preventable. It is caused by rising pressure inside the eye due to obstructed normal fluid drainage; the front part of the eye is filled with fluid, which is constantly produced to maintain the eye's shape and to refract light – if it doesn't drain at the rate at which it arrives, pressure can build up, damaging the optic nerve, which transmits the images we see to the brain.

Although glaucoma is rarely painful or problematic in the early stages, the first sign may be blurred vision, redness, or seeing haloes around lights, but often there is no noticeable change in vision until the condition is well advanced. A simple pressure test can identify the condition in time to arrest the deterioration with eye drops, lazer therapy, or surgery. It is vital to pick it up at this stage, however, since once the optic nerve is damaged, any loss of sight can never be restored.

Checks for glaucoma should be part of every full medical examination after the age of 35 if you have a family history of the disease, which raises the risk tenfold. The American Academy of Ophthalmology recommends routine screening on all persons over age 40.

H

HAIR LOSS

It is not just men's hair that thins with age. A woman's hair also becomes finer in texture, and may start to thin out over the top of the scalp. In midlife, one in ten women experiences the sort of hormonally induced hair loss (androgenic alopecia) that usually affects men. This number increases substantially after the menopause, when a woman's ratio of androgen, the hair-thinning hormone, increases relative to estrogen. It is usually most apparent on the front and crown of the head, and clever hairstyling can do much to disguise the problem.

Most hair thinning is caused by disruption of the hair's normally prolonged growing phase, which becomes shorter and shorter, lasting for months rather than years.

Replacement hairs may not even reach cutting length as their growing phase is curtailed. Eventually the follicle may die off and cease to produce any hair at all.

Researchers have recently found a link between thinning hair and iron deficiency, with marked improvements in the volume of the hair achieved after several months' supplementation with iron. Pronounced hair loss can also be caused by thyroid dysfunction, some common drugs – among them anti-coagulants, anti-arthritis drugs, anti-depressants, and beta-blockers – or dramatic losses (or gains) of weight.

HEADACHE

Everyone experiences headaches, but for a few people they can become almost a way of life, striking as often as daily and bringing a train of problems in their wake, such as insomnia, memory problems, and depression. The usual response, to give painkillers, only perpetuates the problem. In one study at the Houston Headache Clinic in Texas, patients who stopped using medication reported a 60 per cent improvement in headache severity and frequency in three months; specifically targeted prophylactic drugs were then given, with marked success in about three-quarters of patients.

Many dentists and headache specialists are increasingly finding the cause of frequent headaches to lie in a faulty bite. If the upper and lower jaws do not mesh perfectly, spasms and muscular tension are inevitable as the muscles try to pull the jaw into line to compensate. Signs of this so-called TMJ (temporomandibular joint) syndrome are frequent headaches and neck and shoulder pains. Suspect a dental cause if headaches are accompanied by nocturnal tooth grinding, jaw clicking, or excessive wear on the biting surfaces.

HEMORRHOIDS

Very common in midlife, and usually the consequence of years of unhealthy eating, chronic constipation, and, especially, straining, hemorrhoids can cause anything from mild discomfort to intense soreness and maddening itching. It used to be thought that hemorrhoids were veins that had become distended with blood, but it is now realized that they are displaced cushions of vascular tissue normally located in the anal canal. Pressure caused by straining or pregnancy forces them down until they protrude visibly and/or can be felt as a hard lump.

At an early stage, hemorrhoids can be prevented from getting worse, and sometimes even persuaded to disappear, by eating a high-fiber diet. Small ones can be successfully treated by injecting a sclerosing fluid around them, though in some cases surgery may be necessary.

HOT FLASHES

One of the classic signs of the menopause, hot flashes are intense sensations of heat which spread upward over the chest, neck, and face and can last for anything from a few seconds to 30 minutes or more (though this is unusual). Typically, they start just before the periods stop and continue for about a year afterward, though in about one in ten women they persist for five to ten years. In one study of 1000 menopausal women, nearly half reported having hot flashes but only 15 per cent were bothered by them.

Hot flashes are thought to be the response to some sort of thermoregulatory disruption in the brain, and are the body's way of resetting its thermostat. As the blood vessels expand, there is a surge of blood to the skin, together with sensations of heat and flushing and, sometimes, weakness or dizziness, palpitations, or skin prickliness. Although the peripheral (skin) temperature rises, the internal temperature drops as heat is eliminated via sweat. This is why the flashes are often followed by shivery chills.

Hot flashes vary enormously – ranging from transient sensations of warmth that are quite manageable, even pleasant, to overwhelming waves of heat and drenching sweats. At best disconcerting and at worst life-disrupting, very pronounced temperature changes are more common in women who have had their ovaries or womb surgically removed, and hence a more abrupt menopause, with intense attacks usually continuing for about six months after surgery.

Simple self-help measures can make life more tolerable. These include having fans and water sprays to hand, wearing layers of clothes so that you can swiftly subtract and add as the temperature changes take place, and applying cool compresses to the wrists, temples, and forehead (keep an ice bag handy so it can be filled with ice and applied at a moment's notice). Eliminating caffeine, alcohol, sugar, spicy foods, hot soups and drinks, and very large meals may also help. Some medicines may make the problem worse.

Britain's childbirth guru, Sheila Kitzinger, advises greeting hot flashes with one's breathing instead of resisting them or pretending that they are not happening. "It helps if you let the breathing flow right down into the pelvis," she counsels, "so that not only the abdomen, but also the pubis, moves slightly, rising up as you breathe in and descending a little as you give a long, slow breath out." It sounds poetic but a trial of the technique, known as controlled respiration, achieved a 40 per cent diminution of severity of flashes, according to a recent paper in the *American Journal of Obstetrics and Gynecology*.

While the use of sedatives and sleeping pills to calm the anxiety and make up for the disrupted nights is widespread, hormone replacement is much more effective and will completely abolish both flashes and sweats in nine out of ten women. Relief can be noticed in as little as a week, though it may take three months to get the full effect.

Also try: vitamin E, starting with 100 IUs and rising to a maximum of 400 IUs (check with your doctor first if you are diabetic or have high blood pressure); dong quai ("female ginseng," a Chinese herb containing plant com-

pounds with estrogen-like effects) or agnus castus (a homeopathic remedy) – since herbal remedies can be potent, be sure to keep within the recommended dose.

HYPERTENSION/HIGH BLOOD PRESSURE

The heart sends the blood through the arteries with considerable force in order to keep it moving around the body. The peak pressure on the heartbeat is known as the *systolic*, and the lowest pressure, reached when the heart relaxes between beats, the *diastolic*. These are expressed like a fraction – 120/80 being the classic "norm."

There is no absolute cut-off that divides normal blood pressure from a high one. The American Heart Association defines all systolic pressures over 140 as "abnormal," which would apply to well over 40 per cent of the U.S. population (58 million Americans), but actual hypertension is generally said to exist above pressures of 160 and 90 respectively. Blood pressure must be checked two-yearly, oftener if there is a family history of high blood pressure or heart disease, or if the person is diabetic. Unchecked, high blood pressure damages the artery wall, allowing atherosclerosis to take hold, increases the risk of heart attack, stroke, and kidney disease. If blood pressure rises too high, the blood vessels are in danger of bursting, particularly in the brain, leading to a cerebral hemorrhage (stroke).

Although raised pressure can sometimes provoke headaches, dizziness, and nosebleeds, there is often not the slightest sign that anything is amiss. Do-it-yourself home-testing kits can be unreliable – as indeed are one-off surgery measurements. Fat arms may give falsely high readings. If on the high side, blood pressure should always be checked again on a different day, since it can fluctuate widely. It also changes during the day, being highest in the morning and gradually falling later in the day and especially at night. Always make sure blood pressure is measured when you are sitting down after five minutes' rest and have taken no vigorous exercise within the last hour.

Women with a family history of hypertension should adopt certain preventive lifestyle measures, even if their own pressures are normal, and those with borderline high blood pressure should aim to lower it without drugs. Mildly raised pressures can often be brought down to near normal by stopping smoking, losing weight where appropriate, taking regular moderate exercise, and strictly limiting the amount of salt in the diet. About half of all hypertensives are sensitive to salt, which holds water and increases blood volume. Not adding salt when cooking or at the table and avoiding high-sodium, highly processed foods can produce lowering effects in as little as two months. There is some evidence that women respond especially positively to cutting down on salt. Eating more fresh fruit and vegetables and taking vitamin C (up to one gram a day) may also help avoid, or reduce, the need for medication.

Although the "tension" part of hypertension suggests the condition is stress-induced, the idea that people are responsible for their own blood pressures and can lower them by being more relaxed about life is largely mistaken, though helpful effects have been gained with biofeedback, yoga, and other forms of relaxation therapy.

Adopting a healthier lifestyle and so avoiding the need for medication is especially worthwhile for white women, for whom the value of treating high blood pressure remains controversial. Although the dangers of raised blood pressure apply every bit as much to women as to men, especially as regards their susceptibility to stroke, women may not benefit as much from having their pressures lowered by drugs. One review of the major trials so far, published in 1991 at the Bronx-Lebanon Hospital Center in the United States, came to the worrying conclusion that drugs that work for men, and for black women (who are more susceptible to the condition and get it at younger ages), may be ineffective or even harmful for white women. It pointed up the need for more research to establish which women should be treated and which should not and what the thresholds for starting treatment should be. Answers, unfortunately, are unlikely to be forthcoming for several years.

All drugs that are used to lower blood pressure have side-effects. Diuretics, which are often given first and to which women generally respond quite well, reduce the sodium load and hence blood volume, sparing the heart; the side-effects are fatigue, muscle weakness, leg cramps, and an increasing need to urinate. Beta-blockers lower the heart's demand for blood and slow the whole metabolism down; the side-effects include nausea, tiredness, dizziness on rising out of bed or change of posture, bad dreams, and tiredness. Vasodilators open up the blood vessels; with these, the side-effects are flushing and, sometimes, constipation.

If you have high blood pressure, inform exercise instructors and avoid prolonged contractions when working out, especially when using weights or weight-training equipment. A contracted limb steps up heart and breathing rate and raises blood pressure, a stress the healthy cardiovascular system can deal with but hypertensives should avoid.

I

INSOMNIA

Sleep-needs diminish dramatically with age – from 18 hours as a baby to six hours or less as an octogenarian. As the quantity drops, the quality changes too, with a shift away from the sledge-hammer slumber of youth to a lighter sleep, in which periods of wakefulness are punctuated with catnaps during the day as well as the night.

Older individuals drop off more readily and are more easily awakened because they get more of the shallow stage-one sleep and less of the deep stage-four sleep.

In stage-four sleep, the brain is just ticking over while the body is super-active – mobilizing its repair and renewal processes and pouring out growth hormone, recently much in the news for its supposed rejuvenating effects when given to a group of middle-aged men (see page 11). This deeper phase of sleep is thought to transform mood and energies, wiping the slate clean, so that individuals who drop into bed feeling spent and exhausted, wake refreshed. The shallower, dozing stages of sleep do not seem to be restorative. Individuals who do not get stage-four sleep, which can happen as a consequence of age or of taking certain sleeping tablets, can feel washed-out the next day.

Surveys show that almost half of all women over 60 complain of difficulty in falling or staying asleep. For such women, all that may be needed is to free themselves from the oppressive eight-hour rule and to stop interpreting being awake as a problem. Wakefulness can then stop being a torment and instead become a treasured opportunity to be up and about in a sleeping world.

To meet their excessive expectations, sleeping pills are still routinely prescribed for the over-60s, even though the extra "sleep" is unlikely to be worth very much (see page 120). They may just result in the individual feeling heavy and hung-over the following morning. Research carried out by the U.S. Institute of Medicine established that the benzodiazepines, which account for nine out of ten sleeping pill prescriptions, give no more than 30 or 40 more minutes' "sleep" a night. Unfortunately, older individuals, who tend to metabolize all drugs less efficiently, are particularly prone to their side-effects – namely daytime drowsiness and confusion, impaired memory, and a generally unpleasant "hangover effect."

Although the medical consensus now is that sleeping pills should be used only for acute insomnia over short periods (around two weeks), and even then not continuously but, say, on every third night, the vast majority are repeat prescriptions. Although these drugs are preferable to the old barbiturates, which were highly addictive, dependency problems arise when they are prescribed for extended periods. Withdrawal after long-term use can cause a range of frightening effects (see anxiety/agitation), along with a rebound insomnia that is often mistakenly interpreted as the old problem resurfacing, rather than a new one caused by taking the drugs out of the system too quickly. Physicians recommend a carefully staged withdrawal strategy, with phased reductions in dose; it generally takes as many months as the number of years patients have been taking the drugs, they say, to get sleep patterns back to normal.

Since the problems of sleeping pills are myriad, going *with* the changes age brings is better by far than submitting to the bottomless pit of the pharmacological route. Rests can be scheduled during the day and a shorter sleep at night simply accepted as the new norm. "Sleep hygiene" principles can also be useful. The cardinal rules are: not to go to bed until sleepy; to get up at a fixed time rather than extending sleep into the day; not to languish in bed awake, but to get up instead and distract the mind – reading a book, doing a jigsaw puzzle, writing letters – returning only when sleepy; to avoid alcohol, coffee, and big meals near bedtime; and to keep the bedroom reserved for sleep (and sex).

Insomnia may not just be a consequence of getting older; underlying physical or psychological disorders can interfere with sleep. Depression, for example, typically causes early wakening and feelings of not having had sufficient sleep. Sudden losses of weight can also disrupt sleep patterns: in one research study of 375 psychiatric outpatients, those who had lost more than 10 pounds (4.5 kilograms) were found to have dislocated sleep patterns, while those who had gained weight actually slept more than normal.

IRRITABLE BOWEL SYNDROME

. . . really exists! And one in three people suffers it at some time in their lives. Also known as "mucus colitis" and "spastic colon," this all-too-real disorder is often dismissed as "psychological," with sufferers said to be more neurotic, tense, obsessive, anxious, and depressed than the general population. This is hardly surprising when they are having to put up with intractable constipation and/or explosive diarrhea, bleeding, uncomfortable bloating, and embarrassing rumblings – and finding so little in the way of medical help. The good news is that IBS usually resolves on its own over time; one survey revealed that up to seven out of ten sufferers are free of symptoms five years after first consulting a doctor.

Food intolerance is thought to blame for about two-thirds of irritable bowel cases, especially where diarrhea is involved. Milk in particular may cause abdominal pain, flatulence, and diarrhea in people who are intolerant (not the same as allergic) to lactose, due to reduced concentration of the lactose enzyme in the gut. This can be overcome by using a commercial preparation whenever dairy foods are taken.

Certainly, an elimination diet is a sensible self-help measure for any IBS sufferer. Cut out all the following food groups from your diet for a two-week period, and see whether symptoms improve, before "challenging" the system by re-introducing them, one group at a time, leaving a clear week between each. Omit wheat, dairy products, citrus fruits, coffee, tea, cola drinks, eggs, chocolate, and onions. If there is no change, follow with brassica-type vegetables (such as cabbage and turnips), potatoes, peanuts, bananas, and corn. If you are intolerant of any of these foods, lack of them may initially lead you to feel worse before any change for the better sets in.

Perhaps the mose widely used treatment for IBS is the use of fiber to increase the bulk of the stool. While some studies show it to be no better than a placebo, it does help relieve the problem for some patients.

A change of bowel habit, particularly with bleeding, should always be thoroughly investigated to rule out the possibility of colorectal cancer or a benign polyp (growth) in the bowel wall, which is how nine out of ten of these tumors are thought to start. Never accept a diagnosis of "irritable bowel syndrome" until these checks have been carried out.

Also try: oil of peppermint capsules; oil of evening primrose (especially where IBS is related to the menstrual cycle); hypnotherapy; homeopathy.

ITCHINESS

Skin gets drier and itchier with age. A problem that can become acute in cold weather, and that afflicts at least half of all older women, it is caused by extreme dryness and cracking of the top, dead layer of the skin, known as the stratum corneum. Since hot water cleanses by stripping oils from the skin, a long hot soak in the bath every day becomes a luxury in later life that many women can ill afford.

The first solution is simply to wash less often and more speedily in cooler water (just a few degrees up from tepid) and save the soap for those areas that really need cleaning – the feet, hands, underarms, genitals. Avoid bath additives, whatever they promise, with the exception of colloidal oatmeal, which does appear to soothe irritated and itching skin.

Moisturizers are very helpful. Experiment with a range of emollient creams (ask your doctor/dermatologist for suggestions), using them on different parts of the body to determine which is most effective, and continue on a daily basis with the one that suits you best. A humidifier may also help by keeping sufficient water in the air to prevent your own escaping from the skin.

L

LIVER SPOTS

Also known as lentigines or "senile freckles," these freckle-like blotches appear on the skin from midlife as a direct result of too much sun. They appear only on exposed skin (most commonly hands, forearms, and face) and are caused by ultraviolet light overstimulating pigment cells in the epidermis which then clump together to produce irregular blotches of dark. The development of further spots can be prevented by using a high-SPF sunscreen on hands and face at all times. Existing spots can be gently frozen with liquid nitrogen to produce a peeling of the surface, or removed by certain lazers. Bleaching products containing hydroquinone (more effective when combined with an alpha hydroxy acid) or the use of retinoic acid may lighten liver spots and so make them less obvious, but results are often disappointing; they can, however, be improved by using both approaches together.

M

MACULAR DEGENERATION

The commonest reason for vision loss in later life in the Western world, macular degeneration is caused by the accumulation of debris within the macula, the key focusing area of the retina. Its causes still mystify, but it appears to be commoner in those with light-colored eyes. Vision is usually not lost entirely, peripheral sight being retained, but the area of sharpest vision gradually distorts and blurs to a point where detail is hard to distinguish and reading becomes difficult. Sufferers with advanced disease often find it hard to recognize faces, even when very close to them, or to read print. It accounts for much of the skepticism about elderly people's eyesight – that "they just see what they want to see," such as failing to recognize someone yet spotting a coin in the corner of the room. In fact MD can severely affect quality of life, compromising the ability to read, drive, and watch television, though sufferers rarely forfeit their independence entirely. It can be diagnosed by a sight test. Macular degeneration cannot be cured, but the process can occasionally be slowed by lazer therapy when the condition is picked up early. Although MD cannot be corrected by fitting a lens to the eyes, low-vision aids such as large print books, magnifying spectacles, and other devices can be very helpful.

MENORRHAGIA (HEAVY MENSTRUAL BLEEDING)

In the years leading up to the menopause many women find their periods become longer, heavier, and more erratic: torrential bleeding, or "flooding," often with blood clots, can really be a "curse," requiring a change of tampon or pad every few minutes. In addition, there is a real risk of anemia (qv), which can be debilitating. After a few years of embarrassing overflows, some women, heartily fed up with the whole thing, beg for a hysterectomy. Although many of these operations are still performed for this reason, there are now a number of equally effective and less radical alternatives.

Proper investigation is essential. Even though in at least half of cases nothing abnormal will be found, menorrhagia can be a complication of endometriosis, fibroid tumors, an underactive thyroid gland, and, very occasionally, endometrial hyperplasia or cancer. Sometimes, it may be a side-effect of injectable contraceptives, such as Depo–Provera, and other progestin-only forms of contraception. A blood test for anemia, a pelvic examination, a

Pap smear and biopsy are usually necessary to rule out anything sinister. Although D & Cs ("womb scrapes") are commonly performed, any improvement is usually only temporary and periods soon become heavy again.

A number of drug therapies, some of which, like mefenamic acid, need to be taken only during menstruation, dramatically reduce blood loss in about half of all women. Progestins on their own, while commonly prescribed, do not appear as effective as danazol, a synthetic hormone similar to the male hormone testosterone. When taken continuously, this blocks and actually lowers natural hormone levels in the body, cuts down radically on the degree of blood lost, and can even prevent periods entirely, but it often has unpleasant side-effects, such as bloating, acne, hot flashes, increased facial hair, and voice changes, the last of which can be irreversible. The Pill is another option that is often very effective. The new levonorgestrel-releasing IUD has been found greatly to reduce blood loss and duration of bleeding in most women after three months of use, but it is not yet available in the United States.

If the bleeding does not respond to medical treatment, a relatively new technique, known as endometrial ablation, can often help by shaving away the cells of the womb lining with an electrically charged wire loop. A lazer can be used to exactly the same effect. Since 99 per cent of the cells of the lining of the womb are obliterated, periods become much lighter and usually stop altogether. In one survey of the procedure, less than one in six patients asked for any pain relief afterward, most were up and about within a few days, and 64 per cent had a complete cessation of periods. Although both methods generally lead to infertility, and should only be contemplated if no (further) children are desired, effective contraception continues to be a must, as conception is still possible and there may be a small increased risk of ectopic pregnancy. An experienced operator is also essential, however, since the procedure carries a small risk of severe, even life-threatening, complications.

Also try: evening primrose oil; acupuncture (several sessions); homeopathy.

MIGRAINE

These excruciating, throbbing headaches affect twice as many women as men, with some 17 per cent said to suffer them. Frequently linked to fluctuating estrogen levels, migraines are often at their worst in early midlife (30 to 45) and can be provoked by birth control pills, pregnancy, the menopause, and hormone replacement therapy. Often accompanied by nausea and vomiting, as well as numbness and visual disturbances such as flashing lights, the headaches are triggered by a wide range of stimuli. These include bright lights, especially sunlight; lack of sleep; stress and hunger; certain odors, such as tobacco, paint, and perfume; dental problems; loud noises; foods like cheese, yogurt, bananas, alcohol (especially red wine), chocolate, caffeine, and anything containing monosodium glutamate (MSG) or nitrates.

Although a measure of control can be gained by avoiding these triggers, it is difficult to eliminate the headaches without medical help. Most treatment still centers around drugs made with ergotamine, which constricts blood vessels. Unfortunately, they can cause nausea, vomiting, and, ironically, withdrawal headaches, as well as having other potentially dangerous side-effects. Preventive medicines such as beta-blockers can help many sufferers. But side-effects are still a concern as the medication may need to be taken continuously. Regular low-dose aspirin may also help. A 20 per cent reduction in migraine has been noted among men taking the drug every other day, and trials are now underway to test the effect on women, though results are not due in till the close of the decade.

A self-administered injection, imigran/sumatriptan, spells new hope for migraine sufferers. A pre-filled syringe is placed against the thigh at the first signs of an attack and a button pressed to release the drug under the skin. The drug, which binds to specific sites in the brain, causes dilated blood vessels to constrict, aborting an imminent migraine attack. Trials have shown that, an hour after injection, the pain lightens considerably in nearly three-quarters of those who use it and disappears in half. Side-effects of the drug include tingling and flushing but no nausea.

Also try: the herbal remedy feverfew.

OSTEOARTHRITIS

While rheumatoid arthritis can strike at any age, osteoarthritis is caused by degenerative changes in the joints, gets commoner with age, and is present to some degree in half of most elderly Westernized populations. Osteoarthritis is a result of mechanical wearing down of the joints. The classical signs of OA are persistent pain and stiffness in the hands, neck, knees, spine, hips, and ankles.

While usually not crippling, OA can render movement difficult. Light exercise, though often avoided because of the discomfort, is essential to break the vicious circle of pain, muscular inactivity, muscular degeneration, joint instability, and worsening of the arthritis. Non-weight-bearing exercises such as swimming and cycling are ideal, but twisting movements on weight-bearing joints, such as squash, will only worsen the condition. Osteoarthritis can follow previous damage to, or overuse of, the joints, and is a common complication of obesity, which loads the joints with more weight than they can stand.

Symptoms can often be relieved with painkillers, anti-inflammatory drugs, and heat treatment. Non-surgical treatment includes weight reduction (if necessary), physi-

cal therapy, and activity modification. In extreme cases, surgery, in the form of new replacement joints, can turn a housebound cripple into a fully active person once more and is an example of the life-enhancing impact of modern medical techniques. Trials of alternative dietary approaches, on the other hand, such as taking fish oils or oil of evening primrose have proved disappointing.

Also try: acupuncture.

PREMENSTRUAL SYNDROME (PMS)

One advantage of the menopause is that, as periods stop and hormonal fluctuations level out, PMS sufferers can look forward to a relief from their trials. They may have to endure a crescendo of malaise, irritability, and headaches for the five or six years before it, however, since this is often when hormone levels are at their most erratic.

About 150 different symptoms have been associated with PMS, from breast tenderness to bloating, irritation, and suicidal thoughts. The time-honored theory is that it is caused by imbalance in the estrogen and progesterone levels in the run-up to the period. Progesterone and synthetic progestins are still commonly prescribed although they are generally considered ineffective.

An increasing number of gynecologists, believing that PMS is caused by hypersensitivity to the hormonal processes of ovulation rather than menstruation itself, are prescribing hormones which prevent ovulation, such as the Pill. Severe PMS-linked depression can be lifted by specific anti-depressants that enhance the action of the neurotransmitter serotonin.

Alternative dietary strategies involve avoiding foods to which one may be intolerant (see page 369) and following a regular eating schedule. Eating small carbohydrate snacks (wholewheat crackers, a baked potato, half a slice of bread or toast) at regular intervals throughout the day, and never letting more than three hours elapse between meals, except, of course, when asleep, is helpful for some women.

If consulting a doctor, take a symptom chart with you. Simply make out a calendar for three menstrual cycles and use letters to denote the specific problems you suffer: SB for sore breasts, BT for breast tenderness, BL for bloating, H for headaches, I for irritability, etc. At the end of the day mark up any symptoms you had and award each a severity score (between 1 and 5, with 1 being mild and 5 intolerable). Shade in days when menstruation takes place.

Also try: oil of evening primrose (six capsules a day for six months), 100 mg of vitamin B6 (pyridoxine) throughout the cycle, calcium with vitamin D, a strong magnesium-based multivitamin and mineral supplement, vitamin C; cutting out tea, coffee, saturated fat, sugar, and chocolate.

PROLAPSE

Also called a "dropped womb," a prolapse occurs when the supporting sling of muscles and ligaments which holds the womb and other pelvic organs in position gives way. As the uterus and cervix sag, they may press on other pelvic organs, usually the bladder or the rectum, which may then bulge into the vagina. There is often a sensation of something "coming down." Prolapse can cause backache, a sensation of wanting to urinate all the time, difficulty in controlling the bladder and occasionally the bowel, and discomfort during intercourse.

Prolapse can be caused by childbirth, particularly if labor was prolonged, and by excessive strain, especially lifting and particularly when pregnant. A chronic cough and chronic constipation can also provoke it. It is more common after the menopause, when the female hormones responsible for maintaining uterine tone drop. Kegel exercises done daily (see page 182) are a woman's best prevention, since they prevent the muscles from becoming lax. Good tone is also of great value before and after surgery. A repair operation, performed through the vagina, can reposition the uterus, tighten the muscles, and return the other organs to their proper places. If only the womb has dropped, and everything else is unaffected, a plastic ring pessary can be pushed up into the vagina to hold it in place.

PSORIASIS

A common skin condition, psoriasis is characterized by crusty patches of skin and caused by some still-unidentified factor accelerating the rate of cell turnover in the skin – so that the 28 days it normally takes one skin cell to pass from the basal layer to the surface, where it sloughs off, dives to a mere seven. It is neither infectious nor malignant, but it cannot be cured – just managed or controlled, so that the condition becomes tolerable. Sometimes just a few parts of the body are affected – most commonly the elbows, knees, and scalp, where it may be mistaken for dandruff or eczema. Rarely, outbreaks can be extensive, seeming to cover the whole body. At best psoriasis is an irritation; at worst profoundly distressing, embarrassing and disfiguring.

Surveys reveal widespread dissatisfaction with current treatments. Those involving tar (best on small numerous patches) or anthralin (best on larger patches) are effective but messy – the messier, in fact, the better. Recently, a more cosmetically acceptable vitamin D-derived cream, calcipotriol, which is colorless and odorless, does not stain, and appears to delay the proliferation of cells. In trials noticeable improvements were seen in nine out of ten patients after six weeks' use. Since skin irritation can be a common side-effect, however, it is not suitable for the face. More powerful drugs can be used to treat very severe psoriasis but they all have side-effects.

Sunlight can help psoriasis heal: certain wavelengths of ultraviolet and certain parts of the world – most notably, the Dead Sea in Israel – are linked with complete clearance of patches and long remissions. Light therapy can be effective in the UVB range, or with UVA and psoralens (plant derivatives that make the skin more receptive to sun), but it must be carefully controlled. Unsupervised sessions on sunbeds are not advised.

In general, use emollients such as aqueous creams instead of soap, which tends to dry the patches out, aggravating any itchiness, and avoid alcohol.

Also try: Chinese herbs, acupuncture.

S

SENSITIVE TEETH

Teeth become sensitive when the outer enamel wears away or the gums recede, uncovering the sensitive gum/tooth margin. Both expose the inner layer of dentin to daylight. Since this layer has millions of tiny tubules that lead directly to the nerve, hot, cold, sweet, or acidic foods and drinks and even air can trigger pain as they hit it.

Women are more likely to suffer from sensitive teeth than men, and the problem is very common in midlife. There are several effective treatment options, all of which work by blocking the tubules and preventing the transmission of external stimulants to the nerve. Regular use of a toothpaste containing strontium acetate, strontium chloride or potassium salts or daily rinsing with fluoride mouthwashes can help seal the holes. A more effective option is to ask your dentist to paint a dentin bond over the offending teeth. Use of a certain type of lazer, known as a yag, may also turn out to be effective in smudging over these microscopic holes. As sensitive teeth are so often caused by a wrong (usually over-vigorous) brushing technique, see page 74 for details of the correct method, and ask your dentist or dental hygienist for guidance.

SWOLLEN ANKLES

As youth fades, the ankles tend to swell by the end of the day. A little swelling is normal but if the ankles are visibly puffy and the skin tight and shiny, the metabolic balance of the body may be out of kilter and a doctor should be consulted since it can, very occasionally, signal liver, kidney, or even heart malfunction. Where ankles return to size after a night's sleep or a few hours with the feet up, the problem is likely to be due to raised pressure in the veins of the legs, which pushes fluid out of the capillaries into the tissues, which then become waterlogged. Although aggravated by standing, the swelling can be relieved by brisk walking since the contractions of the leg muscles squeeze the veins and get the blood flow working against gravity and back up to the heart. This swelling, known as edema, may affect other areas of the body too.

T

TELANGIECTASIA (SPIDER VEINS)

These small dilated capillaries on the face, thighs, and lower legs are not, as is generally thought, usually caused by "broken" blood vessels, but by a loss of elasticity in the capillary wall which causes them to stay dilated, and hence visible. They are genetically influenced, but in the legs they are invariably made worse by pregnancy, substantial overweight, and prolonged sitting or standing. They can be treated by sclerosing injections which provoke an inflammatory reaction that seals off the capillary. (Larger capillaries generally respond better than smaller ones.) Each vein may require several injections, spaced two to three weeks apart, so patience is required. Veins often appear more prominent for several weeks afterward, but most will disappear with adequate treatment. A competent operator is essential. The most common side-effect of sclerotherapy is hyperpigmentation, a darker spot of pigmentation, which may resolve or may be permanent.

A recently developed form of treatment is low-powered lazer therapy: a hand-held device, aimed directly at the vessels, emits a millisecond pulse that vaporizes them in a couple of sessions, with no more than a mild pinprick sensation and a transitory crusting following treatment. But a skilled operator is essential, since scarring is a risk. Unfortunately, this technique is not yet widely available.

THYROID PROBLEMS

Ten times commoner in women than in men, thyroid disorders are surprisingly prevalent and are notorious for striking women in midlife out of the blue. Thyroid hormone is vital for all bodily processes, from weight regulation and heart function to maintaining fluid balance, immunity, and mental composure. The main symptom of an underactive thyroid gland (also called myxoedema or hypothyroidism) is a slowing-down of the entire system, which manifests itself in lethargy, listlessness, unusual sensitivity to cold, constipation, and weight gain – all of which may creep up so insidiously that the underlying biochemical disorder goes unsuspected or is mistaken for depression.

Hypothyroidism becomes commoner with age, but there is no specific connection with the menopause. Any woman who is feeling excessively weak, miserable, and lethargic should not allow herself to be turned away from a consultation with a "menopausal" label without first raising the question of thyroid function and seeing that she gets tested for possible thyroid deficiency. After the age of 60, when thyroid problems may afflict as many as one in ten women, sometimes with no obvious symptoms, regular blood checks may be warranted.

Although delays of months, sometimes even years, are common before the correct diagnosis is made, therapy is important, since continual undersupply of thyroid hormone can affect blood fats and increase the risk of heart disease. After just a few weeks on additional hormone, thyroxine, sufferers begin to feel revitalized. Usually therapy has to be continued for life, but it is important to have regular checks to assess circulating levels of thyroid hormone and not to take more of the medication than necessary since over-high doses accelerate bone breakdown and have been linked with osteoporosis. (Researchers at Cornell University Medical College, New York, found some women taking ten times the necessary amount because they liked the zippy effects of the hormone so much.)

Hyperthyroidism (also called thyrotoxicosis and Graves's disease) is caused by excessive thyroid hormone and is sometimes accompanied by prominent eyes and/or a swelling, or goiter, in the throat. Other signs include sensations of speediness, racing heartbeat, intense heat as though one is burning up inside, wild, rushed thoughts and driving anxieties, and losing weight despite eating a lot. Treatment is more problematic than for its metabolic opposite. It involves either giving radioactive iodine to kill off overactive tissue, surgery to remove part of the thyroid gland itself, or taking medication (propylthiouracil methimazole) which rapidly controls the condition in most cases. Recovery may be far from smooth, however, and sufferers may yo-yo between hypothyroidism and its opposite until some stability is achieved.

V

VAGINAL DRYNESS

A common problem throughout life when sexual arousal is insufficient, vaginal dryness is exacerbated by hormonal changes at menopause. With decreasing levels of estrogen – the hormone responsible for maintaining vaginal tone and lubrication – the vagina becomes thinner, shorter, drier, and more prone to infection. This makes sex more uncomfortable if not outrightly painful – though it may not be a problem for all women and may not start for years after the menopause.

Over-the-counter lubricants can supply the slipperiness that menopausal women are often without until arousal takes hold and a woman's own natural lubrication takes over. Most are used at the time of love-making, and with confidence and a little imagination can become an integral and pleasurable part of sex. Always buy a lubricant formulated specifically for the purpose. Oil-based lubricants, such as baby-oil, Vaseline, cooking oils, and massage oils, can be irritating and can also cause condoms to degrade with potentially disastrous results. If deep thrusting is causing discomfort, a specifically formulated lubricant applied to the penis as well, or inserted high into the vagina with the plunger-type applicator provided with spermicidal jellies can often give relief. Alternatively, use vaginal lubricating suppositories, giving them a few minutes to melt before penetration begins; or try one of the newer formulations, such as Replens, that work on a slow-release principle and lend lubrication to the vagina for days at a time.

If the problem persists or a more permanent solution is required, a low-dose estrogen cream will plump up the vaginal walls, making them stronger and more infection-resistant, and increase sexual responsiveness. Happily, women suffering quite pronounced problems years after the menopause can be helped substantially by estrogen creams or (a new advance) a hormonal ring, as the body never loses its capacity to respond to the hormone. Some good knock-on effects may be gained on the bladder muscle too, maintaining holding capacity. Use of an estrogen cream does not have to be a lifelong strategy, however, nor very often does it have to be applied in the amounts recommended by the manufacturer, since as little as one-eighth of the official dose may be effective. Most gynecologists now recommend daily application for the first couple of weeks to reverse the vaginal atrophy (more if the problem is a longstanding one) and then a maintenance twice-weekly dose. Since estrogen is a powerful medication that is swiftly absorbed through the skin, it should never be applied like a lubricant just before love-making, as the man's penis can absorb it; cases of abnormal breast enlargement have been reported in the male partners of women who use vaginal creams.

After the menopause, the vagina also tends to become more susceptible to infection. If this is a problem, twice-weekly use of an over-the-counter preparation, acetic acid jelly, can render the vagina less alkaline and so bolster its natural resistance to infection. Estrogen replacement therapy will cause a similar beneficial change in vaginal pH.

VARICOSE VEINS

Varicose veins are very common in mid and later life, and getting commoner, due it's thought to an unrefined diet, overweight, and, especially, an inactive lifestyle. Pregnancy, in particular, predisposes to them as a result of hormonal changes that cause the vein walls to relax and dilate, as well as the hugely increased blood volume and the pressure of the enlarging uterus on the blood vessels going to and from the legs.

The blood supply to the legs has to be considerable in order to meet the demands of the muscles. It also has to work against gravity when returning to the heart through the veins. The normal action of breathing, plus the pumping action of the muscles, provides the stimulus to get it there via deep veins buried in the muscles of the legs. Smaller, "perforating" veins link this system up with the superficial veins you see under the skin. The perforating veins contain one-way valves to prevent backflow.

Varicose veins start when the valves fail and the blood pools. As the pressure rises due to the obstruction, the veins dilate and lengthen and then twist and become knotted. When valves are severely damaged they may lead to leg ulcers. These open sores can be very painful and may take months to heal.

Most common on the insides of the legs and the backs of the calves, varicose veins are disfiguring. They also cause throbbing, "heavy" legs, and swollen ankles – sensations that are aggravated by standing, and relieved by walking, which gets the blood flowing back to the heart again. Pressure rises quickly once activity stops, however, and the aching returns. Medical-grade support stockings can prevent the condition from getting worse but will not reverse it. Keeping weight down and avoiding constipation also helps.

Varicose veins can be treated by a sclerosing injection, which causes an inflammatory reaction that, hopefully, seals them off for good, although after a couple of years the veins may reopen under the pressure of blood. The recurrence rate after ten years is as high as 90 per cent.

Surgery via tiny stab incisions is more likely to give a permanent result. These veins are literally stripped out, in part or in their entirety, without affecting the circulation because the blood will always find other routes through which to return to the deep veins. The technique sounds savage but, in fact, even the worst cases require no more than 24 hours in hospital and dressing with pressure bandages for a week. Walking after the first 24 to 48 hours is usually strongly advised to get the circulation moving again. Complications include lasting discoloration where bruising does not entirely resolve, some temporary numbness and tingling, and, occasionally, the appearance of spider, or thread, veins (see telangiectasia), which are more likely if you already suffer from these. Although the vein, once removed, cannot cause any further trouble, the tendency to develop them remains, and further veins are therefore likely to appear in time.

Also try: a homeopathic substance, Poikiven, which has been found in trials to improve aching and ulceration and even to slow the progress of the condition.

Y

YEAST INFECTIONS

Few women escape without one vaginal yeast infection in their lives, and many suffer persistent infection or recurring attacks. Symptoms range from mild to maddening and include itching, soreness, redness, and, characteristically, a white, cheesy, usually inoffensive-smelling discharge. Yeast infections can make sex uncomfortable and can cause pain on passing urine. They are caused by the overgrowth of a fungus, candida albicans, which is always present in the vagina, intestines, and mouth. Normally kept in check by the body's immune system, it can become rampant after broad-spectrum antibiotic therapy (which kills off the restraining good bacteria, allowing thrush to get a hold) and in pregnancy (which also changes the bacterial balance of the vagina). Recurrent infections can occasionally be a sign of undetected diabetes. If more than two attacks occur within six months, and there is no obvious reason such as pregnancy, this possibility should always be checked out.

Some women find their attacks are commoner before a period or in hot, humid conditions. A tendency to yeast infections can be aggravated by tight pants and nylon underwear (which prevent air from circulating, keeping the vagina hot and humid), the use of bubble baths (which can change the pH balance of the vagina) and perfumed soaps, and frequent sex with the use of the spermicide nonoxynol-9.

The only effective treatment is antifungal therapy in the form of tablets, cream, or pessaries, which are inserted high into the vagina. A single-dose cream is now available without prescription. Relief is usually swift and the infection clears within days. Time-honored approaches such as eating quantities of yogurt or putting a clove of garlic into the vagina (which smells revolting) soothe at best and have no impact at worst; douching with vinegar, as sometimes advised, may intensify the irritation.

Also try: superdolphus.

OVERLEAF: Many disorders of midlife and later respond well to a range of approaches – alternative as well as mainstream.

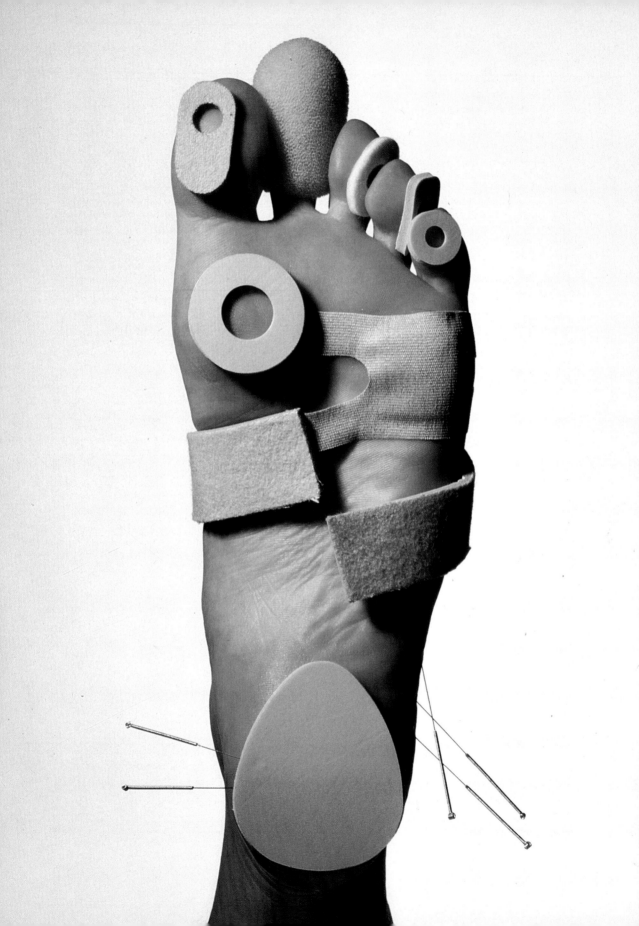

NOTES

VISIBLES

SKIN
1 (p 33) J S Weiss and others, "Topical tretinoin improves photoaged skin: a double-blind vehicle-controlled study," *Journal of the American Medical Association* (JAMA), 21 (1988), 638-44.
2 (p 33) J Bhawan and others, "Effects of tretinoin on photodamaged skin: a histological study," *U.S. Archives of Dermatology*, 127 (1991), 666-72.
3 (p 34) S J Jick and others, "First trimester use of topical tretinoin and congenital disorders," *The Lancet*, 341 (1993), 1181-2.
4 (p 38) Hugo Vickers, *Gladys, Duchess of Marlborough* (London, Weidenfeld and Nicolson, 1979).
5 (p 39) Daly, 1979, cited in Sara Arber and Jay Ginn, *Gender and Later Life: a sociological analysis of resources and constraints*, (London, Sage, 1991).
6 (p 41) Saville Jackson, "Submitting to the scalpel," British *Vogue*, March 1992.

HAIR
1 (p 62) S H Zahm and others, "Use of hair colouring products and the risk of lymphoma, multiple myeloma and chronic lymphocytic leukemia," *American Journal of Public Health*, 82 (1992), 990-997.
2 (p 62) Judy Sadgrove, "Shades of grey," British *Vogue*, June 1993.

SHAPE
1 (p 92) R R Wing and others, "Weight gain at the time of menopause," *Archives of Intern Medicine*, 151 (1991), 97-102.

STYLE
1 (p 110) Simone de Beauvoir, *The Second Sex* (New York, Vintage Books, 1952).

PHYSICALS

BRAIN
1 (p 121) Elizabeth Taylor, *Mrs Palfrey at the Claremont* (London, Chatto & Windus, 1971).

SENSES
1 (p 127) A A McKechnie and others, "Anxiety states: a preliminary report on the value of connective tissue massage," *Journal of Psychosomatic Research*, 27 (1983), 125-9.
2 (p 127) Catherine Bennett. "Professional touch: in search of a good massage," British *Vogue*, June 1987.

BREASTS
1 (p 132) S J London and others, "A prospective study of benign breast disease and risk of breast cancer," *Journal of the American Medical Association* (JAMA), 267 (1992), 941-4.
2 (p 132) Quoted in Alisa Solomon, "The politics of breast cancer," *Voice*, May 14, 1991.
3 (p 133) W Willett and others, "Fat and fiber in relation to the risk of breast cancer. An 8-year follow up," *Journal of the American Medical Association* (JAMA), 268 (1992), 2037-2044.
4 (p 135) M Le Geyte and others, "Breast self examination and survival from cancer," *British Journal of Cancer*, 66 (1993), 917-18.
5 (p 137) A Stacey-Clear and others, "Breast cancer survival among women under age 50: is mammography detrimental?" *The Lancet*, 340 (1992), 991-4.
6 (p 138) A B Miller and others, "Canadian National Breast Screening Study: 1. Breast cancer detection and death rates among women aged 40 to 49 years," *Canadian Medical Association Journal*, 147 (1992), 1459-76.
7 (p 138) Nyström and others, "Breast cancer screening with mammography: overview of Swedish randomised trials," *The Lancet*, 341 (1993), 973-978.

HEART
1 (p 143) S Haynes and M Feinleib, "Women, work and coronary heart disease: prospective findings from the Framingham heart study," *American Journal of Public Health*, 73 (1980), 113-41.
2 (p 145) S B Hulley, "Health policy on blood cholesterol: time to change direction," *Circulation*, 86 (1992), 1026-9.
3 (p 147) K Anastos and others, "Hypertension in women: what is really known?" *Annals of Intern Medicine*, 115 (1991), 281-293.
4 (p 149) K F Gey and others, "Inverse correlation between vitamin E and mortality

from ischaemic heart disease and cross cultural epidemiology," *American Journal of Clinical Nutrition*, 53 supplement 1 (1991), 326-45.
5 (p 149) M J Stampfer and others, "Vitamin E consumption and the risk of coronary disease in women," *The New England Journal of Medicine*, 328 (1993), 1444-9.
6 (p 150) M J Stampfer and others, "Postmenopausal estrogen therapy and coronary heart disease: ten-year follow-up from the nurses' health study," *The New England Journal of Medicine*, 325 (1991), 756-62.
7 (p 151) S N Blair and others, "Physical fitness and all-cause mortality – a prospective study of healthy men and women," *Journal of the American Medical Association* (JAMA), 262 (1989), 2395-2401.
8 (p 152) Anti-Platelet Trialists Collaboration, "Collaborative overview of randomised trials of anti-platelet treatment," *British Medical Journal*, January 8, 1994.

MUSCLES AND JOINTS
1 (p 155) Susan Sontag, "The double standard of aging," *Saturday Review*, September 23, 1972.
2 (p 155) "Physical activity and aging," *American Academy of Physical Education Papers* (Champaign, Human Kinetics Publishers), 22 (1989).
3 (p 156) B Vellas and others, "Malnutrition and falls," letter to *The Lancet*, 336 (1990), 1447.
4 (p 158) Gloria Steinem, *Revolution from Within* (New York, Little Brown, 1992).
5 (p 158) Elizabeth Taylor, *Mrs Palfrey at the Claremont* (London, Chatto & Windus, 1971).

BONES
1 (p 163) M Law and others, "Strategies for prevention of osteoporosis and hip fracture," *British Medical Journal*, 303 (1991), 453-9.
2 (p 164) R L Prince and others, "Prevention of postmenopausal osteoporosis – a comparative study of exercise, calcium supplementation and hormone replacement therapy," *The New England Journal of Medicine*, 325 (1991), 1189-95.
3 (p 166) B Dawson-Hughes and others, "A controlled trial of the effect of calcium supplementation on bone density in postmenopausal women," *New England Journal of Medicine*, 323 (1990), 878-84.
4 (p 166) T L Holbrook and E Barrett-Connor, "A prospective study of alcohol consumption and bone mineral density," *British Medical Journal*, 306 (1993), 1506-9.
5 (p 170) Mary Roach, "Inner strength," American *Vogue*, May 1991.

GUT
1 (p 173) Judy Sadgrove, "Gut reactions," British *Vogue*, September 1992.
2 (p 175) J V Selby and others, "A case controlled study of screening sigmoidoscopy and mortality from colorectal cancer," *The New England Journal of Medicine*, 326 (1992), 653-7.
3 (p 175) J S Mandel and others, "Reducing mortality from colorectal cancer by screening for fecal occult blood," *The New England Journal of Medicine*, 328 (1993), 1365-71.

BLADDER
1 (p 178) T M Thomas and others, "Prevalence of urinary incontinence," *British Medical Journal*, 281 (1980), 1243-5.
2 (p 178) Quoted in Pauline Chiarella, *Women's Waterworks – curing incontinence* (Gore & Osment, for the Disabled Living Foundation, 1991).
3 (p 183) J A Fantl and others, "Efficacy of bladder training in older women with urinary incontinence," *Journal of the American Medical Association* (JAMA), 265 (1991), 609-613.

REPRODUCTIVE TRACT
1 (p 185) Johanna Roeber, "The Forever Therapy," British *Vogue*, June 1990.
2 (p 187) W Willemsen and others, "Ovarian stimulation and granulosa-cell tumour," *The Lancet*, 341 (1993), 986-988.

PRACTICALS

INTRODUCTION
1 (p 194) S N Blair and others, "Physical fitness and all-cause mortality – a prospective study of healthy men and women," *Journal of the American Medical Association* (JAMA), 262 (1989), 2395-2401.

MOVING
1 (p 201) Bernard van Oven, 1853, quoted in Peter Laslett, *A Fresh Map of Life* (Cambridge, Massachusetts, Harvard University Press, 1991).

2 (p 205) Charles Darwin, *The Origin of Species by Means of Natural Selection* (London, John Murray, 1859).
3 (p 207) L Clarkson-Smith, "Relationship between physical exercise and cognitive abilities in older adults," *Psychology and Aging*, 1989.
4 (p 208) R S Pfaffenbarger and others, "Physical activity, all-cause mortality and longevity of college alumni," *The New England Journal of Medicine*, 64 (1986), 541-6.
5 (p 209) A E Hardman and others, "Brisk walking and plasma high density lipoprotein cholesterol concentration in previously sedentary women," *British Medical Journal*, 299 (1989), 1204-5.
6 (p 212) *The Times*, September 15, 1991.
7 (p 212) M A Fiatarone and others, "High intensity strength training in nonagenarians: effect on skeletal muscle," *Journal of the American Medical Association* (JAMA), 263 (1990), 3029-34.
8 (p 213) Professor Paul Thompson, quoted in Christopher Connolly and Hetty Einzig, *The Fitness Jungle* (London, Century Hutchinson, 1986).

TAKING TIME OUT
1 (p 223) Nan Talese, "Spa break," American *Vogue*, June 1982.

EATING
1 (p 233) G Block and others, "Nutrient sources in the American diet: quantitative data from the NHANES II survey I, vitamins and minerals," *American Journal of Epidemiology*, 122 (1985), 27-40.
2 (p 239) P M Horvath and others, "Synergistic effect of vitamin E and selenium in the chemoprevention of mammary carcinogenesis in rats," *Cancer Research*, 43 (1983), 5335-41.
3 (p 240) P Knekt, "Serum vitamin E level and risk of female cancers," *International Journal of Epidemiology*, 17 (1988), 281-8.
4 (p 240) M J Stampfer and others, "Vitamin E consumption and the risk of coronary disease in women," *The New England Journal of Medicine*, 328 (1993), 1444-9.
5 (p 242) K F Gey and others, "Inverse correlation between vitamin E and mortality from ischaemic heart disease and cross cultural epidemiology," *American Journal of Clinical Nutrition*, 53 supplement I (1991), 326-45.
6 (p 243) W C Willett and others, "Relation of serum vitamins A and E and carotenoids to the risk of cancer," *The New England Journal of Medicine*, 310 (1984), 430-4.

DRINKING
1 (p 250) Editorial published in connection with C Renaud and M de Lorgeril, "Wine, alcohol, platelets and the French paradox for coronary heart disease," *The Lancet*, 339 (1992), 1523-5.
2 (p 251) C Renaud and M de Lorgeril, "Wine, alcohol, platelets and the French paradox for coronary heart disease," *The Lancet*, 339 (1992), 1523-5.
3 (p 251) M J Stampfer and others, "A prospective study of moderate alcohol consumption and the risk of coronary disease and stroke in women," *The New England Journal of Medicine*, 319 (1988), 267-73.
4 (p 252) O G Brooke and others, "Effects on birth weight of smoking, alcohol, caffeine, socioeconomic factors and psychosocial stress," *British Medical Journal*, 298 (1989), 795-801 and N D Sulaiman, "Alcohol consumption in Dundee primigravidas and its effects on outcome of pregnancy," *British Medical Journal*, 296 (1988), 1500-3.

SMOKING
1 (p 258) E A Krall and B Dawson-Hughes, "Smoking and bone loss among post-menopausal women," *Journal of Bone Mineral Research*, 6 (1991), 331-7.

SCREENING
1 (p 263) A B Miller and others, "Canadian National Breast Screening Study: breast cancer detection and death rates among women aged 40 to 49 years," *Canadian Medical Association Journal*, 147 (1992), 1459-76.

HORMONALS

SEXUALITY
1 (p 277) R L Winn and N Newton, "Sexuality in ageing: a study of 106 cultures," *Archives of Sexual Behaviour*, 11 (1982), 288.
2 (p 277) Suzanne Lowry, "Middle age," British *Vogue*, June 1987.
3 (p 278) Simone de Beauvoir, *La Force de l'Âge* (1960), translated as *The Prime of Life* (London, Weidenfeld & Nicolson, 1962).
4 (p 278) A D Mooradian and V Grieff, "Sexuality in older women," *Archives of Intern Medicine*, 150 (1990), 1033-8.
5 (p 283) Joanna Day, "Sex differences," *The Independent*, September 14, 1992.
6 (p 284) Janet Spencer-Mills, "The spirit is willing . . .," British *Vogue*, October 1992.

CONTRACEPTION
1 (p 285) Marie Stopes, *Contraception – theory, history and practice* (John Bale Sons & Danielsson Ltd, 1923).

2 (p 292) T Cundy and others, "Bone density in women receiving depot medroxyprogesterone acetate for contraception," *British Medical Journal*, 303 (1991), 13-16.
3 (p 294) W Bounds and others, "Preliminary report of unexpected local reactions to a progestogen-releasing contraceptive vaginal ring," *European Journal of Obstetrics & Gynaecology and Reproductive Biology*, 48 (1993), 123-125.

FERTILITY
1 (p 301) G S Berkowitz and others, "Delayed childbearing and the outcome of pregnancy," *The New England Journal of Medicine*, 322 (1990), 659-64.
2 (p 303) B M van Noord-Zaadstree and others, "Delayed childbearing: effect of age on fecundity and outcome of pregnancy," *British Medical Journal*, 302 (1991), 1361-5.
3 (p 306) Quoted in J Berryman and K Windridge, "Having a baby after 40: 1. a preliminary investigation of women's experience of pregnancy," *Journal of Reproductive and Infant Psychology*, 9 (1991), 3-18.
4 (P 307) H S Cuckle and others, "Estimating a woman's risk of having a pregnancy associated with Down's syndrome using her age and serum alphafetoprotein level," *British Journal of Obstetrics and Gynaecology*, 94 (1987), 387-402.
5 (p 307) P A Baur and others, "Maternal age and birth defects: a population study," *The Lancet*, 337 (1991), 527-30.
6 (p 311) Quoted in Anne Merewood, "Last-minute mother," British *Vogue*, May 1992.

MENOPAUSE
1 (p 316) Bungay and others, "Study of symptoms in middle life with special reference to the menopause," *British Medical Journal*, 281 (1980), 181-3.
2 (p 317) Gloria Steinem, *Revolution from Within* (London, Bloomsbury Publishing, 1992).
3 (p 318) Cited in Judy Hall and Dr Robert Jacobs, *The Wise Woman* (London, Element Books, 1992).
4 (p 320) Gail Sheehy, *The Silent Passage* (New York, Random House, 1992).
5 (p 321) Quoted in Angela Lambert, "Serious writing for fun," *The Independent*, September 1991.

HORMONE REPLACEMENT
1 (p 325) Dr Lewis Kuller, quoted in Gail Sheehy, *The Silent Passage* (New York, Random House, 1992).
2 (p 330) M J Stampfer and others, "Postmenopausal estrogen therapy and coronary heart disease: ten-year follow-up from the nurses' health study," *The New England Journal of Medicine*, 325 (1991), 756-62.
3 (p 332) K Hunt and others, "Long-term surveillance of mortality and cancer incidence in women receiving hormone replacement therapy," *British Journal of Gynaecology*, 94 (1987), 620-635.

PSYCHOLOGICALS

1 (p 338) Carl Jung, "Aims of psychotherapy," *Modern Man in Search of a Soul* (London, Routledge, 1933).
2 (p 338) Doris Lessing, *The Summer Before the Dark* (London, Jonathan Cape, 1973).
3 (p 338) Barbara MacDonald and Cynthia Rich, *Look Me in the Eye* (New York, Spinsters Ink, 1983), quoted in Paula Brown Doress and Diana Laskin Siegal, *The Midlife and Older Women Book Project, Ourselves Growing Older* (New York, Simon & Schuster, 1987).
4 (p 339) Germaine Greer, "Letting go," American *Vogue*, May 1986.
5 (p 341) Elliott Jaques, "Death and the mid-life crisis," *International Journal of Psychoanalysis*, 1965.
6 (p 342) Erica Jong, "Is there sexy after 40?" American *Vogue*, May 1987.
7 (p 344) J Aronson, "Women's perspectives on informal care of the elderly: public ideology and personal experiences of giving and receiving care," *Ageing and Society*, 10:1 (1990), 61-64.
8 (p 346) Sigmund Freud, "On psychotherapy," *Collected Works 13* (1905).
9 (p 347) P H M King, "Notes on the psychoanalysis of older patients," paper delivered to the Society of Analytical Psychology, January 15, 1973.
10 (p 349) G McCracken, "Culture and consumption among the elderly," *Ageing and Society*, 7:2 (1987), 203-24.
11 (p 349) Elliott Jaques, "Death and the mid-life crisis," *International Journal of Psychoanalysis*, 1965.
12 (p 353) L Harris and associates, *The Myth and Reality of Aging in America* (the National Council on Aging, Inc, 1975).
13 (p 353) Alex Comfort, *A Good Age* (London, Mitchell Beazley, 1977).
14 (p 355) Paper presented by the Dublin Royal College of Surgeons at the annual meeting of the British Psychological Society, April 1992.
15 (p 357) H Evers, "Old women's self-perceptions of dependency and some implications for service provision," *Journal of Epidemiology and Community Health*, 38 (1984), 306-9.

INDEX

Page numbers in *italic* refer to illustrations.

ACKNOWLEDGMENTS

Thanks are due to the following for providing information and inspiration and for checking the text: Lisa Armstrong, Kevyn Aucoin, Unity Barnes, Mr Dev Basra, Dr Michael Beverly, Professor Alan Boyde, Ms Linda Cardozo, Mr John Cochrane, Dr Jean Coope, Gillian Crosby at the Centre for Policy on Ageing, Barbara Daly, Marianna Falconer, Dr Tim ffytche, Dr Ignac Fogelman, Karl Forsythe-Gray, Mr Nigel Graves, Dr Robert Howard, Dr John Hunter, Professor Howard Jacobs, Andrew Jose, Philip Kingsley, Michael Landon, Professor James Leyden, Vanessa de Lisle, Sonia Lushington, Dr Adam Magos, Sarah Mower, Professor Kypros Nicolaides, Linda Allen Schoen and Dr Mitchell Wortzman at the Neutrogena Corporation in California, Lizzie Radford, Joan Raphael-Leff, Research into Ageing, Mr John Reuter, Johanna Roeber, Polly Sellar, Dr Dev Singh, Dr Howard Swanton, Maxine Tobias. I am grateful to Anna Wintour, editor-in-chief of American *Vogue*, and Alexandra Shulman, editor of British *Vogue*, for their support and encouragement. Especial thanks are due to Dr Anne Szarewski, who received an unfair share of the manuscript, Anne Merewood, who provided a critical U.S. perspective, Dr. Valerie Ulene for her thorough checking of the U.S. edition, Alison Wormleighton for her patient editing and re-editing of the text, Shirley Breen, for making my absence such fun for my children, Charlie Stebbings for continually stepping into the breach and Archie and Romilly Stebbings for displaying patience beyond their years and only switching off my computer once.

PICTURE CREDITS

Michel Arnaud: 60 (bottom right); Rick Baid: 328 (Gloria Steinem); David Bailey: 88; Diana Cochran: 60 (center top and bottom); Michael Comte: 350-1; Clark Edwards: 24-5, 56, 84, 91; Arthur Elgort: 202, 225, 256-7, 312; Fabrizio Ferri: 52; Tim Green: 60 (left); Xavier Guardans: 343; Michel Haddi: 276 (top right); Steven Klein: 101; Andrew Lamb: 13 (bottom and left); Nathalie Lamorel: 348; Lancôme: 45; Roxanne Lowitt: 60 (top right); Andrew MacPherson: 107; Irving Penn, courtesy American Vogue copyright 1988, 1989, 1990, 1991 by The Conde Nast Publications Ltd: 9, 16, 40, 76, 116, 193, 241, 273, 336, 376; Andre Rau: 97; Rex Features: 276 (Sharon Stone, Demi Moore, Tina Turner), 328 (Germaine Greer, Joan Collins, Teresa Gorman, Kate O'Mara); Science Photo Library: 125 (top: Dr John Mazziotta et al/Neurology; middle: Hank Morgan; bottom: National Institute of Health), 128, 136 (top left: Kings College School of Medicine; right: Breast Screening Unit, Kings College Hospital, London), 144 (top: CNRI; bottom: Manfred Kage), 148, 153, 157, 164, 165, 169 (both J. C. Revy), 176 (both Biophoto Associates), 189, 264-5 (Cecil H. Fox), 288 (Sidney Moulds), 293 (Sidney Moulds), 304 (CNRI), 305 (St Bartholomews Hospital); Snowdon: 211, 227, 340, 345, 352; Charlie Stebbings: 197, 216-221, 301; P. Therme: 13 (right); Nick Towers: 13 (top center); Tessa Traeger: 229, 236